The Yearbook of South Asian Languages and Linguistics

1998

South Asia is home to a large number of languages and dialects. While the number of linguists working on South Asia has grown considerably in the recent past, there is as yet no recognized international forum for the exchange of ideas among them.

The Yearbook of South Asian Languages and Linguistics is designed to be just that forum. It will consolidate empirical and theoretical research and provide a testing ground for the articulation of new ideas and approaches grounded in a study of South Asian languages but which have universal applicability.

The Yearbook of South Asian Languages and Linguistics

1998

Chief Editor

RAJENDRA SINGH

Sage Publications
NEW DELHI ■ THOUSAND OAKS ■ LONDON

First published in 1998 by

Sage Publications India Pvt Ltd
M–32 Market, Greater Kailash Part–I
New Delhi–110 048

Sage Publications Inc
2455 Teller Road
Thousand Oaks, California 91320

Sage Publications Ltd
6 Bonhill Street
London EC2A 4PU

Published by Tejeshwar Singh for Sage Publications India Pvt Ltd, phototypeset by Line Arts, Pondicherry and printed at Chaman Enterprises, Delhi.

ISSN: 0971–9539

ISBN: 0–7619–9231–6 (US-hb)
81–7036–685–2 (India-hb)

Sage Production Team: Shukla Basu, Shashi Sharma and Santosh Rawat

Contents

Commentum Editoris

South Asia is home to a large number of languages and dialects. While the number of linguists working on South Asia has grown considerably in the recent past, there is, unfortunately, no recognized international forum for the exchange of ideas amongst them. Hence *The Yearbook*.

The aim of *The Yearbook of South Asian Languages and Linguistics* is to consolidate empirical and theoretical research on South Asian languages and dialects and, hopefully, provide a testing ground for the articulation of new ideas and approaches that have universal applicability but are firmly grounded in a study of South Asian languages.

All issues of *The Yearbook* will have the same structure as this inaugural issue. They will contain four major sections:

Section 1 (Invited Contributions): Distinguished linguists from around the world will be invited to critically assess the research being done on South Asian languages, contribute state-of-the-art surveys, and write about what they think the study of South Asian languages can contribute to our understanding of the nature and structure of human language. This issue contains invited contributions by K.A. Jayaseelan, Paul Kiparsky and Bh. Krishnamurti.

Section 2 (Open Submissions): This section will contain articles, selected from open submissions, dealing with a wide range of topics. We are happy to present contributions by Abel, Agha and Vasishth in this issue.

Section 3 (Reports, Reviews and Abstracts): This section will contain (a) abstracts of recently completed doctoral dissertations, (b) review articles, (c) reviews, and (d) some reports on research on South Asian languages around the world. This issue contains four dissertation-abstracts, six regional reports (from Africa, Europe, Japan, North America, Pakistan, and Southeast Asia), and four book reviews.

Section 4 (Dialogue): This will consist of brief but substantive notes on matters of importance and on significant research published in *The*

Yearbook. This year, it was necessary to invite contributions to this section to give our readers some idea of the sorts of things needed for it. Professor Comrie and Associate Editor Dasgupta have contributed these invited pieces. Future contributions to this section will, however, have to be somewhat shorter.

The last couple of pages will contain housekeeping and other announcements, including announcements regarding relevant conferences and job openings. This issue contains an announcement regarding a rather special prize.

Committed to breadth, we are interested in extending the contribution that South Asian languages have already made to our understanding of language, society, and language in society. Other than excellence and non-isolationism, we have no agenda and no thematic priorities.

I wish to thank Sage Publications, New Delhi for their confidence in this long-term venture. I am particularly grateful to Mr Tejeshwar Singh, its Managing Director, for having guided me, with patience and kindness, throughout the initial stages of this venture.

I am delighted to put the first issue of *The Yearbook* in your hands. It would not have, however, seen the light of day without the help, far beyond the call of duty, of our Editorial Assistants, and Ms Shukla Basu and Jaya Chowdhury, my editors at Sage. I am grateful to them.

RAJENDRA SINGH
Chief Editor

A

■ Invited Contributions ■

Blocking Effects and the Syntax of Malayalam *Taan*[†]

■ K.A. JAYASEELAN ■

Malayalam long-distance reflexive *taan* (which requires a 3rd person antecedent) shows blocking effects if there is any non-3rd person pronoun in its 'neighborhood'. We account for this by saying that *taan* is bound by Perspective. We postulate a Perspective Phrase in the COMP system. A clause's Perspective, normally indexed by its subject, is pre-empted by the Speaker/Hearer, if the latter is mentioned in the clause. *Taan* must adjoin to Perspective in LF; when long-distance bound, it must climb by successive–cyclic adjunction to Perspective. If it adjoins to a non-3rd person Perspective, a mismatch of features results and the derivation is canceled.

■ 1. Some Preliminaries and the Special Status of the Person Feature in Blocking

Malayalam has a long-distance reflexive anaphor *taan* which is 3rd person, singular and [+human], but is unmarked for gender. (The Malayalam pronominal system does mark gender.) It has a plural form *taŋŋaḷ*. *Taan* (or *taŋŋaḷ*) is subject-oriented like most long-distance anaphors. It is also anti-local, which means that it cannot be bound by the minimal subject (i.e. the subject of the phrasal head of which *taan/taŋŋaḷ* is an argument) but must be bound by a

† A part of this paper was presented at the 18th South Asian Language Analysis (SALA) Roundtable at Jawaharlal Nehru University (New Delhi), January 1997. I wish to thank the following: Bao Zhiming for very kindly responding to my urgent appeal and giving me some Chinese data that I needed; P. Madhavan, G. Radhakrishna Pillai and M.T. Hany Babu for "cross-checking" my grammaticality judgments in Malayalam; K.G. Vijayakrishnan for information about blocking effects in Tamil; and Probal Dasgupta for some comments on the analysis.

subject "higher up". *Ṯaan/ṯaŋŋaḷ* has a complex form *ṯaan ṯanne/ṯaŋŋaḷ ṯanne* which is not anti-local and so can be coindexed with the minimal subject. See Jayaseelan (1997) for a discussion of these (and some other) properties of *ṯaan*.

We are concerned here with the blocking effects exhibited by *ṯaan*.[1] *Ṯaan* (we said) is 3rd person; cf.,

1. John$_i$ / *ñaan$_i$ / *ṉii$_i$ ṯan$_i$-te bhaarya-ye ṉuḷḷi
   I you self-gen. wife-acc. pinched
   'John$_i$ / *I$_i$ / *you$_i$ pinched self's$_i$ wife.'

In (1), *ṯaan* is embedded within a DP; but when *ṯaan* is an argument of a verb, it must be long-distance bound owing to the anti-locality property we mentioned, cf.,

2. *John$_i$ ṯan$_i$-ne sneehik̈k̈uṉṉ-illa
   self-acc. love(Pres.)-neg.
   'John$_i$ does not love self$_i$.'
3. John$_i$ wicaariccu [Mary$_j$ ṯan$_{i/*j}$-ne sneehik̈k̈uṉṉ-illa eṉṉə]
   thought self-acc. love(Pres.)-neg. COMP
   'John$_i$ thought that Mary$_j$ does not love self$_{i/*j}$.'

However, when it is long-distance bound, every intervening subject must be 3rd person; otherwise the coindexing is blocked:

4. John$_i$ wicaariccu [Mary / kuṭṭikaḷ / *ñaan / *ṉii ṯan$_i$-ne
   thought (the) children I you self-acc.
   sneehik̈k̈uṉṉ-illa eṉṉə]
   love(pres.)-neg. COMP
   'John$_i$ thought that Mary / the children / *I / *you do(es) not love self$_i$.'

As (4) shows, only the non-identity of the person feature of the intended long-distance antecedent and the intervening subject, results in blocking; a mismatch of their number or gender feature does not affect the long-distance binding.

Now this (in itself) is puzzling for some contemporary accounts of blocking which make blocking contingent on an anaphor seeking its "missing" features.[2] Thus Huang and Tang (1989) propose that a long-distance-bound reflexive identifies its missing phi-features in the local domain, from its potential antecedent in the minimal clause and that it (then) matches these same features with the corresponding features of its potential antecedent in each of the higher clauses it moves into (see op. cit. for details). Such an account predicts that only the missing phi-features of a long-distance anaphor are relevant to blocking. We should therefore expect that gender, which is the only missing phi-feature of *ṯaan*, should be relevant to blocking; but that the person feature, for which *ṯaan* is already lexically marked, should not be relevant to blocking. But we find that the opposite is the case.

Actually (however), it might very well be the case that (universally) only the person feature of a long-distance anaphor ever plays a role in blocking. The Chinese long-distance anaphor *ziji* is unmarked for person, number or gender. Huang and Tang (1989) note that mismatch of the gender feature of an intervening potential antecedent and the actual antecedent does not result in blocking. They attribute this to the fact that the Chinese pronominal system does not mark the gender feature. And they claim that mismatch of either person or number results in blocking. But this last claim may be incorrect: Cole and Wang (1996: 360) say (speaking of *ziji*) that "[n]umber and gender are irrelevant to blocking".

The fact that only the person feature matters for blocking is expressed in Battistella's (1989) alternative account of blocking by means of a stipulation. Battistella generates *ziji* (which, as we said, is inherently unmarked for phi-features) with an arbitrary person feature—*only* a person feature—in D-structure. When *ziji* adjoins to I (see fn. 2 for Battistella's account of successive cyclic adjunction), it acts like an AGR and checks the person feature of the subject in the specifier of I. Therefore all the subjects "along the path" of *ziji* must agree with respect to the person feature.[3] Given this latter account, it would appear that all that we need to say about blocking in Malayalam is the following: whereas Chinese *ziji* must be generated with an arbitrary person feature in D-structure, Malayalam *t̲aan* is lexically marked as 3rd person. The rest of the account can remain unchanged.

Unfortunately, we go on to show that a solution along these lines is inadequate for *t̲aan*. Because the biggest puzzle about *t̲aan* is the following: it is not only potential antecedents which can affect the long-distance binding of *t̲aan*.

■ 2. Blocking by Non-Subjects

Consider the following sentences:

5\. a. *John$_i$ wicaariccu [Mary n̲in-ne-(y)um t̲an$_i$-ne-(y)um
thought you-acc.-conj. self-acc.-conj.
paricayappedut̲t̲-um en̲n̲ə]
introduce-Fut. COMP
'John$_i$ thought that Mary would introduce you and self$_i$.'

b\. John$_i$ wicaariccu [Mary Bill -ine-(y)um t̲an$_i$-ne-(y)um
thought -acc.-conj. self-acc.-conj.
paricayappedut̲t̲-um en̲n̲ə]
introduce-Fut. COMP
'John$_i$ thought that Mary would introduce Bill and self$_i$.'

c\. John$_i$ wicaariccu [Mary n̲in-ne-(y)um awan$_i$-e-(y)um
thought you-acc.-conj. he-acc.-conj.
paricayappedut̲t̲-um en̲n̲ə]
introduce-Fut. COMP
'John$_i$ thought that Mary would introduce you and him$_i$.'

In (5a), the coindexing of *ṯaan* and the matrix subject is blocked. In (5b), the same coindexing is fine. The difference is that *ṯaan* is conjoined with a non-3rd person DP in (5a), but not in (5b). (5c) has the regular pronoun *awan* instead of *ṯaan*, and regular pronouns show no blocking effects.

Consider also (6) and (7):

6. a. *John$_i$ wicaariccu [Mary eni-k̇k̇ə ṯan$_i$-ne
   thought I-dat. self-acc.
   paricayappeḍuṯṯ-um eṉṉə]
   introduce-Fut. COMP
   'John$_i$ thought that Mary would introduce self$_i$ to me.'
   b. John$_i$ wicaariccu [Mary Bill-inə ṯan$_i$-ne
   thought -dat. self-acc.
   paricayappeḍuṯṯ-um eṉṉə]
   introduce-Fut. COMP
   'John$_i$ thought that Mary would introduce self$_i$ to Bill.'
   c. John$_i$ wicaariccu [Mary eni-k̇k̇ə awan$_i$-e
   thought I-dat. he-acc.
   paricayappeḍuṯṯ-um eṉṉə]
   introduce-Fut. COMP
   'John$_i$ thought that Mary would introduce him$_i$ to me.'
7. a. *John$_i$ paRayuṉṉu [ṯaan$_i$ ṉin-ne orikkalum
   says self you-acc. never
   kaṇḍiṭṭ-illa eṉṉə]
   have seen-neg. COMP
   'John$_i$ says that self$_i$ has never seen you.'
   b. John$_i$ paRayuṉṉu [ṯaan$_i$ Mary-(y)e orik̇kalum
   says self -acc. never
   kaṇḍiṭṭ-illa eṉṉə]
   have seen-neg. COMP
   'John$_i$ says that self$_i$ has never seen Mary.'
   c. John$_i$ paRayuṉṉu [awan$_i$ ṉin-ne orikkalum
   says he you-acc. never
   kaṇḍiṭṭ-illa eṉṉə]
   have seen-neg. COMP
   'John$_i$ says that he$_i$ has never seen you.'

In (6a), *ṯaan* has a non-3rd person DP as a co-argument, while this is not the case in (6b). The coindexing of *ṯaan* with the matrix subject is blocked in (6a) but not in (6b). (6c), which has the regular pronoun instead of *ṯaan*, shows no blocking effect.

The sentence (7a) is especially interesting because *ṯaan* itself is the embedded subject and so there is no intervening subject between it and its antecedent. It also shows that there is no need for the non-3rd person DP to c-command *ṯaan* for a blocking effect to obtain.

(8) and (9) (below) show that blocking (in Malayalam) is not confined to long-distance binding;[4] also, (9) once again illustrates the fact that whatever is happening in blocking has nothing to do with c-command of the anaphor by the non-3rd person DP or vice versa.

8. a. ?*John$_i$ ṉin-ne ṯan$_i$-te wiiṭṭ-ileekkə kšaṇiccu-oo?
   you-acc. self-gen. house-to invited-Q
   'Did John$_i$ invite you to self's$_i$ house?'
   b. John$_i$ Mary-(y)e ṯan$_i$-te wiiṭṭ-ileekkə kšaṇiccu-oo?
   -acc. self-gen. house-to invited-Q
   'Did John$_i$ invite Mary to self's$_i$ house?'
   c. John$_i$ ṉin-ne awan$_i$-te wiiṭṭ-ileekkə kšaṇiccu-oo?
   you-acc. he-gen. house-to invited-Q
   'Did John$_i$ invite you to his$_i$ house?'
9. a. ?*John$_i$ en-te bhaarya-ye ṯan$_i$-te amma-kkə
   I-gen. wife-acc. self-gen. mother-dat.
   paricayappeḍuṯṯi
   introduced
   'John$_i$ introduced my wife to self's$_i$ mother.'
   b. John$_i$ Bill-inte bhaarya-ye ṯan$_i$-te amma-kkə
   -gen. wife-acc. self-gen. mother-dat.
   paricayappeḍuṯṯi
   introduced
   'John$_i$ introduced Bill's wife to self's$_i$ mother.'
   c. John$_i$ en-te bhaarya-ye awan$_i$-te amma-kkə
   I-gen. wife-acc. he-gen. mother-dat.
   paricayappeḍuṯṯi
   introduced
   'John$_i$ introduced my wife to his$_i$ mother.'

(10) (below) shows that *ṯaan* and the non-3rd person pronoun need not be in the same minimal clause for blocking to take place:

10. a. *Mary$_i$ ṉin-nooḍə paRaññiṭṭ-uṇḍ-oo [ṯaan$_i$ wiwaaham
   you-to told-have-Q self marriage
   kazhikk-aan pookuṉṉ-a kaaryam]?
   do-Inf. go(Pres.)-Relativizer matter
   'Has Mary$_i$ told you (the fact) that self$_i$ is going to get married?'
   b. Mary$_i$ Bill-inooḍə paRaññiṭṭ-uṇḍ-oo [ṯaan$_i$ wiwaaham
   you-to told-have-Q self marriage
   kazhikk-aan pookunn-a kaaryam]?
   do-Inf. go(Pres.)-Relativizer matter
   'Has Mary$_i$ told Bill (the fact) that self$_i$ is going to get married?'
   c. Mary$_i$ ṉin-nooḍə paRaññiṭṭ-uṇḍ-oo [awal$_i$ wiwaaham
   you-to told-have-Q she marriage

kazhik̈k-aan pookunn-a kaaryam]?
do-Inf. go(Pres.)-Relativizer matter
'Has Mary$_i$ told you (the fact) that she$_i$ is going to get married?'

In (10), *ṯaan* is in the embedded clause, and the non-3rd person pronoun is in the matrix clause which also contains the antecedent. But when the case is the reverse, i.e. when the non-3rd person pronoun is in the embedded clause and *ṯaan* is in the matrix clause which contains the antecedent, there is no blocking:

11. John$_i$ ṯan$_i$-te anuyaayikaḷ-ooḍə paRaññu [awar-aarum
self-gen. supporters-to said they-no one
eni-k̈kə wooṭṭə ceyy-aruṯə enn̲ə]
I-dat. vote do-neg. COMP
'John$_i$ told self's$_i$ supporters that none of them should vote for me.'

Again, as (12) and (13) show, there is no blocking if the non-3rd person pronoun is outside the minimal clause which contains the antecedent:

12. n̲ii keeṭṭu-oo [John$_i$ ṯan$_i$-te bhaarya-ye nuḷ̈ḷi-(y)a
you heard-Q self-gen. wife-acc. pinched-Relativizer
kaaryam]?
matter
'Did you hear (the fact) that John$_i$ pinched self's$_i$ wife?'

13. ñaan wicaariccu [John$_i$ aRiññiṭṭ-illa en̲n̲ə [ṯaan$_i$ man̲ṯRi
I thought have known-not COMP self minister
aay-a kaaryam]]
become-Relativizer matter
'I thought John$_i$ hadn't come to know (the fact) that self$_i$ had become a minister.'

Apparently there is a notion of "closeness" involved here. In (10), the non-3rd person pronoun is "closer" to the antecedent than *ṯaan*, if we measure "closeness" in terms of intervening CP (or IP) boundaries. In (11), *ṯaan* is "closer" to the antecedent than the non-3rd person pronoun. (12) and (13) show that only the c-command domain of the antecedent counts for blocking.

■ 3. The Role of Perspective in Long-Distance Binding

We saw that the mere presence of a non-3rd person pronoun which is as close as *ṯaan* (in terms of intervening CP or IP boundaries) to the antecedent, blocks *ṯaan*'s ability to access the antecedent. In none of the examples (5)–(10), which illustrate blocking, is the non-3rd person pronoun a subject and therefore a potential antecedent of *ṯaan*. Furthermore, there need be no c-command relation (either way) between *ṯaan* and this pronoun. These facts seem to indicate that the interaction of these elements is not direct but mediated by a third element.

Our proposal is that this mediator is Perspective. It is an old and familiar claim in linguistics that "point of view" plays a role in the interpretation of anaphors. Thus the English reflexive *X-self* (*himself*, *herself*, etc.) is known to be capable of being "logophorically" bound (see, among others, Cantrall (1974), Kuno (1972, 1983, 1987), and Zribi–Hertz (1989), for data and analyses). Logophoric binding is defined by Clements (1975) as the interpretation of an anaphor as referring to the person "whose speech, thoughts, feelings, or general state of consciousness are reported" in the clause or sentence in question. All (or most) subject-oriented reflexives—e.g. Chinese *ziji*, Japanese *zibun*, Korean *caki*, and Icelandic *sig*—are also amenable to logophoric binding. (14) (below) illustrates the logophoric binding of *t̲aan*:

14. a. John$_i$ manassilaakki, ii band̲ham awasaaniccu
 understood this relationship finished
en̲n̲ə. T̲aan$_i$ ini Mary-(y)e orikkalum kaaṇ-illa
COMP self in the future -acc. never will see-not
'John$_i$ understood that this relationship was finished. Self$_i$ would never see Mary again.'

Notably, this binding too is disturbed by the presence of a non-3rd person pronoun:

b. *John$_i$ manassilaakki, ii band̲ham awasaaniccu
 understood this relationship finished
en̲n̲ə. T̲aan$_i$ ini n̲in-ne orikkalum kaaṇ-illa
COMP self in the future you-acc. never will see-not
'John$_i$ understood that this relationship was finished. Self$_i$ would never see you again.'

There are some Malayalam verbs which show *taan*'s special relationship to Perspective. Malayalam has two verbs, *koḍukk* and *t̲ar*, both of which mean 'give'; however they exhibit a complementarity of distribution, cf.,

15. John ii pust̲akam Mary-k̇k̇ə / *eni-k̇k̇ə / *n̲in-akkə koḍukk-um
 this book -Dat. I-Dat. you-Dat. give-Fut.
 'John will give this book to Mary / *me / *you.'
16. John ii pust̲akam *Mary-k̇k̇ə / eni-k̇k̇ə / n̲in-akk t̲ar-um
 this book -Dat. I-Dat. you-Dat. give-Fut.
 'John will give this book to *Mary / me / you.'

The usual explanation given for this distribution is that when the Goal argument of 'give' is 1st or 2nd person, i.e. the speaker or the hearer of the utterance, one uses *t̲ar*; otherwise, one uses *koḍukk*. But this is not entirely correct, cf.,

17. John$_i$ wicaariccu [Mary t̲an$_i$-ik̇k̇ə aa pust̲akam *koḍukk-um /
 thought self-Dat. that book give-Fut.

ṯar-um ennə]
give-Fut. COMP
'John$_i$ thought that Mary would give that book to self$_i$.'

18. John$_i$ wicaariccu [Mary awan$_i$-ə aa pusṯakam koḍukk-um /
thought he-Dat. that book give-Fut.
*ṯar-um ennə]
give-Fut. COMP
'John$_i$ thought that Mary would give that book to him$_i$.'

When the Goal argument is *ṯaan*, one must use *ṯar*; and when it is the regular pronoun *awan* (he), one must use *koḍukk*—even though both *ṯaan* and *awan* are 3rd person. So, *ṯaan* patterns with 1st and 2nd person pronouns with respect to the choice between the verbs *ṯar* and *koḍukk*.[5]

How do we state the condition on *ṯar* and *koḍukk*? Their meaning difference seems to relate to the point of view from which the event of 'giving' is viewed. *Ṯar* requires the event to be viewed from the point of view of the Goal argument; *koḍukk* requires it to be viewed *not* from the point of view of the Goal argument. In other words, *ṯar*'s selectional frame marks its Goal argument as identical with the clausal Perspective and *koḍukk*'s selectional frame marks it as distinct from the clausal Perspective.[6]

What, we might now ask, are the rules for determining the Perspective of a clause? It would appear that the Speaker or the Hearer of the utterance, if mentioned in the clause by means of 1st or 2nd person pronouns, pre-empts Perspective. If both are mentioned, either of them can be Perspective, as suggested by (19):

19. a. ñaan nin-akkə oru pusṯakam ṯar-aam
I you-dat. a book give-shall
'I shall give you a book.'
b. nii en-ikkə oru pusṯakam ṯar-um-oo?
you I-dat. a book give-Fut.-Q
'Will you give me a book?'

Here, *ṯar*'s requirement that the Goal argument be the Perspective is presumably satisfied in both sentences. We shall give 1st and 2nd person pronouns the value 2 on a scale of "preference" for Perspective—making it the highest value of the scale.[7]

In a logophoric context, the person whose thoughts or feelings are reported in the clause or sentence—the logophoric antecedent—can be Perspective. But this element's claim to be Perspective seems to be only equal to that of the subject of the clause; the choice between them appears to be free (as will appear subsequently). Let us (then) give both the logophoric antecedent and the subject of the clause the value 1 on our scale. All other elements have the value 0. The rule for choosing Perspective is the following: choose an element such that no other element in the clause has a higher value on the "preference" scale.

A caveat: the assignment of value 1 to the subject is not a completely straightforward affair. In fact, the subject's choice as Perspective seems actually to be determined by a hierarchy of theta-roles. As is well-known, in clauses with a "psych verb", the DP bearing the Experiencer theta-role shows "subject-like" properties; in our terms, it is chosen for Perspective, as evidenced by *ṯaan*'s being anteceded by it in a sentence like (20):

20. ṯan$_i$-te makkal-ude perumaattam John$_i$-ine weedanippiccu
    self-gen. children-gen. behavior -acc. pained
    'Self's$_i$ children's behavior pained John$_i$.'

Again, the subject should be a volitional subject (Agent) in order to be Perspective, contrast (21a) and (21b):

21. a. *Mary$_i$ [John ṯan$_i$-ne ṯaḷḷi-(y)appooḷ] wiiṇu
       self-acc. pushed-when fell
       'Mary$_i$ fell when John pushed self$_i$.'
    b. Mary$_i$ [John ṯan$_i$-ne ṉuḷḷi-(y)appooḷ] uRakke karaññu
       self-acc. pinched-when loudly cried
       'Mary$_i$ cried loudly when John pinched self$_i$.'[8]

Given our "preference" rules, we can explain the choice between *ṯar* and *koḍukk* in (15) and (16). If *Mary-k̈k̈ə* (to Mary) is the Goal argument, it cannot be the Perspective because the subject has a higher value on our preference scale. Therefore *ṯar* cannot be chosen, and *koḍukk* can be chosen. But if *eni-k̈k̈ə* 'to me' or *ṉin-akkə* 'to you' is the Goal argument, it supersedes the subject's claim to be the Perspective; and *ṯar* can be chosen, and *koḍukk* cannot be chosen.

Now in (17) and (18), we get *ṯar* if the Goal argument is *ṯan-ik̈k̈ə* 'to self', and *koḍukk* if the Goal argument is *awan-ə* 'to him'. We can extend our explanation to these examples if we may assume that *ṯaan* is related to the Perspective of the embedded clause, and *awan* is not.[9]

■ 4. The Representation of Perspective

This brings us to the important question of how Perspective is represented in the clause. Most studies of point-of-view phenomena—e.g. Banfield (1982), Kuno and Kaburaki (1977), Sells (1987)—assume that point-of-view is represented as a "parallel" system. Our contention will be that such a representation of it, which is unintegrated into syntax, is inadequate.

For concreteness, consider Sells (1987), arguably the most articulated account of logophoricity that we have at present. In Sells' system, the discourse roles of a complement clause are determined by the matrix verb; e.g. in the complement of *say*, all the discourse roles are identified with the subject of *say*.[10] If now an anaphor (in the complement of *say*) is identified with a discourse role (e.g. PIVOT, see fn. 10), it would indirectly corefer with the matrix subject, giving rise to "long-distance binding". However, it is unclear how the system would allow an anaphor in a multiply embedded clause to access an antecedent "across" an intervening clause, as in (22):

22. John$_i$ paRaññu [Bill$_j$ paRaññu en̯n̯ə [Mary tan$_{i,j}$-ne
         said   said   COMP   self-acc.
    sneehikkun̯n̯-illa en̯n̯ə]
    loves-neg.   COMP
    'John$_i$ said that Bill$_j$ said that Mary does not love self$_{i,j}$.'

In order to get the reading in which *taan* refers to 'John', the system will have to be extended by incorporating some further mechanism for the "inheritance" of discourse roles from a higher to a lower clause. The nature of such a mechanism must remain highly speculative at present.

Another problem is clausal adjuncts, cf., (23):

23. [John   tan$_i$-ne   nul̯l̯i-(y)appool] Mary$_i$ uRakke karaññu
         self-acc. pinched-when   loudly cried
    'Mary$_i$ cried loudly when John pinched self$_i$.'

If the embedded clause of (23) adopts Mary's point of view, as Sells would claim,[11] it cannot be for any semantic reason since the clause is not a complement of a verb of propositional attitude; in fact, it is not in the subcategorization frame of any verb. The reason therefore must be structural. But Sells' DRSs offer no ready means of expressing a structural reason.

We propose that Perspective is a structural position represented in the syntax; and that the seeming "inheritance" of discourse roles from higher to lower clauses, is best represented by successive-cyclic adjunction of an anaphor to higher and higher Perspective positions.[12]

■ 5. The Syntax of *Taan*

We assume that Perspective is a functional head, which projects a Perspective Phrase, in the "left periphery" of the clause. Like Topic Phrase and Focus Phrase, Perspective Phrase is also optionally generated as part of the COMP system; specifically, it is generated when needed to license an element in the clause which is marked [+ Perspective]. *Taan* (we assume) is marked [+Perspective].

Before we proceed, we must say something about the nature of *taan*'s anaphoricity. Huang and Tang (1989) analyze the Chinese reflexive anaphor *ziji* as a form that lacks both phi-features and reference; and which therefore needs to get two indices—an R-index (referential index) and a phi-index. (*Ziji*, they say, is a "double anaphor".) Italian *pro*, we may say, has an R-index and lacks only a phi-index. *Ṯaan* (we saw) lacks only one phi-feature of the Malayalam pronominal system, namely gender. What distinguishes it from the regular pronouns, and makes it an anaphor, is not (we think) so much its lack of gender as the fact that it has no inherent reference. In other words, what it needs to get is an R-index.

This situation makes it look rather like the English reflexive *himself*, which Huang and Tang argue lacks only an R-index. An R-index (by itself) can apparently be received from any c-commanding element (including Perspective—recall cases of the logophoric binding of *himself*). Therefore, *himself* is not "subject-oriented". *Ṯaan*, however, is marked [+ Perspective]; its features must adjoin to Perspective in LF (a "Perspective Criterion"). Since, in the majority of cases, a volitional subject gives its index to Perspective, we derive the result that *ṯaan* is "subject-oriented".

Perspective requires (minimally) a referential index; a point of view must be the point of view of someone. We shall assume that a search algorithm (of which more directly) will give it the index of the referent who has the highest value on our scale of "preference". Along with the index, it can get the phi-features of that referent. But let us say that Perspective (as compared with pronouns) has a "restricted" phi-feature matrix: it has a slot only for the person feature. Therefore only the person feature of the referent in question is copied onto Perspective. This last assumption, we shall see, will enable us to explain why only the person feature of the intervening potential antecedents of a long-distance-bound anaphor plays a role in blocking.

Note that this last assumption is also natural: a point-of-view is crucially differentiated as that of the Speaker of the utterance, the Hearer of the utterance, or "another" person; it is *not* differentiated with respect to number or gender. But the same cannot be said for the functional head AGR (more broadly, INFL), which is known to check the subject's full range of phi-features. Therefore theories which seek to derive the "subject orientation" of long-distance reflexives by adjoining them to INFL cannot explain why only the person feature of the intervening potential antecedents of the anaphor ever figures in blocking.

The search algorithm mentioned above (we assume) considers all the referents of a clause and gives them a value according to the system we mentioned; if the clause is in a logophoric context, it also considers the "logophoric antecedent". It then marks Perspective with the index (and person feature) of one of the referents, such that no other referent has a higher value. Importantly, it does not "go down" into an embedded clause; otherwise, we shall have multiple subjects—all with the value 1—"competing" for Perspective, and it should be possible for an anaphor in a matrix clause to be interpreted as coreferential with an embedded subject. This stricture also enables us to explain why, in Malayalam, a 1st or 2nd person pronoun in an embedded clause does not block the ability of a *ṯaan* in the matrix clause to access its antecedent (cf. [11]).

Ṯaan (we said) must adjoin to Perspective in LF. It can move up into superordinate clauses by successive-cyclic adjunction to Perspective. At each adjunction site, it must copy the phi-features of—or otherwise match phi-features with—the element it adjoins to; this means (in effect) that it must copy (match) the person feature of each Perspective it adjoins to. But it can "defer" the copying of the R-index. When it copies the R-index of a Perspective, it will be interpreted as coreferential with the referent that gave the R-index to that Perspective. Given these mechanisms, we have an explanation of the long-distance binding of *ṯaan*.

Given (in addition) our "preference" rules for Perspective, we also have an explanation of blocking. Consider (8a) (repeated below), which shows blocking in a case of local binding:

8a. ?*John$_i$ ṉin-ne ṯan$_i$-te wiitt-ileekkə kšaṇiccu-oo?
you-acc. self-gen. house-to invite-Q
'Did John$_i$ invite you to self's$_i$ house?'

The second-person referent (here) gives its index and person feature to Perspective, "overriding" the subject's claim to Perspective. When *ṯaan* adjoins to Perspective and copies its phi-feature, it gets contradictory phi-features since *ṯaan* is 3rd person; and the derivation crashes.[13]

This explanation holds good for all the instances of blocking given in (5)–(10) (as the reader can check). It also explains why there is no blocking in (11)–(13). Consider (11) (repeated below):

11. John$_i$ ṯan$_i$-te anuyaayikaḷ-ooḍə paRaññu [awar-aarum
self-gen. supporters-to said they-no one
eni-kkə wooṭṭə ceyy-aruṯə eṉṉə]
I-dat. vote do-neg. COMP
'John$_i$ told self's$_i$ supporters that none of them should vote for me.'

The embedded clause's Perspective has the R-index and phi-feature of the first person referent. But this does not matter since the anaphor is in the matrix clause. The search algorithm that tries to determine the Perspective of the matrix clause does not "go down" into the embedded clause. The matrix clause's Perspective gets the index and phi-feature of the matrix subject, and *ṯaan* can corefer with the latter quite unproblematically. In (12) and (13), the non-3rd person pronoun is in the matrix clause, and *ṯaan* and its antecedent is in the embedded clause. The embedded clause's Perspective has the index and phi-feature of the embedded subject, with which *ṯaan* can corefer.

■ 6. *Ṯaan* and "Subject Orientation"

The fact that we relate *ṯaan* to Perspective (rather than INFL) also enables us to give a more nuanced account of *ṯaan*'s 'subject orientation'. As we know, it is not the case that all subjects, or only subjects, can be the antecedent of *t̲aan*. In our account of the "preference" rules for Perspective, we said that the value 1 is given (on a par with the logophoric antecedent), not directly to the subject, but to the highest argument on a scale determined by a hierarchy of theta-roles. In most cases, the subject is Agent and therefore the highest argument; which is why *t̲aan* is considered "subject-oriented". But a non-volitional subject is not Agent. Therefore a non-volitional subject does not qualify to be the antecedent of *t̲aan*.[14] Similarly, in a clause with a "psychological" predicate, the argument with the Experiencer theta-role is the highest argument; therefore it antecedes *t̲aan*, superseding the subject. Data involving a non-volitional subject or a "psych" verb are a problem for theories which relate a long-distance reflexive to the subject (e.g. by adjoining it to INFL, which is invariably coindexed with the subject). But these data require no special treatment in our account.

We also have no problem dealing with a logophoric antecedent. In our "preference" rules for Perspective, a logophoric antecedent and a volitional subject have the same value; so that the choice between them is free. This latter fact is illustrated by (24):

24. (John$_i$ bhayappeṭṭu Bill$_j$ oru d̲urmaargi aayirikk-aam en̲n̲ə.)
    feared one immoral person be-may COMP

    Bill$_j$ t̲an$_{i,j}$-te bhaarya-ye n̲uḷḷ-aam
    self-gen. wife-acc. pinch-may

    '(John$_i$ was afraid that Bill$_j$ might be an immoral person), Bill$_j$ may pinch self's$_{i,j}$ wife.'

Here, *t̲aan* can be anteceded (equally) by 'John' or by 'Bill'.

Now, regarding a logophoric antecedent, current accounts which relate long-distance reflexives to the subject are constrained to say that this is an instance of "another" type of binding—a type of binding which obeys very different rules from syntactic binding.[15] But we do not need any such dichotomy. We can offer a unified account of the binding of *t̲aan*.[16] This account has obvious implications for a theory of long-distance anaphora.[17]

■ NOTES

1. What we say here about the blocking effects of *t̲aan* apply equally to *t̲aŋŋaḷ* and *t̲aan t̲anne/t̲aŋŋaḷ t̲anne*.
2. It is now widely acknowledged that long-distance anaphors are elements which lack inherent reference and also one or more phi-features, and that it is this "deficit" which makes them anaphors; see Burzio (1991), Huang and Tang (1989), Reinhart and Reuland (1991, 1993), Jayaseelan (1997). Another common assumption is that a long-distance-bound reflexive must "move up close" to its antecedent by successive-cyclic adjunction. (A current debate is about whether the adjunction is to IP—as is the position of Huang and Tang [1989]—or to I—as maintained by Pica [1987], Battistella [1989], and several others.)

3. Cole, Hermon and Sung (1993) and Cole and Sung (1994) have a slight variant of this account, in which *ziji* when adjoined to I, "percolates" its person feature to I. This "percolation" variant is meant to capture a generalization that only languages with no overt subject-verb agreement (e.g. Chinese) show blocking effects; languages with overt subject-verb agreement (e.g. Italian) do not. This follows from the proposed account: if AGR has a feature-matrix which is already filled, the anaphor's features cannot percolate to it.

   The generalization (however) seems to be questionable. Tamil, which has a rich system of subject-verb agreement, shows blocking effects (K.G. Vijayakrishnan, p. c.).
4. But many speakers judge the blocking effect to be somewhat weaker in cases of local binding, like in (8a) and (9a).
5. The Japanese verbs *yaru* 'give' (subject-centred), and *kureru* 'give' (dative-centred), discussed by Kuno and Kaburaki (1977) do not show a similar complementarity of distribution; thus they can replace each other in the same sentence, although with a difference of perspective:

   i. a. Taroo wa Hanako ni okane o yatta (Subject-Centred)
   to money gave
   b. Taroo wa Hanako ni okane o kureta (Dative-Centred)
   to money gave
   'Taroo gave money to Hanako.'

   This sentence can be said in Malayalam only with *koḍukk* (not *ṯar*).

   The Japanese verbs seem to be like the much-investigated English verbs 'come' and 'go' (or their counterparts in other languages), which seem to be able to 'project' the sentential perspective required by their interpretation. Thus 'come' requires the movement it signifies to be towards Perspective; but consider a sentence like (ii):

   ii. (You) come to Mary's house.

   Here, 'come' projects an abstract 'I' whose point of view is adopted in the sentence, and whose presence at 'Mary's house' at the time of the arrival of 'you' is implied.

   The verbs *koḍukk* and *ṯar* (on the other hand) simply adopt the point of view yielded by the rules for the choice of Perspective which we outline below.
6. We actually need to stipulate a stronger condition on *koḍukk*, namely that the Goal argument should be *not a possible* Perspective, because of data like (i):

   i. ñaan ṉin-akkə oru pusṯakam ṯar-aam / *koḍukk-aam
   I you-dat. a book give-shall give-shall
   'I shall give you a book.'

   Since the 1st and 2nd person pronouns are equally "preferred" for being Perspective (as we argue directly), it should be possible to make the subject the Perspective of this clause; and since the Goal argument would now be distinct from the Perspective, it should be possible (without this stronger condition) to use *koḍukk* in this sentence—but it is not.

   This stronger condition can be restated as follows: *koḍukk* requires its Goal argument to be lower on the "preference" scale (for determining Perspective) than the Perspective.
7. We may recall here an "empathy hierarchy" postulated by Kuno and Kaburaki (1977: 652):

   (i) *Speech-Act Participant Empathy Hierarchy*:
   It is easiest for the speaker to empathize with himself; it is next easiest for him to empathize with the hearer; it is most difficult for him to express more empathy with third persons than with himself or with the hearer:
   Speaker > Hearer > Third Person

   But in Malayalam, in view of evidence like (19), we are unable to rank the speaker higher than the hearer.
8. As has been pointed out (e.g. by Huang and Tang [1989]), data like these should be a problem for any theory of long-distance anaphora which relates anaphors automatically to the subject—say, by adjoining them to INFL.

9. One might ask why *awan* may not be related to the Perspective in (18) the same way as *ṯaan* is in (17). The embedded clause reports a thought of 'John'; the latter therefore qualifies as a logophoric antecedent and is a possible choice for Perspective in that clause. Suppose we adopt this option. Since *awan* corefers with 'John', it would now also corefer with Perspective. Apparently coreference is not enough. While *awan* would corefer with Perspective, it would not either determine Perspective (as 1st and 2nd person pronouns do), nor be in a chain with Perspective. On the other hand, *ṯaan* (we shall argue) adjoins to Perspective in LF.
10. Sells analyzes the notion of "logophoric antecedent" into three distinct notions: the SOURCE (the person whose utterance the clause reports); the SELF (the person whose thoughts or feelings the clause reports); and the PIVOT (the person from whose "point of view" the report is made). These roles are represented in a 'Discourse Representation Structure' (DRS), like the following:

    (i) (= Sells' (37))

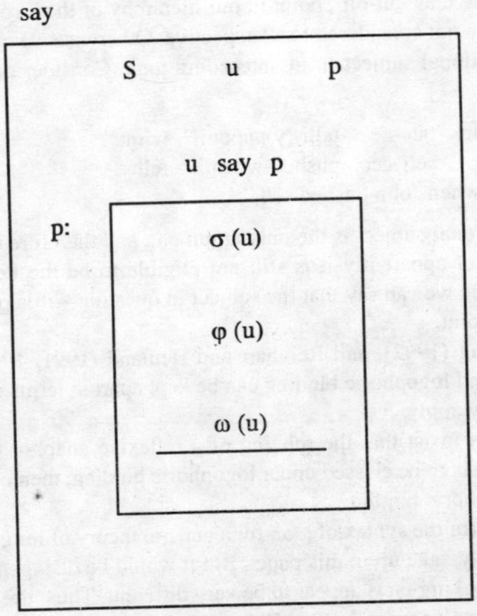

(*S* represents the external speaker; *u* is an individual variable and *p* a propositional variable; σ is SOURCE, φ is SELF and ω is PIVOT.) (i) is a representation of the discourse structure of the verb *say*.
11. The embedded clause does not represent something uttered by Mary, or a thought or feeling of Mary; i.e. in Sells' terms, Mary cannot be the SOURCE or SELF of the embedded clause. In such cases (called "3POV", or third-person-point-of-view, contexts by Sells), the claim is that the matrix subject may become the PIVOT of the embedded clause. But no explanation is offered, of how this may come about.
12. It also seems to us that for logophoricity, the crucial notion is only PIVOT (point of view); a referent's being the SOURCE or the SELF of a clause only helps it to become the PIVOT. Sells' evidence to show that SOURCE and SELF can be separately targeted by the interpretation of certain types of elements, is not entirely convincing. A "speaker-evaluative" phrase, Sells claims, is ascribed to the SOURCE; but in (i), 'Mary' is neither the SOURCE nor the SELF of the embedded adverbial clause, and yet the highly preferred reading is that the description of 'John' as 'that rogue' is Mary's.

i. [aa ṯemmaaḍi John ṯani-ne ṉuḷḷi-(y)appooḷ] Mary$_i$ uRakke karaññu
that rogue self-acc. pinched-when loudly cried
'When that rogue John pinched self$_i$, Mary$_i$ cried loudly.'

Our notion of 'Perspective' most closely corresponds to Sells' PIVOT.

13. If LF-movement is feature-movement, and if successive-cyclic movement can be formulated as a single operation of "Form Chain" (Chomsky 1995), we can reformulate our account as follows: the features of *ṯaan* are free to adjoin to any c-commanding Perspective, but locality considerations force the operation to leave a trace of these features on each of the intervening Perspectives. If we can say that, in every case of head-to-head adjunction, the phi-features of the heads must be "amalgamated", we have an alternative account of one sub-case of checking, namely the checking of heads: incompatible features derived from the two heads will make the derivation crash. Blocking now falls out from checking: since *ṯaan* is 3rd person, an intervening Perspective which is non-3rd person will give rise to a contradictory feature-matrix and the derivation will crash.
14. We may need to have a "cut-off" point in our hierarchy of theta-roles, such that theta-roles below that point are not considered for Perspective. Otherwise we may not always be able to *prevent* a non-volitional subject from anteceding *ṯaan*. Consider our earlier example (i) (= [21a]):

i. a. *Mary$_i$ [John ṯani-ne ṯaḷḷi-(y)appooḷ] wiiṇu
self-acc. pushed-when fell
'Mary$_i$ fell when John pushed self$_i$.'

Here the non-volitional subject is the only argument, and therefore the highest argument, of the matrix verb. But apparently it is still not eligible to be the Perspective of the matrix clause. In such cases we can say that the subject in question—it is possibly Theme here—is below the cut-off point.

15. See Pollard and Sag (1992), and Reinhart and Reuland (1991, 1993), for a proposal that syntactic binding and logophoric binding can be kept apart in terms of the syntactic environments in which they apply.
16. If someone were to insist that the relating of a reflexive anaphor to the clausal "point of view" (Perspective) is to be classed under logophoric binding, then our claim is that all binding of *ṯaan* is logophoric binding.
17. These implications (of the syntax of *ṯaan* for a general theory of long-distance anaphora), we cannot, unfortunately, take up in this paper. But it would be disingenuous if we did not note that the Chinese blocking facts appear to be very different. Thus, the following Chinese sentences are fine (examples given by Bao Zhiming, p.c.):

i. Zhangsan$_i$ yiwei Lisi hui jieshao wo he ziji$_i$
think would introduce I and self
'Zhangsan$_i$ thought that Lisi would introduce me and self$_i$.'

ii. Zhangsan$_i$ yiwei Lisi hui ba ziji$_i$ jieshao gei wo
think would BA self introduce to I
'Zhangsan$_i$ thought that Lisi would introduce self$_i$ to me.'

iii. Zhangsan$_i$ shuo ziji$_i$ mei jian-guo ni
say self not see-ASP you
'Zhangsan$_i$ said that self$_i$ has not seen you.'

Obviously, 1st and 2nd person pronouns do not supersede the subject's claim to Perspective. The Chinese subject is more "prominent" (for Perspective) than the Malayalam subject, in some way which needs to be understood. Another puzzle is that the BEI-phrase (the equivalent of the agentive *by*-phrase of English) and the BA-phrase (BA marks a preverbal object) are as "prominent" as the subject; these phrases can be an alternative antecedent for *ziji*, as illustrated in Cole and Wang (1996).

A 1st or 2nd person pronoun which is *part* of the subject can apparently induce blocking (in our terms, "override" the subject's claim to Perspective), cf.,

iv. ? Zhangsan$_i$ shuo wo didi xihuan ziji$_i$
say I brother like self
'Zhangsan said my brother likes self.'

A question to be investigated is whether a non-3rd person pronoun which is not a subject (nor part of a subject) and not in a BEI- or BA-phrase, can antecede *ziji*. The fact—noted by Cole and Wang (1996)—that a 1st/2nd person pronoun in a BEI-/BA-phrase of the embedded clause does not block *ziji*'s ability to corefer with the matrix subject, should not be a problem for an account of blocking in terms of Perspective: if the embedded subject can always be chosen for the embedded Perspective in Chinese, *ziji* would "have its way clear" into the matrix clause.

■ REFERENCES

Banfield, A. 1982. *Unspeakable sentences*. Boston, Massachusetts: Routledge and Kegan Paul.

Battistella, E. 1989. Chinese reflexivization: a movement to INFL approach. *Linguistics* 27.987–1012.

Burzio, L. 1991. The morphological basis of anaphora. *Journal of Linguistics* 27.81–105.

Cantrall, W.R. 1974. *Viewpoints, reflexives, and the nature of noun phrases*. The Hague: Mouton.

Chomsky, N. 1995. *The minimalist program*. Cambridge, Mass.: MIT Press.

Clements, G.N. 1975. The logophoric pronoun in Ewe: its role in discourse. *Journal of West African Languages* 2.141–177.

Cole, P. and **L.M. Sung.** 1994. Head movement and long-distance reflexives. *Linguistic Inquiry* 25.355–406.

Cole, P. and **C. Wang.** 1996. Antecedents and blockers of long-distance reflexives: The case of Chinese ziji. *Linguistic Inquiry* 27.357–390.

Cole, P., G. Hermon and **L.M. Sung.** 1993. Feature Percolation. *Journal of East Asian Linguistics* 2.91–118.

Huang, C.-T.J. and **C.-C.J. Tang.** 1989. The local nature of the long-distance reflexive in Chinese. *Proceedings of NELS* 19.191–206.

Jayaseelan, K.A. 1997. Anaphors as pronouns. *Studia Linguistica* 51(2). 186–284.

Kuno, S. 1972. Functional sentence perspective: A case study from Japanese and English. *Linguistic Inquiry* 3.269–320.

———. 1983. Reflexivization in English. *Communication and Cognition* 16.65–80.

———. 1987. *Functional syntax: anaphora, discourse and empathy*. Chicago: Chicago University Press.

Kuno, S. and **E. Kaburaki.** 1977. Empathy and syntax. *Linguistic Inquiry* 8.627–672.

Pollard, C. and **I. Sag.** 1992. Anaphors in English and the scope of the binding theory. *Linguistic Inquiry* 23.261–303.

Pica, P. 1987. On the nature of the reflexivization cycle. *Proceedings of NELS* 17.483–497.

Reinhart, T. and **E. Reuland.** 1991. Anaphors and logophors: an argument structure perspective. *Long-Distance Anaphora*, ed. by J. Koster and E. Reuland, 283–321. Cambridge: Cambridge University Press.

———. 1993. Reflexivity. *Linguistic Inquiry* 24.657–720.

Sells, P. 1987. Aspects of logophoricity. *Linguistic Inquiry* 18.445–479.

Zribi–Hertz, A. 1989. Anaphor binding and narrative point of view: English reflexive pronouns in sentence and discourse. *Language* 65.695–727.

Aspect and Event Structure in Vedic

■ PAUL KIPARSKY ■

The aspectual, temporal, and discourse uses of the Vedic aorist are derivable from a basic resultative perfect function. The perfect and imperfect cover the other function of the perfect (existential/universal and present perfect) and past tense, respectively. As it stands, the Reichenbachian approach is not rich enough to distinguish the different uses of the perfect. I argue that this is to be done by specifying the relationship between a predicate's event structure and the perfect's temporal parameters. The proposed representation provides a new solution to the "present perfect puzzle", predicts the co-occurrence of the different readings of the perfect with classes of adverbs, and explains why the existential perfect triggers sequence of tenses in English, and seemingly functions as a backshifted past.

■ 1. The Vedic Past Tenses

■ 1.1. Introduction

Sanskrit presents a classic case of the evolution of aspect to tense.[1] For Proto-Indo-European, the aorist and perfect are reconstructed as purely aspectual categories, with respectively perfective and stative value.[2] In the language described by Panini and used in the Brahmana literature, on the other hand, the aorist serves as a general past tense, while the imperfect and the perfect designate remote or historical past, the perfect being furthermore restricted to events not witnessed by the speaker.[3] In the intervening stage of Vedic Sanskrit, the past tenses show a complex mix of temporal, aspectual, and discourse functions. On top of that, Rigvedic retains the injunctive, a chameleon-like category of underspecified finite verbs whose many uses partly overlap with those of the past tenses. The present study of the Rigvedic system is offered as a preliminary step towards the reconstruction and theoretical interpretation of this aspect-to-tense trajectory.

The issues of tense/aspect theory that this forces us to face are of considerable interest in their own right as well. The "two-dimensional" framework introduced by Reichenbach (1947) has proved illuminating for English and other languages,[4] but its application to Vedic Sanskrit runs into a serious problem. It cannot provide a unitary representation for the aorist or for the perfect, or even distinguish them from each other in terms of the primitives that it provides. A less obvious variant of this problem arises even in English, where the distinction that Sanskrit makes overtly in the morphology appears covertly in the syntax. The solution I propose in this paper involves two refinements. The first is to specify, as part of the representation of certain tense/aspect categories, a particular assignment of the verbal predicate's event structure to the parameters that define their temporal relations. The second is to assume that general categories are *blocked* by specific categories, a move fairly standard in modern morphology (and, of course, in Paninian grammar), but so far not exploited in the analysis of tense. With these added tools, the theory can make sense of most of the intricate data of Vedic, and succeeds in relating its seemingly exotic tense inventory to categories long since known from other languages. Some famous problems of the English tense/aspect system find new solutions too, including tense shift in subordinate clauses and the "present perfect puzzle".

The remainder of section 1 presents the outlines of Vedic tense usage. Readers already familiar with the facts or primarily concerned with the general issues may wish to proceed directly to section 2, which lays out the Reichenbachian theory with the modifications I propose. Section 3 develops the analysis of Vedic and English and shows how it supports the modified theory.

■ 1.2. The Aorist

The Vedic aorist[5] is said to have four main uses.[6] In non-finite and modal verb forms, it marks **perfective aspect**. In the indicative, on the other hand, it has a range of temporal meanings. In main clauses, it most often refers to the **immediate past**:[7]

1. a. vásann araṇyānyā́m sāyám ákrukṣad íti manyate
   staying forest-Loc at-night scream-**Aor**-3Sg unquote think-3Sg
   'In the forest at night, one imagines that someone has just screamed.' (10.146.4)

   b. citráṃ devā́nām úd agād ánīkam, …ā́prā
   bright god-GenPl up rise-**Aor**-3Sg face, …fill-**Aor**-3Sg
   dyā́vāpr̥thivī́ antárikṣam
   heaven-and-earth-Acc middle-abode-Acc

'The bright face of the gods has risen, …it has filled heaven and earth and the air between them.' (1.115.1)

But it also functions like the English pluperfect, to mark the **relative anteriority** of a subordinate clause with respect to the main clause. The event in this case need not be recent, either in relation to the time of speech or to the reference time of the main clause.

2\. a. víśve deváso amadann ánu tvā; śúṣṇam píprum
all gods rejoice-**Impf**-3Pl to you Suṣṇa, P.-Acc,
kúyavaṃ vṛtrám indra yadā́vadhīr ví púraḥ
K.-Acc, V.-Acc, I.-Voc when smite-**Aor**-3Sg apart forts-Acc
śámbarasya
Ś.-Gen
'all the gods cheered you, Indra, when you had smashed Śuṣṇa, Pipru, Kuyava, Vṛtra and the forts of Śambara' (1.103.7–8)

b\. ugrám ayātam. ávaho ha kútsaṃ
terrible-Acc go-**Impf**-3Du took-**Impf**-2Sg Part Kutsa-Acc
sáṃ ha yád vām uśánā́ranta deváḥ
together Part when you-PlAcc Uśana-Instr bring-**Aor**-3Pl gods
'The two of you went to the terrible one. You took Kutsa, when the gods had united you with Uśanā.' (5.31.8)

c\. sávanaṃ vivér apó yáthā purā́ mánave
oblation work-**PresInj**-3Sg work-Acc as formerly Manu-Dat
gātúm áśret
way-Acc provide-**Aor**-3Sg
'The oblation has fulfilled its purpose, as it once prepared the way for Manu.' (10.76.3)

The fourth traditionally recognized use of the Vedic aorist is to make a **statement of fact** (*Konstatierung*, Hoffmann 1967: 155).[8] The aorists said to have this function typically occur amidst imperfects, often at the end of a narrative, or with a change in point of view, as in (3c). They may carry the story forward or summarize it and comment upon it. Hoffmann contrasts this function of the aorist with the imperfect's function of "reporting narration" (*berichtende Erzählung*) (p.160) and with the injunctive's function of "mention" or "mentioning description" (*erwähnende Beschreibung*) (p.163).

3\. a. nā́tārīd asya sámṛtiṃ vadhā́nāṃ
not bear-**Aor**-3Sg his impact-Acc weapon-GenPl
'He failed to withstand the impact of his weapons.' (1.32.6)

b\. satrā́bhavo vásupatir vásūnāṃ dátre
totally become-**Impf**-3Sg wealth-lord wealth-GenPl portion-Dat
víśvā adhithā indra kṛṣṭī́ḥ
all-AccPl put-Mid-**Aor**-3Sg I.-Voc people-AccPl

'You have become the supreme overlord of wealth, you have supplied all peoples with their portion, Indra' (4.17.6)

c. ní āvidhyad ilībíśasya dṛḷhā́ ví śṛṅgíṇam
down strike-**Impf**-3Sg I.-Gen forts-Acc apart horned-Acc
abhinac chúṣṇam índraḥ …vájreṇa śátrum
split-**Impf**-3Sg Śuṣna-Acc Indra …thunderbolt-Instr enemy-Acc
avadhīḥ pṛtanyúm
slay-**Aor**-2Sg hostile-Acc
'Indra struck down Ilībiśa's forts and split apart the horned Śuṣna…you have slain the enemy (O Indra)' (1.33.12)

The link between these four functions is certainly not obvious. What exactly do the temporal meanings "recent past" and "relative anteriority" have to do with one another? What does either of them have to do with the discourse function of "statement of fact"? And what do any of these have to do with the telicity that the aorist marks in non-indicative contexts? Part of the problem is to discover what *kind* of connection we should be looking for: a basic meaning from which the several functions are synchronically derivable? Or a natural diachronic path that connects them, grounded in principles of language change? And the answer to that depends on whether the tenses have a single lexical meaning with structural ambiguity, a single meaning with different pragmatic uses, or are genuinely polysemous.

I will argue that the tenses have synchronically unitary meanings, that these meanings give rise to distinct readings through alternative assignments of event structure into the temporal parameters, and that each such reading determines a particular range of discourse functions. Aside from the empirical evidence, this is more likely than the opposite direction of dependency[9] for several conceptual reasons. First, temporal relations make better descriptive primitives because they are invariant across sentence types and literary genres, which such discourse categories as "narration", "statement of fact", and "mention" are not. The latter do not even describe the functions of the tenses across all their indicative uses, being applicable only to declarative main clauses, though the tense distinctions in questions and restrictive relative clauses are in fact entirely parallel. But even for declarative main clauses the discourse categories are far from well-defined. (We can identify a narrative well enough by its sequential progression of temporal reference points, but what exactly is a "statement of fact", as opposed to a "mention"?) For tenses and aspects, on the other hand, there exist reasonably well worked out descriptive frameworks, most prominent among them the Reichenbachian theory, a modified version of which I will be adopting here. It has the added virtue of giving us a handle on the co-occurrence restrictions between the individual tenses and various classes of adverbs, and on the restrictions of certain tenses to particular aspectual classes of verbs, because it provides an explicit way of relating the meanings of the tenses to the meanings of the adverbs and of the verbs that they are associated with. I believe that this approach also furnishes a promising starting point for an understanding of the diachrony.

■ 1.3. Imperfect and Perfect

Returning to our review of the Vedic past tenses, the imperfect is comparatively straightforward.[10] It is used for narrating sequences of past events, and picks out a specific, localized past time of the historical or remote past (Delbrück 1876: 90 ff., 1897: 268 ff., Hoffmann 1967: 151).

4.

ástabhnāt	síndhum	arṇavám̥	…viśvā́mitro	yád	
stay-**Impf**-3Sg	river-Acc	flowing-Acc	…V.	when	
ávahat	sudā́sam	ápriyā́yata		kuśikébhir	índraḥ
carry-**Impf**-3Sg	Sudas-Acc	be-pleased-**Impf**-3Sg		K.-InstPl	I.

'(the sage) dammed the flowing river … When Viśvamitra brought Sudas, Indra was pleased with the Kuśikas.' (3.53.9)

The perfect, on the other hand, seems even more heterogeneous than the aorist.[11] From a class of achievement verbs, it forms **stative presents**, very likely the Indo-European perfect's primordial function (Cowgill 1972: 928):

5. *veda*, *ciketa* 'knows' (from *vid*, *cit* 'find out'), *jujoṣa* 'enjoys', *cakāna* 'likes', *bibhāya* 'fears', *taṣṭhau* 'stands', *śiśrāya* 'rests on', *dadhāra* 'holds', *ānaśa* 'has', *babhūva* 'is'.

These perfects predicate only the state itself, not the change of state that may have brought it about. They have strictly present time reference, and are coordinated with regular present tense verbs:[12]

6.

ká	īṣate	tujyáte	kó bibhāya
who	flee-**Pres**-3Sg	rush-**Pres**-3Sg	who fear-**Perf**-3Sg

'Who is fleeing and rushing, who is afraid?' (1.84.17)

In all other uses, the perfect refers to the past. Some of these are shared with the aorist, others are the exclusive domain of the perfect. To begin with the latter, the most salient perfect-specific function is to introduce an existential or universal *quantification over past times*. Predicates interpreted distributively, denoting multiple events, nearly always have the perfect in reference to past time (Renou 1925: 23). The text in (7) nicely illustrates of the contrast between the perfect with distributive reading and the imperfect with individual/collective (single-event) reading.

7.

dáme-dame	…agnír	hótā	ní	ṣasāda	
house-Loc-house-Loc	…Agni	priest	down	sit-**Perf**-3Sg	
yájīyān	agnír	hótā	ní	asīdad	yájīyān
more sacrificing	Agni	priest	down	sit-**Impf**-3Sg	more sacrificing
upásthe	mātúḥ				
lap-Loc	mother-Gen				

'Agni the expert priest sat down in every house.' [Several sittings, perfect.] 'Agni the expert priest sat down on his mother's lap.' [One sitting, imperfect.] (5.1.5)

(8) shows an analogous contrast between the individual/collective aorist in (8a) and the distributive perfect in (8b), both with the verb *vad* 'speak', and both referring to recent past.

8. a. prá maṇḍū́kā avādiṣuḥ
Pref frog-Pl speak-**Aor**-3Pl
'The frogs have spoken.' [in chorus, aorist] (7.103.1)
b. drúna íd bhūtím ūdima
wood-Gen just origin-Acc speak-**Perf**-1Pl
'We have just spoken about the origin of wood.' [each of us in turn, perfect] (1.161.1)

The distributive reading typically occurs with plural or collective subjects or objects. Indeed, with universally quantified plurals, the perfect is mandatory:

9. tám evá víśve papire suvardṛ́śo bahú sākáṃ
that-Acc Prt all-Pl drink-**Perf**-3Pl sun-seeing-Pl much together
sisicur útsam udríṇam
pour-**Perf**-3Pl source-Acc watery-Acc
'All who see the sun have drunk from that (well). They have all drawn deeply from the abundant water source' (2.24.4)

A telling contrast occurs in the creation hymn 10.129. It first says that certain things did not exist — being did not exist, death did not exist (*āsīt*, imperfect) — and then concludes: nothing existed (*āsa*, perfect).

The perfect is obligatory with respect to past time, even with singular nominal arguments, when the verb is modified by a adverb of quantification, either universal (such as 'always' in [10] or existential, such as 'many times' [Renou ibid.]):[13]

10. a. sádā kavī sumatím ā́ cake vāṃ
always seer-DuVoc favor-Acc Part enjoy-**Perf**-1Sg you-DuGen
'I have always sought your favor, O seers.' (1.117.23)
b. śáśvat puróṣā́ ví uvāsa deví
always formerly Dawn Part shine-**Perf**-3Sg goddess
'The goddess Dawn has always shone forth in the past.' (1.113.13) [Contrast (1b), about the particular current sunrise.]
c. purutrā́ vā́cam pipiśur vádantaḥ
in many ways voice-Acc ornament-**Perf**-3Pl speaking-Pl
'In speaking, they have modulated their voices in many ways.' (7.103.6)

The perfect is also the normal past tense of generic and habitual sentences:[14]

11. a. ná sóma índram ásuto mamāda
not soma Indra-Acc unpressed please-**Perf**-3Sg
'Unpressed soma has not [ever] pleased Indra.' (7.26.1)
b. tuvám̥ jigetha ná dhánā rurodhitha
you win-**Perf**-3Sg not prize-Pl retain-**Perf**-3Sg
'You have [always] won and not kept the booty' (1.102.10)

This holds also for generalizing relative clauses ('whoever', 'whatever', 'in whatever way'), e.g. (12a),[15] and generalizing questions (who [all], whatever etc.), e.g. (12b).[16]

12. a. yác ca papaú yác ca ghāsím̥
what-Acc and drink-**Perf**-3Sg what-Acc and food-Acc
jaghā́sa
eat-**Perf**-3Sg
'Whatever it (the horse) has drunk and whatever food it has eaten' [let it all be for the gods] (1.162.14)
b. ká īm̥ dadarśa
who him see-**Perf**-3Sg
'Who has (ever) seen him?' [Implication: no-one has.] (8.100.03)

In contrast, questions about specific past occasions, asking for particular answers, and relative clauses with referential heads, have imperfect tense.[17]

13. a. kó apaśyad indram
who see-**Impf**-3Sg Indra-Acc
'Who saw Indra?' [Implication: I did.] (5.30.1)
b. káḥ kumārám ajanayad; rátham̥ kó nír
who boy-Acc engender-**Impf**-3Sg cart-Acc who Pref
avartayat
make-**Impf**-3Sg
'Who conceived the boy? Who made the chariot?' [Implication: someone did.] (10.135.5)

Aorist-like uses of the perfect include simple 'statements of fact' similar to (3), interspersed in aorist-like fashion with imperfects in a narrative context.

14. a. ā́ dade vas trí yuktā́n
to give-**Perf**-Mid-3Sg you-PlDat three-Acc yoked-Acc
'I received three (chariots) in harness for you.' (1.126.5)
b. yé cid dhí pū́rva r̥tasā́pa ā́san sākám̥
who-Pl Prt Prt ancestors truth-seeking be-**Impf**-3Pl together
devébhir ávadann rtā́ni té cid ávāsur
gods-Instr speak-**Impf**-3Pl truths-Acc they Prt stop-**Aor**-3Pl
nahí ántam āpúḥ
not end-Acc reach-**Perf**-3Pl
'Our ancestors, who after all were committed to the truth, and

spoke the truth with the gods, even they ceased, even they never reached the end.' (1.179.2)

c. urú kṣáyā́ya cakrire
wide-Acc dwelling-Dat make-**Perf**-3Pl
[They conquered (impf. *ataran*) heaven, earth, and the waters,]
'they made themselves a wide homeland.' (1.36.8)

A case can be made for the stronger claim that the perfect's potential uses include *all* uses of the aorist. Even the recent past and anterior past, the prime territory of the aorist,[18] seems to be in principle available to the perfect as well. The evidence is that if a root for one or another reason lacks aorist forms, and there is no suppletive root to fill the gap, its perfect forms are used in the aorist's functions. Such roots are *ruc* 'shine' and *su* 'press', whose basic diatheses make no aorists in the Rigveda[19], and *vakṣ* 'grow'.[20] The place of their missing aorists is taken by the perfect, as in the following examples with recent past meaning:[21]

15. a. úpo ruruce yuvatír ná yóṣā
forth Prt shine-**Perf**-3Sg young like woman
'(Dawn) has shone forth like a young woman' (7.77.1)

b. putráḥ káṇvasya vā́m ihá suṣā́va somiyám mádhu
son Kanva you-Dat here press-**Perf**-3Sg somic juice-Acc
'[come here, gods, for] the son of Kanva has pressed some *soma* juice for you here.' (8.8.4)

The challenge of providing a unitary characterization, then, seems even more formidable for the perfect than for the aorist. But even the perfect's apparent functional diversity is nothing compared to that of the injunctive.

■ 1.4. The Injunctive

This most various of verbal categories, retained from Indo-European in early Vedic but lost in later Sanskrit, can assume virtually any temporal and modal value in context. It marks only aspect (by the contrast of present stem vs. aorist stem) and person/number (by means of secondary endings). Injunctive forms typically pick up their tense/mood reading from a fully specified verb in their discourse context:[22]

16. a. ádhvānayad duritā́ dambháyac ca
smoke-out-**Impf**-3Sg fortresses-Acc sack-**Inj**-3Sg and
'He smoked out the fortresses and sacked them.' (6.18.10)

b. ā́d ít paścā́ bubudhānā́ ví ā́khyann, ā́d
the Part afterwards awakened around look-**Aor**-3Pl, then

íd rátnaṃ dhārayanta dyúbhaktam
Part jewel-Acc hold-**Inj**-3Sg heaven-bestowed-Acc
'Then, when they had afterwards woken up, they looked around and held on to the jewel that heaven had bestowed on them.'
(4.1.18)

Injunctives also fill in for missing forms in the paradigm of the imperative (Hoffmann 1967: 269, fn. 5), and appear optionally in several other functions that can be considered temporally unmarked performatives (Hoffmann 1967: 251 ff.),

17. a. índrasya nú vīríyani prá vocam
I.-Gen Part exploits Pref call-**AorInj**-1Sg
'I hereby proclaim the heroic deeds of Indra.' (1.32.1) [proem]
b. subaddhā́m amútas karam
well-tied-Acc from there make-**AorInj**-1Sg
'I hereby tie her firmly from there.' (10.85.25) [wedding liturgy]

generic and universally quantified sentences that do not have specifically past time reference (Hoffmann 1967, Ch. 3),

18. a. divé-dive sū́riyo darśató bhūt
day-Loc-day-Loc sun visible become-**AorInj**-3Sg
'Every day the sun appears.' (6.30.2)
b. tuváṃ vikṣú pradívaḥ sīda āsú
you peoples-Loc continually sit-**Inj**-2Sg these-Loc
'You continually sit among these peoples.' (6.5.3)

and prohibitions, where the particle *mā* is joined with the present injunctive to prohibit an ongoing event ("inhibitive" prohibitions), and with the aorist injunctive to prohibit a future event ("preventive" prohibitions), (Hoffmann 1967, Ch. 2). It is clear that the injunctive should be treated as a form which has no tense and mood specifications. The question for any theory which treats the present as zero tense, and the indicative as zero mood, is this: how should we distinguish the present indicative from the more radically underspecified category of the injunctive?

■ 2. Tense Theory

■ 2.1. The Reichenbachian Framework

Temporal relations hold among three *temporal parameters*, E, R, P and a constant, S:

19. a. E (event time, the time during which the event unfolds)
b. R (reference time, the time referred to)

c. P (perspective time, the "now" point of temporal deixis)
d. S (speech time, the actual moment of utterance)

Following Dowty (1979), I assume that the values of the parameters are intervals, and treat points as degenerate intervals. S will be assumed to be a point.

Most versions of the theory treat S as a parameter rather than as a constant relative to a speech act. They rather uncomfortably divide the function of P time between R and S, in a way which precludes a consistent interpretation of both. The simplest motivation for distinguishing speech time S and "now" time P is the historical present, where they are obviously different times.[23] Even if the historical present were treated as a stylistic convention outside of the theory of grammar, the analytical "overload" of S is undeniable in analyses of complex sentences which assign distinct S times to main and subordinate clauses even when the latter do not denote speech acts (e.g., Hornstein 1990, see section 3.3 below). In the present analysis, it is P that temporally links main and subordinate clauses, while S remains fixed to actual speech time. The idea of adding a parameter of P time is due to Kamp and Reyle (1993: 594) and Eberle and Kasper (1994: 157), who show that Reichenbach's R parameter is also trying to do too many things at once.[24] This said, for purposes of most of the present discussion, we will consider only the case where S and P coincide, and omit S from the tense formulae.

Temporal relations are defined by the relations of immediate precedence (A—B, read "A immediately precedes B") and temporal inclusion ($A \subseteq B$, read "A is included in B"). The default temporal relations for verbs unmarked for tense and aspect are the following inclusion relations:

20. a. $P \subseteq R$
b. $E \subseteq R$
c. $S \subseteq P$

A finite verb not marked for tense will thus be assigned a present tense reading. Morphologically marked tenses and aspects function to defeat these defaults. Morphology that defeats (20a) by specifying a precedence relation between R and P may be called *tense* (E, R—P = past tense, P—E, R = future tense). Morphology that defeats (20b) by specifying a precedence relation between E and R may be called *aspect* (E—P, R = perfect, P, R—E = prospective[25]). In addition, marked aspects may specify the assignment of a predicate's event structure into the temporal parameters in the four ways detailed in the next subsection. This makes aspect a semantically more diverse category than tense, and allows a language to have several 'perfects'.

For English, the present, past, perfect, and past perfect have the specifications shown in (21). The first line shows the underspecified lexical representations of the tense-aspect combinations, the second shows the default assignment by (20), and the third shows the resulting fully specified temporal relations.

21.

	Present	*Past*	*Pres. Perfect*	*Past Perfect*
Specification		E, R—P	E—R, P	E—R—P
Default	$E \subset R$, $P \subseteq R$	$E \subseteq R$	$P \subsetneq R$	
Output	$E \subseteq R$, $P \subseteq R$	$E \subseteq R$, R—P	E—R, $P \subseteq R$	E—R—P

For easier visualization of the temporal relations in complex sentences, I will sometimes show temporal inclusion as vertical alignment, like this:

22. a. Past: E
|
R— P

b. Present Perfect: P
|
E—R

Note that (20) does not include a default relation $P \subseteq E$, and if it did, the specifications for the past and for the present perfect in (21) and (22) would come out wrong. This means that for present tense the system does not specify an intrinsic inclusion relation between E and S/P. I take this to be the correct result because of cases such as *the boat leaves tomorrow*, where we clearly have S, P—E. Rather, I assume that present tense is an unmarked tense which covers those temporal relations for which there is no marked tense in the system. In other words, the interpretation of present tense is the result of *blocking* by tenses with temporally more restricted meanings. We shall see several cases below where the blocking mechanism is necessary to avoid complex or even impossible specifications of tense categories.

Vedic shares with English the categories of past tense (R—P, the Vedic imperfect) and perfect aspect (E—R). The two languages diverge in how they divide the perfect into a marked and an unmarked subcategory. English distinguishes past perfect (pluperfect) from present perfect, Vedic distinguishes the resultative perfect (its aorist "tense") from the unmarked perfect-at-large (its perfect "tense").

In the terminology adopted here, the Vedic aorist and perfect are aspects, not tenses. However, there will be no harm in continuing to refer to them together as tenses, in keeping with traditional terminology, as long as we don't forget that they are both aspectual in the sense that they mean that event time precedes reference time (E—R), whereas the imperfect means that reference time precedes perspective time (R—P).

■ 2.2. Perfect Aspect

Any analysis of the perfect must account for its apparent polysemy. The Vedic aorist and perfect divide among themselves all the readings (23a–d) of the English perfect,[26] plus another, the stative present perfect:

23. a. **Resultative**: The police have caught the suspect in Berkeley.
    b. **Existential**: Fred has been to Paris.
    c. **Universal**: I have known Max since 1960.

d. **Recent Past**: General Mohammed Aidid has died in Mogadishu at age 61. (From an obituary.)
e. **Stative Present**: (I've got [=I have] something to tell you.[27])

Opinions are divided on whether there are several structurally and semantically distinct kinds of perfect (McCawley 1971, 1981, Mittwoch 1988, Michaelis 1994) or a single perfect which receives several pragmatic interpretations (McCoard 1978, Matthews 1987, Declerck 1991, Klein 1992). Vedic strongly supports the former view. The fact that it groups the readings into two morphologically distinct categories, aorist and perfect, shows that the relevant readings must be grammatically distinct. As for how that distinction is to be made in the grammar, the Vedic data support a semantic approach in the spirit of Mittwoch's, over both McCawley's syntactic approach and Michaelis' construction grammar approach. In the particular semantic account I will defend, the different types of perfect correspond to different ways of relating the event structure specified by the lexical content of the verb to the temporal structure E—R denoted by perfect aspect. A particular perfect category in a language can be specified for which of these possible temporal interpretations it requires or allows.

a. The **resultative** reading, also called the state reading, is confined to accomplishment and achievement predicates, which are characterized by a change of state component in their lexical semantic form (Vendler 1957, Dowty 1979, Foley and van Valin 1984, Rappaport Hovav and Levin 1997). An accomplishment predicate, such as *catch*, *hide*, denotes an event ε consisting of an activity leading to a change of state. An achievement predicate, such as *die*, *arrive*, denotes an event consisting of a change of state. The resultative reading of the perfect arises when the change of state corresponding to an accomplishment or achievement predicate is temporally located at the edge between time E and time R in the perfect's temporal schema. Because the change of state is temporally located at the onset of R time, the activity leading up to it in accomplishment predicates must immediately precede R. For example, in (23a) *catch the suspect*, the activity of pursuing the suspect is located at E, i.e. it extends from some time prior to R up to R, the change of state is located at the edge between E and R, and the result state begins at that point. Because $P \subseteq R$, the sentence entails (or at least implicates) that the suspect is currently in custody—the so-called "current relevance" property of the resultative reading. In the case of achievement predicates, the change of state is again temporally located at the onset of R time, with the same "current relevance" implications, but no activity is located at E.

b. The **existential** reading, also known as the experiential reading, is obtained when the whole event denoted by an atelic or an iterative telic verbal predicate (a state or process) is fully contained in the interval E. The resulting predicate asserts that one or more events of that type occurred during that interval. The event does not have to extend throughout the entire interval E to the beginning of R (as in the universal reading), and the implicature is that it does not. For example, (23b) asserts that Fred has visited Paris on one or more occasions during a period E extending from some past time up to time R, and implicates that he is not currently visiting Paris.[28]

c. The **universal** reading (or continuing reading) arises when the event denoted by an atelic or an iterative telic verbal predicate is coextensive with the interval E. For a sentence with a perfect to be true in the universal reading, the state or process must last for the entire duration of the period terminating at R. For example, (23c) means that the knowing extends through the entire time from 1960 up to R, which in this case is the present.

The universal reading requires an adverb specifying a duration (such as *always, since 1960* or *for two years*) and so it is tempting to derive it as a special case of the existential reading, resulting from cancellation of the existential reading's implicature that the event does not obtain throughout E, by the explicit adverb. Such a unification of the universal and existential readings would have to overcome at least three prima facie objections. First, the boundaries that define the duration are understood in an inclusive way in the existential reading but in an exclusive way in the universal reading (Mittwoch 1988). The sentence

25. I have been in Hyderabad since 1977.

is false on the existential reading if I last was in Hyderabad in 1977 or if I have just landed on my first visit there; it is the intervening time that counts (exclusive boundaries). For the universal reading of (25) to be true I must have been there in 1977 and I must be there now (inclusive boundaries). This difference between the universal and existential readings constitutes a bar to the proposed unification (unless it can be shown to follow somehow from the interpretation of existential and universal quantification). The second objection is that some languages (such as German) do not allow the universal reading of the perfect (or allow it only in restricted circumstances). Any claim that the universal reading is derived from the existential perfect would then have to be complemented with an explanation for why the derivation fails in German. The third objection is that there are, conversely, languages with a special perfect that is restricted just to the existential reading, such as the Hungarian indefinite tense discussed by Piñon (1996). At least in these languages the existential perfect cannot be an implicature of the universal perfect.

d. The status of the **recent past** or "hot news" reading is dubious. Michaelis (1994: 127, fn. 4) suggests that it is an implicature of the resultative reading.[29] This is plausible because the resultative reading situates an event at a time which verges on P time, and locates the result state at P time. It would fit well with Vedic, where the aorist has precisely the resultative and recent past functions. I will adopt this idea here and treat the recent past and resultative readings as special cases of a single reading, here referred to as the R-reading.[30] It is this reading which characterizes the Vedic aorist. The other three readings devolve by default onto the perfect.

e. In the **present state** reading, the reference interval is included in the result state corresponding to the verbal predicate. The change of state is not assigned to any temporal parameter, but remains implicit. It is thus not part of this reading of the perfect, though it may be pragmatically inferred. This yields a purely stative interpretation, and strictly present time reference.[31]

Let ε be the event denoted by a verbal predicate, *e* the temporal trace of the activity leading up to the change of state, and *r* the temporal trace of the result state. Then we can depict the four different temporal structures of the perfect as follows:

26. a. R-reading:

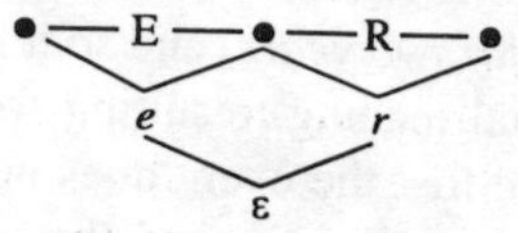

b. Existential reading:

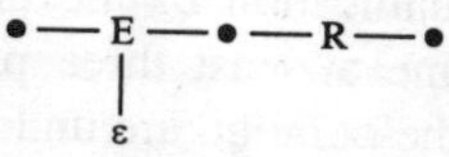

c. Universal reading:

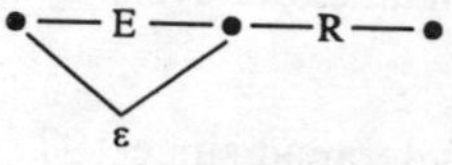

d. Present state reading:

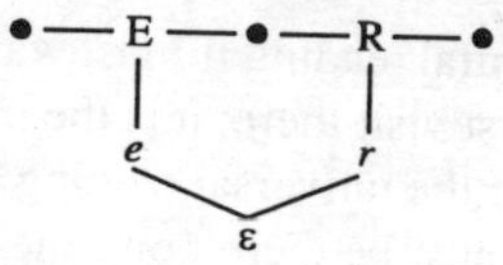

We are now ready to lay out the specifications of the Vedic past tenses. The aorist's distinctive property over and above the perfect is that it requires the R-reading ([26a], symbolized in the table by the ad hoc notation E—R_r).

27.

	Present	*Past*	*Perfect*	*Aorist*
Specification		R—P	E—R	E—R_r
Default	E⊆R, P⊆R	E⊆R	P⊆R	P⊆R
Output	E⊆R, P⊆R	E⊆R, R—P	E—R, P⊆R	E—R_r, P⊆R

It is the R-reading that lies behind the four temporal and aspectual functions of the aorist listed in section 1.2. The "recent past" and "current relevance" implications of the R-reading are consequences of the particular way the R-reading maps telic events into E and R time. They are not properties of the perfect generally, but of the R-reading in particular.

Once the aorist is so specified, it is not necessary to restrict the meaning of the perfect to exclude the R-reading. In fact, it is not possible to do so because the perfect has in principle the full range of perfect functions. It is simply that the aorist, being specifically restricted to the R-reading, blocks the perfect from being assigned that reading. The perfect picks up the remaining perfect readings consistent with the temporal schema (E—R), viz. the existential, universal, and present state readings ([7], [9]–[12], and [6] respectively). And in those few verbs which lack an aorist (see [15]), the perfect picks up the R-reading as well.

■ 2.3. The Injunctive as a Tenseless Verb

The Reichenbachian representational schema provides a ready means of assimilating the tenselessness of the injunctive to the tenselessness of the other non-indicative verb forms. Their common characteristic is that they are not specifiable, inherently or by the default rule (20), for the parameter P. Thus they have no past tense (R—P), no future tense (P—R), and no present tense ($P \subseteq R$, $S \subseteq P$). But they can be aoristic (E—R), because aspect does not involve specification of the parameter P. In discourse, injunctives may become temporally localized via another verb form's P by what we can think of as temporal anaphora, as in (16). They can also be localized at speech time by the temporal equivalent of deixis, as in (17), or remain temporally unlocalized, in which case they are interpreted as "timeless" generic verb forms, as in (18). Since the neutralization of the P parameter provides a basis for the injunctive's different uses, the postulation of a special discourse function of "mentioning" for it is unnecessary.

■ 2.4. Why the Imperfect is the Narrative Tense

Default discourse conventions on temporal sequencing relate to reference time (R). In the absence of information to the contrary, successive R times 'move forward' (Dowty 1982, Partee 1984). Thus, letting R_a and R_b stand for the reference times of sentences A and B,

28. a. $R_a = R_b$, if at least one of them denotes a state or process;
    b. If $R_a \neq R_b$, and A precedes B, then R_a—R_b.

(28) is defeasible in the sense that it provides only a default inference about the order of narrated events. It can be thwarted by specifying a contrary sequencing through adverbs and other temporal information.

Purely pragmatic accounts of these phenomena (such as Lascarides and Asher 1993) fail to address the fact that languages differ systematically in whether they allow inferences based on real-world knowledge to override order of narration. English tolerates texts such as *John came to work late yesterday. He got up only at 10.* The German translation requires a past perfect in the second sentence.[32] In Vedic, as well, (28) seems to be more rigorously enforced; I have found no example where imperfects narrate events in the "wrong" order. This suggests the following generalization:

29. a. *Vedic, German*: R must be fixed by temporal adverbs or narrative context.

b. *English*: R must be fixed by temporal adverbs, narrative context, or inference.

The extra option of fixing R by inference in English would also allow such 'out of the blue' cases as *Oops, the lights just went out.*, *Did you see that huge wasp fly by?*, or *I didn't hear. I had the water running.* (cf. Michaelis 1994: 146). Because there is no narrative context or adverbial specification of time, German would here use the perfect and Vedic the aorist. For the same reason, English can use past tense in reference to an indeterminate remote past time, (e.g. *Who killed Julius Caesar?*, Partee 1984), where German would tend to use the perfect.

The fact that the past but not the perfect is used in narrative can then be explained as follows. Verbs in the same stretch of discourse have the same P time. But the perfect's P time is included in R time (see [21] and [27]). Therefore, if two perfects fall in the same discourse, the R time of one cannot precede the R of the other (for both R_i and R_j include P). Even though the perfect places an event in the past, a sequence of perfects cannot provide the succession of R times that "drives the narrative forward", because the R times of all perfects in a stretch of discourse necessarily overlap, so that perfect aspect cannot be subject to (28). This contrasts with past tense (the Vedic imperfect). Each past tense can have its own R time, because there can be arbitrarily many successive intervals R_i, R_j... which all precede P. Each reset R time includes a new E time. This unlimited supply of R/E times is exploited by the narrative convention (28), which makes each new R point in a narrative sequence (and therefore each E included in it) a temporal successor of the last one. A sequence of telic past tense verbs is thus understood as referring to successive events. Consequently, Vedic narrative, which is governed by (28), uses the imperfect but not the perfect or aorist.

This much establishes why the imperfect (and only the imperfect) is used for narrative in Vedic. We must still explain its other salient property, that it typically refers to the remote past, clearly not simply a consequence of its narrative function. Nor can it be due to an inherent meaning such as "remote past", at least on the minimal theory of tense assumed here, which simply does not allow for such a meaning. To be sure, we could add machinery for specifying degrees of temporal distance, and this may indeed be necessary for other tense systems (Comrie 1981). But for Vedic at least there is a more attractive account which is consistent both with the simple theory and with the simple representation of the imperfect as a general past (R—P). This is to derive the imperfect's restriction to remote past as a *blocking* effect. The idea is that reference of the imperfect to the recent past is pre-empted by the aorist, which is restricted to recent past in virtue of its resultative meaning. Expression of the remote past then falls by default to the imperfect. As often, when the semantic range of a category is complex or impossible to specify positively, it turns out that the blocking mechanism assigns it the "elsewhere" function relative to one or several more specific categories.

To see in detail how this blocking of the perfect by the aorist works in Vedic, we must take a closer look at the functions of the aorist. Our goal is to derive them from the aorist's temporal schema E—R,.

■ 3. Event Structure and The Aorist

■ 3.1 The Aspectual Function of The Aorist

The Vedic aorist is restricted to *telic* verbs (Delbrück 1897: 239). The telicity of the aorist is a consequence of its resultative character. The aorist requires the R-reading of the perfect (E—R), which maps the change of state to the edge between E and R. Telic predicates have an event structure which provides such a change of state. Atelic predicates do not, hence cannot be assigned an R-reading, so their aorist would be uninterpretable.[33]

Specifically, Vedic verb roots can be grouped into three *Aktionsart* types:[34]

30. a. Telic (achievements and accomplishments, so-called 'aorist roots'): *vṛt* 'turn, become', *vṛdh* 'row', *sthā* 'stand up', *krand* 'cry out', *hṛ* 'take', *bhū* 'become', *dyut* 'flash', *skand* 'leap', *bhī* 'become scared', *budh* 'wake up, take notice', *vap* 'strew', *jan* 'be born', *ram* 'calm down', *tyaj* 'leave'.
    b. Atelic (states and processes): *as* 'be', *vas* 'dwell', *śī* 'lie', *ās* 'lie', *iṣ* 'move', *iṣ* 'desire', *bhā* 'shine', *vā* 'blow' (wind), *rud* 'weep', *plu* 'float', *jīv* 'live'.
    c. Telic/atelic. These verbs are lexically compatible with both a resultative and an irresultative reading. They may be aspectually specified either syntactically at the VP level (e.g. indefinite bare plural objects force an atelic reading on the VP) or morphologically (by aspectual affixes): *bhar* 'bring, carry', *kram* 'step', *ruh* 'climb', *dhāv* 'run', *pū* 'cleanse'.

In principle, all inherently telic verbs form aorists, often directly from the root (or with a semantically empty thematic suffic *-a*). Telic/atelic verbs also form aorists, but normally by means of a perfectivizing stem-forming suffix *-s*. Inherently atelic roots do not form aorists in Rigvedic. On the other hand, many atelic verbs form a present tense without a stem-forming suffix with either perfectivizing or imperfectivizing function.

Originally, stative present perfects probably also did not occur with inherently atelic verbs. Such perfects as (5) were formed from achievement predicates by making their result state coextensive with R and suppressing the change of state component. However, the same mechanism of change by which middles become underlying statives can operate for present perfects as well. When an underlying achievement predicate changed in meaning, or went out of use in the other tenses, the stative present perfect derived from it could be reinterpreted as a basic stative verb with perfect inflection. For example, when the present tense *bibheti* changed its meaning from 'become afraid' to 'be afraid', there would no longer have been any reason to treat the perfect *bibhāya* as containing an implicit change of state component.

Thus, even when temporally interpreted as in the indicative, aorist and perfect are subject to constraints based on their aspectual nature.

The clearest aspectual contrast between aorist and non-aorist injunctives appears in prohibitions. As noted earlier, preventive prohibitions take the aorist injunctive, while inhibitive prohibitions take the present/imperfect injunctive:

31. a. mā́ párā gāḥ
    not away go-**AorInj**-3Sg
    'Don't go away' (3.53.2) [Addressed to someone who is present]
  b. akṣaír mā́ dīvyaḥ
    dice-Instr not play-**Inj**-3Sg
    'Don't gamble (any more).' (10.34.13) [Addressed to a gambler]

Assume that prohibitions, like all modal verb forms, are tenseless, i.e. they are not specified for the parameter P.[35] The injunctive's basic property is precisely that it is not specified for the parameter P (section 1.4). Suppose further that the imperative and the prohibitive request the addressee to bring it about that the event denoted by the verb respectively should and should not obtain at R. Applied to a non-aorist predicate ($E \subseteq R$), the prohibitive, marked by the particle *mā*, yields an inhibitive prohibition, for $\neg (E \subseteq R)$ is true for any time R at which the event is not taking place. Applied to an aorist predicate (E—R), it yields a preventive prohibition, since ¬ (E—R) on the R-reading can be true at R only if the event has never occurred.

■ 3.2. Adverbs

The co-occurrence of adverbial modifiers and tense depends on several dimensions of the adverbs' meaning: whether they quantify over times, whether they denote points or non-point intervals, whether they denote times anterior to, included in, or posterior to P, and whether they are deictic or not.

The Vedic data in (8)–(12) showed that the aorist is excluded with adverbs requiring universal or existential quantification over times. With past time reference, such adverbs require the perfect.[36] The relevant class of adverbs is that which is semantically incompatible with the R-reading. Compare the English examples in (32):

32. a. I have broken my leg. [Salient R-reading.]
  b. I have often broken my leg. [No R-reading.]
  c. Whenever I have tried this run, I have broken my leg. [No R-reading.]

While (32a) has an R-reading, implying that my leg is still broken, (32b,c) do not have such a reading. In Vedic, since the aorist is restricted to the R-reading, it is incompatible with quantificational adverbs. They require the perfect, which allows the universal and existential readings.

The R-reading of the English present perfect admits deictic adverbs that specify a point included in P (33a).[37] It excludes adverbs that denote a point anterior to P (33b), and those that denote an interval (33c,d).

33. a. The convict has escaped now (already, at this point). [*Now* specifies a point included in P; R reading OK.]
    b. #The convict has escaped three hours ago (yesterday, in 1960). [*Three hours ago* specifies a point that precedes P; no acceptable reading.[38]]
    c. #The convict has escaped twice nowadays (currently, these days). [*Nowadays* specifies an interval that includes P; no acceptable reading.]
    d. The convict has escaped recently (in the past, during the Reagan administration). [*In the past* specifies an interval that precedes P; existential reading only.]

We can understand this distribution if we suppose that the R-reading temporal adverbs specify the edge between E and R, the point at which the change of state is located. The R-reading of the present perfect is then incompatible both with adverbials denoting a time anterior to R and with adverbs denoting an interval.

The same restriction holds by and large for the aorist of recent past in Vedic, as befits its status as a perfect with an R-reading. It is readily accompanied by adverbs denoting an interval that includes present time, such as *idā* 'now', *adya* 'today', and *(u) nu* 'just now, already', as in (34).[39]

34. a. ā́po adyā́nv acāriṣaṃ
    water-PlAcc today Prt go-**Aor**-1Sg
    'I have visited the waters today' (1.23.23)
    b. asmā́bhir u nú praticákṣiyābhūt
    we-Instr Prt now regard-Ger become-**Aor**-3Sg}
    'Now she has become visible to us' (1.113.11)

It does not occur with adverbs denoting an anterior time (such as *purā* 'in the past'), or with adverbs denoting a present interval, such as *nūnam* 'nowadays', which always take the perfect:[40]

35. yáṃ gā́va āsábhir dadhúḥ purā́ nūnáṃ ca
    which-Acc cows mouths-Inst suck-**Perf**-3Pl before now and
    sūráyaḥ
    sponsors
    'which formerly the cows sucked with their mouths, and these days the sponsors of the sacrifice do' (9.99.3)

So far we have seen how the aorist comes by its recent past function and its telic/perfective aspectual value. We must now say how the aorist gets its second main temporal function, of expressing relative anteriority. For that, a short detour into the interpretation of tense in subordinate clauses is necessary.

■ 3.3. Subordination of Tense

For tenses in complements and relative clauses we require three additional rules:

36. a. *Tense subordination*: P_{sub} coincides with the temporal trace of the event denoted by the main clause.
    b. *Independent tense*: P_{sub} may include P_{main}. (optional)
    c. *Sequence of tense*: If P_{sub}—P_{main}, the verb of the subordinate clause has past tense.

where P_{sub} and P_{main} respectively symbolize the P times of subordinate and main clauses. The main difference with respect to other Reichenbachian treatments (such as Hornstein 1991) is that (36a) does not anchor the P time of the subordinate clause to the E time of the main clause, but to the event itself. The different ways of relating event structure and the temporal parameters shown in (26) then predict different temporal relations between main and subordinate clause. Of course, (36a,b) apply both in English and in Vedic, whereas (36c) does not apply in Vedic.

Consider first a future subordinated to a past:

37. a. John said that he would leave. [(i) ... and he did; (ii) ... and he will.]
    b. John said that he will leave. [(i) *... and he did; (ii) ... and he will.]

(37a) and (37b) both assert that John said that he would leave at some time after he spoke; (37b) in addition places this departure after P time: it can be true only if John has not yet left.[41]

Writing the main clause above the subordinate clause in the temporal representations of complex sentences, (37a) and (37b) look like this:

38.

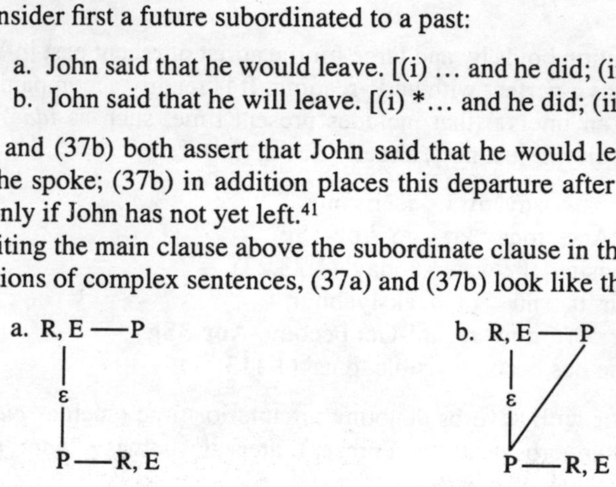

The rules in (36) derive (38) as follows. By (36a), the P_{sub} time relative to which the leaving is in the future is anchored to the saying event ε. The past tense *said* locates the saying event (and P_{sub} with it) at E_{main}/R_{main} preceding P_{main}. This renders the temporal relations of (37a), where P_{sub} precedes P_{main}, so that we get past tense by (36c). A second reading is derived by letting P_{sub} include P_{main} by the optional rule (36b). This locates the leaving event after P_{main}, which is to say after the current speech time. In this reading, P_{sub} overlaps P_{main}, and (36c) is therefore inapplicable, yielding (37b).

Both (37a) and (37b) are unambiguous, because the past tense by (36c) identifies the application of (36b) in (37b), and (36c) is the only source of (36b), for *would* is not an independent past tense. Ambiguities are created whenever (36b) applies without bleeding (36c), and also whenever a subordinate past tense has an independent source.

As an example of the first type of ambiguity, let us take (39).

39. John will say that he lives in California.

By (36a), P_{sub} is anchored to the saying event, which is temporally located in the future. Therefore, all readings of (39) imply that John will say at some future time that he lives in California at that time. In addition, (36b) allows P_{sub} to be synchronized with P_{main}, yielding a second, more restrictive reading (40b) with the additional entailment that he lives in California now.

40. a. b.

Because neither reading shows the relation P_{sub}—P_{main}, (36c) is inapplicable and the two interpretations of (39) are morphologically identical.

As an example of the second type of ambiguity, consider the examples in (41), discussed by Enç 1987.

41. a. John knew that Mary is pregnant.
    b. John knew that Mary was pregnant.

For (41a) to be true, Mary must have been pregnant both when John knew she was and she must still be pregnant at the current P time (here including S time). (36a) always anchors P_{sub} to the knowing event, which is temporally located in the past. In this reading, the subordinate clause is temporally unmarked ("present"). (36b) applies, bleeding (36c).

42.

If (36b) does not apply, the subordinate clause gets past tense by (36c), and we derive the reading of (41b) on which Mary was pregnant when John knew she was (see [43a]).

43. a. b. c.

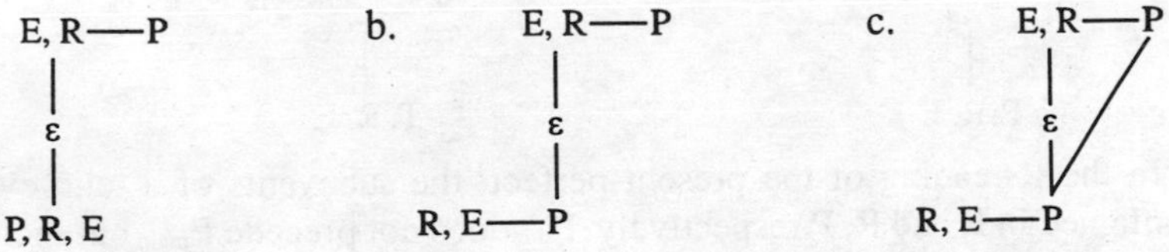

If the subordinate clause is past (R—P), (36b) may again apply or not, yielding (43b) and (43c), both of which mean that Mary was pregnant before John knew it, and she was no longer pregnant when John came to know it. In either case, P_{sub}—P_{main}, so (36c) applies, with the result that (41b) has three readings. ([43b,c] can be distinguished by whether deictic time adverbs in the subordinate clause [such as *three weeks ago*] refer to the time of the embedded event or to current P time.)

Subordinate past perfects show a similar ambiguity.

44. a. John heard that the convict has escaped.
    b. John heard that the convict had escaped.

In addition, both sentences are ambiguous between the usual readings of the perfect (existential, resultative etc.). On the R-reading, (44a) implies that the convict is still at large at speech time. Sentence (44b), even on the R-reading, does not.

Sequence of tense provides another argument that the distinction between the R-reading of the perfect and the existential/universal readings is structurally represented. Declerck (1991: 174) points out that while the resultative perfect never triggers tense shift from present to past in subordinate clauses, the existential and universal readings can, citing contrasts of the type:

45. a. #I have finally realized that the earth was round. [Resultative]
    b. I have always known that the earth was round. [Universal]
    c. I have often thought that the earth was round. [Existential].

Such data refute the view that sequence of tense is a purely morphological phenomenon, as Declerck makes clear. They are incompatible with all classical Reichenbach-style theories, which traffic only in the temporal parameters and assign perfects the single representation E—R, P. In these, the interpretation of tense in subordinate clauses must be a matter of associating one of their temporal parameters with a temporal parameter of the main clause.[42] The problem is solved if the P time of the subordinate clause is anchored not directly to one of the temporal parameters of the main clause, but to the event itself, which is then interpreted as discussed in section 2.2. The contrast seen in (45) is then accounted for by the respective representations of the R-reading and the existential and universal perfects that we already motivated above:

46. a.
```
E——R, P
   |
   ε
   |
P, R, E
```
b.
```
E——R, P
|
ε
|
P, R, E
```

In the R-reading of the present perfect, the subevents of a telic event are contained in E and R, P respectively. P_{sub} does not precede P_{main} but includes it, and (36c) is inapplicable. In the existential and universal readings, the entire event is respectively contained in and coextensive with E (the simplified notation in [46b] collapses the latter two readings). In this case, P_{sub} precedes P_{main} and (36c) duly applies to give a past tense in the subordinate clause.

What it means for Sanskrit to lack sequence of tense, then, is that rule (36c) does not apply. More generally, its subordinate clauses are deictically independent with respect to the main clause, with no shift of person, spatial orientation, or any other deictic category.

A sentence with a telic predicate, such as (47a), has only the independent past tense reading. The shifted reading is not available because resultative predicates do not allow the temporal relation E, P ⊆ R, a prohibition which applies to the plain and shifted present alike, as (47b) shows.

47. a. John heard that the convict escaped. [The escape preceded the hearing.]
    b. #The convict escapes. [OK only as a historical present.]

(36) should probably be generalized to main clauses in the scope of *implicit* perspectival predicates. Several authors have interpreted main clause past perfects in "flashbacks" and free indirect speech along these lines (Banfield 1982, Declerck 1991, Ch. 2, Kamp and Reyle 1993: 594, Eberle and Kasper 1994: 157):

48. John came to work at noon yesterday. He had woken up at 10. He had made coffee and eaten breakfast.

If each past perfect in (48) has the same R as the past tense of the first clause, then how can they constitute a narrative progression? On the other hand, if each has a different R, why do they all denote events anterior to the event of first clause? The solution is to assume that such past perfects are governed by the perspective time of the first clause, even though they are not syntactically subordinated to it. We can think of them as subordinated to a perspectival operator which extends over a stretch of discourse. Even apart from past perfects, this is clearly necessary anyway for past tenses in such cases as:

49. a. What was your name again?
    b. Tarzan was not yet king of the jungle. That would come later.[43]

Sequences of past perfects allow distinct R times, and that enables them to advance the narrative (just like sequences of plain past tenses, see section 2.4). But the successive R times of the past perfects all precede the P time of their clause, and this is anchored to the event denoted by of the first clause, and so cannot advance beyond it.[44]

■ 3.4. The Past Perfect

With respect to point-denoting adverbials in the R-reading, the past and future perfects differ from the present perfect in a surprising way. The present perfect is not compatible with adverbials denoting a specific past time (see [33b]). But the past perfect is not only compatible with such adverbials, it even allows two distinct readings with them! The time adverbial may be read as specifying either the *terminus ante quem* of the event (reading 1) or the culmination of the event itself:[45]

50. The convict had escaped at 3.
 Reading 1: At 3, the convict had already escaped [the actual time of escape may have been earlier].
 Reading 2: The convict had escaped, and the escape took place at 3.

These data pose a famous problem for the theory of tense (Klein 1992). The ambiguity of the past perfect illustrated in (50) has been taken to show that in the representation of the past perfect, redisplayed in (51a), the adverb can associate either with the reference time R (reading 1) or with the event time E (reading 2). But then, why is even the latter reading unavailable in the present perfect, which has the representation (51b)?

51. a. **Past perfect:** E—R—P
 b. **Present perfect:** E—R, $P \subseteq R$

Klein suggests a pragmatic constraint to the effect that event times and reference times cannot be simultaneously fixed to specific intervals. But this does not look like a pragmatic constraint because it is neither motivated by rational communicative principles nor defeasible by explicit contrary information. Michaelis (1992) also points out that the constraint is undermined by the well-formedness of discourses such as (52), in which these two times are in fact fixed.

52. [It was 1972.] Harry had joined the navy in 1960.

Still, why cannot both times be specified by time adverbials in a sentence? Michaelis proposes placing a construction-specific constraint on the R-reading. But we can do better than that.

Consider first the analysis (50) embedded under a past tense, which also has two readings:

53. John heard that the convict had escaped at 3.
 Reading 1: John heard that at 3, the convict had already escaped [the actual time of escape may have been earlier].
 Reading 2: John heard that the convict had escaped, and that the escape took place at 3.

The reading as an embedded perfect with sequence of tense from (36c) is excluded by the constraint mentioned in fn. 37 (erasing the adverb or substituting a deictic adverb such as *then* would render it acceptable). The reading as an embedded past perfect is fine, though, with R_{sub} = *at* 3:

54.
```
          E, R—P
            |
            ε
            |
E—R—P
```

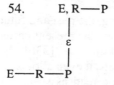

But as we know already from section 2.2, this representation has two readings. In the existential reading (reading 1 of [53]), there was an escape during the interval E_{sub}. In the R-reading (reading 2), there was an escape that culminates at time R. As this analysis correctly predicts, reading 1 does not entail that the convict was still at large at 3 (he or she might have been caught again by that time), while reading 2 does entail that.

The upshot is that there is no shift of past to past perfect in sequence of tenses as many writers have supposed. The apparent "past perfect as back-shifted past" is really the existential reading of the past perfect. This fits well with our previous observation (see [45]) that the existential reading of the present perfect functions like a past tense in triggering sequence of tense. As for the present perfect, its R time cannot be modified by past tense adverbs because it includes P time and S time.

The assumption that (36) is triggered by implicit operators (section 3.3, see [48]) makes it possible to extend the analysis of the overtly embedded case in (53) to explain the ambiguity of (50). Again, the existential reading yields reading 1 of (50), and the resultative reading yields reading 2.

The ambiguity of the future perfect follows analogously from its temporal specification E—R, P—R.

55. The convict will have escaped tomorrow at 3.
Reading 1: Tomorrow at 3, the convict will already have escaped.
Reading 2: The convict will complete an escape tomorrow at 3.

As before, reading 1 is the existential reading (the escape falls within E, before 3) and reading 2 is the R-reading (the escape culminates at the E/R edge, i.e. at 3).[46] Again, there is no need to assume that the past tense "becomes" a perfect in infinitives. The perfect's own meaning is responsible for all its uses.

We are at last ready for the Vedic aorist of relative anteriority. Let us suppose that temporal conjunctions relate the reference times R of the main clause and the subordinate clause. In particular, the conjunction *when*, and its Sanskrit counterparts *yat* and *yadā*, align R_{sub} and R_{main}, so that "A when B" and "B when A" both mean that the R times of A and B coincide. If A and B have the same tense, then their E times will be included in the same R time.[47] But if the tenses of A and B differ, their E times can diverge. Taking (2b) as our example, let A = "You took Kutsa", and B = "The gods had united you". Then (57) diagrams the temporal relations asserted by "You took Kutsa when the gods had united you". Given the meanings of the tenses, the culmination of the uniting event at the E_{sub}/R_{sub} edge must precede the taking event at E_{main}, which is the right temporal interpretation of the sentence.[48]

57. E, R—P
|
ε
|
E—R, P

The analysis of the Vedic aorist of relative anteriority as the functional analog to the English (or more accurately, the German) past perfect makes some additional predictions. First, if implicit operators can trigger (36) over a stretch of discourse, we predict that the aorist of relative anteriority should occur also in main clauses, to mark relative anteriority with respect to a previous event in the discourse. Such a use of the aorist of anteriority was suggested in passing by Hoffmann (1967: 158), and the following seem plausible examples of it:[49]

58. a. yújaṃ hí mā́m ákr̥thāḥ
ally-Acc but me make-**Aor**-2Sg
'But you had made me your ally!' (5.30.8)
b. antár hí ákhyad ubhé asya dhéne
among for see-**Aor**-3Sg both-Du-Acc his breast-Du-Acc
'For he had seen both his breasts among them.' (5.30.9)
c. stómena hí diví devā́so agním ájījanan
praise-Instr for sky-Loc god-Pl fire-Acc engender-**Aor**-3Sg
'For the gods had engendered Agni in heaven with praise.' (10.88.10)

Second, our analysis of the aorist of anterior time predicts that the aorist of relative anteriority (unlike the aorist of recent past, see section 3.2) might occur with adverbs that specify a past point in time. This expectation is confirmed as well.[50]

59. yáthā purā́ mánave gātúm áśret
as previously Manu-Dat path-Acc provide-**Aor**-3Sg
'in the same way that it had previously readied a path for Manu' (10.76.3)

In this section I have sketched out a semantic account of the temporal relation between subordinate and main clauses, in which rules (36a,b) do most of the work, coupled in English with the sequence of tense rule (36c). With the additional assumption that tenses can be subordinated to abstract operators in discourse, the account generalizes to free indirect discourse and flashbacks. It also solves the present perfect puzzle without positing either unmotivated pragmatic constraints or construction-specific grammatical properties of the R-reading. The aorist of relative anteriority is the result of applying (36a,b) to the aorist's tense specification. This completes my argument that the temporal and aspectual uses of the aorist are specializations of the R-reading.[51]

■ 3.5. Questions

In the presence of adverbial Wh-questions, the existential reading, however far-fetched, is always available. As noted by Michaelis (1994), the R-reading is crisply excluded unless the adverbial relates to the result state:

60. a. Where have the police caught the suspect? [No R-reading, only the existential reading "In what places have the police caught the suspect (over the years)?"]
   b. #Where has general Aidid died? #At what age has general Aidid died? [No R-reading; the existential reading presupposes resurrection[52]]
   c. Where have you hidden my watch? [R-reading OK.]
   d. (#)Where have you found my watch? [Existential reading only.]
   e. (#)When have you hidden my watch? [Existential reading only.]
   f. How have you worded the letter? [R-reading OK.]
   g. (#)How have you found the letter? [Existential reading only.]

The subcategorized adverbials associated with *hide* and with *word* in (60c,e,f) specify a property that comes to obtain when the change of state takes place, while non-subcategorized adverbials associated with *die* and *find* in (60b,d,g) specify a property that obtains at the time when the activity leading up to it terminates. For example, the locative in (60c) specifies the location of the watch from the time it was hidden, whereas the locative in (60d) specifies the location of the watch at the time it was found.

According to a suggestion by Michaelis, in the R-reading the change of state is an assertion and the activity leading up to it is a presupposition, and the unacceptable Wh-questions in (60) are ruled out because an element in a presupposition has been questioned. This is known on other grounds to be unacceptable:

61. a. What did Mary believe / #know that John took?
   b. Who did John read a / #the book by?

Why should this be so? Looking back at (26) we see that the R-reading is the only reading of the perfect in which the change of state and the activity leading up to it are temporally distinguished. In the existential and universal readings, the entire event is respectively contained in or coextensive with E. Thus it is only when the activity and the resulting change of state are temporally distinguished that they are separated into an assertion and a presupposition.

Analogous facts hold in Vedic. The aorist is rare in Wh–questions, as well as in adverbial relative clauses (e.g. *yatra*, *yathā*). The cases that do occur seem to conform to the restriction that the Wh–question should be about the resultant state.[53]

62. a.

kám̐	svid	árdham	párāgāt
which	Prt	side	Pref turn-**Aor**-3Sg

'Which way has she turned?' (1.164.17)

b.

kúva	tyā́	valgū́	puruhutā́
where	those-DuAcc	handsome-DuAcc	much-invoked-DuAcc

adyá	dūtó	ná	stómo	avidat
today	messenger	like	praise	find-**Aor**-3Sg

'Where has the song of praise reached the two beautiful much-invoked ones today?' (6.63.1)

■ 4. Conclusion

Vedic supports Reichenbach's two-dimensional theory of tense and aspect with two modifications. The first modification is to allow tenses and aspects to be characterized at a finer level of granularity, by specifying the relation of the predicate's event structure to the temporal parameters. This allows the different readings of the perfect to be represented grammatically, a move necessary because these readings correspond to distinct aspect categories. In Vedic, while the imperfect is a past tense (R—P), the aorist and perfect constitute two distinct species of perfect aspect (E—R), the former a specialized resultative perfect and the latter a general perfect. The aorist's diverse temporal and aspectual functions were shown to follow from a particular assignment of the event structure of telic predicates to the perfect's temporal parameters E and R.

For the Vedic perfect, on the other hand, there is no simple positive characterization that picks out all its functions to the exclusion of those of the aorist. It just covers what is left of that aspect's territory when the specific functions of the aorist are subtracted. In this respect, the unification of the tenses relies crucially on the blocking of general categories by special categories. So does the analysis of the imperfect remote past function. Only if the aorist pre-empts the imperfect in the recent past temporal function, and the perfect in the resultative aspectual function, can the meaning of all three categories be specified in a way compatible with the theory. The beauty of blocking is that it eliminates complex and unnatural disjunctive categories by reducing them to general "elsewhere" cases relative to more narrowly specified categories with unitary properties.

The discourse functions of the tenses were argued to be consequences of their temporal and aspectual properties. Such categories as "mentioning", "reporting", and "statement of fact", previously used to define the Vedic tenses' functions, prove to be epiphenomenal.

In section 3, I showed that the proposed structural distinction between the resultative and existential/universal readings of the perfect solves several long-standing difficulties in the English tense system, in particular, the "present perfect puzzle", the problem of tense shifting when the main clause has perfect tense, and the relation of past and past perfect in sequence of tense contexts.

■ NOTES

1. Thanks to Cleo Condoravdi and Henriette de Swart for their searching comments on a draft. Naturally I am responsible for any remaining errors.
2. Hoffmann 1970, Cowgill 1972, Beekes 1995: 252.
3. Pāṇini 3.2.110 ff. See Speijer 1886: 246 ff., Liebich 1891, Renou 1925, Apte 1946: 141–145. The reader should keep in mind that the Western names of the Sanskrit tenses are simply taken from the cognate tenses in Greek and must not be understood literally. While the Sanskrit

'imperfect' is the etymological counterpart of the Greek imperfect, it has none of its imperfective semantics.

4. See e.g. Dowty 1982, Partee 1984, Hornstein 1990, Kamp and Reyle 1993, Klein 1994, Schopf 1987, 1989, and Thieroff and Ballweg 1994; also Comrie 1976, 1985, Declerck 1991, and Binnick 1992 for critical discussion and alternative approaches.
5. The aorist is formed from a special aorist stem, with augment and secondary P/N endings.
6. The basic doctrine on Vedic tense was worked out by Delbrück 1876, 1897, with refinements by Renou 1925 and Hoffmann 1967. For a concise summary, consult Macdonell 1916: 341–343.
7. All examples are from the Rigveda (text according to van Nooten and Holland 1994, translation following Geldner 1951). To save space, my interlinear glosses omit the unmarked categories Nominative and Singular for nouns, and Active voice and Present tense for verbs.
8. Delbrück refers to this as the historical aorist (1876), or the aorist of 'assertion' (*Behauptung*) (1897).
9. Attempts to base the theory of tense on discourse categories include Weinrich 1964, and (in a completely different tradition) Lascarides and Asher 1993.
10. Morphologically, it consists of the present stem plus the augment (prefixed *a-*) and secondary (short) P/N endings.
11. The perfect is formed athematically from its own special stem (normally reduplicated), with a set of special P/N endings. The classification of the perfect's meanings and uses presented here follows Delbrück 1876: 6–88, 1897: 178–229, 269–275; see further Renou 1925 and Hoffmann (1967: 155, 160).
12. Unlike most other uses of the perfect, the stative present perfect has a past form, the 'pluperfect', formed from the perfect stem with augment and secondary P/N endings, and functionally equivalent to an imperfect. The non-finite counterparts of stative present perfects are 'passive' participles such as *sthita* 'standing', *śrita* 'leaning, depending on', similar to English 'adjectival passives' such as *seated*, *broken*, *interested*, *tired*.
13. Such adverbs include *purutra* 'in many places, in many ways' (2.18.7, 3.61.7, 7.1.9, 7.1.16, 8.33.8), *purudhā* 'in many ways' (3.55.19), *viśvadhā* 'at all times' (5.8.4) *bhūri* 'many times' (1.120.10, 1.165.7, 2.29.5, 7.56.23, 8.62.10), *satrā* in the meaning 'always, everywhere' (3.51.6, 3.51.6, 5.60.4, 6.34.4), *nahi* in the meaning 'never' (1.24.6, 1.39.4, 1.167.9, 6.25.5, 8.3.13, 10.131.3, and distributive (*āmreḍita*) compounds (e.g. 1.131.5, 1.168.1, 3.29.15, 3.36.1, 3.38.7, 3.38.7, 4.54.5, 5.52.17, 5.61.1, 6.15.8, 6.27.3, 6.30.2, 6.32.5, 6.36.5, 6.47.18, 6.47.21, 6.74.1, 7.6.3, 7.15.2, 7.18.24, 7.26.2, 8.4.10, 8.13.7, 8.48.9, 8.70.14, 9.77.3, 9.107.19, 9.110.5, 10.27.22, 10.28.7). Contrast e.g. 2.23.17, 5.11.6, 10.46.3 (single event, imperfect tense).

    The imperfects in 10.43.6, 9.110.4, and 10.56.5 seem to be genuine exceptions to the generalization. An apparent exception is *sóme-soma ā́bhavaḥ* 'you have appeared at every soma' in 8.93.17, if the Padapatha's analysis *ā́ ábhavaḥ* (imperfect) is right. However, the meter does not support a disyllabic reading of *ā́-*, and so a possible alternative reading is *ā bhavaḥ*, with a generically interpreted injunctive, meaning 'you appear at every soma'. Even though the Rigveda's text and the Padapatha analysis must have been edited into final shape very early, the injunctive was then no longer a live grammatical category, and so the compilers have tended to supply missing augments in their morphological analysis wherever this could be done without changing the actual wording of the text (Hoffmann 1967: 146).
14. Delbrück 1876: 107. See also 1.23.22, 1.102.10, 1.162.14, 10.11.5.
15. See also 1.162.9, 1.179.5, 5.85.5, 8.45.25.
16. See also 1.164.4, 1.165.2, 4.13.5, 4.23.2, 4.25.1–2, 5.74.7, 8.100.3, 10.10.6, 10.51.2, 10.102.10, 10.114.9.
17. The implications indicated are clear from the context. See also 8.45.37, 10.135.5.
18. When the reference time of a subordinate clause is a definite anterior point of time, it sometimes has imperfect tense, e.g. 'since (*yad*) the rains came…, (*āyan*, imperfect), the frogs'

croaking resounds (*sam eti*, present)' (7.103.2), similarly 10.43.7. The imperfect is also possible when the events are contiguous; see below.

19. What does occur are passive aorists (*aroci* 3x, *asāvi* 7x) and causative aorists (*arūrucat* 3x).
20. No aorist except for the late and obviously secondary *aukṣīs* (10.27.7).
21. Other examples of perfects of recent past with these verbs are: 3.61.5, 4.5.15, 6.62.2, 9.83.3 (*ruc*); 9.107.1, 1.137.1, 4.16.1, 7.22.1, 8.17.1, 9.107.1 (*su*); 1.146.01, 3.5.7, 3.9.3, 7.8.2, 8.12.4, 8.12.7 (*vakṣ*). Perfects of anteriority of these verbs (paralleling the other main use of the aorist) are: 4.16.4, 4.45.5, 4.7.11. Since *hu* 'sacrifice' has no aorist in Vedic, the anterior perfect (*juhve* 6.2.3) should perhaps be interpreted in the same way.
22. See Kiparsky 1968. However, I now prefer to treat the phenomenon semantically, rather than by a syntactic rule of 'conjunction reduction'.
23. For Vedic examples of the historical present, see Macdonell 1916: 340, Whitney 1889: 278.
24. Their demonstration involves 'extended flashbacks' (section 3.4 below).
25. English *be going to* (Matthews 1989) and the second (remote) future of Sanskrit are perhaps instances of this category.
26. At this point only the most salient reading of each example is relevant. Most of the examples are in fact ambiguous; in particular the Existential reading is almost always available. The reader is asked to disregard the other readings for the moment; we will be returning to them shortly.
27. The only example in English, and probably not synchronically a perfect anyway: speakers who use *gotten* as the past participle of *get* still say *have got.*
28. Of course, the previous example (23a) can be assigned an existential reading too. For (23a) to be true on the existential reading, there must have been at least one complete catching event within a subinterval of E extending from some past time up to time R. Thus the existential reading of (23a), unlike its more salient R–reading we considered earlier, does not entail that the suspect is currently in custody.

    The existential reading is associated with the presupposition that a recurrence of the event type in question is possible (McCawley 1981, Piñon 1996). In particular, the referents of the NP arguments must exist at P time, and the event must be of a repeatable type. (23c) thus implies that Fred is still living and that Paris exists, and that he might visit it again. In contrast, (24a) is incongruous because Nazi Germany no longer exists, and (24b) is incongruous because one can only be born once.

    24. a. #Fred has been to Nazi Germany. [Uttered in 1997]
        b. #Fred has been born in Paris.

29. It has also been claimed that it is a variant of the existential perfect (McCoard 1978, McCawley 1981), but the problem with that is that recent past perfect is not subject to the above mentioned constraint on the existential perfect that the re-occurrence of the event type should be possible. Moreover, the Hungarian existential perfect has no recent past reading (Piñon 1996).
30. This does not imply a commitment to Michaelis' treatment of the R-reading (or any of its other readings either) as conventionalized constructions or 'formal idioms' whose properties cannot be derived from the semantics of the perfect. I believe that the present analysis shows that the types of perfect represent the possible assignments of event structure to the perfect's temporal parameters, that each type's properties are predictable, and that the types are cross-linguistically represented.
31. There is an analogy between the present state reading and the middle (such as *this wood cuts easily*). In the middle, it is the causal component of an accomplishment predicate that is left implicit. Only the change of state is syntactically visible. This could be the rationale behind the probable historical identity of the Indo-European perfect and middle.
32. See Matthews 1994: 87–88 for illuminating remarks on this point.
33. It would not be possible to conversely derive the resultative character of the aorist from its restriction to telic predicates. The assumption that the aorist is simply a perfect that happens

to be restricted to telic predicates would allow existential and universal perfect readings for those predicates, contrary to fact.

34. A caveat is in order here: in addition to the synchronic variation due to the aspectually flexible class of telic/atelic roots, there is much ongoing historical change. At any given stage of the language, the morphological properties for a given verb may in part reflect its Aktionsart at an earlier period.
35. This generalization seems to be empirically correct but would of course itself have to be explained.
36. Similarly, reference to time that extends from the past into the present requires the perfect, e.g. 6.34.1 *purā́ nūnáṃ ca* 'formerly and now' (Renou 1925). The adverb *jyok* (*jiyok*) takes the aorist in what could be interpreted as the universal reading ('for a long time now'), but Hoffmann (1967: 157) suggests that the Rigvedic instances (except perhaps for 1.33.15) are resultative ('long since').
37. The requirement that the point included in P must be specified deictically, rather than by adverbs denoting an absolute point of time, is not special to the perfect, but a general constraint on reference to any time that includes P time. For example, *on Friday* means last Friday or next Friday, not the current day, even if it happens to be a Friday.
38. Such sentences can be amnestied under rather special conditions (Crystal 1966: 19, fn., and Meyer 1992, Ch. 8, Declerck 1991: 333). For example, (33b) is OK if the adverb is read as a separate intonational phrase.
39. Other examples of this kind are 1.124.1, 4.34.4, 4.54.1, 6.47.22, 7.20.2, 8.27.11.
40. *purā* can also occur with present tense even if it refers to the past, a fact for which I know of no explanation. In two interesting examples (8.66.7, 8.99.1) it occurs with *both hyaḥ* 'yesterday' and *idā* 'now' combined asyndetically; on Geldner's translation 'yesterday at this time' these would be problematic; however, the translation 'yesterday and now', which would be consistent with my proposal as a universal perfect, seems equally possible to me. The aorist *avṛṣata* in 8.1.29 seems to refers to a repeated action, so perfect tense would have been expected.
41. John might have explicitly stated that he would leave some time after the current P time, or he might have left the time open, in which case the extra component of futurity in (37a) is an assertion by the speaker.
42. For example, Hornstein's (1990) sequence of tense rule associates the subordinate clause's P with the main clause's E, and shifts the morphological tense from present to past when the main clause's E is a past time. For the perfect, this would predict that tense shift would be triggered not only by the existential and universal perfect (45b,c), but also by the resultative perfect (45a), contrary to fact.
43. I owe this example to a lecture by J. McCawley.
44. But if the last sentence in (48) is changed to past tense (*He made coffee and ate breakfast*), the inference is that the event took place *after* John came to work.
45. I assume the same would be true in Vedic, but I cannot offer any evidence one way or the other.
46. Note that the constraint of fn. 37 has no effect on future and modal perfects.
47. Things are not quite so simple, of course. (56) could mean that the party was held just before John's departure (a goodbye party), right after it (a good riddance party, perhaps), during his departure, though surely not years earlier or later.
    (56) When John left, Mary threw a party.

    In Vedic as well, contiguous events do not require the aorist of anteriority, e.g. 'when the gods put (*adadhur*, imperfect) the sun into the sky, then (= from that point onwards) all the worlds could see (*prāpaśyan*, imperfect)' (10.88.11), similarly 8.12.30. The imperfect is possible for the same reason that the English and German translations allow the simple past rather than the pluperfect, namely that no temporal separation between the main clause and subordinate clause events is intended.

48. Being subject to rule (36c), English would here use the past perfect.
49. Others are 1.24.8, 4.1.8, 4.18.5, 5.30.4, 10.45.4.
50. Another example is *ajaniṣṭa* 'had been born (then)' in 5.32.3.
51. The analysis could be extended to *before* and *after* clauses, but since Sanskrit does not have them, they can be bypassed here.
52. Because of the 'repeatability' property of atelic predicates mentioned at (24).
53. Rhetorical, exclamative questions seem to be exempt from the constraint, e.g. 1.54.1, 4.23.1, 3–5 (see Grassmann's comments *s.v. kathā*). (The English examples in (60) may have such readings too). *aśret* in 10.76.3 is not a conterexample because it is an aorist of relative anteriority (see [59]).

■ REFERENCES

Apte, Vaman Shivaram. 1946. *The student's guide to Sanskrit composition.* Eighteenth edition. Poona: V.G. Ketkar.

Banfield, Ann. 1982. *Unspeakable sentences: narration and representation in the language of fiction.* Boston: Routledge and Kegan Paul.

Beekes, Robert S.P. 1995. *Comparative Indo-European linguistics: an introduction.* Amsterdam: Benjamins.

Binnick, Robert I. 1991. *Time and the verb: a guide to tense and aspect.* Oxford: Oxford University Press.

Comrie, Bernard. 1976. *Aspect.* Cambridge: Cambridge University Press.

———. 1981. On Reichenbach's approach to tense. *CLS* 17.24–30.

———. 1985. *Tense.* Cambridge: Cambridge University Press.

Cowgill, Warren. 1972. More evidence for Indo–Hittite: the tense-aspect systems. *Proceedings of the Eleventh International Congress of Linguists.* 922–34.

Crystal, David. 1966. Specification and English tenses. *Journal of Linguistics* 2.1–34.

Declerck, Renaat. 1991. *Tense in English.* London: Routledge.

Delbrück, Berthold. 1876. *Altindische Tempuslehre.* Halle: Verlag der Buchhandlung des Waisenhauses.

———. 1897. *Vergleichende Syntax der indogermanischen Sprachen, Zweiter Theil.* Strassburg: Trübner.

Dowty, David R. 1979. *Word meaning and Montague grammar.* Dordrecht: Reidel.

———. 1982. Tenses, time adverbs, and compositional semantic theory. *Linguistics and Philosophy* 5.23–33.

Eberle, Kurt and **Walter Kasper.** 1994. French past tenses and temporal structure. *Tense systems in European languages*, ed. by Rolf Thieroff and Joachim Ballweg, 149–72. Tübingen: Niemeyer.

Enç, Mürvet. 1987. Anchoring conditions for tense. *Linguistic Inquiry* 18.633–57.

Foley, William A. and **Robert van Valin.** 1984. *Functional syntax and universal grammar.* Cambridge: Cambridge University Press.

Geldner, Karl Friedrich. 1951. *Der Rig-Veda.* Cambridge, Mass: Harvard University Press.

Hoffmann, Karl. 1967. *Der Injunktiv im Veda.* Heidelberg: Winter.

———. 1970. Das Kategoriensystem des indogermanischen Verbums. *Münchener Studien zur Sprachwissenschaft* 28.19–41.

Hornstein, Norbert. 1990. *As time goes by: tense and universal grammar.* Cambridge, Mass: MIT Press.

Kamp, Hans and **U. Reyle.** 1993. *From discourse to logic: introduction to model-theoretic semantics of natural language, formal logic, and discourse representation theory.* Kluwer: Dordrecht.

Kiparsky, Paul. 1968. Tense and mood in Indo-European syntax. *Foundations of Language* 4.30–57.

———. 1997. Partitive case and aspect. *The projection of arguments: lexical and syntactic constraints*, ed. by M. Butt and R. Geuder. Stanford, CA: CSLI.

Klein, Wolfgang. 1992. The present perfect puzzle. *Language* 68.525–52.

———. 1994. *Time in language*. London: Routledge.

Langendoen, D.T. and **C.J. Fillmore** (eds). 1971. *Studies in linguistic semantics*. New York: Holt, Rinehart, and Winston.

Lascarides, Alex and **N. Asher.** 1993. Temporal interpretation, discourse relations and commonsense entailment. *Linguistics and Philosophy* 16.437–93.

Liebich, Bruno. 1891. *Panini*. Leipzig: Ein Beitrag zur Kenntnis der indischen Literatur und Grammatik.

McCawley, James D. 1971. Tense and time reference in English. *Studies in linguistic semantics*, ed. by D.T. Langendoen and C.J. Fillmore, 97–113. New York: Holt, Rinehart, and Winston.

———. 1981. Notes on the English perfect. *Australian Journal of Linguistics* 1.81–90.

Macdonell, Arthur Anthony. 1916. *A Vedic grammar for students*. Oxford: Oxford University Press.

Matthews, Richard. 1987. Present perfect tenses: towards an integrated functional account. *Essays on tensing in English*, Vol. 1. ed. by Alfred Schopf. Tübingen: Niemeyer.

———. 1994. Das englische Tempus- und Akzentsystem. Tense systems in European languages, ed. by Rolf Thieroff and Joachim Ballweg, 69–92. Tübingen: Niemeyer.

McCoard, Robert W. 1978. *The English perfect: tense choice and pragmatic inferences*. Amsterdam: North-Holland.

Meyer, Matthias. 1992. *Das englische Perfekt*. Tübingen: Niemeyer.

Michaelis, Laura A. 1994. The ambiguity of the English present perfect. *Journal of Linguistics* 30.111–57.

Mittwoch, Anita. 1988. Aspects of English aspect: on the interaction of perfect, progressive and durational phrases. *Linguistics and Philosophy* 11.203–54.

van Nooten, Barend and **Gary B. Holland.** 1994. *Rig Veda: a metrically restored text with an introduction and notes*. Cambridge, Mass: Harvard University Press.

Partee, Barbara. 1984. Nominal and temporal anaphora. *Linguistics and Philosophy* 7.243–86.

Piñon, Christopher. 1996. The existential tense in Hungarian. Presented at the conference Sémantique non-lexicale (de préference), Paris, 21.6.1996.

Rappaport Hovav, Malka and **Beth Levin.** 1997. Building verb meanings. *The projection of arguments: lexical and syntactic constraints*, ed. by M. Butt and R. Geuder. Stanford, CA: CSLI

Reichenbach, Hans. 1947. *Elements of symbolic logic*. New York: The Free Press.

Renou, Louis. 1925. *La valeur du parfait dans les hymnes védiques*. Paris: Librairie ancienne Édouard Champion.

Schopf, Alfred. 1987, 1989. *Essays on tensing in English, Vols. 1, 2*. Tübingen: Niemeyer.

Speijer, J.S. 1886. *Sanskrit syntax*. Leiden: Brill.

Thieroff, Rolf and **Joachim Ballweg** (eds). 1994. *Tense systems in European languages*. Tübingen: Niemeyer.

Vendler, Zeno. 1957. Verbs and times. *The Philosophical Review* 66.143–60.

Weinrich, Harald. 1964. *Tempus*. Kohlhammer: Stuttgart.

Patterns of Sound Change in Dravidian[†]

■ BH. KRISHNAMURTI ■

The major sound changes in Dravidian are classified into Historical and Typological. The historical changes are classified into (1) those internal to Proto-Dravidian, and (2) innovations confined to major branches, sub-branches, and individual languages, e.g. palatalization of velars, $c > s > h > \phi$, umlaut, apical displacement, etc. Some of these are common in human languages and others, peculiar to Dravidian. Typological changes include the unconditional merger of PD *ñ- and *y- with *n*- and *ø*-, the gradual merger and elimination of PD *ṯ yielding a five-point stop system, the emergence of two syllable types, CV; C and CVCV, and single–double stop contrast becoming voiced–voiceless contrast. These changes have led to convergence between Dravidian and Indo-Aryan phonological systems within the Indian linguistic area. Criteria for distinguishing the historical from the typological have been stated. It is proposed that typologically motivated changes in phonology tend to be more regular than the products of historical change.

■ 1. Introduction

The twentieth century has seen remarkable progress in comparative Dravidian studies, mainly in the area of phonology. The major contributors to this devel-

† I am grateful to M.B. Emeneau and Hans H. Hock for their valuable comments on this paper when it was first presented at a symposium on Language and Prehistory in South and Southeast Asia organized by the Center for South Asian Studies at the University of Hawaii at Manoa in March, 1995. I express my gratitude to the Director of the Center for South Asian Studies, Professor Cromwell Crawford, the Executive Committee of the Center and the Dean of SHAPS for selecting me for a Watumull Fellowship which made it possible for me to spend the spring of 1995 at the University of Hawaii in the stimulating company of many eminent linguists. I must express my thanks to Ms. Karina Bingham for her help in converting, editing and laser-printing this paper in time for the Symposium. Thanks are due to Brett Benham of UTA for incorporating the final corrections and revisions.

opment are K.V. Subbiah, L.V. Ramaswami Aiyar, T. Burrow and M.B. Emeneau, Bh. Krishnamurti, P.S. Subrahmanyam, Kamil Zvelebi, and N. Kumaraswami Raja. Thanks to *A Dravidian Etymological Dictionary* by Burrow and Emeneau (1961, rev. edn. 1984), it has both inspired and facilitated much of the research on comparative phonology during the past three decades. Although some problems still remain unsolved, we now have a reliable knowledge of the phonological system of Proto-Dravidian and the processes of sound changes which have shaped the modern Dravidian languages. These have not been presented in a systematic manner in any one place, and therefore, have not attracted the attention of historical and comparative linguists at large.

The Dravidian phonological changes (in the form of rules) are organized in this paper in two categories—historical and typological. The historical ones are subclassified as: (a) changes internal to Proto-Dravidian, (b) phonological innovations shared by one or more subgroups, (c) innovations shared by more than one language within a subgroup, and (d) innovations peculiar to individual languages. The typological changes are classified as follows: (a) unshared common changes which cut across different subgroups with a common direction and output, e.g. **ḷ*, **ṇ* to *l*, *n* in SCD, CD and ND, (b) universal changes, i.e. processes found in several language families in the world, e.g. *s* > *h*, palatalization of velars, vowel harmony, etc., (c) changes predominantly found in the South Asian area, e.g. assimilative retroflexion, (d) changes peculiar to the Dravidian family, e.g. apical displacement, or to certain subgroups within Dravidian.

The twenty-four or so Dravidian languages are divided into four geographic-cum-genetic subgroups, i.e. South Dravidian (SD): Tamil, Malayāḷam, Koḍagu, Toda, Kota, Iruḷa, Kannaḍa, Tuḷu; South–Central Dravidian (SCD): Telugu, Gondi, Koṇḍa (Kūbi), Kui, Kuvi, Pengo, Manḍa; Central Dravidian (CD): Parji, Kolami, Naiki, Ollari and Gadaba; North Dravidian (ND): Kurux, Malto, Brahui. The South (SDI) and South–Central (SDII) have developed from an original major branch, which I call Proto-South Dravidian (PSD) [see Figure 1].

■ 2. Historical Changes

■ 2.1. Proto-Dravidian

Proto-Dravidian had ten vowels, *i e a o u* plus their long counterparts, and sixteen consonants, as shown in Table 1. In addition, a laryngeal **H* is needed for some reconstructions.

PD roots have the shape $(C)V_1(C) = V_1$, CV_1, V_1C, CV_1C (V_1 = long or short). There are some bases of $(C)V_1CC$-type contrasting with $(C)V_1C$. There are no prefixes in Dravidian. Alveolar and retroflex consonants do not begin a word. Any consonant can occur as C_2 root-finally, other than **ñ*. Word-initial

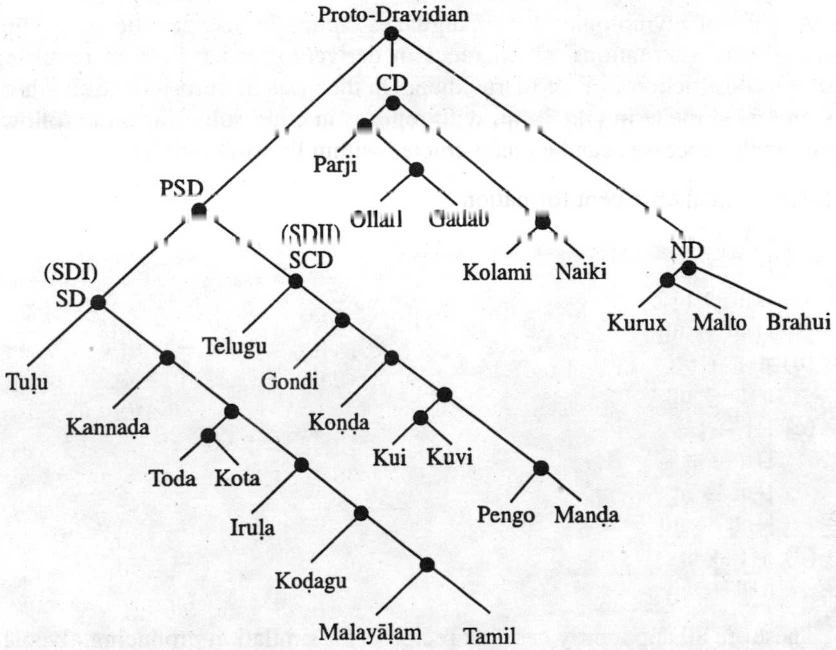

Figure 1: Family Tree of the Dravidian Languages

Table 1: Proto-Dravidian Consonants

Obstruents	p	t	ṯ	ṭ	c	k	
Nasals	m	n		ṇ	ñ		
Laterals			l	ḷ			
Flap/Tremulant			r				
Frictionless continuant				ẓ			
Semi-vowels	w				y		(H)

*y and *ñ occur only before *ă/*ĕ which is an archiphoneme. Word-initial *w is not followed by rounded vowels. All consonants except r and ẓ can be geminated post-vocalically. The vowel-ending roots may take formative suffixes of the shape C, CV, CCV, CCCV. Roots ending in C take formative suffixes of the above types preceded by V_2 = *a, i, u*. A base-final stop is followed by an enunciative *u*. There are no consonant clusters word-initially. Post-vocalic clusters are either geminates or sequences of nasal (N) + stop (P) (+ stop (P)). The obstruents had lenis allophones when intervocalic [w d ḏ/ṟ ḍ s g]; after a nasal, they were voiced stops, and geminates were always voiceless. Except for Tamil and Malayāḷam and to some extent Toda, the descendant languages have maintained this pattern, but have also developed word-initial voicing and aspiration through sound changes and borrowing from Indo-Aryan.

A study of etymologies from languages cutting across genetic subgroups shows stem alternations which recur in derivation and inflection requiring their reconstruction in Proto-Dravidian. On the basis of verb-inflection which is preserved intact in Old Tamil with reflexes in other subgroups, the following sandhi processes can be reconstructed within Proto-Dravidian.

Rule 1. Apical obstruent formation

(a) l+t → ṯ
l+tt → ṯṯ
l+nt → nṯ
l+ntt → nṯṯ

(b) n+t → nṯ
n+tt → nṯṯ

(c) ḷ+t → ṭ
ḷ+tt → ṭṭ
ḷ+nt → ṇṭ
ḷ+ntt → ṇṭṭ

(d) ṇ+t → ṇṭ
ṇ+tt → ṇṭṭ

These are all apparently cases of reciprocal assimilation producing alveolar and retroflex consonants secondarily. There are, however, many more lexical items in which alveolar and retroflex obstruents are primary. The following alternations are attested and distributed widely in different subgroups:

Rule 2a. Alternations **l*: **ṯ*: **ṯṯ*

1. PD ***nil*** (past *ninṟ-*) 'to stand'. SD: Ta. *nil* (*ninṟ-*), Ma. *nil* (*ninn-*), Ko. *nil-/nin-* (*ninḏ-*), To. *nil-* (*niḏ-*), Ka. *nil* (*nind-*), Kod. *nil-* (*nind-*); PD ***nil*** (past *niṯṯ-*): SCD. Go. *nil* (*nitt-*), Koṇḍa *nil-* (*niR-*); PD ***nil*** (past *nil-tt-*): Ka. *nil* (*nilt-*); CD: Pa. Oll. Gad. *nil-* (*nilt-*), Kol. Nk. *nil-* (*nilt-*); SCD: Pe. *nil* (*nilt-*), Manḍa *li-* (*lit-*); ND *il-* (*il-c-*). PD **niṯ-* (< **nil-t-*). SD: Ta. Ma. *niṟu* 'to put, place'; PD **niṯṯ-*. SCD: Go. *nitt-/nit-* 'to stand', Kui *nisa* (*nisi*); CD: Pa. *nit-* (*nit-it-*) [DEDR 3675].

Another such case is **kal* (*kaṯṯ-*) beside **kaṯ-* 'to learn', the former in SD and the latter in SCD and CD. Note that in the above cases, **niṯ*, **niṯṯ*, and **kaṯ* are represented as bases within Proto-Dravidian, perhaps restructured with the past suffix incorporated as a derivative at a later stage, still within PD. Such alternations are also noticed in non-verbs, e.g. PD **kil/*kiṯ-V* 'small' with cognates in SD and SCD [DEDR 1577, 1594].

Rule 2b. Alternations **l*: **ṯ*: **nṯ*

2. PSD **kil-* (*kinṯ-*) 'to be able'. Tamil and Malayāḷam have cognates. The Tamil present tense suffix *-kiṟ-/-kinṟ-* is traced to this root (Steever 1993: 172–78) [DEDR 1570].
3. PD **el*, **enṯu* 'sunshine, sun': SD, SCD and CD [DEDR 829, 869].

4. PD **niṯ-V-* 'to be full'. SD: Ta. Ma. Ko. To. Ka. Tu.
   PD **ninṯ-* v.i. 'to be full', *ninṯṯ-* v.t. 'to fill'; SCD: Te. Go. Koṇḍa, Kui, Kuvi, Pengo, Manḍa; ND: Kur. Malt. [DEDR 3682]

Rule 2c. Alternations *ḷ : *ṇṭ : *ṭṭ : *ṇṭṭ

5. PD **koḷ* (*koṇṭ-*) 'to receive, seize, buy'. SD: Ta. Ma. *koḷ* (*koṇṭ-*), Ko. *koḷ-/koṇ-* (*koḍ-*), To. *kwïḷ-* (*kwïḍ-*), Koḍ. *koḷḷ-* (*koṇḍ-*), Ka. *koḷ-* (*koṇḍ-*), Tu. *koṇ-* (*koṇḍ-*); SCD (past **koḷ-ntt-*): Te. *kon-* (*koṇṭ-*), tr. *kolupu*, Koṇḍa *koṛ-/kol-* (*koṇ-*, *koṭ-*), Kui *koḍa* (*koḍi*), Kuvi *koḍ-* (*koḍ-it-*), Pe. *koṛ-* (*koṛ-t-*), Manḍa *kṛag-* (*kṛakt-*); CD: Kol. Nk. *kor-/ko-* (*kott-*) [DEDR 2151].

Similarly, PD **kaḷ-* (*kaṭṭ-*) 'to steal', **kēḷ-* (*kēṭṭ-*, *kēṇṭṭ-*) 'to hear, ask', **wēḷ* (*wēṇṭ-*, *wēṇṭṭ-*) 'to desire, want', **kāṇ-* (*kaṇṭ-*) 'to see' are widely represented in different subgroups.

Contraction of two syllables into one, i.e. $(C_1)V_1C_2\text{-}V_2\text{-}$ to $(C_1)\bar{V}_1\text{-}$ (where C_2 is **y*, **w* or **k*) is reconstructable to PD, e.g.

Rule 3. Syllable contraction

$$(C_1)V_1 \begin{Bmatrix} y \\ w \\ k \end{Bmatrix} \text{-}V_2\text{-} > (C_1)V_1[+\text{long}]$$

6. PD **tiy-am* > **tē-m*/**tī-m* 'honey'. PSD **tey-am* > *tē-m*: Ta. Ma. *tēn*, Ko. *tēn*, To. *tȫn*, Koḍ. *tēnï*, Ka. *tēnu*, *jēn*. Tu. *tīya*; SCD: Te. *tēne*, Go. Koṇḍa *tēne*; CD **tiy-am* > *tī-m:* Pa. Oll. Gad. *tīn* (Kol. Nk. borrowed *tēne* from Telugu); ND **tiyam* > *tīn:* Kur. *tīn-ī* 'bee', Malt. *tēni* 'honey, bee' [DEDR 3268b].

Other such cases are **tok-al* > **tō-l* 'skin, peel' [DEDR 3559], **mic-al*/**miy-al* > **mē-l* 'above, high' [DEDR 5086], **kic-ampu* > **kiy-ampu* > **kē-mpu*/*kī-mpu* [DEDR 2004]. Note that the last case has *ī* and not *ē* as expected in CD and ND.

All Dravidian languages carry evidence of alternation between heavy and light, root syllables, when a 'formative' vowel follows as V_2, or when a monosyllabic root becomes disyllabic:

$(C)\bar{V}_1C : (C)V_1C\text{-}V_2\text{-}$
$(C)V_1CC : (C)V_1C\text{-}V_2\text{-}$

Contrasting with the above, there are non-alternating pairs like:

$(C)V_1C : (C)V_1C\text{-}V_2\text{-}$

Therefore, in the neutralizing environment, i.e. $\text{-}V_2$, a heavy syllable is said to have merged with a light syllable, by internal reconstruction within PD.

Rule 4. Quantitative variation
$(C)\bar{V}_1C\text{-}/(C)V_1CC\text{-} > (C)V_1C\text{-}/\#\_\_+V_2\text{-}$

7. PD **pāṯ-*: **paṯ-V-* 'to run, flee'. SD: Ta. Ma. *pāṟu*, *paṟ-a*, Ko. *parn-*, To. *pōṟ*, Ka. *pāṟu*, *paṟi*, Koḍ. *pār*, Tu. *pāruni*; SCD: Go. *parī-*, Te. *pāṟu*, *paṟacu*, Kui *pāsk-*, Kuvi *prāḍ-* [DEDR 4020].
8. PD **cupp*: **cuw-ar* (< **cup-ar*) 'salt'. SD: Ta. Ma. Ka. Tu. Te. *uppu*, Ko. To. *up*, Koḍ. *uppï*; also Ta. *uvar* 'to taste saltish, brackish', n. 'brackishness, saltishness', Ma. *uvar*, n., Ka. *ogar*, Te. *ogaru* 'astringent taste', Tu. *ubarï*, *ogarï* 'brackishness'; SCD **cow-ar*. Go. *sovar*, *sawwor*, *hovar*, *ovar* (dial.), Koṇḍa *sōru*, Kui *sāru*, Kuvi *hāru*, Pe. *hōr*, Manḍa *jār*; CD: Kol. Nk. *sup*, Pa. *cup*, Oll. *sup*, Gad. *cuppu* [DEDR 2674].

G.S. Rao suggested that Rule 4 operates systematically if the underlying and derived forms belong to the same grammatical class, e.g. both verbs, or both nouns, etc. (for further details, see Subrahmanyam 1983: 182–86).

■ 3. Sound Changes in Subgroups

■ 3.1. Proto-South Dravidian

Rule 5. Umlaut

$$\text{PD} * \begin{bmatrix} i \\ u \end{bmatrix} > \begin{bmatrix} e \\ o \end{bmatrix} /\#(\text{C})\_\_\text{C}+a \text{ (PSD)}$$

When PD *-V_2 is [+low], the preceding root vowels which are [+high] become mid [–high, –low] in PSD (i.e. SD or SDI and SCD or SDII), e.g.

9. PD **tur-a-* 'to push, drive away.' SD: Ta. Ma. *tura*, *turattu* v.t., n. *turappu*, Ka. Tu. *dobbu* (< *tor-pp-*); SCD: Te. *trōcu*, *drobbu*, Go. *ro-*, *ropp-* (< *tro-*), Kui, Kuvi *trō-* (*trō-t-*); CD: Pa. *turkip-* (*turkit-*), Gad. *turus key-*, *turuyp-* [DEDR 3340].
10. PD **wil* 'to sell': **wil-ay* n. 'price'. SD: Ta. *vil* (v.), *vil-ai* (n.), Ma. *vil* (v.), *vilai* (n.), Ko. *vel* (n.), To. *pïl* (n.), Ka. *bil* (v.), *bele* (n.); Koḍ. *bele* 'cost', Tu. *bilè*, *belè* (n.); SCD: Te. *wil(u)cu* (v.), *wela* (n.) [DEDR 5421].

Old Tamil and Malayāḷam had changed these mid vowels to high vowels and again to mid vowels in modern times. In the above examples Ta. Ma. *i*, *u* are derived from PSD **e*, **o*, respectively (see below under South Dravidian, Rules 8a and 8b).

Rule 6. Deaffrication and sibilant reduction

a. PD **c* > **s*/#__V (PSD, PCD, irregular)
b. SD **s* > **h* > Ø/#__V (*h*-stage is pre-historic)
c. SCD **s* > *h*/#__V (Go.-Kui-Kuvi-Pe.-Manḍa dial.)
d. *h* > Ø/#__V (Hill Maria and Koya dial. of Go.)

In SD *c is phonetically represented as [ś] in spoken Tamil, [s] in Kannaḍa, Tuḷu and non-standard Telugu; in CD it is [c] in Parji, [c/s] in Gadaba and [s] in Kolami, Naiki and Ollari. In SCD all languages except Telugu have [s]. It is assumed here that those lexical items which had *s-* variants at the reconstructed stage in SD changed [s] to [h] which tended to become Ø. This rule was shared by SD and SCD, although Telugu, because of the areal influence, goes with SD in losing *c in cognate items. In Middle Indo Aryan (MIA) *s* becomes *h* in Sinhala (non-finally), e.g. *satta* > *hatta* 'seven'; palatal *c* becomes *s* regularly, e.g. *chā(y)ā* > Si. *seya* 'shade' (Masica 1991: 205–207). This is certainly an areal trend involving Dravidian and Indo-Aryan.

11. PD **ciy-/*cī-* 'to give'. SD: Ta. Ka. *ī*, SCD: Te. *icc-/iy-/ī-*, Go. *sī-*, *hī-*, *ī-*, Koṇḍa *sī-*, *si-*, Kui *sī-*, *jī-*, *hi-*, Kuvi *hi-*, Pe. *sī-*, Manḍa *hi-*; CD: Kol. *sī-*, Nk. *s'ī-*, Pa. *ci-*, Oll. Gad. *si*, ND: Kur. *ciʔ-* (*cicc-*), Malt. *ciy-* (*cic-*) [DEDR 2598]. Also cf. (8) above.

3.1.2. South Dravidian

Rule 7. Palatalization

PD *k > c/#__ [+V, -back][+C, –retro] (Ta. Ma.)

12. PD **key* 'to do, make'. SD: Ta. Ma. *cey*, Ko. *key*, *gey*, To. *kïy*, Koḍ. *key*, Ka. *key*, *gey*, Tu. *gey*; SCD: Te. *cēyu*, Go. *kī-*, Koṇḍa *ki-*, Kui *ki-/gi-*, Kuvi *kī-*, Pe. Manḍa *ki-*; ND: Brah. (*kann-*), pres. tense *kē-* [DEDR 1957].

Rule 8. Dissimilation and umlaut

a. $\begin{bmatrix} *e \\ *o \end{bmatrix} > \begin{bmatrix} i \\ u \end{bmatrix}$ /#(C)__(C)+*a*- (OTa. Ma.)

b. $\begin{bmatrix} i \\ u \end{bmatrix} > \begin{bmatrix} e \\ o \end{bmatrix}$ /#(C)__(C)+*a*- (spoken Ta. Ma.)

The output of PSD Rule 5 is input to Rule 8a; the output of 8a is input to 8b. Unlike in (9) and (10), in (12) and (13) PD *e, *o[C-*a* > PSD *e, *o[C-*a* > Pre-Tamil *i*, *u*[C-*a*.

13. PD **weḷ-V-*, PSD **weḷ-a-*, SD: **weḷ-a* 'to shine': Ta. *veḷi* (adj.) 'white', *viḷ-aŋku* (v.i.), Ma. *veḷi* 'light', *viḷ-aŋŋuka* (v.i.), Ko. *veḷ*, To. *pöḷ* (adj.), Ka. *beḷagu* (v. & n.), Te. *velũgu* (v. & n.); all other subgroups point to **weḷ* [DEDR 5496].
14. PD **col-V-*, PSD **col-ay*, SD: **col-a/*ol-a* 'fireplace, furnace': Ta. *ulai*, Ma. *ula*, Ka. *ole*, Koḍ. *ole*, Tu. *ule*; SCD: Koṇḍa *solu*, Kui *soḍu*, Pe. *hol*; CD: Pa. *colŋgel* (*kel* 'stone') 'fireplace' [DEDR 2857].

Changes in Individual Languages A. CONSONANTS:

Rule 9. Nasal assimilation

NP [NB] > NN/#(C)V__V, (C)VCV__V (Middle Malayāḷam, mainly in velar, palatal, dental and alveolar series; also in Koḍagu in a few cases. For details, see Subrahmanyam 1983: 309–312.)

15. PD **ponku* 'to boil'. SD: Ta. *ponku* [*poŋgu*], Ma. *poŋŋu*, Ka. *pongu*, Koḍ. *poŋŋ-*, Te. *pongu* [DEDR 4469].

Rule 10. Deaffrication
SD **c* > *t*/#__V (Toda regularly; Tuḷu dialectally)

16. PD **cuṭu* 'to be hot'. SD: Ta. Ma. *cuṭu* (*cuṭṭ-*) 'to be hot', Ka. *suḍu* (*suṭṭ-*), Koḍ. *cuḍ* (*cuṭṭ*), Tu. *suḍu*, *tuḍu*: To. *tuṛ* (*tuṭṭ*) [DEDR 2654].

Rule 11. Labial spirantization
p > *h*/#__V (Old Kannaḍa within historical period)

17. PD **pāl* 'milk', Ka. *pāl*, *hāl* [DEDR 4096].

Rule 12. Labial glide to stop
w > *b*/#__V (Old Kannaḍa within historical period;? extended to Koḍagu and Tuḷu through diffusion). See 10.

There are numerous changes of consonants in Toda and Kota, both synchronically and diachronically, which have not been treated here owing to constraints of space; also several changes of Tuḷu and Koḍagu are skipped.

B. VOWELS:

Rule 13. Vowel assimilation (Assimilation of a vowel to an adjacent vowel and/or consonant):

a. *Umlaut*

1. $\begin{bmatrix} e \\ o \end{bmatrix} > \begin{bmatrix} i \\ u \end{bmatrix}$ /#(C)__C-*i/u* (Kannaḍa)

18. PSD **keṭ-u* (*keṭṭ-*) 'to perish': Ka. *kiḍu* (*keṭṭ-*) [DEDR 1942].
19. PSD **koṭ-u* 'to give to 3rd person': Ka. *kuḍu* (*koṭṭ-*) [DEDR 2053]. The underlying midvowels in Kannaḍa can be recovered through internal reconstruction.

2. $\begin{bmatrix} o \\ \bar{o} \end{bmatrix} > \begin{bmatrix} e \\ \bar{e} \end{bmatrix}$ /#(C)__C-*e* (*-*e* < *-*ay*; Pre-Kota). The final vowel -*e* is lost after the sound change. Exceptions abound. See Emeneau (1994).

20. PSD **koṭ-ay* 'umbrella': Ta. *kuṭai*, Ma. *kuṭa*, Ka. *koḍe*: Ko. *keṛ*, *koṛ* [DEDR 1663].

3. $\begin{bmatrix} u \\ \bar{u} \end{bmatrix} > \begin{bmatrix} i \\ \bar{i} \end{bmatrix}$ /#(C)__C(C)-*e* (Pre-Kota).

21. PSD **kupp-a* 'heap': Ta. *kuppai*, Ma. *kuppa*, Ka. *kuppa*: Ko. *kip* (< **kipp-e* < **kupp-e*) [DEDR 1731a].

4. $\begin{bmatrix} a \\ \bar{a} \end{bmatrix} > \begin{bmatrix} o \\ \bar{o} \end{bmatrix}$ /#(C)__C_2-V_2 (V_2 is not *-*a*/*-*ay*; for the short vowel C_2 is [–alveolar, –nasal]; Pre-Toda).

22. PD **kaṇ* 'eye': To. *koṇ* [DEDR 1159(a)]; here there is no **ay* in the second syllable.

23. PSD **pakal* 'day': To. *poxol* (C_2 is non-alveolar) [DEDR 3805]; elsewhere PD **a*, *ā* remain (see Subrahmanyam 1983: 54–60).

b. *Labialization*

5. $\begin{bmatrix} i \\ \bar{i} \\ e \\ \bar{e} \end{bmatrix} > \begin{bmatrix} u \\ \bar{u} \\ o \\ \bar{o} \end{bmatrix}$ /#(C_1)__C_2-V_2

(C_1 = labial stop, C_2 = retroflex or alveolar **ṯ*; V_2 = [–low]; Pre- Koḍagu, Tuḷu)

24. PSD **piṭ-i* 'to catch; n. handle': Koḍ. *puḍi*, Tu. *puḍi*.

c. *Vowel-lowering*

6. *e* > *a*/#(C_1)__C_2-*a*/*ay* (C_1 = **k*, **c*, **p*; C_2 = retroflex; Pre-Koḍagu)

25. SD **piḷḷ-ay* 'child': Koḍ. *paḷḷe* [DEDR 4194].

d. *Vowel retraction*

7. $\begin{bmatrix} i \\ \bar{i} \\ e \\ \bar{e} \end{bmatrix} > \begin{bmatrix} \ddot{i} \\ \bar{\ddot{i}} \\ \ddot{e} \\ \bar{\ddot{e}} \end{bmatrix}$ /#C_1__C_2-V

(C_1 is not labial or palatal, C_2 = retroflex or **ṯ*; Pre-Koḍagu)

26. SD **kiḷi* ~ **kiṇi* 'parrot': Ta. *kiḷi*, *kiḷḷai*, Ma. *kiḷi*, Ka. *giḷi*, *giṇi*: Koḍ. *giṇi*.

8. [*e*] > [*ö*]/#C_1__C_2 (C_2 = [–alveolar]; Pre-Toda)

27. SD **etir* 'opposite': To. *ö θïr* [DEDR 795]; SD **eṇṭ* 'eight': Ta. *eṭṭu*, Ka. *eṇṭu*: To. *öṭ* [DEDR 784].

9. *ĕ* > *ŏ̈*/#C_1__C_2- (C_2- is not (C)y); Pre-Toda)

28. SD **cēr*(*cēr-nt-*) 'to reach': To. *sȫr* (*sȫd-*).

10. *i* > *ï*/#C_1__C_2- (C_1 or C_2 is not a palatal or sibilant)

29. PSD *iru* 'to be': Ta. *iru* (*iru-nt-*), To. *ïr* (ïθ-) 'to sit, live'.

e. *Back vowel fronting and rounding*

11. *u* > *ü*/#C_1__C_2-V_2 (C_2 = **y*, or V_2 = [–back, +high]; Pre-Toda)

30. SD **puli* 'tiger': Ta. Ma. Ka. *puli*; To. *püṣy* [DEDR 430].

f. *Glide formation*

12. $\begin{bmatrix} o \\ \bar{o} \end{bmatrix} > \begin{bmatrix} wa \\ w\bar{\ddot{a}} \end{bmatrix}$ /#(C_1)__C_2-*ay* ($C_1 \neq p$; Pre-Toda)

13. $\begin{bmatrix} o \\ \bar{o} \end{bmatrix} > \begin{bmatrix} w\ddot{i} \\ w\bar{\ddot{i}} \end{bmatrix}$ /#(C_1)__C_2-*i*/*u* / (Pre-Toda)

31. PSD **oṭ-ay* 'to break': Ta. *uṭai*; To. *waṛ* (*waṛ-θ*) [DEDR 946].

32. PD **onṯu* 'one'; Ta. *onṟu*; To. *wïḏ* [DEDR 990(d)].

g. *Dissimilation*

14. *u* > *ï*/#C_1__C_2-V_2 (C_1 or C_2 is [+labial] and V_2 = [+low]; Pre-Toda)

33. PD **puẓ-ay*, SD **poẓ-ay* 'hole': Ta. *puẓai*, Ma. *puẓa*, Ka. *poẓe*; To. *pïṭ* 'drainage hole in wall' [DEDR 4317].

The above changes show how vowels are influenced in their quality by adjacent vowels or consonants or both, creating variation between features such as front–back, high–low, and rounded–unrounded. Since Toda and Kota have lost the conditioning factors (most of the non-initial vowels and sometimes the original consonants), changes have to be recovered (only) from earlier historical stages by applying the comparative method. (For a detailed discussion of these changes, see Subrahmanyam 1983, Emeneau 1994.)

3.1.3. South-Central Dravidian

Rule 14. Apical displacement

a. $(C_1)\begin{Bmatrix} a \\ e \\ o \end{Bmatrix} C_2 - a -> (C_1)C_2 \begin{Bmatrix} \bar{a} \\ \bar{e} \\ \bar{o} \end{Bmatrix} -$

b. $(C_1)\begin{bmatrix} i \\ e \\ o \\ u \end{bmatrix} C_2 + \begin{Bmatrix} i \\ u \end{Bmatrix} > (C_1)C_2 \begin{bmatrix} \bar{i} \\ \bar{e} \\ \bar{o} \\ \bar{u} \end{bmatrix} -$

c. $(C_1)\begin{bmatrix} i \\ e \\ a \\ o \\ u \end{bmatrix} C_2 \begin{Bmatrix} i \\ u \end{Bmatrix} C_3 -> (C_1)C_2 \begin{bmatrix} i \\ e \\ a \\ o \\ u \end{bmatrix} - \emptyset - C_3C_3 -$

(Conditions: 1. $C_1 = \emptyset$; C_2 = [+apical, –nasal], i.e. **ṯ*, **r*, **l*; **ṭ*, **ḷ*, **ẓ*: All languages of SCD; 2. C_1 = **p*, **t*, **c[s]*, **m*, **w*; C_2 = **ṯ*, **r*, **ẓ*: Telugu and Koṇḍa; 3. C_1 = **p*, **t*, **c[s]*, **k*, **m*, **n*, **w* or Ø; C_2 = [+apical, –nasal]: Kui, Kuvi, Pengo, Manḍa)

Rules 14a–c represent an atypical sound change or complex of changes innovated by the members of the SCD (SDII) branch of PSD—Telugu, Gondi, Koṇḍa, Kui, Kuvi, Pengo and Manḍa. This is an areally and lexically diffused sound change which shifted intervocalic apical consonants of PD to the word-initial position (not allowed in PD) and also created word-initial consonantal clusters with apicals as second members (also not allowed in PD). As we proceed from South to North and East (Kui, Kuvi, Pengo, Manḍa), the structural conditions widen and more and more lexical items got involved in the change. Gondi and Koṇḍa are much less affected by these changes than the others. A subsequent series of sound changes simplified the clusters by dropping either C_1 or C_2 in different languages (for details, see Krishnamurti 1978). In 14a–b, the root vowel V_1 and suffix vowel V_2 are contracted to lengthen V_1. In 14c, the unaccented suffix vowel V_2 is lost in heavy syllables.

34. PSD **ūẓ/*uẓ-u* 'to plough'. SCD (SDII): OTe. *ḍukki* 'ploughing' (> Mdn. *dukki*), Go. *uṛ-*, Koṇḍa, Kui, Kuvi *ṛū*, *rū*, *lū-*, Pe. Manḍa *ṛū* (PD **ūẓ/*uẓ-u*) [DEDR 688].

35. PSD **carac*/**tarac* 'snake'. SCD (SDII): OTe. *trācu* (> Mdn. *tācu*) 'cobra', Go. *tarāsh*, *taras*, Koṇḍa *saras*, (dial. *srāsu*), Kui *srās*, *srācu*, Kuvi *rācu*, Pe. *rāc*, Manḍa *trehe* (cf. Ta. Ma. *aravu* 'serpent' [DEDR 2359].

Rule 15. Retroflex-alveolar merger (apical fronting?)

PD **ṭ* > **ṯ*/#(C)V̆̄__(SCD). Even post-nasal **nṯ* is involved in this change.

36. PSD **nāṭu* 'country, village, location, cultivated land'. SDI: Ta. Ma. *nāṭu*, To. *nōṛ*, Ko. *nāṛ*, Ka. *nāḍu*; SCD **nāṭ*: (Te. *nāḍu*), Go. *nār* (pl. *nāhku*), Koṇḍa *nāṟu* (pl. *nāRku*), Kui *nāju* (pl. *nāska*), Kuvi *nāyu*, Pe. *nāz*, *nās*, Manḍa *nāy* (obl. *nāṭ-*) [DEDR 3638].

In Telugu, only a few lexical items are affected by this change.

Rule 16. Retroflex mergers and deretroflexion

a. $\left\{\begin{matrix} z. \\ ḍ \end{matrix}\right\}$ > *ṛ*/#C₁__ (All SCD languages except Telugu; Kui has *ḍ*-, if C_1- is Ø).

b. *ḷ* > *l*/#C__ (Kui dial.)
   > *ṛ*/#C__ (All SCD except Te. and Koṇḍa)
   > *ṇ*/#C__ (Kuvi dial. where C = *m*)

c. *l* > *r*/#C__ (Pe. Manḍa, sometimes Kui-Kuvi; all retain *l* if C = Ø)

37. PD **puẓ-V-* 'worm, insect'. OTe. *pruwwu*, *purwu*, MTe. *purugu*, Go. *puṛī*, Koṇḍa *piṛvu* (pl. *piṛku*), Kui *pṛiu* (pl. *pṛīka*), Kuvi *prī-* (*prīka*) [DEDR 4312].
38. PD **kaḷ-am* 'threshing floor': Go. *kaṛā*, Koṇḍa *kaṛan*, *kalan*, Kui *klai*, Kuvi *kṛānu*, Manḍa *kāṛa* [DEDR 1376].

Rule 17. Cluster simplification

a. C_1 > Ø/#__C_2... (C_1 = *n*); All SCD languages except Te. and Koṇḍa; where C_1 = *s* (< *c*), or *w*, all but Kui; when C_2 is **ṛ* (< **ṭ*) then C_1 is Ø in Kuvi, Pengo and Manḍa, see 14 above.

Rule 18. Mid-vowel-lowering in Kui-Kuvi

$\left\{\begin{matrix} \bar{e} \\ \bar{o} \end{matrix}\right\}$ > *ā*/#(C)(C)__ (The mid vowels must have resulted from vowel contraction with a low vowel *-a-* as -V_2 in the original form, e.g. PSCD **sow-ar* 'salt' > *sōru* in Koṇḍa, but *sāru* in Kui and *hāru* in Kuvi; see Rules 3 and 14).

Changes in Individual Languages

Rule 19. Apical mergers

a. SCD $\left\{\begin{matrix} ẓ \\ ṯ[r] \end{matrix}\right\}$ > *r*/#C__ (Early Old Telugu)

b. SCD **ẓ* > *ḍ*/#__ (Old Telugu)

c. OTe. *ṯ[ṟ]* > *r*/#__ (Middle and Mdn. Telugu)
d. OTe. *ḍ* > *d*/#__ (Middle and Mdn. Telugu)
e. OTe. *r* > Ø/#C_1__ (Middle and Mdn. Telugu)

Sub-rules 19c–e operate on apicals resulting from displacement rules 14a–c and 19a–b.

Rule 20. Palatalization

a. PD **ay* > *ē*/#(C)__ (Pre-Telugu)
b. PD **k* > *c*/#__ [+V, –back] (Pre-Telugu). This rule is independent of a similar rule (Rule 7 above) in Tamil and Malayāḷam. The palatalizing environment includes *ē* resulting from 20a; the following retroflexes do not inhibit palatalization as in Ta. -Ma.

Rule 21. Sonorant deretroflexion

$\begin{bmatrix} \text{ḷ} \\ \text{ṇ} \end{bmatrix} > \begin{bmatrix} l \\ n \end{bmatrix}$ /#CV__ (Old Telugu). Even geminated ones are affected by this change. It appears to be an areal change in SCD, CD and ND (see below).

■ 3.2. Central Dravidian

There are no significant shared sound changes in CD. The ones which need mention refer to C_2- obstruents which are treated separately. A single PD **ṯ[ḏ]* is represented as a stop, i.e. *d/ḍ* in Kolami, Naiki and Parji, further softened to *y* in Oll. and Gad. PD **ẓ* develops to *ṛ* in Pa.-Oll.-Gad. subgroup, to *r* in Kol. and to *l, r, y* in Nk. (Ch.). Word-initial **n*- is generally lost in Kolami-Naiki as a shared innovation.

Changes in Individual Languages
Rule 22

a. *Low vowel raising*

PCD $\begin{bmatrix} {*a} \\ {*\bar{a}} \end{bmatrix} > \begin{bmatrix} e \\ \bar{e} \end{bmatrix}$ /#(C)__ [+C, +alveolar] (pre-Parji)

b. *Sonorant deretroflexion*

PCD $\begin{bmatrix} \text{*ḷ} \\ \text{*ṇ} \end{bmatrix} > \begin{bmatrix} l \\ n \end{bmatrix}$ /#(C)V__ (Pre-Parji)

c. *Alveolar merger with dental or retroflex reduction*

PCD $\begin{bmatrix} \text{*ṯṯ} \\ \text{*nṯ} \end{bmatrix} > \begin{bmatrix} \text{tt / ṭṭ} \\ \text{nd / nḍ} \end{bmatrix}$ /#CV__ (Parji in different dialects).

The above three are chronologically ordered rules. The Vowel-raising Rule 22a took place before 22c; 22a will not apply to the output of 22b; e.g. PCD **kal* > Pa. *kel* 'stone', PCD **man* > Pa. *men* 'to be', but PCD **kaḷam* > Pa.

kali 'threshing floor', PCD **kaṇ* > Pa. *kan* 'eye', PCD **waṯ-* > Pa. *ved-p* (*ved-t-*) 'to dry'.

■ 3.3. North Dravidian

Rule 23.

a. *Velar spirantization*
PD **k* > *x*/#__ [+V, –high] (Kurux, Malto, Brahui)

39. PD *kaṇ* 'eye': Kur. Malt. Br. *xan* [DEDR 1159(a)].

b. *Velarization of palatal*
PD **c* > *k*/#__ [+V, +back, +high] (North Dravidian, irregular)

40. PD *cuṭu* 'be hot': Kur. *kuṛ* (*kuṭṭ-*), Malt. *kuṛe* 'embers' [DEDR 2654].

Changes in Individual Languages

Rule 24. *Denasalization*

$$\text{PND} \begin{bmatrix} *n \\ *m \end{bmatrix} > \begin{bmatrix} d \\ b \end{bmatrix} /\#\_\_ \text{ [+V, –back] (Pre-Brahui)}$$

Rule 25. *Midvowel loss*

$$\text{PND} \begin{bmatrix} *e \\ *o \end{bmatrix} > \begin{bmatrix} i/a/\bar{e} \\ i/a/\bar{o} \end{bmatrix} /\#(\text{C})\_\_ \text{ (Pre-Brahui)}$$

Brahui lost the mid short vowels under the areal influence of Baluci, etc.

41. PD **ne(y)tt-V-* 'blood': Br. *ditar* [DEDR 3748].
42. PD **mēy* 'to graze': Br. *bei* 'grass fit for grazing' [DEDR 5093].

■ 3.4. Patterns of Change of Intervocalic Obstruents

It is not possible to find consistently shared innovations in the case of intervocalic consonants, particularly the obstruents. Therefore, they are depicted as patterns in Figure 2 with an indication where they appear to be shared ones. The most common reflex is shown in bold.

■ 4. Typological Classification

■ 4.1. Unshared but Widespread Changes

A number of sound changes have occurred or are occurring in contiguous languages at different times, producing a final result, which, if we looked back after many years, would give the impression that they were shared innovations. These are different from the sound changes discussed so far in two respects: (1) they do not have a fixed, definable time frame, except that they are

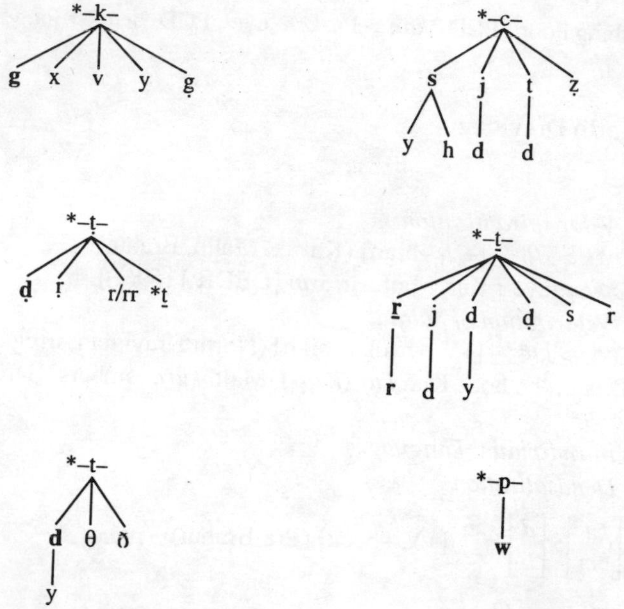

Figure 2: Developments of PD Intervocalic Obstruents

all post-PD; (2) there is evidence that they have been occurring in different languages at different times; some are on-going; (3) they cut across the sub-groups set up on the basis of shared innovations; (4) it seems possible that their spread can be defined in terms of broad geographical regions. For these reasons, they are not formulated as rules below, although it is possible to do so.

1. PD root final *-ay*, develops to *ĕ* and *ĭ* in almost all SCD, CD and ND languages (see etymologies 11 and 12 above).
2. PD **y-* is lost in all languages except Old Tamil; Mdn. Tamil and Malayāḷam also do not have it. The vowel following **y-* was **Ă*, which is represented as *e/ā* in SD, as *ē/ā* in SCD, as *a/ā* in CD and as *e/ē* in ND. Similarly PD **ñ* merged with *n* in all languages except in Malayāḷam which retains some items with **ñ* and not all.
3. PD **ẓ* is lost in all languages consequent on splits and mergers during historic times, except in Standard Tamil and Malayāḷam. In Parji of CD, it develops to *ṛ* distinctively. It merges in different languages with *ḍ ṛ l ḷ r y š ṣ θ*. No clear isoglosses seem possible.
4. PD **ṇ* **ḷ* became deretroflexed as dental/alveolar *n l* in SCD, CD and ND. They are internally reconstructable in certain languages of SCD and CD. All SD languages preserve them. The change, however, is a sweeping one.
5. PD **ṯ* **ṯṯ* **nṯ* are preserved only in Toda and Kota and, to some extent, as *ṯṯ* in Malayaḷam in SD and in Koṇḍa in SCD. In the rest of the languages,

ṟ merged with the flap *r* and *ṯṯ nṯ* with dental *tt nd* or retroflex *ṭṭ ṇḍ*. Some of these changes are datable within the literary languages; no common historical stage can be postulated.

6. Two syllable types have become normalized in all languages except Tamil and Malayāḷam, viz. (C)VCCV or (C)V̄CV. A number of phonological changes have occurred leading to this typological goal Such a shift is also evidenced in Indo-Aryan (Krishnamurti. 1991. Masica 1991: 187–188, 198). PP > P, NP > B/#(C)V̄__ is part of this strategy. Loss of a high vowel *i u* in the medial (unaccented) syllable has led to the creation of disyllabic forms from underlying trisyllabic ones, e.g. **mar-untu* 'medicine': Te. *mandu*, Ka. *maddu*, *mardu*, Pa. *merd-* (< **mar-nt-*). Consequent on changes in canonical shapes, obstruent voicing became phonemic in almost all the languages except Tamil, Malayā-

PD	*P–	*–P–	*–PP–	*–NP–	*–NPP–
post-PD	?	–B–	–P–	–NB–	–NP–

ḷam, and Toda, as follows:

The initial position is filled by secondary voicing and through borrowings from Indo-Aryan. The older single vs. double contrast became voiced vs. voiceless.

7. PD **w-* > *b-* in Kannaḍa, Koḍagu and Tuḷu in SD and in Kurux and Malto of ND. A similar sound change is found in Indo-Aryan in the Northern and Eastern languages, viz. Hindi, Rajasthani, Nepali, Bihari, Bengali (Masica 1991: 202).

■ 4.2. Some Suggestions on Areal Types

The elimination of the alveolar in all its occurrences has led to the emergence of a five-point obstruent system in most of the languages which has then produced a common Indo-Aryan Dravidian type in phonology. Secondary retroflexion of dentals in word-initial position through assimilative changes in SCD, CD and ND is another type which looks suspiciously IA. The opposite tendency is noticed in the case of retroflex sonorants, word-initial or non-initial retroflexes—*ḷ ṇ ẓ*; they merged with alveolars in CD and SCD and ND. Apical displacement (Rule 14) seems to be the only atypical Dravidian development.

■ 4.3. Observations and Questions to be Addressed

1. Most of the historically identifiable shared innovations have exceptions. The typologically motivated ones are extremely regular (those in 4.1 as opposed to the changes proposed as rules).

2. It is likely that shared innovations generally spread through lexical diffusion. Typologically triggered sound changes spread without exception but are spatially gradual.
3. Is it necessary or possible to make a distinction between these two types of changes? What are the implications of such a distinction to the comparative method?

Questions of this kind have not been seriously addressed by language typologists and historical linguists. It is claimed that typology imposes certain constraints on reconstructed states of a language or a family in order to make it conform to what is plausible in human languages (Fox 1995: 250–60).

What is claimed here is that certain changes (mainly sound changes) are motivated or caused by system-internal pressures and such changes tend to be much more regular than the changes caused by sporadic shifts in the speech habits of speakers. For instance, in Dravidian, the palatalization of a velar before front vowels (Rules 7, 20) is a change of this latter kind. There is nothing system-internal to this change, although it may have brought about changes in the distribution of certain phonemes. But the replacement of PD *ṯ either by a dental *t or retroflex *ṭ is typologically motivated; hence its spread is sweeping and there are hardly any exceptions after its operation.

In Austronesian languages, Proto-Oceanic (POC) had word-final consonants as well as vowels, while some of the derived subfamilies and languages became totally vowel-ending in two ways: (1) either the final consonants are lost, or (2) an 'echo vowel' which harmonizes with the preceding vowel is added, e.g. (1) POC **manuk* 'bird' > (Southeast Solomonic languages) *manu*; similarly, **ikan* 'fish' > *iɣa*, *iʔa*, **niuR* 'coconut' > *niu*; (2) > (Northwest Solomonic languages) *manuɣu*; *viɣana*, *iana*; *niunu*, respectively. Final vowels of POC remain in the derived languages, **bebe* 'butterfly' > Southwest and Northwest Solomonic languages *bebe*, **kutu* 'louse' > *ɣutu*, *utu* (communication from Robert Blust and Malcom Ross, the latter mainly for the examples). What is important to note is that the vowel-ending descendant languages have no items being retained as consonant-ending. This is a case of a regular typological change. These could have been shared innovations (I have not checked!), but still they were clearly, typologically motivated or triggered.

■ REFERENCES

Burrow, T. and **M.B. Emeneau.** 1984. *A Dravidian etymological dictionary [DEDR]* (2nd ed.). Oxford: Clarendon Press.

Emeneau, M.B. 1970. *Dravidian comparative phonology: a sketch.* Annamalainagar: Annamalainagar University.

Emeneau, M.B. 1994. *Dravidian studies: selected papers.* Delhi: Motilal Banarsidas Publishers.

Fox, A. 1995. *Linguistic reconstruction: an introduction to theory and method.* Oxford: Oxford University Press.

Krishnamurti, Bh. 1961. *Telugu verbal bases: a comparative and descriptive study (UCPL 24)*. Berkeley and Los Angeles: The University of California Press.

———. 1978. Areal and lexical diffusion of sound change: evidence from Dravidian. *Language* 54.1–20.

———. 1991. The emergence of syllable types of stems (C)VCC(V) and (C)VC(V) in Indo-Aryan and Dravidian: conspiracy or convergence? *Studies in the Historical Phonology of Asian Languages*, ed. by William G. Boltz and M.C. Shapiro, 160–75. Amsterdam: John Benjamins.

Kumaraswami Raja, N. 1969. *Post-nasal plosives in Dravidian*. Annamalainagar: Annamalainagar University.

Masica, C.P. 1991. *The Indo-Aryan languages*. Cambridge: Cambridge University Press.

Schiffman, H.F. and **C. Eastman** (eds). 1975. *Dravidian phonological systems*. Seattle: Institute for Comparative and Foreign Area Studies, University of Washington.

Steever, S.B. 1993. *Analysis to synthesis*. Oxford: Oxford University Press.

Subrahmanyam, P.S. 1983. *Dravidian comparative phonology*. Annamalainagar: Annamalai University.

B

■ Open Submissions ■

Diglossia as a Linguistic Reality

■ P. REKHA ABEL ■

This paper argues for a view of diglossia that treats it not as a contingent pathology observable in some languages in some developing nations, but as a universal fact about language which has been underexplored by theoreticians because of factors that need to be understood and overcome. It is suggested that the transition to the new perspective on diglossia be seen as part of the aftermath of structuralism.

■ 1. Introduction

This paper traces the development of diglossia studies—a gradual process, from Ferguson to Britto and beyond, of outgrowing the early view of diglossia as an interesting aberration. Once seen as a contingent and pathological relic of the past in certain third world cultures, diglossia in the story we tell begins to look like a constitutive necessity rooted in discourse coupling, a universal of language use. We begin with a simplistic presentation of the old and new views; refinements are offered as the paper progresses.

The old ideas of diglossia studies reflected a stance of linguistic naturalism. This attitude on the one hand declared Low language alone to be natural, and therefore real. And on the other hand it accepted the model of High language, a teachably organized/structured means enabling US to understand THEIR reality. Such a bifurcation into an US of describing culture and a THEM of describable nature was complicit with a modernization/development agenda, though not always consciously so. The global elite sponsoring that agenda assumed that the better organized northern societies must, by effective pedagogy, aid the societies of the south to structure themselves along northern lines.

The new ideas say: language is both a spontaneous Low learning and a self-structuring High knowledge validation. The key transition that makes this shift possible is from old pictures of normal languages having one Code and some odd languages having two Codes—two lexical mappings between sound and meaning—to new pictures. These new pictures show that language use regularly couples two discourses on a High-to-Low basis for the purpose of knowledge transmission from a knowledge-validating High discourse to a knowledge-using Low conversation which the coupling treats as a discourse (a discourse is a flow of verbal exchanges that sets its own rules for handling knowledge and other resources). The general two-coding of diglossia becomes a functional fact. Structural two-coding—the coexistence in one language of two structural mappings from sounds to meanings—turns into a special and occasional effect of such discourse couplings. Nothing now prevents any discourse D-i from playing different roles—playing High to D-j's Low, but Low to D-k's High.

Diglossia in this generalized sense becomes a body of evidence—morphological evidence in the case of the structural two-coding which alone in the older view counted as "diglossia"—showing that code-variation within a single language is something of which speakers have linguistic knowledge, which their normal language acquisition endowment must have enabled them to acquire. This evidence requires mainstream linguistic attention. The material of diglossia therefore belongs to the core of language study and not to its periphery. This reasoning forces contemporary work to seek an explanatory account of diglossia as a matter of universal linguistic principle and not just at some language-specific level of description.

In this paper we narrate how diglossia studies have reached their contemporary level of thematic potential—high but as yet underutilized by many linguists. To this end we trace the development of diglossia theory from the formalism of Ferguson (1959), over the functionalist bridge of Fishman (1968a), to the substantivism of Britto (1986). The development of diglossia studies begins by characterizing certain speech communities in terms that are formal in that they imply a linguistics of codes, of mappings between sound and meaning. It ends, so far, at a substantivist view which detects latent diglossia in every community, working for a linguistics of discourses where speakers and their actions of speaking and understanding provide the substantive underpinnings for the systems of their linguistic and other knowledge.

Section 2 of this paper critiques Ferguson's theory of diglossia from the perspective provided by later work. Section 3 construes Fishman's conceptualization of diglossia as using DOMAINS to move away from the naturalist formalism of Ferguson. Section 4 presents Britto's diasystemic approach to validation using the H and L concepts of diglossia theory but redefining them in terms of primary speech as authentic. In section 5 we extend the theoretical breakthrough in Britto and draw conclusions of our own.

■ 2. Ferguson: A Critique

This section suggests that Ferguson's (1959) naturalist assumptions underpin a formalist account construing diglossia as a third world pathology unrelated to serious linguistic principles. The formalist approach to language planning and development neglects in description and seeks to side-step in prescription the pluralities generally found in the real world—a distortion most clearly seen in Ferguson (1968). For a fuller treatment of the Fergusonian corpus from a post-formalist standpoint, see Britto (1986).

Ferguson (1959) identifies the diglossic situation as an unusual kind of standardization. He suggests that diglossia is an ultimately nonsustainable situation as it burdens the speech community with communicative tensions that will need to be resolved sooner or later by going monoglossic. His description of diglossia in terms of the traits of function, prestige, standardization, stability, grammar, lexicon and phonology makes the form of language the locus where one identifies a diglossic situation—by finding, if diglossia is indeed present, that one superposed variety shows at least some of those diagnostic traits.

Why does this model ask us to find two varieties coexisting throughout the speech community and playing specific and differentiated roles? Because the point is to draw a complementary distribution picture: two form-sets A and B neatly play two sets of roles P and Q. This implements the formalist program of beginning with form and looking for correlates that warrant setting up a formal grid.

To see that this program drives the Fergusonian framework, consider the following questions:

1. Why is it that two formally divergent varieties work in distinct sets of situations?
2. In spite of the prediction (from general linguistics) that both varieties should be equally resourceful in referring to the external world in its entirety, why is there a marked pairing of certain realms with one variety and others with another?

The framework answers these questions in terms of the notions listed above (prestige, standardization and the like). A diagnosis of diglossia as a pathological situation follows, for one insinuates that the natural (L) languages of some speech communities lack the resources to talk about the Higher spheres of life.

Such a diagnosis reflects the formalist preoccupation with referring expressions rather than objects referred to or persons who give and take these references. If a language as a code is one's point of departure, one assumes that the language precedes a speech community which emerges around it. Any coexistence of language varieties in the community looks unnatural and is assumed to stem from some social–hierarchical archaism. And one tends to synchronically 'understand' this archaic bifurcation by stating a complementary distribution pattern that freezes H and L in their respective contexts of use, unable to meet or interact.

Is this a caricature of Ferguson? His work did fall within the overall functionalist program in that it paired structurally different codes with separate functions. But Ferguson's formalism is evident in his definition of diglossia on the basis of structural differentiation. The specificity of functional differentiation goes unrecognized within such a view.

Ferguson examines only what we may call structural or more accurately morphological diglossia. Not even as a projected continuation of his program does he envisage any generalization from this morphological core. For diglossia is considered a deviant relative to the norm of monolingualism. This judgement stems from an exclusive concern with the formal mapping from expression to content and non-concern with substance. Hence the use of systematic two-coding of morpho-lexical structure as the chief diagnostic for diglossia. Such a stance is typical of formal-naturalist linguistic methodology. It takes the language and not the speaker's actions as a natural object for analysis and regards a study of form as a complete research program.

However, Ferguson does record some phenomena which show readers today where such a program fails. In speaking of the use of H in the domain of formal education Ferguson says:

> The situation in formal education is often more complicated… In the Arab world, for example, formal university lectures are given in H, but drills, explanations, and section meetings may be in large part conducted in L, especially in the natural sciences as opposed to the humanities. Although teachers' use of L in secondary schools is forbidden by law in some Arab countries, often a considerable part of the teacher's time is taken up with explaining in L the meaning of the material in H which has been presented in books or lectures (1959: 431).

For Ferguson this is a place where his neat complementary distribution leaks, an example where L is used even in what he would expect to be H situations. For a substantivist or postformal view, this 'exception' to Ferguson's formal pattern instantiates the real 'rule'. No sharp boundary separates the two kinds of knowledge system which underlie the H and L discourses. Knowledge flows between them when they are coupled. Diglossia then becomes a study of knowledge transmission as teaching/learning.

In Ferguson, diglossia was a formal fact about certain speech communities marked by pathological language use. His classification of H domains and L domains was dictated by different phonological and grammatical forms correlated with degrees of learnedness. That there might be other factors involved in such differentiation of domains completely escapes such a net.

With the advantage of hindsight, we see today that a study of 'domains', in a sense sharpened by the work of Fishman discussed in section 3, leads us away from Ferguson's formalist approach. We move towards the view that types of knowledge, ways to validate it, modalities for transmitting and receiving it belong within the scope of diglossia studies. One cannot formulate a purely linguistic program of diglossia research which would work out the formal alternation of codes in correlation with some extralinguistic contextual variation left unanalyzed because it lies outside language.

Ferguson's dire predictions about the consequences of maintaining a diglossic situation belong to the monistic package of language modernization. Unlike such a model, standardization seems a necessary part of language modernization. Diglossia theory, of the Fergusonian kind, maintained that progress would involve eliminating diglossia, since variation of any kind within the standard was considered a pathology and monolithic standardization was considered the optimal goal or an inevitable result.

Thus Tauli (1977) maintains that all diglossia is uneconomical. The aim of language planning should be to work for its elimination. Such a view stems from Tauli's essentially monistic outlook. The sociological assumption that monolithic standardization should be the norm comes from classical modernization theory. The cognate naturalist assumption in linguistics that pluralism is a pathology (since form should be biuniquely connected to a single reality-substance) leads to an imperative of eliminating diglossia during modernization.

These implications of the naturalist methodology of linguistics merit careful study even by readers not interested in sociolinguistics per se. Structuralists assumed—and generativists largely agree, except that they make the sets infinite—that since a language is a single pairing of a set of sound signals with a set of meaning messages, a semantics should be able to offer a single mapping specifying this pairing. In such a view of the world, which one might call the modernist view, the world was devoid of variation in principle and progress was seen as essentially eliminating plurality. This belief in monolithic standardization again stems from the assumption that one-to-one mapping of form and substance is possible and indeed natural. Form is therefore the object of knowledge. What you know is form.

Is it his linguistics that makes Ferguson subscribe to such a view of diglossia? We would like to suggest that, indeed, his overall view stems from a methodology which analyzes a language as a morpholexical code and not in terms of the minds of persons. If language is its morpholexical forms alone, we cannot speak of various referential substances the form may hook up with in different uses. Fergusonian diglossia is then based on the one-to-one mapping between form and substance. Such a formal perspective confines diglossia to languages where it has morpholexical effects. Within such a framework we cannot refer to whatever underlies or drives the contexts in which forms so differentiated are used. The study of contexts calls for generalizations beyond the morpholexical facts. Fergusonians cannot do this since diglossia for them is about the morpho-lexis. Generalizations which lead to the postulation of diglossia as a universal or a linguistic principle cannot be made.

Another way to approach this limitation is to say that Ferguson describes speech as the use of a code and regards a code as a normative entity—in the sense of Khubchandani (1983), whose important contribution considerations of space prevent us from discussing here (Khubchandani 1997 provides a representative sample of his relevant writings). Once the process of speech is seen as a normative entity, we lose the agency of the participants in a speech situation and the situated message-content of their speaking. Such a formal view treats the speech situation as unamenable to specific description, totally subordinating it to alleged rules governing the forms deployed in speech. For a critique of this view that reads Khubchandani's work as initiating a postformal approach, see Dasgupta (1997).

■ 3. Fishman

Moving away from the naturalist formalism of Ferguson, Joshua Fishman shifts the scene of diglossic variation from the old codes to his new 'domains' of language use.

Fishman's willing acceptance of the inherent communicative heterogeneity of a speech community, be it structurally monolingual or multilingual, yields an entirely different picture of diglossia. Taking as a point of departure *societal interaction* rather than language variation, Fishman (1968a,b,c) describes diglossia in terms of functionally differentiated language uses for varied purposes. This contrasts with Ferguson's model showing one code as *superposed* on another. Fishman's analysis emphasizes societal patterns which govern language use, not language alone. Structurally monolingual and multilingual societies are taken to be essentially similar at the functional level. This similarity is based on common causes for communicative heterogeneity in all speech communities. Sociolinguistic differentiation is seen as merely less morphologized in monolingual societies and not as absent. Membership in either type of society, according to Fishman, 'results in norm-regulated communicative interaction such that certain usage is considered appropriate (and is, therefore, effective) in certain contexts' (Fishman 1968b: 154). It is thus the social organization of behavior, and not language alone, which is the primary concern. And this gives "attitudes of the users" the right of entry into the general theory.

With Fishman, diglossia is no longer an isolated pathological phenomenon restricted to a few societies and meriting empirical description as an ethnographic curiosity. Instead, it becomes a theoretically interesting manifestation of social behavioral patterns in language and betokens the complexity of human society. All patterns, for Fishman, arise from concrete settings of face-to-face verbal interaction. Social patterns emerge from individual behavior, taking into account facts concerning the speaker, the hearer, their relationship to each other, the locale and the topic of communication. The formulation of societal regularities which can be utilized to study linguistic variation is the basic task of sociolinguistic research.

Fishman defines societal regularities, which can be organized into 'domains', "in terms of institutional contexts and their congruent behavioural co-occurrences" (Fishman 1968c: 248). These societal regularities are drawn from the *data of talk*.

A society's linguistic repertoire, accordingly, includes all varieties of language it uses in various domains it recognizes. Acknowledgement of domains entails the acceptance of correspondingly differentiated varieties of language. It also entails that every individual of that society is functionally diglossic or bilingual. This leads to Fishman's assertion that

> diglossia exists not only in multilingual societies which officially recognize several *languages*, and not only in societies that utilize highly divergent and even genetically different vernacular and classical varieties, but also in societies which employ *separate dialects*, *registers*, or *functionally differentiated language varieties of whatever kind* (Fishman 1968a: 136).

One important difference between Ferguson and Fishman is the latter's acceptance of *functionally differentiated language varieties of whatever kind* as terms in a diglossia, in contrast to Ferguson's exclusive focus on structurally different varieties of the same language. Diglossia therefore becomes for Fishman "a characterization of the societal allocation of functions to different languages or varieties" (Fishman 1968a: 145), while for Ferguson diglossia characterizes only societies which employ two or more varieties of one language and differentiate their functions. We detect in Fishman the shift from language as a code to language use as a social process. This type of characterization more directly commits Fishman to functional inquiry than Ferguson, who in contrast appears merely to have been forced by his forms into a reluctant study of some function-tangent issues.

Unlike scholars concerned directly with the nature and role of functions, Ferguson views the contexts hierarchically, overgeneralizing from the exemplary languages which mark his—and the field's—first encounter with diglossia. He finds it striking that in those languages the H variety is more archaic than the L variety genealogically derived from it; and that this archaic variety is used for what the society traditionally regards as Higher functions. Generalizing, Ferguson's diglossia requires an L subcode genealogically related to an H code, and imposes a hierarchy placing H contexts above L.

Fishman's Domains, though they inherit the core of the contexts where Ferguson's two codes are deployed, do not replicate their hierarchical arrangement. He stresses that every speech community gives its members ready access to a range of compartmentalized roles and is thus endowed with domains. But his account imposes no rank order *a priori* on these domains, or on the role-relations obtaining within them. The implication, that any ordering along those lines must be formulated *a posteriori* by the speech community for itself, is consistent with the general picture of intra-group interaction that has been emerging in the literature.

However, note that though an adoption of the fully functionalist characterization potentially makes diglossia look like a universal phenomenon, Fishman does not make this explicit. His main concern is to separate diglossia from bilingualism and make it easier to study bilingual speech communities as well as those in which linguistic diversity involves varieties of one language. His study of diglossia is geared towards showing that all speech communities possess a diversified linguistic repertoire and are thereby diglossic and/or bilingual. This enables him empirically to stress the non-existence of monovarietal speech communities, a crucial result that poses the theoretical challenge which subsequent diglossia theory must derive from deeper linguistic principles. Furthermore, his study of domains visualizes a complex speech community which has undergone modernization-induced compartmentalization of roles. Modernization studies therefore feed the analysis of domains, forcing sociolinguistics into a closer engagement with the social sciences, another methodological consequence of some importance.

In raising the question "who speaks what language to whom and when?" and formulating potential answers to it in terms of domains, Fishman relates the form of language material directly to the substance of language use. The emphasis placed on *talk* and the attempt to link rules governing talk with rules governing other aspects of social behavior testifies to his belief in the fundamental role of language variation at the Form (language system)/Function (language use) interface. It is such a postformal or substantivist vision that gives conceptual depth to Fishman's (1968a,b, and c) empirical claim that, once bilingualism has arisen from repertoire diversification (an inevitable process, given the inherent complexity of speech communities) and become a societal norm, it ends up as a diglossia. This claim is methodologically unpacked in terms of various local answers to what we can only call "Fishman's Problem": who speaks what language to whom and when? Positing domains and role repertoires within domains paves the way for a serious redescription of the diversities known as bilingualism and diglossia.

Moving away from the overemphasis on the pattern of every L being historically derived from and synchronically subordinate to its H, a functionalist account stresses domains and the use of different speech variants in different domains. This marks an advance over the structural H/L dichotomy. The hierarchical dichotomy remains significant only to the extent that it helps to make a certain type of sense of the structuring of domains.

For Fishman, diglossia as a speech community feature functionally differentiates the speech of individuals playing various roles in different domains. The existence of domains in this account is linked to that of roles, not to codes or subcodes as a matter of linguistic form. Individuals' roles are variables depending on relationship dyads. Different kinds of dyads obtain in different domains. This leaves one individual playing various roles, with diversified linguistic consequences. The domain is thus an abstract of interactive relations. Hence the non-hierarchical and non-genealogical (non-derivational) form of linguistic differentiation. To the extent that such a portrayal makes discursive (knowledge-negotiating) interaction intrinsically plural in the unmarked case, we thus arrive at some preliminary idea of a possible general basis for the non-existence of truly monocodal speech communities. This idea, though preliminary, is recognizably relational and represents a decisive break with the formal approach. If no monocodal community can be usefully imagined, the idea of a perfect description of one code does not amount to a complete linguistics, and structuralism can provide only partial descriptions.

The studies of Fishman and other post-Fergusonians not discussed in detail here (see especially the works of Gumperz and Khubchandani) enable contemporary research to visualize diglossia as a language universal and thus to bring its study to bear on fundamental principles. Fishman's domain-based characterization of diglossia takes the essential step of drawing a map of various ways of talking in different interactive situations. The next step is to ask why these different ways of talking exist.

One answer originates in the work of Bernstein (1972) who sees different meaning systems as generating different codes in a dynamic sense he gives to this term. He pioneers a new approach to the relationship between the use of codes and the socialization process, to which we return in section 5. But more comprehensive answers are developed in the diglossia theory proper, in the work of Francis Britto.

■ 4. Britto

Using the case of Tamil diglossia as the foundation for his conceptualization, Britto (1986) builds a new framework around the following key concepts: USOC (Use-Oriented Code) vs. UROC (User-Oriented Code), diasystems, optimal distance, authentic vs. nonauthentic domains, and markedness as an H within a diglossia for which "the functional norms related to H and L are almost universal, and observed by the whole community" (1986: 37). Here the H variety becomes the property of the entire speech community rather than that of a privileged few, thus undercutting the tendency towards a hegemonic relationship between the H and L varieties. Such an H is a Use-Oriented Code, a USOC, and not an example of particular users imposing their form of speech on another group which cannot identify with that form. Since the entire speech community neutrally identifies with the H variety there is no occasion for resentment or hostility. Such a speech community displays a total functional and acquisitional superposition of the H variety, as against the partial superposition evident in the case of UROCs.

The H is a UROC or user-oriented code when the functional norms relating to H and L are *not* universally observed. It is in such a situation that oppression, imposition and resultant antipathy arise. While USOC is a form of diatypical diglossia, i.e. a diglossia where "H is superposed for every member of the diglossic community, being learnt subsequent to the primary dialect and being used for high functions" (1986: 306), in contrast UROC is a form of dialectal diglossia best illustrated by the case of standard-with-dialects, with the *standard* as the dialect of a certain region, religion or class. UROC can be described as a pathological situation which reflects social inequality and creates unjust diversity within a speech community, while USOC represents equality and unity within a speech community.

His USOC vs. UROC distinction enables Britto to argue against the account that brands all diglossia as pathological.

DIASYSTEM replaces the older Fergusonian notion of VARIETY. 'Variety', in Ferguson, is used in two senses: it can refer to any code within a code-set; it may also refer to the H and L poles of a diglossic system. Britto notes that a diglossic language may have several varieties, not just two. Within H and L subsystems there are hyponymous varieties. Ferguson himself does not rule out cases of more than two varieties constituting a diglossic situation, though he limits himself to the examination of those that do involve two varieties—H and L. Britto's use of the notion of diasystem allows heterogeneity within H and L. He defines a diasystem as "an emic variety that together with the other diasystem(s) constitutes a situation of diglossia" (1986: 127). It thus becomes an abstract collective label subsuming all varieties of language which contextually complement each other.

This notion of diasystem is implicit in Ferguson, who says: "For convenience of reference the superposed variety in diglossia will be called the H ("high") variety or simply H, and the regional dialects will be called L ("low") varieties or *collectively* simply L" (Ferguson 1959: 430). Britto distinguishes between diasystems and varieties. Diasystems are poles or components in a diglossic situation. Varieties are subsystems or codes within a diasystem. A system may involve more than two diasystems in Britto's account. This shift away from the dualism of H and L is the beginning of a more systematic questioning of the dichotomous approach to diglossia. Britto uses Tamil to illustrate and develop his argument.

Tamil has three structurally different varieties, which can be set up as distinct diasystems functionally complementing each other—Classical Tamil, Literary Tamil and Colloquial Tamil. One can envisage a diglossia continuum from H proper to L proper with varieties of the H/L diasystems in between:

Diglossic continuum:

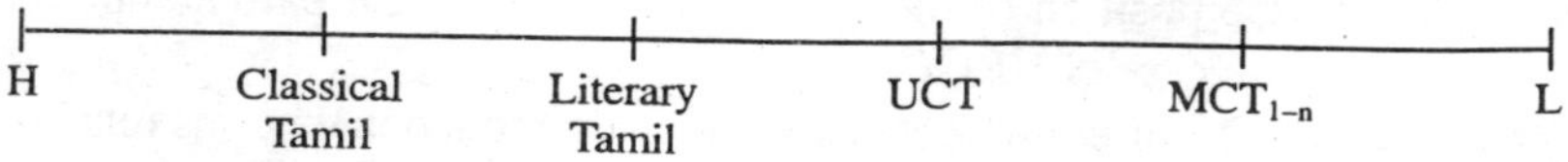

In Britto's system functional complementation draws boundaries between diasystems, and close linguistic relatedness groups varieties into a diasystem. His discussion of Tamil diglossia makes a distinction within the L diasystem between Unmarked Colloquial Tamil (UCT) also called standard colloquial Tamil and Marked Colloquial Tamil (MCT) also called substandard colloquial Tamil. These two varieties form a single diasystem, and not two, as they are in functional complementation.

The primary difference between UCT and MCT is that, while UCT is free of social markings, in the sense of being neutral as to social class, caste or region, speaking MCT always means speaking some particular dialect of MCT that reveals the social/regional background of the user. Hence the term 'marked'. For Britto, then, MCT—or rather each of several MCT codes—counts as a UROC (user-oriented code) while the uniquely neutral code UCT is a USOC (use-oriented code).

Having differentiated it from the MCTs, Britto proceeds to characterize UCT as a variety that is superposed and not acquired naturally by speakers of Tamil. UCT is not taught in the 'formal' educational system the way H is. But the use of UCT is semi-formally learned in social interaction. It is MCT which is acquired at the primary level of a child's acquisition of Tamil and later UCT is superposed. This superposing is total, affecting every member of the Tamil speech community, cutting across MCT subcommunity boundaries. Every member of the speech community can comprehend the UCT. While the productive performance level may vary, receptive competence is reasonably uniform.

This empirical base of Britto's account seems independently plausible—to me as a speaker of Tamil—and will need to be handled adequately by backers of alternative theories of diglossia, including the conservative pre-Britto alternatives. It is indeed difficult to give UCT a coherent theoretical location in a Tamil diglossia if one does not adopt something at least as nuanced as Britto's model.

Another crucial notion in Britto's system, *optimal distance*, unpacks Ferguson's assumption that the relatedness between the two poles in a diglossic polarization should be close enough to count as varieties of one language and yet distant enough to count as more than mere 'styles'. Relatedness here must be structural, emphasizing the genealogical criterion. This admits only intralanguage diatypical diglossia. For Fishman, on the other hand, functional complementarity rather than structural relatedness determines a diglossic situation. Thus any two or more codes coexisting in functional complementarity constitute a Fishman-diglossic situation. Britto's delineation of three levels of inter-pole distance fuses Ferguson's and Fishman's notions.[1] He envisages diglossias involving three levels of pole-to-pole distance—superoptimal, optimal, suboptimal. Diasystems superoptimally distant are a case of two-language diglossia; optimally distant diasystems constitute a classical Fergusonian single-language diglossia; when (as in, say, 'Standard English' in some national context) the diasystems are suboptimally distant it is a case of a single-language diglossia where the differentiation is into officially invisible functional varieties such as styles, registers, etc.

The optimal distance scale refers to the degree of linguistic relatedness between the diasystems. Britto claims that if optimal distance could be determined objectively by quantifying cross-variety linguistic differences, then one could begin to evaluate the *diglossicness* of a particular situation. If, as one suspects, such formalization is always subjective and arbitrary, then the cut-off point between diglossia and non-diglossia will remain arbitrary. Britto quotes Wexler (1971: 337)—"At best, then, the difference between Arabic and English is one of degree and not of kind" (1986: 20)—in support of his proposal of three optimality levels. His recognition of the three levels allows him to build a subarchitecture—not discussed here—of embedded diglossia or diglossia within diglossia.

The use of the notions of *authentic* and *nonauthentic domains* in explaining functional complementation seems one of Britto's most significant contributions to the theory of diglossia. This distinction reflects the relation between differentiated adult language use and child language acquisition. It marks a theoretical advance over the formal/informal dichotomy suggested by Ferguson and commonly accepted by most researchers.

How is it an advance? Isn't Britto merely renaming the two poles? No, for his distinction marks a rethinking of the relation between primary acquisition and social differentiation as well as a new approach to the task of explaining diglossia. As he notes, 'the dichotomy suggested by Ferguson seems to be not diglossia-universal but diglossia-specific' (1986: 147). Britto argues that a formal/informal dichotomy which starts from the standpoint of the formal systems encoding the requirements of institutional power (and thus starts by legislating what can count as a formal domain) cannot deal with actual H/L polarizations across languages. For there is cross-societal variation as to the domains in which the respective H and L are appropriate. It is in response to this problem and the need to relate the theory to the givens of primary acquisition that Britto introduces the concept of authentic vs. nonauthentic domains of language use. In pursuit of "a principle of generality that underlies functional complementarity" (1986: 147), Britto suggests:

> The authentic domain is that domain of language use in which one speaks spontaneously, in natural or real-life situations, without assuming any 'role'; it is the whole domain of language use excluding writing and public discourses… The Nonauthentic domain is that domain of language use in which one uses language before a passive audience, takes on a role, or uses artificial means of communication such as pen and paper, or a microphone (1986: 298).

Naturalness is a markedness-linked mediator between contemporary thinking on child language acquisition and the socially differentiated field of adult competence where speakers have to negotiate with the specificities of context and power. So equipped, the authentic—nonauthentic distinction can take on the abstract task of characterizing the range of language use domains on the basis of what is naturally given. Specifically, Britto proposes that among the nonauthentic uses of language, some types make it a point to mimic the authentic domain itself, introducing a visible mediation—taking the form of UCT in the Tamil case:

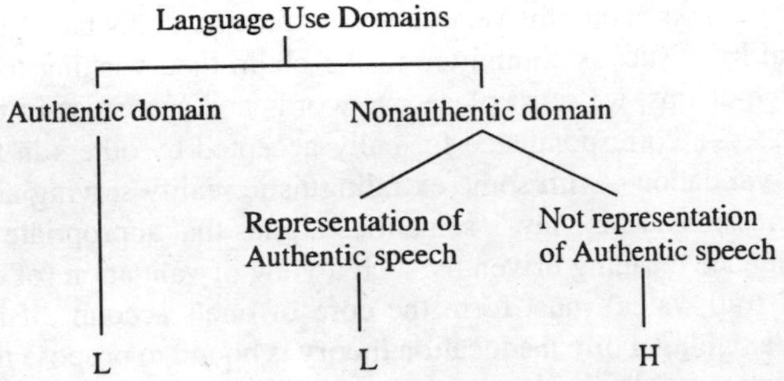

(Britto 1986: 151)

This dichotomy serves as the basis of Britto's detailed descriptive account of Tamil diglossia (not repeated here).

Britto empirically stresses functional complementation as the defining criterion for diglossia. Here he seems to rely on Fishman rather than Ferguson, who makes linguistic relatedness paramount in the identification of diglossia.

Conceptually, Britto begins to address the issue of why language is diglossic. We read him as the first specifically postformal scholar in this field. On our reading, he breaks with earlier work mainly by making the L pole the Authentic centre of the linguistics of the system, and by raising a new question: does a given variety in the H sector seek to mimic the form of L? These moves permit the following account to emerge. In any community, people speak, for reasons of UG, but it need not follow that a 'language' picks up and codifies this speech. If a codification exists, it does so for reasons of power. So far, we have got an L, the Authentic givens of speech, and an extreme H, the Nonauthentic givens of education. Britto adds that, at a certain mid-point, L comes to terms with H in the people's reception of the knowledge that comes through the codified educational system, and H comes to terms with L by mimicking it, but this mid-point must itself work within the H sector, as 'discourse' in our sense and not as 'conversation'.

To bring out the radical potential of these moves is to work our way past these beginnings. Fishman's domains could be read as 'multiple conversations' or as 'multiple discourses', or as some mix that needs to be analyzed. Britto introduces a principle that can underwrite analysis of this sort.

■ 5. Beyond Britto

If formalism was a suitable term for the Fergusonian beginnings of diglossia description, we find substantivism a usable attitude for those trying to develop postformal theories that can help explain diglossia and not just describe it.

The present essay reads the development of diglossia studies as a transition from a formal-interventionist view of diglossia—wedded to the coded naturalisms—towards a relational-interactive view that thematizes discourses and not codes. A few remarks about this version of the transition may be useful.

Any formal linguistics is committed to the claim that, wishing to validate our knowledge-claims, we must place our words and sentences in cognitive correspondence—a correspondence formally accepted by others in the same enterprise of validation—with some extralinguistic reality serving as content for these expressions. This view's semantics argues that appropriate formalizations of sentence meaning driven by such a view of validation (of checking propositional truth-value) must form the core of one's account of how language means anything. Formal education theory is bound to propose that some of us can validate our knowledge and should intervene in the lives of those less lucky; a teaching network should endow the haves who know more with interventionist power over the have-nots who know less. Formal-interventionist sociolinguistics must suggest that social classes capable of knowledge-laden speech should benevolently teach the dispossessed. Internationally, this means developed societies should aid pre-modern societies to sweep away the cobwebs of non-knowledge.

Not all these features of such a methodology appear as visible moves on the surface of mainstream writings in the linguistics of codes (expression-content contracts). But some reflection will convince many readers that these basic moves, perhaps somewhat stylized or exaggerated here, do follow from the decision to focus linguistic study on codes, i.e. sound-meaning mappings. The usual idealizing assumption that a language is a single such mapping quickly becomes complicit with social prescriptions that favour a standard variety and wish away all variation by rendering the other varieties invisible to theory and—through pedagogy designed to eliminate them in favor of the standard—eventually non-existent in practice.

Note that the elite-run interventions such a view tends to favor correspond to the standard prescriptions of the Western-sponsored models of development and modernization that India, for instance, has tried to follow in the early decades of its independence. Conventional education systems rest on such a formal-interventionist approach.

In this paper we move away from the code-based view of language and reconceptualize the diglossic poles High (H) and Low (L) in terms of 'high discourse' and 'low conversation'. Our exposition here starts with the following preliminary explication of this substantivist (relational-interactive) alternative that we prefer to the formalist (formal-interventionist) view. For a more general discussion of the shift in language studies from a past overemphasis on form to a growing reorientation to the substance of language production and understanding, see Dasgupta (1997, 1998).

An H norm and its L counter-norm emerge in and sustain an H/L discourse-coupling in the social crucible of language use. Such a coupling links H as a site of teaching or giving knowledge to L as a site of learning or taking knowledge. Such a view makes any given code only relationally an 'H' or 'L' norm. H names a donor code and L names a receptor code. Any given code is capable of serving simultaneously as L and as H, but only in different discourse-couplings, a point illustrated empirically in Dasgupta (1993) whose discourse coupling concepts are invoked here. For a code serving as an L site of learning must refer its validity-claims to the H source or sources it draws upon. Conversely, if less obviously, an H site of teaching must appeal to L audiences whose reception re-validates its knowledge claims. Call this the relational-interactive view of validation. Our conceptualization of diglossia in terms of a relational approach thus leads us to re-examine the usual sociolinguistics of diglossia as well as the standard semantic account of meaning and truth. The received view of validation is the formal-interventionist one.

Received precepts of development and planning took it that modernization would be brought about by universalizing an education predicated on the knowledge that drove the industrialization of the West. Such prescriptions underlay the early perception of structural diglossia as a third world pathology. Here we have surveyed the evolution of these precepts in terms of the changing faces of diglossia from Ferguson (1959) through Fishman (1968a,b,c) to Britto (1986). Something like a postmodern rejection of the grand narrative and a corresponding celebration of plurality or decentralization as essential to language emerges from readings of diglossia available in such works as Britto (1986), Singh, Dasgupta and Lele (1995), Singh (1986, 1992), Singh and Maniruzzaman (1983) and Dasgupta (1993). Such a reading arises quite naturally from, and helps makes sense of, the cultural and linguistic plurality in a country like India—a characterization that builds on the rich work of Khubchandani (1983, 1985, 1991, 1997), Pattanayak (1985, 1986) and other Indian linguists.

Even at this relatively promising theoretical conjuncture, one task contemporary sociolinguistics has yet to take up is that of understanding and extending the theoretical breakthrough made by Britto.

Attention in diglossic studies has consistently been focused on speech behavior and speech variation. Diglossia has always been defined relative to the speech behavior of a speech community. It has been assumed that distinct 'codes' make up the verbal repertoire of a speech community, and that communities tend towards a functional codification of the constituents of the repertoire. Where such functional codification is officially visible, one declares a state of diglossia.

Britto shows that—regardless of the patchy incidence of such overt two-coding—covert two-norming is a universal. There is 'discourse' as knowledge encoded in the code-sponsoring H norm that appears in education and other embodiments of official power. There is speech as spontaneous 'conversation' available on the social ground because humans acquire primary speaking without official instruction. And there is a mediating 'discourse' where discourse proper, H, meets conversation proper, L; this mediation is itself a discursive norm, an H, as it works out the terms of trade between the knowledge available in H and the way this knowledge is used in the flow of L. That working-out sets its own rules and counts as a discourse, a self-controlling flow embodying a knowledge. In Britto, it makes sense that there should be such a mediating discourse; an H or a discourse does not have to be a codification formalizable only as a fixed mapping; it can be a going-along, a negotiation, which makes up its mappings as it proceeds. This was not possible before Britto. Going beyond him involves finding out how best to use the potential that he releases in everybody's work.

Britto's work encourages us to anchor the universal occurrence of diglossia in a theory of social structuration as an on-going traffic of this sort between norms. Such a perspective can pose and eventually answer questions related to the explanation for such arrangements of language variation. Apart from mere functional complementation, different codes seem to provide access to different ranges of meanings. Here recourse to some version of Bernstein seems inevitable. For convenience, we are using the standard version; readers should feel free to replace this with their favorite revisions.

Bernstein's theory of elaborated and restricted codes seems a natural adjunct to the work explored here. For Britto and other diglossia theorists, different codes/diasystems/varieties are seen as existing for purely functional reasons. For them, meaning remains a neutral substance codified differently in H or L depending on the domains of use. This seems to attest to a kind of unified (or single) 'world-view' of an entire group of people who constitute a single speech community, regardless of an individual's social background or her primary linguistic code. But serious, postformal study of substance will lead us to view not only linguistic forms but also meaning-substances as diverse. We may choose to agree with Bernstein, for instance, that different forms of social relations generate different communication codes.

> As a child learns his speech, or...specific codes which regulate his verbal acts, he learns the requirements of his social structure.... The social structure becomes the substratum of the child's experience essentially through the manifold consequence of the linguistic process (Bernstein 1972: 473).

On this account the child's world-view is shaped by her social identity which in turn is shaped and reinforced in the child by the linguistic processes of being socialized into a particular code. The social role of the individual thus becomes "a complex coding activity controlling both the creation and organization of specific meanings and the conditions for their transmission and reception" (1972: 474). This gives the users of different codes access to different ranges of meanings. That particular social classes have demonstrably unequal access to these ranges of meanings indicates a relationship between the social identities of the individuals and their 'cognitive expression'.

Britto makes the transition from a monolithic view of the world to a world where the fact of plurality is regarded as natural and pluralism, an explicit recognition of plurality, is part of a theoretical understanding of naturalness. This shift enables us to move away from monolithic standardization as the goal of social planning towards optimal differentiation guided by a pluralism. This shift can be observed with special reference to South Asia in such writings as Singh (1986), Dasgupta (1988), and other references given above.

These are some of the consequences of the realization that diglossia is not an isolated morpholexical curiosity restricted to certain speech communities, but is the linguistic instantiation, at functional and discursive levels, of the macro/micro duality characterizing all modes of social organization. Other consequences will become clearer if we sharpen our tools. Is it useful to look at how the tools that came out of the study of a few cases turned into potentially universal means of analysis? Is the universalization of diglossia a sociolinguistic counterpart to the trend in recent syntax to extend the theory of case from the morphology of richly inflected languages to the grammar of language in general?

The diglossia studies enterprise did begin by analyzing certain overtly diglossic languages as segregating 'H' code from 'L' code phenomena formally. Early work asked what functions such codes have. From this formal phase, the theory moved to a functional phase which focused on the question of whether two codes formally unrelated to each other but coexisting in a community and used for complementary functions in different domains could constitute diglossia. Finally, Britto's postformal theory locates the problem in the theory not of morphological form but of linguistic substance by focusing on an abstract diglossia—whose concrete form may be overt, as in the old diglossias, or covert, as in an English or a French, this formal question is no longer the issue—now seen as a language universal. And we are raising questions of differentiation within substance by invoking the familiar apparatus of Bernstein. There is indeed a clear parallel with what happened to morphological case in formal syntax research as it began to treat Case as an abstract universal, only optionally showing up in concrete case affixes in some languages.

Perhaps the really interesting avenues of further research will pertain to the differences between speech and writing. We are proposing a discourse vs. conversation reading of the poles H vs. L of this new universal, diglossia. This reading—whose flexible account of discourse is a response to Britto's notion of the middle term where the H mimics and incorporates the L material—works within the relational-interactive view of H and L. This view invites comparison with the formalist-interventionist view of diglossia inherent in the Fergusonian characterization.

Our "substantivist" or "beyond Britto" proposal, which we hope can serve as a prolegomenon to certain types of research in fields like literacy and the sociolinguistics of education, comes from the assumption that every language is used in ways that range over a spectrum. This spectrum features a textual or discursive pole organized around an H code (in the dynamic Bernsteinian, non-naturalist sense of 'code') at one end and a conversational or interactive pole organized around an L code at the other. The advantage of positing this type of spectrum in place of Ferguson's formal-to-informal scale or even Britto's authentic-to-nonauthentic scale (which continues to assume that meaning is a single substance) is that we can refer differentially to the referential apparatuses available to an individual at some specific point in social space. We see directly how the referring mechanisms differ in the two systems of interaction. While reference is textual in H or the discursive code, i.e. spelt out explicitly in the archive of the "language" as a codification with an educational system attached, reference in L or the conversational code is contextual, drawing on pragmatic notions of the speaker's intention, shared assumptions and negotiation. For one account of these notions, see the study by Gumperz and Gumperz (1982) of verbal interaction in modern societies.

Our debt to Britto's authentic vs. inauthentic dichotomy is obvious. But we see the notion of authenticity as still adhering to the hegemonic view of diglossia, with H as power and L as powerless. With such a view one retains a lingering aftertaste of the formal-interventionist style. H as the seat of power dictates terms to L. There is no reciprocal interaction between H and L. Seeing L as a series of disconnected, powerless conversations cannot help us to understand how conversation can be a domain-shaping praxis, and thus does not serve as a true foil to H. However, if we perceive H as the source of teaching and L as the site of a learning that must co-occur with and modify the teaching, then H becomes dependent on L for its revalidation. It then follows that knowledge is relevant to the characterization not only of H but of L also. L-knowledge incorporates (i) the received and revalidated H knowledge and (ii) the other kinds of knowledge which are not normally recognized as 'Knowledge', but are the noncomputational 'bits of information' which are not built into the larger, formal system. These 'bits of information' or 'stories of the street' are validated by 'non-formal H' systems in the community, the oral social history and the like. This is the way one can make productive use of the relational-interactive view, where H and L appeal to each other for validation of their respective claims. But we present this material mainly to exemplify the potential of the approach, not to claim that these proposals are The Implementation.

Rewriting the H/L dichotomy in terms of discourse vs. conversation provides an advantage in terms of the social-scientific anchoring of our linguistics. Notice that we refer to the two kinds of knowledge-systems available to a speaker—each of which is authenticated or validated by various subsystems and by each other. The H system of knowledge is validated by *institutions* such as science, the state, etc. and the L system of knowledge is validated through networks of interpersonal relations. This context gives the micro/macro duality real teeth in the methodology of diglossia research. Societal norms (a macrofact/H) and individual norms (a microfact/L) are seen at play in an interactive fashion. And this interaction is not simply a verbal matter.

Meaning in the H mode centres round the notion of context-freedom and is situated outside the life of the participants in a speech situation. As we have seen earlier, reference in H is explicitly or 'seriously' spelt out. The knowledge transmitted through the H mode is held to be uniquely legitimate. In such a situation there is no opportunity for either of the interlocutors to construct his/her own context using the tools provided by language. The H mode of reference and predications are not negotiated on-line but are assumed to be able to draw on a pre-existing fund of options given by the textual body, the archive, prior to all possible contexts. In contrast, in the L mode, which is context-bound, reference is negotiated between speakers and hearers with respect to a shared or accepted availability of precepts and concepts in the referential context. The speakers and hearers actively engage in the construction of contexts.

Once such a distinction is made we can see that discourse/H sponsors styles of language use that exhibit asymmetry while conversational/L styles of speaking are symmetric. Theories based on the formal-interventionist model put the theoretician in the position of uncritically upholding the official validity of H/discourse styles of speaking (and, more usually, writing). In the H mode, given that negotiation is not possible, the speaker is the teacher who with the *authority* of pre-contextual texts hands knowledge to the hearer/learner who receives it. Such a teaching-oriented asymmetry denies the notion of a speech situation where learning is done *on-line* in a negotiable context. This also denies the fact that most interaction is an encounter of negotiation or learning, where speakers and hearers interactively and interdependently engage in the process of problem solving. The H style of discourse seen in the formal discursive practices such as writing, teaching and public speeches is based on such an asymmetric notion of communication while the L style of conversation seen in normal everyday face-to-face encounters is based on a symmetric notion of communication.

What a serious social theory needs to recognize is that H and L interactively contribute to the process of validation. The L style is also a full system of communication. For learning to take place or for communication to be effective there is a constant shifting of ground between H and L—the rendering of H notions in an L style of speaking. Educational theories proposed by Bernstein (1971, 1972) and the poignant *Letter to a Teacher* (1970) written by students of the Barbiana school testify to the problems which arise from a strict adherence to a context-free H mode of lecturing. H and L function as H and L relative to each other and depend on each other for their validation.

Such an asymmetric conceptualization, or a formal-interventionist view, of H and L has had negative consequences in the area of language planning also. Language planning has centred round the H axis leading to standardization practices of a kind which favor H and ignore the existence of L. This is evident in the prevalent image of the West as the developed teacher from whom the poor cousins in the third world need to learn the practices of industriality. The present survey indicates that the further development of diglossia theory, with possibly universal implications, depends on deepening our understanding, in the community of linguists, of matters in the third world, from a theoretical perspective shaped in recent years by linguists located there. The enterprise that sought to promote one standard variety in the name of efficiency—on formal-interventionist grounds—failed to see that codes in old sense were an artefact reflecting discursive forces that need to be examined and tackled. Current work enables us to visualize diglossia as a manifestation of the division of linguistic labor vis-à-vis different knowledge-flows. We need not stay trapped in a mind-set which favors one particular language as more developed or modern, and hence uniquely suited to system-oriented domains of communication, relegating its poor relations to the menial task of sweeping the local, person-oriented arenas of communication.

■ NOTES

1. Though Ferguson claims, in his foreword to Britto's book, that Britto recognizes optimal varieties as comprising a diglossic situation, it is not clear if Britto really does that, since he refers to Fishmanian inter-language diglossia also as a possible case of diglossia.

■ REFERENCES

Barbiana, School of. 1970. *Letter to a teacher*. Harmondsworth: Penguin.

Bernstein, B. 1971. *Class, codes, and control. Vol. 1*. London: Routledge and Kegan Paul.

———. 1972. A sociolinguistic approach to socialization: With some reference to educability. *Directions in sociolinguistics: the ethnography of communication*, ed. by J.J. Gumperz and D. Hymes, 465–97. New York: Holt, Rinehart and Winston.

Britto, F. 1986. *Diglossia: a study of the theory with application to Tamil*. Washington, DC: Georgetown University Press.

Dasgupta, P. 1988. Sanskrit and Indian English: some linguistic considerations. *Explorations in Indian sociolinguistics*, ed. by R. Singh, P. Dasgupta, and J.K. Lele, 160–75. New Delhi: Sage.

———. 1989. *Projective syntax: theory and applications*. Pune: Deccan College Postgraduate and Research Institute.

———. 1993. *The otherness of English: India's auntie tongue syndrome*. New Delhi: Sage.

———. 1997. Foreword. *Revisualizing boundaries: a plurilingual ethos*, ed. by L.M. Khubchandani, 11–29, New Delhi: Sage.

———. 1998. Knowing the word/trikkhe/: against purism in the study of language. *The Yearbook of South Asian Languages and Linguistics*, ed. by Rajendra Singh. New Delhi: Sage.

Dil, A.S. (ed.) 1972. *Language in sociocultural change*. Stanford: Stanford University Press.

Ferguson, C.F. 1959. Diglossia. *Language in culture and society*, ed. by D. Hymes, 1964. New York: Harper and Row.

———. 1968. Language development. *Language problems of developing nations*, ed. by J.A. Fishman et al. New York: John Wiley.

Fishman, J.A. 1968a. Societal bilingualism: stable and transitional. *Language in sociocultural change*, ed. by A.S. Dil, 1972, 135–52. Stanford: Stanford University Press.

———. 1968b. The description of societal bilingualism. *Language in sociocultural change*, ed. by A.S. Dil, 1972, 153–61. Stanford: Stanford University Press.

———. [illegible]. The relationship between micro- and macrosociolinguistics in the study of who speaks what language to whom and when. *Language in sociocultural change*, ed. by A.S. Dil, 1972, 162–84. Stanford: Stanford University Press.

Gumperz, J.J. and **J.C. Gumperz.** 1982. Introduction: language and communication of social identity. *Language and social identity*, ed. by J.J. Gumperz, 1–21. Cambridge: CUP.

Khubchandani, L.M. 1983. *Plural languages, plural cultures: communication, identity and sociopolitical change in contemporary India*. Honolulu: The East–West Centre.

———. 1985. Diglossia revisited. *For Gordon M. Fairbanks*, ed. by V.Z. Ascon and R.L. Leed, 197–211. Honolulu: University of Hawaii Press. Repr. in: Khubchandani 1997, as 'Indian diglossia'.

———. 1991. *Language, culture and nation-building: challenges of modernization*. Shimla: Indian Institute of Advanced Study.

———. 1997. *Revisualizing boundaries: a plurilingual ethos*. New Delhi: Sage.

Pattanayak, D.P. 1985. Diversity in communication and languages: predicament of a multilingual nation state: India, a case study. *Languages of inequality*, ed. by N. Wolfson and J. Manes, 399–407. Berlin: Mouton de Gruyter.

———. 1986. Educational use of the mother tongue. *Language and education in multilingual settings* ed. by B. Spolsky, 5–15. Cleveland, England: Multilingual Matters.

Singh, R., P. Dasgupta, and **J.K. Lele** (eds). 1995. *Explorations in Indian sociolinguistics*. New Delhi: Sage.

Singh, U.N. 1986. Diglossia in Bangladesh and language planning problems. *The Fergusonian impact Vol. 2*, ed. by J.A. Fishman et al. The Hague: Mouton.

———. 1992. *On language development and planning: a pluralistic paradigm*. Shimla: Indian Institute of Advanced Study/New Delhi: Munshiram Manoharlal.

Singh, U.N. and **Maniruzzaman**. 1983. *Diglossia in Bangladesh and language planning*. Calcutta: Gyan Bharati.

Tauli, V. 1977. *Language planning*. The Hague: Mouton.

P. Wexler. 1971. Diglossia, language standardization and purism. *Lingua* 27.330–54.

Form and Function in Urdu–Hindi Verb Inflection†

ASIF AGHA

The paper presents a comprehensive analysis of the inflectional categories of the Urdu–Hindi verb, focusing in particular on tense-aspect-mood categories. The basic tense contrast is shown to be 'past'/'nonpast'; the so-called 'future' is shown to be a complex mood construction. Aspect categories include 'perfective' and 'imperfective', as well as a third category, the 'telic', not distinguished in earlier work. Apart from the 'indicative' and 'interrogative' moods, six additional mood constructions are traditionally distinguished; these constructions are shown to be reflexes of three basic mood categories. The paper shows that once the basic verbal categories are isolated, certain dependent phenomena (such as tense-aspect-mood co-occurrence restrictions, 'split' and 'fluid' case marking patterns) permit a straightforward account.

■ 1. Introduction

Our understanding that categories of tense, mood and aspect can be isolated as grammatical categories of a language is based on three distinct kinds of assumptions. First, that certain linguistic forms—morpheme configurations in specifiable syntactic constituency—can be isolated as segmentable markers of certain grammatical functions. Second, that such grammatical functions have a clear analysis within a theory of predicate modalization, a theory which

† I am grateful to Elena Bashir, Colin Masica, and Yamuna Kachru for written comments on earlier versions of this paper, and to audiences at two conferences for many helpful suggestions: the 8th Annual Meeting of the Linguistics Society of Nepal (Kathmandu, November 1987) and the 27th Annual South Asia Conference (Madison, November 1988). The basic research was supported by grants from the Social Science Research Council and the Committee on Southern Asian Studies of the University of Chicago.

clarifies the functional interpretation of criterial forms. The third assumption is that the interpretation of each grammatical category—*qua* pairing of form and function—remains invariant across utterance events in a specifiable way; this is tantamount to the assumption that the specific functional effects of grammatical forms can be isolated from the (contextually superimposed) effects of co-occurring forms. These three assumptions motivate three distinct perspectives on categories of verb inflection. The first assumption, considered by itself, constitutes a perspective on the analysis of *form categories*; the first and the second assumptions jointly constitute a perspective on *grammatical categories*; and all three assumptions taken together constitute a perspective on the *specific and differential coding* characteristics of grammatical categories.

The categories of tense, mood and aspect in Urdu–Hindi have traditionally proved to be recondite to grammatical analysis, especially with respect to form segmentability.[1] Several mood categories are not locally segmentable. The telic aspect exhibits partial formal overlap with certain forms of the infinitive, and is not distinguished in most traditional analyses. Although the analysis of past and present tense is clear, the so called 'future tense' is formally and functionally a complex mood construction; but showing this requires an independent analysis of mood categories.

In this paper, I offer a systematic analysis of Urdu–Hindi verb inflection, arguing that problems of form segmentability can straightforwardly be solved if all three of the above analytic perspectives are employed *concurrently* during grammatical analysis. In practice, these criteria are always employed concurrently, of course. Yet the theoretical significance of this fact is typically underestimated. The present analysis of Urdu–Hindi verb inflection demonstrates the importance of this issue, both for linguistic theory and method.

My analysis of the inflectional categories of Urdu–Hindi has several implications for the analysis of dependent grammatical phenomena in the language. These include ergative and dative case marking, and tense-mood-aspect co-occurrence restrictions. Once the analysis of verb inflection is clear, I argue, these dependent phenomena are straightforwardly explained. Let me turn first to the analytic considerations I have raised above, before turning to the data of Urdu–Hindi.

■ 2. Three Perspectives on Grammatical Categories

■ 2.1. Formal Perspective on Grammatical Categories[2]

From the standpoint of the analytic task of deducing the grammatical categories of a language, an ideal language would be one where distinct morphemic constituents coded distinct, non-overlapping domains of grammatical function, as schematized in (1).

1. $[[[[\ m_1]\quad m_2]\quad m_3]\quad [m_4\quad m_5]\ \ldots\ m_n]_s$

$\quad\ \ f_1 \qquad f_2 \qquad f_3 \qquad f_4 \qquad f_5$

In a coding scheme such as this, where each distinct morphemic constituent, m_i, has a distinct grammatical function, f_i—each grammatical category, m_i/f_i, can be segmented directly, as it were, from the surface form. Paradigms of such grammatical categories satisfy three formal conditions: (i) there exists a *one-to-one map* from form to function; (ii) the form coding each function is a single morpheme rather than a combination of elements, so that the formal mark of the category is *localizable* in expression; (iii) the category is marked by an expression identifiable in surface form, so that the category is *surface segmentable*. When all three conditions are met, we have something like an optimal analytic scenario (cf. Whorf 1956 [1945], Silverstein 1979, Gvozdanovic 1991).

While some grammatical categories in every language appear to approach this ideal, it is clear that any general approach to the functional individuation of grammatical categories must take note of their *partial formal syncretism*.

2. $[[\ [m_1]\quad [m_2\quad m_3]\quad m_4\quad m_5]\ \ldots\ m_n]_s$

$\quad\ \ f_1 \qquad f_2 \qquad f_3 \qquad f_4, f_5$

$\qquad\qquad f_6 \qquad\qquad f_7$

In (2), the grammatical categories m_1/f_1, m_2/f_2 and m_3/f_3 satisfy all three conditions noted above; in each case, the formal mark of the category is constituted by a single surface morpheme having a one-to-one mapping relationship with a corresponding grammatical function. However, morpheme m_4 is quite different in that it encodes not one but at least two distinct grammatical functions, f_4 and f_5. Failure of condition (i) leads to a one-to-many map from form to function, thus constituting an instance of the well-known class of *portmanteau* morphemes (e.g. in English, the verbal suffix -s, marking 3rd-singular-nonpast-active-indicative). Such formal categories constitute the simplest kind of departure from the optimal analytic scenario. We might say, then, that the morpheme m_4 is portmanteau of functions f_4 and f_5, and conversely, that functions f_4 and f_5 are syncretic in morpheme m_4.

Function f_6 in (2) is an example of the violation of condition (i) in the other direction, leading to a many-to-one map from form to function. In addition, condition (ii)—the localizability condition—is violated as well. Neither m_2 nor m_3 is a marker of f_6; rather, the two morphemes co-occurring in a particular constituency form a configurative formal category whose mark is the morpheme collocation $[m_2 \ldots m_3]$ itself, and whose function f_6 is something distinct from any function that each morpheme might be said alone to have (e.g. f_2 or f_3). Negation in French and the passive voice in English are common examples of such *configurative* categories.

Violations of conditions (iii)—the surface segmentability condition—constitutes the functional basis of the modern notion of 'underlying' structure, yielding the class of grammatical categories which Whorf termed 'covert' categories. Insofar as some linguistic utterance is analyzable as having more than one type of categorial analysis in grammatical terms, the same 'surface' form has more than one 'underlying' categorial status. Since the surface expression contains no mark distinguishing the two underlying categories, the categorial distinction can only be clarified by appeal to some criterial test which will disambiguate the two possible analyses of the form at issue. Otherwise, the covert distinction remains opaque to grammatical analysis.

These considerations are critical to the analysis of mood and aspect in Urdu–Hindi. Most mood categories have configurative markers; some morphemic elements within these configurations (particularly 'agreement' markers) are portmanteau in function. On the other hand, the formal marker of the 'telic' aspect merges in surface form with certain shapes of the infinitive ending; the underlying covert contrast, however, is easily isolable by appeal to distributional tests. I return to these issues in sections 4 and 5 below.

■ 2.2. From Form to Grammaticalized Function

While such a perspective on the formal organization of grammatical functions constitutes an important component of the theory of grammatical categories, the grammatical functions identifiable with such forms require characterization in content-based terms as well. The simplest such characterization is a notional one, but such characterizations are less precise than cross-linguistically formulated generalizations about grammatical functions (cf. Jakobson 1971 [1957]). Thus, aspect may be characterized as a coding of the interval characteristics of a predicated event; 'tense' as the indexing of a temporal ordering relation between the predicated event and the event of speaking; and 'mood' as the modalization of sentence propositionality relative to some indexically focal participant of the speech event (Agha 1993, Ch. 6).

Such functional characterizations have two important properties that require comment. First, distinct verbal categories modalize distinct domains of sentence-propositional meaning. Thus, aspect and tense categories modalize predicates, whereas mood characterizations clearly require appeal to the proposition as a whole (cf. Palmer 1986, Ch. 1). Second, certain content types, such as aspect, require only a 'sense'-based characterization (Lyons 1968: 427ff., Lyons 1977: 197–206), whereas others, such as tense and mood are of a hybrid content type in that they possess irreducibly indexical properties as well. The indexical component of meaning lies in the fact that the contribution to sentence meaning of such categories is only statable as a function of the conditions of utterance of the sentence: a past tense, for example, is only interpretable as 'past' relative to the moment of speaking; an imperative mood is interpretable as a command only relative to some individual constituted as the addressee of the speech event.

■ 2.3. Specific and Differential Interpretation: Minimal Dimensions of Coding

Although we can describe each grammatical category as a pairing of a particular form (specified by appeal to form-shape and formal distribution) and a functional dimension (specified by appeal to sentence- and utterance-level interpretation), the actual carrying out of such an analysis must take into account the fact that grammatical categories are seldom found in isolation in empirical data, that they tend to co-occur with other grammatical categories. Thus, the analysis of any grammatical category must distinguish the contribution to sentence meaning of the category at issue from the contribution of other co-occurring categories by means of careful permutation tests within grammatical paradigms. Moreover, not all the specific forms of one grammatical category co-occur with all the specific forms of every other. Such asymmetries of combination are part of the data criterial for analyzing the content coded by any particular form itself. They also provide criteria on labeling conventions for grammatical categories.

In particular, given the co-occurrence effects of category combination in sentences, it is absolutely essential to ask after the specific and differential contribution to overall 'content' of any particular form, before that form can be said to encode a distinct grammatical category. An analysis of such *minimal dimensions of coding* involves paring away from the totality of possible signal contents that may be summoned up by the use of a form, seeking only to capture those content dimensions which are specifically and differentially coded by the form itself—as distinct from those which are either coded by some other form(s) in grammatical combination with the first, or are not coded by any form in particular, but emerge as a result of implicatures from the contingent co-occurrence of some assemblage of forms in a given contextualized utterance.

Minimal dimensions of coding are analyzed in terms of a binary privative feature notation in the present study. Forms which are specific in interpretation with respect to a particular minimal dimension are said to *code* that minimal dimension, this fact being represented by the plus value of the feature representing that content dimension. Forms which are non-specific with respect to a category are, in principle, potentially ambiguous. A rule of residual semantic interpretation is used in markedness theory (Jakobson 1971 [1932], 1971 [1936], Silverstein 1976) to capture this fact, and I follow Silverstein's formulation (1976: 118) here:

3. Residual semantic interpretation:
   If grammatical feature [F] codes semantic property S, then
      [+ F] means 'S', and
      [– F] means ~'S'; but residually, ~'S' ⇒ '~S'

Thus, only [+F] is unambiguous. Although [–F] simply means failure to specify the property 'S', it can be construed as a (seemingly 'positive') specification for '~S', though this is by no means necessary. A second property of non-specific categories is that they are subject to considerable variability in interpretation, as a result of interaction effects with other co-occurring categories, a phenomenon discussed at several points in the exposition below.

■ 3. The Structure of the Predicate

In Urdu–Hindi, as in many South Asian languages, the distinction between verb phrase-'internal' arguments and an 'external' subject argument cannot be maintained by the use of any consistent formal criteria. The subject NP can take not only nominative and ergative, but also dative, instrumental, genitive and locative case marking (Kachru 1990); the properties of syntactic 'control' characteristic of subjects are differently distributed across these sentence types [both in Urdu–Hindi as well as in other South Asian languages (Kachru et al. 1976, Mohanan and Mohanan 1990, Gair 1990)]; the verb agrees with the subject in aspectless and imperfective sentences, but with the direct object in sentences with perfective and telic aspect [see (9)ff. below]. These facts motivate a 'flat' constituent structure for sentences, as in (4):

4. $[_{S}\ NP_1 \ldots NP_n\ [MV\ (COMP)]_{V'}\ [AUX]_{V}\ {}_{S}]$

The AUX(iliary) verb—the only verb in the language which shows a distinction between a past and a non-past stem form—is a syntactic sister to a V' constituent, and to a number of NP arguments. The arguments are assigned case by lexical verbs within the V'. The verbs occurring within the V'—usually no more than two—are traditionally termed the main verb (or 'MV') and the complement verb (or 'COMP'). The MV provides the central semantic characteristics of the predication, and functions as primary case-assigner to argument NPs. The COMP verb is a dependent verb; it occurs only if a MV occurs. It must be analyzed in immediate constituency with the MV, since it functions as a semantic operator on it, modifying both inherent lexical content, aktionsart, valence, as well as the case assigning properties of the MV.

It is important at the outset to note that the MV vs. COMP distinction is a distinction between two fully inflected verbs and, as such, must be kept distinct from a rather different kind of verb serialization in the language whereby two verb stems occur in a type of lexical union to form a 'compound' MV, exemplified in (5).

5.

		MV		COMP	AUX
		$stem_1$	$stem_2$		
(a)	laRkā	[bhāg	rah]	-ø-ā	th-ā
	boy-NOM	run	stay	-P-C	PST-C
	'The boy was running'				

(b)	laRkā	[ā	jā]	-y-ā	kar-t-ā	th-ā
	boy-NOM	come	go	-P-C	do-I-C	PST-C
	'The boy used to come'					

In (5a) no COMP verb occurs. The MV, however, is a lexical compound where the two verbal lexemes share word inflection. In (5b), a compound MV occurs, followed by a COMP verb. Compound verb constructions are themselves quite interesting with respect to the analysis of verbal aspect: the stem$_2$ element occurs as an aspectual operator on the stem$_1$, modifying its inherent lexical aspect. I have discussed the aspectual characteristics of this construction elsewhere (Agha 1994). In the following discussion of aspect, I am concerned only with aspect markers which are morphemic suffixes.

■ 4. Tense

The traditional analysis of tense in this language distinguishes three tense categories, past, present and future. I will be arguing, however, that only the first two are true tense functionally—into two minimal mood categories. The future is therefore a complex mood category, not a true category of tense (see [14ff.] below).

The past and present tenses are coded exclusively by a stem alternation of the AUX verb, which may be characterized as *th-* 'past (PST)' vs. *h-* 'present (PRS)'. This is exemplified in (6) below, where (6a) is a past sentence and (6b–d) are in the present tense. Both tense-marking stems are distinguished by boldface in the examples.

6.					
			MV	AUX	
(a)	laRkā	paise	bhej-t-ā	**th**-ā	
	boy-NOM	money-ACC	send-I-C	PST-C	
	'The boy used to send the money'				
(b)	laRkā	paise	bhej-t-ā	**h**–ai	
	boy-NOM	money-ACC	send-I-C	PRS-C	
	'The boy sends money'				
(c)	laRkā	abh	paise	bhej-t-ā	**h**-ai
	boy-NOM	just.now	money-ACC	send-I-C	PRS-C
	'The boy will send the money momentarily'				
(d)	laRkā	jab	tak	paise	
	boy-NOM	then	till	money-ACC	
	[bhej-cuk]-ø-ā	**h**-o-g-ā			
	send finish-P-C	PRS-C-PRSV			
	'The boy will have sent the money by then'				

Although both the past and the present are distinguished by the binary formal distinction, *th-* vs. *h-*, the interpretation of sentences coded by these tenses does not form an equipollent functional contrast. All sentences in past tense are interpreted in a highly uniform way: the predicated event is always understood as occurring at some point prior to the moment of speaking, as in the interpretation of (6a).

Present tense sentences have the characteristic ambiguity of the present in many languages, and are subject to variabilities of interpretation as a result of other co-occurring categories. Sentence (6b) asserts that the predicated event of sending occurs over an interval which contains the present moment but extends well into the past and potentially into the future; this ambiguity of time reference is due to the presence of imperfective aspect. Sentence (6c) asserts that the predicated event occurs at some moment immediately following the moment of speaking, thus marking a 'proximate future' sense; this construal is due to the co-occurrence of a punctuate adverb with a present/immediate-future meaning. In (6d), the 'present' AUX stem, *h-*, is followed by a cross-reference suffix, *-o*, followed by the morpheme string *-g-ā*. The construction marks the 'presumptive' mood, and has an 'expected occurrence' meaning; in this case, the present tense is part of a construction which codes the predicated event as expected/presumed-to-occur at some point after the moment of speaking.

The functional asymmetry between the stems *th-* vs. *h-* can be described as a privative binary contrast: the two forms constitute a simple binary paradigm where one form is specific in time reference, but the other is not. The form *th-* specifically and differentially marks the fact that the predicated event occurs at some point prior to the moment of speaking, and this coding characteristic may be represented as [+past]. The paradigmatic alternant, *h-*, fails to signal the above temporal ordering, and the absence of this specific and differential coding characteristic may be represented as [–past]. The actual interpretations of the latter form are subject to the usual implicature from non-'past' to 'non-past' as noted in (3) above; this yields a 'present' construal as the default, allowing for a 'future' interpretation where other co-occurring elements in the sentence, or in prior discourse, entail such a construal. These facts are summarized in (7).

7. Minimal distinctions of tense

Form and gloss	Minimal distinctive value
th- 'PST'	[+past] = the predicated event occurs at some point/interval prior to the moment of speaking
h- 'PRS'	[–past] = absence of above specification

The [–past] stem, *h-*, is clearly the unmarked form, since it has a less specific time reference than the [+past] category, as well as the wider syntactic distribution characteristic of all unmarked categories: it can occur in all the mood categories in which the [+past] form occurs (i.e. indicative and interrogative) as well as in the presumptive mood in (6d), where the [+past] category cannot occur.

■ 5. Aspect

Most recent analyses of the language have maintained that two categories of morphemic (suffixal) aspect are found in the language. I will be arguing that this is a misanalysis, and that there is in fact a third category of morphemic aspect in the language, which I will call the 'telic' aspect. All three aspectual categories occur as suffixes in paradigmatic contrast after the verb stem. I discuss the perfective imperfective distinction first, turning to the telic thereafter.

The perfective aspect, signaled by the suffix *-ø/-y*[3], codes a highly specific point-like interval for the predication. In contrast, the imperfective, signaled by the suffix *-t*, is like interval for the predication. In contrast, the imperfective, signaled by the suffix *-t*, is less specific in sense value, signaling only the absence of point-like structure. Due to its lesser specificity of meaning, the imperfective aspect can vary in interpretation, such variation resulting from interaction effects with temporal adverbs and with aktionsart of the MV stem.

The meaning of 'point-like completion' is an invariant meaning of the perfective aspect, found in all verbs which are coded for the aspectual category. In the perfective sentence, (8a), each of the two perfectively coded verbs have a meaning of 'point-like completion'.

8. (a) šīšā gir-ø-ā aur TūT ga-y-ā
mirror-ABS fall-P-C and break go-P-C
'The mirror fell and broke'

(b) laRkā har roz axbār paRh-t-ā h-ai
boy-NOM every day newspaper-ACC read-I-C PRS-C
'The boy reads the newspaper every day' (habitual)

(c) use har dafā sharm ā-t-ī h-ai
he-DAT each time shame come-I-C PRS-C
'He feels shame every time' (habitual)

(d) mãĩ das bārāh baras se yahā rah-t-ā h-ũ
I-NOM ten twelve years-ABL here live-I-C PRS-C
'I've lived here for the last ten to twelve years' (durational)

(e) mādā ne nar se kah-ø-ā:
female ERG male DAT say-P-C
xabardār, dušman ā-t-ā h-ai
be.warned enemy come-I-C PRS-C
'The female said to the male: "Be warned! The enemy [now] comes".' (proximate future) [Nihal Chand (1961: 130)]

The imperfective aspect in 8(b–e) yields a range of interpretations, depending on other elements co-occurring in the sentence: the occurrence of iterative adverbs with both active (8b) and stative (8c) main verbs forces a habitual interpretation of the predicate; in (8d), an interval adverb and a stative main verb stem jointly yield a durational interpretation of the predicate; and in (8e) (as in [6e] above), the highly sudden or momentaneous meaning of the adverb combined with an active main verb jointly yield a proximate future interpretation.

The telic aspect is marked by the suffix *-n*, occurring in the same post verb-stem slot. The telic suffix specifies a temporal interval which is bounded by an endpoint in which the interval culminates. The endpoint can be made denotationally explicit by a specific tense coding {e.g. [+past] in (9b)}, or by adverbs (as in [9c–d]). But even in the absence of such explicit markers, the endpoint meaning is clear from the entailments of sentence meaning.

9. (a) tumhẽ sab ko xat likh-**n**-e h-ãĩ
you-DAT all-DAT letters-ACC write-T-C PRS-C
'You have to write letters to everyone'

(b) mujhe vah tasvīrẽ dekh-**n**-ī th-ī
I-DAT those pictures-ACC see-T-C PST-C
'I had to see those pictures'

(c) āj baraf paR-n-ī h-ai
today snow fall-T-C PRS-C
'It is going to snow today'

(d) kal bāriš ho-**n**-ī th-ī, magar nahī̃ hū-ø-ī
yesterday rain happen-T-C PST-C, but not happen-P-C
'It was supposed to rain yesterday, but it didn't'

In the [–past] sentence in (9a), the endpoint is recoverable only relative to entailments of sentence meaning: the addressee's obligation 'to write letters to everyone' holds until he has written to them all. In (9b), the endpoint of the interval is independently bounded by the deictically specific [+past] tense: the speaker's desire or need to see the photographs is construable as valid up to and including some moment in past time, not further specified; the sentence implies that the necessity or desire to see them was canceled beyond this point, whether by the satisfaction of the desire, or by its supercession by other considerations. In (9b) the endpoint is bounded by the interval denoted by *āj* 'today': the expectation of rain holds up to and including any point which falls within the day in which the speech event occurs. In (9d), the endpoint of the interval (during which rain was expected) is specified in the most denotationally explicit manner: it is denoted by [+past] tense and by an explicitly past adverb in the first clause, and by the perfective aspect of the second clause (specifying that it didn't rain). It should be clear from these examples that the endpoint-culmination sense is the only invariant aspectual value of the form; additional specificity is due to co-occurring devices.

In most cases the culminative sense of the telic aspect yields a modal implicature of expectation or desire or necessity for the action. Such an interpretation follows regularly as an implicature from an aspectual coding which specifies an event as culminating in an endpoint. Note that the actual type of modal interpretation *is not specified by the aspectual coding itself*, but depends upon other co-occurring variables. Sentences having animate, especially human, subjects (e.g. 9a–b above) are construed with a deontic modal meaning of 'desire' or 'obligation'. Sentences with inanimate subjects (e.g.

9c–d) are construed with an epistemic modal meaning of expected occurrence. Modality is, therefore, not a minimal dimension coded by the suffix, but an implicature of its endpoint-culminative sense, specified further only through interactions effects with other sentence categories. Moreover, a true deontic modal construction—such as the *cāhie* 'there is need/obligation' construction in (10) below—is not well-formed with perfective or imperfective aspects; it requires a telically marked verb, specifying its endpoint-culminative sense further to yield a deontic modal meaning.

10. tumhẽ sab logõ ko tasvīrẽ {bhej-n-ī/ *bhej-ø-ī/
you-DAT everyone-DAT pictures-ACC send-T-C/ send-P-C/
*bhej-t-ī} ch-iē
send-I-C} be-necessary
'You should send pictures to everyone'

The fact that the telic aspect has not been distinguished in previous studies of this language is apparently due to the fact that the morphemic constituency of the predicate has not been attended to in sufficient detail. Two kinds of confusion are found in the literature.

The first confusion is caused by the existence of a partial formal overlap between the telically coded form of the verb and certain forms of the infinitive. Thus, the finite 3rd singular masculine form of the verb in the telic construction, e.g. *paRh-n-ā*, resembles the infinitive of the same verb, *paRh-nā* 'to read'. Yet the constituency of the two forms is clearly different. In the finite telic form, the last element, *-ā*, is a segmentable morpheme, signaling cross-reference with a 3rd singular masculine noun, as in the case of agreement with the masculine noun *axbār* 'newspaper' in (11a) below. The fact that agreement is involved in (11a) is clear if we look at the minimally contrastive sentence, (11b), where a feminine noun *kitāb* 'book' occurs; here, the verb form gives way to *paRh-n-ī*, where the suffix -ī indicates cross-reference with the feminine noun. The confusion between the finite verb *paRh-n-ā* and the infinitive *paRh-nā* can therefore be clarified by appeal to such a permutation test.

11. (a) mujhe ek axbār paRh-**n**-ā th-ā
I-DAT one newspaper.MSC-ACC read-T-C PST-C
'I had to read a newspaper'
(b) mujhe ek kitāb paRh-**n**-ī th-ī
I-DAT one book.FEM-ACC read-T-C PST-C
'I had to read a book'
(c) mujhe sāre axbār paRh-**n**-e th-e
I-DAT all newspaper.MSC-ACC read-T-C PST-C
'I had to read all the newspapers'
(d) [[sāre axbār paRh-**ne**]$_{N'}$ se paihle]$_{PP}$
every newspaper reading INS before
'before reading all the newspapers'

(e) [[ek axbār paRh-**ne**]$_{N'}$ ke liye]$_{PP}$
one newspaper reading GEN for
'for the sake of reading one newspaper'

Similarly, the 3rd plural masculine form of the telic verb, *paRh-n-e*, illustrated in (11c), is sometimes confused with the oblique infinitive form of the verb, *paRh-ne*, illustrated in (11d–e). Here, again, the same permutation test for agreement clarifies the confusion: whereas the oblique infinitive, *paRh-ne*, occurs with both plural and singular arguments of nominalized clauses (see 11d vs. 11e), the telic verb form *paRh-n-e* occurs only with masculine plural arguments of finite clauses (as in [11c]; singular arguments receive distinctive treatment (*paRh-n-ā* or *paRh-n-ī*, depending on gender, as in [11a] and [11b], respectively). Thus there are really two unequivocal distinctions between the finite telic verb ending, *-n-e*, and the oblique infinitive marker, *-ne*: (i) the latter is not formally segmentable, so that the final vowel cannot be analyzed as an independent agreement marker; and (ii) the oblique infinitive formed by the latter is the head of an N' construction, as in (11d–e), whereas the telic verb in (11a–c) is the head of a V' which unites with an AUX verb to form a finite sentence.

A second type of confusion seems to follow from certain global restrictions on verb agreement in the language. In Urdu–Hindi, a finite verb can agree in person, number and gender only with NPs which are unmarked for case, according to a specific hierarchy: the verb can agree with subject NPs in unmarked case (NOM or ABS); if the subject NP is in a marked case form (e.g. ERG or DAT), the verb can agree with the direct object, but only if the direct object NP is also in unmarked case; if the direct object is in the 'marked accusative' case (formally identical to the DAT), agreement morphology is neutralized to the 3rd singular masculine suffix form.

Moreover, as I argue below, the telic aspect conditions a DAT-ACC case marking split in this language, just as the perfective aspect conditions an ERG-ABS case marking split (see section 6 for details). When the subject of a telic sentence is datively marked, the verb does not agree with it; in such sentences, the verb can agree only with the direct object, but only if the direct object is itself in unmarked case. However, this is not a peculiarity of the telic aspect. It follows from the global case marking restriction noted above, and applies equally to the perfective aspect. Thus, in the two perfective sentences in (12), the verb agrees with the feminine direct object only in (12a), marking cross reference by means of the feminine suffix *-ī*; non-agreement occurs in (12b), because the direct object is in a marked accusative case, formally identical to the dative. The corresponding telic sentences, (11b) and (12c), are exactly parallel to (12a) and (12b) in terms of agreement. Thus, verb agreement in the telic aspect is governed by the same rule as that in the perfective aspect, at least in standard Urdu–Hindi.[4]

12. (a) mãĩne vah kitāb acchi tarāh paRh-ø-ī h-ai
I-ERG that book-ABS carefully read-P-C PST-C
'I have read that book carefully'
(b) mãĩne us kitāb ko acchi tarāh paRh-ø-ā h-ai
I-ERG that book-DAT carefully read-P-C PST-C
'I have read that book carefully'
(c) mujhe unhī kitābõ ko paRh-n-ā th-ā
I-DAT those very books-DAT read-T-C PST-C
'I had to read those very books'

Of the three categories of aspect distinguished by suffixal means in this language, the imperfective is the least specific in interpretation. All tokens of the perfective aspect mark a point-like interval characteristic; all tokens of the telic aspect mark an endpoint to the predicate interval; but imperfectively coded stems are quite variable in interval interpretation, as noted in (8b–e). These facts of specific and differential coding capacity motivate the analysis of (13a) for the minimal aspectual dimensions of the system; the gross labels 'perfective', 'imperfective' and 'telic' correspond to these minimal dimensions as in (13b).

13. Summary of aspect distinctions
(a) minimal dimensions of the aspectual system
[+perfective] = point-like interval characteristic
[+telic] = interval bounded by an endpoint
(b) interpretation of category labels

category label	minimal dimensions coded	interpretation
'perfective'	[+perfective, –telic]	specified only for point-like interval
'telic'	[+telic, –perfective]	specified only for endpoint
'imperfective'	[–perfective, –telic]	not specific as to either dimension

■ 6. Mood

■ 6.1. Form-based Perspective

Before we turn to the analysis of mood categories proper, it is necessary to clarify the analysis of the segmental forms which are used in these constructions. Three points are worthy of note in this regard.

The first point concerns forms of the verb *honā* 'to be'. One form of the verb *honā* has already been noted in the foregoing discussion. This is the stem form *h-* which is restricted in distribution to the AUX verb, occurring as a 'present' tense marker (specifically, [–past]), in paradigmatic contrast to the [+past] marker, *th-*. Distinct from *h-*, however, are two other forms of this verb, *ho-* and *hū-*, which are in complementary distribution with respect to *h-*: whereas *h-* occurs only as an AUX verb stem, *ho-* and *hū-* never occur as part of the AUX. They are restricted to MV or COMP position, as shown in (14).

14.

		MV		COMP	AUX
(a)	kya	**hū**-ø-ā			**h**-ai
	what	be-P-C			PRS-C
	'What has happened?'				
(b)	vahā̃	šor	**ho**-t-ā		**h**-ai
	there	noise	be-I-C		PRS-C
	'[It] is [usually] noisy there'				
(c)	kām	zarūr	**ho**-n-ā		**h**-ai
	work	must	be-T-C		PRS-C
	'The work must get done'				
(d)	vah	vahā̃	baiTh-ø-ā	**hū**-ø-ā	th-ā
	he	there	sit-P-C	be-P-C	PST-C
	'He was sitting over there'				

The stem contrast, *hū-* vs. *ho-*, of the verb *honā* 'to be' is conditioned by the aspectual morpheme immediately following the stem; the verb belongs to the irregular class of 'strong verbs' which show a stem variation, conditioned by the feature [+/– perfective].[5]

The second point concerns the form and interpretation of the so-called 'future' construction. This construction is formed by the occurrence of three morphemic suffixes after the stem (e.g. *bhāg-e-g-ā* '[he] will run'). Some previous analyses have attempted to analyze the last two morphemes as constituting a separate word (e.g. as *g-*, rather than as *-g-ā*), and to stipulate a third AUX verb on analogy with the present and past AUX verbs exemplified in (14), thus proposing a third tense category by formal analogy. But the lack of insertability of emphatic and negative clitics in the so-called 'future' construction shows that the formal analogy is incorrect. Whereas such particles can occur in VP-initial as well as VP-medial positions in both present (cf. [15a/b]) and past constructions (cf. [15c/d]) (the formal alternation here marks a contrast of discourse emphasis), they are only admissible in VP-initial position in the future construction, as shown in (15e–h).

15. (a/b) aur vah paise {**bhī** le-t-ā h-ai/ le-t-ā
and he money {EMPH take-I-C PRS-C/ take-I-C
bhī h-ai}
EMPH PRS-C}
'And he takes money too'

(c/d) vah kām mujh se {**nahī̃** ho-t-ā th-ā/ ho-t-ā
that work I–INS {NEG be-I-C PST-C/ be-I-C
nahī̃ th-ā}
NEG PST-C}
'I was unable to do that work'

(e/*f) aur vah paise {**bhī** l-e-g-ā/ *l-e **bhī** g-ā}
and he money {EMPH take-C-g-C/ take-C EMPH g-C}
'And he'll take money too'

(g/*h) vah ghar {**nahī̃** jā-e-g-ā/ *jā-e **nahī̃** g-ā}
he home {NEG go-C-g-C/ go-C NEG g-C}
'He won't go home'

This fact of inseparability of affixes provides evidence for the absence of a word boundary between the morpheme *-e* and the morpheme string *-g-ā* in verbs like *l-e-g-ā* 'will take' in (15e) and *jā-e-g-ā* 'will go' in (15g). Moreover, functional facts also preclude the analysis of a minimal dimension of 'future' coding in this construction. The *-e* element clearly lacks deictic reference to future time, since it also occurs in the optative construction (see [16m–n] below), which wholly lacks any time reference whatsoever, coding merely the potential or hypothetical possibility of an event to occur. The *-g-ā* element appears to code a reference to future time in a sentence like (15e); but its occurrence in other constructions—e.g. the presumptive in (16k–l) and the prospective imperative, exemplified in (16t–u)—clearly shows that its basic meaning is that of speaker expectation, not of deictic time reference. In fact, both semantically distinct elements of the so-called future construction, namely *-e* and *-g-ā*, really are code minimal categories of mood, a point to which I return in section 5.3.

The third point concerns the analysis of the 'cross-reference' markers represented by the symbol '-C' in all the example sentences in the foregoing discussion. These morphemes are portmanteau forms. On the one hand, they mark agreement with noun phrase arguments, cross-referencing categories of person, gender, number and deference. But in addition to this well-known function, these morphemes also serve as markers of mood categories in the language, a categorial dimension of these forms which has so far escaped any adequate analysis.[6]

As far as the cross-referencing functions of these suffixes are concerned, it may be noted, first, that lexical nouns in Urdu–Hindi are differentiated for the following cross-referenceable distinctions: the usual three categories of person (first, second and third); two categories of number (singular and plural); two categories of gender (masculine and feminine); and three categories of deference-entitlement to addressee (akin to the T/V pronominal distinction in European languages), one marking addressee as 'lower' in deference-entitlement, one marking addressee as 'higher', and a third marking addressee as an 'equal' (not specifically higher or lower). Of course, not all noun phrase types lexically differentiate these categories: grammatical gender distinctions are lexicalized only in third person nouns, deference marking is generally restricted to second person pronouns, and the 'lower' category of deference marking, in particular, to second singular pronouns. These facts are displayed in summary fashion in Table 1.

The table is organized into three sub-boxes or regions: box I. is a display of NP categories, listed by lexical content with examples; box II. lists cross-reference suffixes, distinguishable into five separate form-classes (labeled $-C_1$, $-C_2$, $-C_3$, $-C_4$ and $-C_5$) on distributional grounds; box III., at the bottom, distinguishes those mood categories which are locally coded by the suffixes (additional mood categories require a separate discussion).

Table 1: Classes of cross-reference suffixes

I. NP categories		II. verbal suffixes of cross-reference/mood				
lexical content	*example form*	$-C_1$*(msc/fem)*	$-C_2$	$-C_3$	$-C_4$	$-C_5$
1. 1st sg.	mā̃ī	-ā/-ī	-ū̃	-ū̃	-ū̃	–
2. 1st pl.	ham	-e/-ī̃(-ī)[7]	-ā̃ī	-ẽ	-õ	–
3. 3rd sg.	vah (laRk-ā/-ī)	-ā/-ī	-ai	-e	-o	–
4. 3rd pl.	vah sab (laRk-e/-iyā̃)	-e/-ī̃(-ī)	-ā̃ī	-ẽ	-õ	–
5. lower, 2nd sg.	tū	-ā/-ī	-ai	-e	-o	-ø
6. equal, 2nd sg.	tum	-e/-ī	-o	-o	-o	-o
7. equal, 2nd pl.	tum sab	-e/ī̃(-ī)	-o	-o	-o	-o
8. higher, 2nd sg.	āp	-e/-ī̃(-ī)	-ā̃ī	-ẽ	-õ	-īe
9. higher, 2nd pl.	āp sab	-e/-ī̃(-ī)	-ā̃ī	-ẽ	-õ	-īe
III. Mood categories:		–	*indicative (present)*	*potential*		*imperative*

Note that whereas cross-reference distinctions are differentiated by specific suffixes within each paradigm, mood categories are coded by the *generic* suffixal form-class in each case. For example, *different* members of the paradigm of $-C_2$ forms distinguish different values of cross-reference. However, all the members of this paradigm––considered now as a class of forms—mark the indicative mood. Let me say something, then, about the specific agreement markers, before I turn to a discussion of the generic mood markers in the next section.

From the point of view of noun phrase agreement, $-C_1$ is the most elaborate form-class since it is the only category which disambiguates gender in addition to person, number and deference. Note that verb-argument agreement with respect to gender is, strictly speaking, an indexical category like deference marking since it is not driven exclusively by NP lexical content: even noun phrase types which are not lexically coded for gender (such as first person categories) are nonetheless marked for the gender of the contextualized referent (for first person forms, the speaker). $-C_5$ is the most marked member, in the sense of having the narrowest distribution: it can only mark second person subjects. Form-classes $-C_2$, $-C_3$ and $-C_4$ show a high degree of paradigm-internal parallelism, including regular neutralizations for certain categories of cross-referenced NP (e.g. in rows 1, 6 and 7, all three form-types are identical in shape). Such neutralizations entail considerable loss of information about cross-referenced NP; moreover, the question of which form-class a particular suffix belongs to can only be settled by means of careful permutation tests.

-C_1 is not only the most elaborate class (by criteria of paradigm elaboration), it is the unmarked class as well (by criteria of sentence distribution): it occurs in the largest number of tense/mood categories; -C_5 occurs only in the imperative mood; -C_3 and -C_4 occur only in potential mood constructions; and -C_2 is found only in the present indicative.

■ 6.2. Traditionally Distinguished Categories of Mood

The terminology which is traditionally used to describe mood categories in Urdu–Hindi is not sensitive to the minimal morphemic distinctions in the structure of the mood paradigm, nor to the formal constituency of the elements coding these distinctions. Six mood categories are generally distinguished: the indicative (INDC), the interrogative (INTR), the contingent (CONT), the presumptive (PRSV), the optative (OPTV) and the imperative (IMPV). We will see that the category which is generally called the future 'tense' (FUTR) is also a mood category, albeit complex in structure. It is compositionally analyzable in terms of simpler mood categories. An eighth mood category, sometimes termed the 'polite request' form, also exists. This is built from the imperative mood, and is also formally and functionally complex. I will refer to it as the 'prospective imperative' (PROS-IMPV) since the label reflects its formal composition somewhat more clearly; the 'polite request' meaning is a reflex of this basic sense. These categories are exemplified in (16) below. In each set of examples, the form-configurations which mark the mood category appear in boldface. Interlinear glosses are used to specify the particular form-class to which the cross-reference suffixes in each construction belong, and such glossing may be verified by appeal to Table 1.

16. *(i) indicative (INDC)*
(a/b) {laRkā/laRkī} phūl bec-t-{ā/ -ī} **h-ai**
boy/girl flowers sell-I-C_1 PRS-C_2
'The {boy/girl} sells flowers'
(c/d) {laRkā/laRkī} phūl bec-t-{ā/ -ī} **th-**{ā/ -ī}
{boy/girl} flowers-ACC sell-I-C_1 PST-C_1 flowers'
'The {boy/girl} used to sell

(ii) interrogative (INTR)
(e/f) **kyā** {laRKā/laRkī} phūl bec-t-{ā/ -ī} h-ai
YNQ boy/girl flowers sell-I-C_1 PRS-C_2
'Does the {boy/girl} sell flowers?'
(g/h) phūl **kaun** bec-t-{ā/ -ī} th-{ā/ -ī}
flowers who sell-I-C_1 PST-C_1
'Who {masc./fem.} sells flowers?'

(iii) contingent (CONT)
(i) (agar) vah āy-ā **h-o...**
if he-ABS come-P-C_1 PRS-C_4
'(If) he has come...'
(potential point–like state)

(j) šayed ãp na ā-t-e **h-õ...**
perhaps you NEG come-I-C_1 PRS-C_4
'Perhaps you don't [usually] come...' (potential habitual state)

(iv) presumptive (PRSV)

(k) ãp ā-ø-e **h-õ-g-e**
you-ABS come-P-C_1 PRS-C_4-g-C_1
'You must have come'
(presumptive point-like state)

(l) mãĩ hi rakh-t-ā **h-ũ-g-ā**
you-NOM EMPH put-I-C_1 PRS-C_4-g-C_1
'It must be me who puts it [there]'
(presumptive habitual state)

(v) optative (OPTV)

(m) (agar) tum **ā-e...**
you–NOM come-C_3
'(If) you come...'

(n) šāyed mãĩ vahã-tak na pahunc-ũ
perhaps he-NOM there will NEG arrive-C_3
'Perhaps I won't reach there'

(vi) future (FUTR)

(o) vah na ā-**e-g-ā**
he-NOM NEG come-C_3-g-C_1
'He will not come'

(p) tum DhūnD-t-e rah-**o-g-e**
you-NOM search-i-C_1 remain-C_3-g-C_1
'You will keep searching'

(vii) imperative (IMPV)

(q) DhūnD-**ø**
seek-C_5
'Look (for it)!' [addressee lower]

(r) DhūnD-**o**
seek-C_5
'Look (for it)!' [addressee equal]

(s) DhūnD-**īe**
seek-C_5
'Please look (for it)!' [addressee higher]

(viii) prospective-imperative (PROS-IMPV)

(t) khā-**īe-g-ā**
eat-C_5-g-C_1
'Please do eat!'

(u) na jā-**īe-g-ā**
NEG go-C_5-g-C_1
'Please don't go!'

■ 6.3. The Minimal Distinctions of Mood

In the present section I argue that there are really only three minimal distinctions of mood in the Urdu–Hindi system (these will be labeled by the distinctive features [+/– potential], [+/– imperative] and [+/– prospective]) and that several of the categories traditionally termed 'mood' are really derivative category clusters formed by the asymmetric combination of minimal mood categories, or by combinations of mood and tense.

As far as the indicative mood is concerned, the examples in (16a–d) show that it is not marked by any distinctive morphemic mark, since the present and the past indicative share no recurrent partials. The indicative is in fact, the unmarked, or least specified category in this language—as it is in most, if not all languages. The interrogatives—both yes–no questions as in (e, f), and content question as in (g, h)—are marked by a paradigm of question words whose analysis is well-known; as such, they present no special problems, and I will not discuss them in any further detail here.

The interesting and hitherto puzzling categories are the ones listed in (iii)–(viii), termed contingent, presumptive, optative, future, imperative, and prospective–imperative. As far as the formation of these categories is concerned, the following form proportions should be evident from the examples and their interlinear glosses:

17. Recurrent partials in mood paradigms

CONT: PRSV	:: PRS-C_4	: PRS-C_4-g-C_1
OPTV: FUTR	:: -C_3	: -C_3-g-C_1
IMPV: PROS-IMPV	:: -C_5	: -C_5-g-C_1

The patterning of formal categories shows that the contingent, optative, and imperative are a series of basic categories from which the presumptive, the future and the prospective-imperative are derived by the affixation of the morpheme string -g-C_1. Further clarification is required, then, as to the categorial meaning of the three basic categories (i.e. CONT, OPTV and IMPV) and of the fourth element (-g-C_1, which is used to derive the other three (i.e. PRSV, FUTR and PROS-IMPV) from the first set.

Let me begin with the last of the three basic categories, the imperative, illustrated in (q–s). As the examples show, this category is marked by the suffixal form class -C_5, specifically and differentially coding in all cases a command imposed upon the addressee. Note that whereas *specific* members of this form class differentiate degrees of deference-entitlement to addressee through the mechanism of cross-reference to (optional) second person NP, the imperative marker itself is the *generic* suffixal form-class, -C_5. In terms of our decomposition of the mood system into minimal categories, the meaning of the imperative marker, -C_5, will be represented by the feature [+imperative], to be given a further interpretation below.

The optative mood, exemplified in (16m–n), is coded by the suffix -C_3, which regularly marks an evaluation of the likelihood or possibility of an event's occurrence, relative to some other contextual fact. The interpretation of this category is highly grounded in discursive context and co-text, to the extent that the optatively marked verb with its arguments does not, by itself, form a complete, independent sentence. In order to form a complete sentence, it must occur as part of a biclausal conditional sentence, or as a clause subordinated to various types of expectation clauses (e.g. *ummīd hai ki* 'it is hoped that...') or with some type of modalizing adverb (e.g. *šāyed* 'perhaps' in [16n]). Consequently, optative sentences in Urdu–Hindi always acquire secondary construction-specific meanings in the various category collocations in which they occur.[8] In general, however, the optative marks the evaluation of an outcome relative to the contextual possibility for potential occurrence: in positive sentences, the form is interpreted to mean that the occurrence of the event is a potential possibility; and in negated sentences, such as (16n), that it is not likely, for reasons either contextually presupposable as given, or entailed by the use of the form, and to be elaborated upon. The minimal content of this formal category may be represented, thus, by the feature [+potential], to be characterized further below.

The contingent category, exemplified in (16i–j), is not a pure mood category at all, but a tense-mood complex: it is formed from the present AUX stem, *h-*, and the mood suffix -C_4. The -C_4 element in the contingent construction codes a meaning of potentiality, much in the same way as the -C_3 element in the optative. Since the verb stem *h-* is lexically stative, the meaning of 'potentiality' is always realized here as 'potential state'. This meaning is perfectly transparent in sentence (16i), where the state is further specified as 'point-like' due to the perfective coding of main verb; in (16j), however, the aspectual component of the meaning is not that of a point-like state, but of a 'habitual' state. This reflex is due to the imperfective aspect of the main verb. We may say, therefore, that the basic meaning of the element *h*-C_4 is that of 'potential state', where the element *h-* is specifically 'stative' and the element -C_4 is specifically 'potential' in meaning; and the 'point-like' (vs. 'habitual') meaning derives from independent occurrence of the perfective (vs. imperfective) aspect in the main verb.

Although both -C_3 and -C_4 are markers of the [+potential] mood, they occur in complementary distribution: the suffix -C_4 can only occur on the AUX verb stem *h-*; -C_3, on the other hand never occurs here, only on other verbs. Since the AUX stem *h-* is a tense marker, the complementarity of distribution appears to be conditioned by the tense marking: the -C_4 form occurs only in tensed sentences. A cross-category implicational relationship obtains as a result: whenever the [+potential] mood category occurs in a [+tense] construction (with shape -C_4) the specific value of tense is always [–past]. This cross-category relationship derives from the fact that an event which is perspectivally 'potential' cannot at the same time already have occurred and be coded as deictically in past time. The distributional rule for the formal shape-class of the mood category [+potential] is stated in (18a); the specific cross-categorial implicational relationship is stated in (18b).

18. (a) [+potential] → -C_4/[+tense]__
-C_3 otherwise
(b) mood-tense co-occurrence restriction: $[+\text{potential}]_{\text{mood}} \Rightarrow [-\text{past}]_{\text{tense}}$

Let us turn now to the function of the -g-C_1 suffix which forms a secondary series of three categories derived from the basic three discussed above. For example, the -g-C_1 element forms the future construction, exemplified in (16o–p), by suffixation after the -C_3 [+potential] mood suffix. As noted above, the -g-C_1 element makes the future a complete monoclausal sentence, unlike the optative (cf. [16m]), which requires some additional element (e.g. a biclausal conditional, a modal adverb as in [16n], etc.) to complete it. Second, it adds a meaning of 'definite expectation', in addition to the meaning of 'potential outcome' code by -C_3 itself. We can characterize this specific meaning of 'definite expectation' by means of the minimally distinctive mood feature [+/– prospective], where the presence of the -g-C_1 element specifies the positive value. The future construction, according to this analysis, is specified as a [+potential, +prospective] mood complex derived from the optative (or simply [+potential]) mood.

Similarly, the presumptive category, exemplified in (16k–l), is formed derivationally from the contingent category by suffixing the -g-C_1 element to the [+potential] mood element, -C_4. Given the co-occurrence of two mood-specifying elements, -C_4 and -g-C_1, the presumptive is a complex mood category as well: it has the same feature decomposition as the future [+potential, +prospective], relative to the minimal dimensions of the system. The difference between the future and the presumptive lies in the verb stem which takes mood inflection: the presumptive mood (like the contingent mood) is formed from the AUX stem *h-*, whereas the future (like the optative) is formed from a MV. Observe that in the AUX-based presumptive (16k–l) and contingent (16i–j) sentences, the *independent* possibility of aspectual inflection in the MV yields comparable variability in overall interval characteristics. In the MV-based optative and future, the MV itself takes no aspect markers; as a result, these constructions are less variable in interval characteristics.

Finally, a second type of imperative construction, the prospective-imperative, exemplified in (16t–u), is formed from the simple imperative by suffixation of the -g-C_1 element to the -C_5 marker of [+imperative] mood. However, this is a highly marked and specialized construction: the -C_5 form-class is frozen to a single specific form, the 'addressee-higher-rank' element of the -C_5 paradigm, *-ie*; the -C_1 element is always frozen to its default masculine singular form, *-ā*. Hence, this is a sub-category of the [+imperative], specified for an additional meaning: its meaning is 'prospective' rather than futuristic (as the more commonly used, but rather inappropriate category label 'future imperative' might suggest): the construction lacks any *specific* deictic reference to future time since it can be used to request someone to do something not only at a moment in future time, but also at a hypothetical time as well. The construction can thus be analyzed as [+imperative, +prospective], the meaning of 'polite request' emerging from the $-C_5$ and $-g-C_1$ elements occurring in concert, signaling a command to an addressee indexed as higher in rank, the force of the command muted by a seemingly solicitous and respectful expectation regarding addressee compliance.

We are now in a position to give an analysis of the basic categories of the mood system. The values [+imperative], [+potential] and [+prospective] mentioned above can be identified with isolable forms in the following way.

19. Minimal categories of mood
    (a) $-C_5$ = [+imperative]
    (b) $-C_3$ (*and* $-C_4$) = [+potential] [see (18)]
    (c) $-g-C_1$ = [+prospective]

The interrogative, on the other hand, is marked by a question word, and does not belong to this paradigm. Moreover, the indicative is not specifically and differentially coded by any form, as noted above; it is the unmarked, default mood category. Thus, the suffix $-C_2$ which occurs only in the present indicative after the stem *h-*, codes no mood category *per se*, though it is part of the tense-mood complex which we term the present indicative. Similarly, $-C_1$ codes no distinction of mood by itself. When it occurs in the $-g-C_1$ construct, the *bimorphemic configuration* codes the value [+prospective]; however, $-C_1$ also occurs in a wide range of other environments, as the data in (16) show, where it signals no specific value. The functional interpretation of the minimal dimensions of mood is given in (20). A compositional analysis of the traditionally analyzed category names is given in Table 2. The traditional labels name category clusters, as their decomposition in Table 2—relative to the minimal mood distinctions of (20)—shows.

20. Minimal mood distinctions
    (a) [+/– imperative] = the '+' value indexically entails addressee-compliance; the '–' value fails to index such addressee compliance,
    (b) [+/– potential] = the '+' value indexes speaker's modalization that the proposition may potentially be true, the '–' value fails to index such speaker evaluation,
    (c) [+/– prospective] = the '+' value indexes speaker's evaluation that the proposition is expected to be true, the '–' value fails to index such evaluation.

■ 7. Aspect and Case Marking

In the foregoing, I have argued that in addition to the two traditionally recognized aspect categories, the perfective and the imperfective, a third category of

Table 2: Formal compositionality of traditionally analyzed mood categories

		(a) 'Pure' mood categories		
A. 'Optative'	=	-C_3		
		[+potential]		
B. 'Future'	=	-C_3		-g-C_1
		[+potential]		[+prospective]
C. 'Imperative'	=	-C_5		
		[+imperative]		
D. 'Future imperative	=	-C_5		-g-C_1
		[+imperative]		[+prospective]
		(b) Tense-mood category clusters		
E. 'Contingent'	=	h-		-C_4
		[–past]		[+potential]
F. 'Presumptive'	=	h-	-C_4	-g-C_1
		[–past]	[+potential]	[+prospective]
G. 'Past indicative'	=	th-	-C_1	
		[+past]		
H. 'Present indicative'	=	h-	-C_2	
		[–past]		

grammatical aspect, the telic, must be distinguished on distributional grounds (see [13] above for summary of aspectual distinctions). Moreover, the telic is like the perfective (and unlike the imperfective) in being highly specific in aspectual interpretation. Given a set of aspectual distinctions in a language, we would expect that if there are any aspectually driven splits in case marking in the language, such splits of case marking would be conditioned by the more marked, more categorially specific grammatical aspects, before any are conditioned by the unmarked, non-specific ones. This is just what we find in Urdu–Hindi: case marking splits are in fact conditioned by the perfective and the telic, but not by the imperfective.

The imperfective does not require any case marking pattern specific to its aspectual category: the ACC-NOM case marking pattern, occurring in the imperfective aspect, as in (21a), is the most widely occurring case marking pattern, found even in clauses which lack any aspectual coding whatsoever, such as (21b).

21. (a) laRkā kitābẽ bec-t-ā h-ai
    boy-NOM books-ACC sell-I-C PRS-C
    'The boy sells books'
    (b) laRkā kitābẽ bec-e-g-ā
    boy-NOM books-ACC sell-FUTR
    'The boy will sell books'
    (c) laRke ne kitābẽ bec-ø-ī h-ãī
    boy-ERG books-ABS read-P-C PRS-C
    'The boy has sold books'

(d) laRkā kaī dafā bhāg-**ø**-ā h-ai
boy-ABS many times run-P-C PRS-C
'The boy has run many times'

However, sentences with bivalent, perfectively marked verbs require a distinctive coding of the agent argument, as in (21c). Both conditions must be met jointly, since agents of monovalent verbs do not require ergative case, even if the verb is perfective, as in (21d). The contrast (21a) vs. (21c) yields the usual analysis of Urdu–Hindi as a split-ERG case system.

The DAT case marking of subjects of telically coded verbs, on the other hand, is not traditionally identified as constituting a case marking split. Before I turn to its characterization, however, I should point out that such telically governed DAT case must be distinguished from a more general lexically based pattern of DAT subjects in the language, which is well-known.

22. (a) mujhe abhī tanxā mil-**e**-**g**-ī
I-DAT just.now salary-ACC get-FUTR
'I will get my salary very soon'
(b) mujhe har hafte tanxā mil-**t**-ī h-ai
I-DAT every week salary-ACC get-I-C PRS-C
'I get my salary every week'
(c) mujhe abhī tanxā mil-**ø**-ī h-ai
I-DAT just.now salary-ACC get-P-C PRS-C
'I just got my salary'
(d) mujhe abhī tanxā mil-**n**-ī h-ai
I-DAT just.now salary-ACC get-T-C PRS-C
'I am yet to get my salary'

Certain two-place agentless verbs, like *mil-* 'get, meet with' lexically specify dative case for subject arguments, regardless of grammatical inflection (Kachru 1990). For such verbs, aspectless 'future' sentences ([22a]), as well as aspectually imperfective ([22b]), perfective ([22c]) and telic ([22d]) sentences, all have dative subjects. Such verbs lexically specify a p(D,O) case frame.

However, verbs which are not lexically specified for dative subjects regularly exhibit dative subject case marking in the telic aspect. Sentences (23a), (21a) and (21c) may be compared to confirm that case marking is here split by aspectual inflection.

23. (a) laRke ko kitābẽ bec-**n**-ī h-ãĩ
boy-DAT books-ACC sell-T-C PRS-C
'The boy has to sell books'
(b) mujh ko kitāb paRh-**n**-ī h-ai
I-DAT book-ACC read-T-C PRS-C
'I have to read (a/the) book'

(c) laRke ko bhāg-**n**-ā h-ai
boy-DAT run-T-C PRS-C
'The boy is to (/has to/wants to) run'

(d) musībat ā-**n**-ī h-ai
misfortune-NOM come-T-C PRS-C
'Misfortune is bound to strike (us)'

(e) voh xat abhī ā-**n**-e hai
that letter-NOM yet come-T-C PRS-C
'Those letters are yet to come'

Note, however, that verbal valence is not a co-factor in defining split-DAT case inflection. Thus, whereas monovalent perfective verbs do not require ERG case marking on their single arguments (e.g. 21d), monovalent telic verbs do require the DAT case, as in (23c). It appears, rather, that the co-factor defining split-DAT inflection is the animacy of the criterial argument. Thus, whereas the animate subjects in (23a–c) require DAT case, the inanimate subjects in (23d–e) do not. The condition on split-DAT inflection can be stated more precisely by appeal to Silverstein's hierarchy of lexical features for noun phrase type (Silverstein 1976): verbs which are in telic aspect, and whose subject argument is specified for a lexical feature higher on Silverstein's NP hierarchy than [+animate] require DAT inflection for that argument.

Thus, both the perfectively driven and the telically driven splits in case marking involve co-factors in addition to aspect marking: the former additionally requires that predicate valence be greater than one, and the latter additionally requires that the criterial argument be of a lexical type specifiable as higher than [+animate] on the hierarchy of noun phrase features. Such *complex–global* splits of case marking (cf. Silverstein 1976: 124–5), are describable only in terms of Boolean conjuncts of lexico-grammatical features, as summarized in (24).

24. Splits of case marking in Urdu–Hindi
(a) Perfectively driven splits:
If [aspect = +perfective] & [predicate valence > 1] → agent gets ERG case; otherwise, agent gets ABS
(b) Telically driven splits:
If [aspect = +telic] & [argument ranks above +animate] → subject gets DAT case; otherwise, subject gets NOM

From these two patterns of 'split' case marking in the language—patterns which are conditioned by co-occurring lexico-grammatical categories—two additional patterns of 'fluid' case marking must be carefully distinguished. 'Fluid' case marking patterns are conditioned by discourse rather than grammatical variables. Our ability to distinguish 'split' case marking from 'fluid' case marking is particularly important, since the former type of pattern co-exists with the latter type (in this, as well as in other languages) in what is only seemingly a homogeneous system of surface patterning.

The first such pattern of 'fluid' case marking is the expansive use of the ERG case in environments where ERG case is not obligatory (i.e. not required by any grammatical rule), but optional. Thus, certain *perfectively* marked *intransitive* verbs, like *chīk-* 'sneeze', allow for the optional possibility of ERG case, in addition to the normally expected ABS case (expected by rule [24a]), as shown in (25a/b). The ERG case in (25b) implies a greater degree of volitionality on the part of the actor (or, contrastive reference to actor), than does the ABS case marking in (25a). Similarly, *telically* marked verbs with *animate* arguments, optionally allow ERG case marking in addition to the normal DAT case as shown in (25c/d): this type of case fluidity extends the optional ERG (with its contrastive, volitional reflexes) to environments where DAT case marked subjects are otherwise expected by grammatical rule (see [24b]). Such optional possibilities are probably derived from contact with Punjabi, and are not well-formed in every regional dialect of Urdu–Hindi, as noted by Masica (1990: 235–6).

25. (a/b) {mãĩ/ mãĩ ne} chīk-ø-ā
{I-ABS/ I-ERG} sneeze-P-C
'I sneezed'

(c/d) {us ko/ us ne} jā-n-ā h-ai
{he-DAT/ he-ERG} go-T-C PRS-C
'He has to go'

(e/f) {xat/ xat ko} ā-n-ā h-ai
{letter-NOM/ letter-DAT} come-T-C PRS-C
'The letter is to come'

A second type of 'fluid' case marking pattern involves the *expansive* use of the DAT case in environments where its occurrence is not predictable by grammatical rule. Thus in (25e/f), the *inanimate* subject of the telic verb can optionally take a DAT case marking, in addition to the NOM case, predicted by rule (24b). But this optional DAT case marking is not limited to subject arguments; it occurs also with *inanimate* direct objects, which can optionally take a DAT case, as exemplified in (12a–b) above. In both instances, the optional DAT argument is acceptable only under certain discourse conditions: the referent of the noun phrase in DAT case must be rhematic, presupposed information, relative to prior discourse.

It should be clear, moreover, that both discourse-conditioned types of case marking patterns are entirely independent of the aspectually-driven grammatical phenomena noted in (24). The expansive ERG can occur in both perfective ([25b]) and telic ([25d]) sentences. The expansive DAT can occur on *subjects* of telic sentences (25f), and on *direct objects* of perfective ([12a]), telic ([12c]) or imperfective sentences. These patterns of case marking (along with conditioning factors, and interpretation) are easily distinguished once the categories of verb inflection are themselves analyzed correctly.

■ NOTES

Symbols: The following glossing conventions are used in this chapter: Aspect: P 'perfective', I 'imperfective', T 'telic'; Tense: PST 'past', PRS 'present'; Mood: INDC 'indicative', CONT 'contingent', PRSU 'presumptive', OPTV 'optative', IMPV 'imperative', FUTR 'future', PROS IMPV 'prospective imperative'. Case: NOM(inative), ACC(usative), ERG(ative), INS(trumental), DAT(ive), etc. Cross-reference suffixes are represented by the generic symbol -C in the first part of the paper; in section 5.1, this class of suffixes is distinguished into five sub-classes C_1, C_2, C_3, C_4 and C_5.

1. Early attempts at analysis, such as those of Lienhard (1961), suffer from too great a reliance on an intuitive segmentation of units of word-structure, not distinguished by consistent formal criteria. The effort is limited, further, by the acceptance of traditional notions of Sanskrit or Latin grammar which prove inadequate to the task. Generative grammar approaches, like that of Pray (1970 [1969]), ignore the morphemic constituency of the verb in favor of 'abstract' phonological segments stipulated in order to correlate syntactic structures directly with phonetic outputs. A general disregard of morphemic structure in these approaches precludes the question of what segmental means may actually serve to code these grammatical categories. Van Olphen (1975), on the other hand, does attempt to give a morphemic segmentation but fails to distinguish between stems and affixes, thus analyzing the stem *rah-* 'stay, remain' as a durative aspectual suffix. But the insertability of negative particles and emphatic clitics between *rah-* and the preceding verb clearly shows that it is not a bound form but an independent stem, acting as a complement verb in the construction at issue. Even Kachru (1980), whose analyses are generally the most thorough is unable to resolve the categories of mood, aspect and tense into recurrent partials, saying, for example that '[i]t is not possible to identify one particular form with one grammatical distinction' (1980: 48). However, precisely such an analysis is offered here.
2. The discussion in this section is adapted from Agha (1993: 4–6).
3. The perfective aspect a morphemic category, //ø//, with allomorphs /y/ and /ø/. The /y/ alternant only occurs between two [+tense] vowels, where the first may be /ā/ or /o/, and the second vowel, /ā/; the /ø/ alternant occurs in all other environments. There is one exceptional verb in the language with respect to this rule, the irregular verb *jānā* 'to go': for this verb, the form /y/ occurs with the [+tense] vowel stem variant (e.g. *jā-y-ā kar-o*, *jā-y-ā kar-t-ā*, etc.) as well as with the [–tense] vowel stem variant (e.g. *ga-y-ā* 'went').
4. It seems clear that the telic aspect is being re-analyzed from the infinitive construction just as the perfective and imperfective aspects were re-analyzed from other nominal constructions at an earlier stage in the language. It is interesting to note that during this transitional phase in the re-analysis, grammatical norms vary somewhat in a diglossic way. For some speakers, the older masculine agreement pattern appears to exist as a generalized *alternative* possibility. However, this is a very sociolectally marked construction. With feminine nouns such as *tasvīr* 'picture' and *baraf* 'snow', the standard agreement pattern is the one in (a) and (b).

    (a) mujhe vah tasvīrē dekh-**n**-ī h-āī
    I-DAT those pictures ACC see-T-C PRS-C
    'I have to see those pictures'

    (b) āj baraf paR-**n**-ī h-ai
    today snow fall-T-C PRS-C
    'Its going to snow today'

    (a') *? mujhe vah tasvīrē dekh-**n**-ā h-āī
    I-DAT those pictures ACC see-T-C PRS-C
    'I have to see those pictures' (non-standard)

    (b') * āj baraf paR-**n**-ā h-ai
    today snow fall-T-C PRS-C
    'Its going to snow today' (not possible)

However, (a') exists as a second possibility in the speech of certain speakers, the author not included. Even for such speakers, the alternative masculine pattern appears to be possible only where the verb is predicated-of an animate, particularly human, subject; it appears not to be possible with inanimate subjects, as in (b'). Four other native speakers whom I have consulted regarding this point (all in their thirties, one an Urdu speaker like myself, the other three, Hindi speakers) all agree that (a') does not occur in their speech. Two of them point out, and I would agree, that utterances such as (a') are characteristic of the speech of older speakers from Uttar Pradesh, and has a somewhat upper-class, even aristocratic ring to it. One informant suggests that the same pattern exists in the speech of lower-class speakers from Bihar, though I am unable to comment on this judgement.

5. In addition to ho-n 'to be', five other verbs (*jā-n* 'to go', *de-nā* 'to give', *le-nā* 'to take' and *kar-nā* 'to do') show a distinct stem form in the perfective aspect. For all five verbs, the stem form in the telic and the imperfective aspects is the same as the infinitive stem.
6. For example, in his SPE style treatment of agreement in Urdu–Hindi, Pray (1970, [1969]) does not distinguish the morphemic classes to which these forms belong, treating them instead as derivable by rule from a single underlying 'abstract' segment (op. cit. 67–68). This analysis is motivated partly by the existence of neutralizations of forms for certain values across the five paradigms; what Pray fails to appreciate, however, is that such phonological identity is 'systematic' not 'accidental', to put it in the terms of Zwicky (1991). Thus, his attempts to deal with morphemic variants solely by morphophonemic rule completely obscures the fact that distributionally distinct form-classes of such segmentable morphemes also differentiate distinct grammatical categories of mood.
7. The general rule for the shape of the 3rd feminine plural marker, *-ī̃*, is that when it occurs serially on successive verbs, the nasalization is deleted in all but the last case.
8. Thus, for example, when the OPTV occurs in the protasis of conditional clauses, it acquires a 'hypothetical condition' sense, clearly a composite, construction-specific meaning. An additional category collocation with a resulting derived meaning occurs in optative clauses with 2nd pers. sg, deferentially 'higher' pronoun subjects (the polite pronoun, p, is optional). In this construction the form yields a polite injunction or request to addressee (polite due to the indexing of deference): e.g. *(āp) khā-ẽ* '(you) please eat', *(āp) dekh-ẽ* '(you) please see/note', *(āp) āge cal-ẽ* '(you) go ahead'; the corresponding polite imperative forms *khā-ie*, *dhek-ie*, *cal-ie* also exist, of course, and are more pointed as polite requests. The same -C_3 suffix can yield a 'hortative' meaning: *(ham) cal-ẽ* 'let (us) go', with optional ellipsis of pronoun subject. The identity of verb forms in the injunctive and hortative constructions is due to a neutralization of the second-sg.-'addressee-higher' and first-plural forms in the -C_3 paradigm. The underlying shape of the latter construction may be seen clearly in questions—*kyā ham cal-ẽ* 'shall we go?', where only the first plural pronoun may occur. However, both the injunctive and the hortative are construction-specific derived meanings of the mood category [+potential]: both may be analyzed in terms of the root meaning of conditional possibility, co-occurring with the speaker- and addressee-indexing by first plural or second person polite pronouns.

■ REFERENCES

Agha, Asif. 1993. *Structural form and utterance context in Lhasa Tibetan: grammar and indexicality in a non-configurational language*. New York: Peter Lang.

———. 1994. The semantics and pragmatics of verb classifiers in Urdu–Hindi. *Proceedings of the Berkeley Linguistics Society* 20.14–27.

Dixon, R.M.W. 1979. Ergativity. *Language* 55.59–138.

Gair, James W. 1990. Subjects, case & INFL in Sinhala. *Experiencer subjects in South Asian languages* ed. by M.K. Verma and K.P. Mohanan, 13–41. Stanford: Center for the Study of Language and Information.

Gvozdanovic, Jadranka. 1991. Syncretism and the paradigmatic patterning of grammatical meaning. *The economy of inflection*, ed. by Frans Plank, 133–60. Berlin: Mouton de Gruyter.

Jakobson, Roman. 1971 [1932]. Zur Struktur des russischen Verbums. In: Jakobson 1971: 3–15. [*Charisteria Gvilelmo Mathesio...oblata*, 74–83. Prague: Cercle Linguistique]

———, 1971 (1936). Beitrag zur allgemeinen Kasuslehre, Gesamtbedeutungen der russischen Kasus. In Jakobson 1971: 23–71 [T.C.L.P. 6.240–288]

———. 1971 (1957). Shifters, verbal categories and the Russian verb. In Jakobson 1971: 130–47 [Mimeo, Department of Linguistics, Harvard University].

1971. *Selected Writings of Roman Jakobson Vol. 2: Word and Language*. The Hague: Mouton.

Kachru, Yamuna. 1980. *Aspects of Hindi Grammar*. New Delhi: Manohar.

———. 1990. Experiencer and other oblique subjects in Hindi. *Experiencer subjects in South Asian languages*, ed. by M.K. Verma and K.P. Mohanan, 59–75. Stanford: Center for the Study of Language and Information.

Kachru, Yamuna, Braj B. Kachru and **Tej K. Bhatia.** 1976. The notion ‘subject’: a note on Hindi-Urdu, Kashmiri and Panjabi. *The notion of subject in South Asian languages*, ed. by M.K. Verma, 79–108. Madison: Dept. of South Asian Studies, University of Wisconsin.

Lienhard, Siegfried. 1961. *Tempusgebrauch und Aktionsartenbildung in der modernen Hindi*. Stockholm: Almqvist and Niksell.

Lyons, John. 1968. *Introduction to theoretical linguistics*. Cambridge: Cambridge University Press.

———. 1977. *Semantics. Vol. 1*. Cambridge: Cambridge University Press.

Masica, Colin. 1990. Varied case marking in obligational constructions. *Experiencer subjects in South Asian languages*, ed. by M.K. Verma and K.P. Mohanan, 335–42. Stanford: Center for the Study of Language and Information.

Mohanan, K.P. and **Tara Mohanan.** 1990. Dative subjects in Malayalam: semantic information in syntax. *Experiencer subjects in South Asian languages*, ed. by M.K. Verma and K.P. Mohanan, 43–57. Stanford: Center for the Study of Language and Information.

Nihal Chand. 1961. *Mazhab-i Ishq*. Khalil-ur-Rahman Da’udi (ed.). Lahore: Majlis-Taraqqi-i Adab.

Palmer, F.R. 1986. *Mood and modality*. Cambridge: Cambridge University Press.

Payne, Thomas E. 1984. Split-S marking and Fluid-S marking revisited. *Papers from the parasession on lexical semantics*, 222–32. Chicago: Chicago Linguistics Society.

Plank, Frans (ed.). 1991. *Paradigms: the economy of inflection*. Berlin: Mouton de Gruyter.

Pray, Bruce. 1970 [1969]. *Topics in Hindi–Urdu Grammar*. Research monograph series no. 1, Center for South and Southeast Asia Studies, University of California, Berkeley. [Agreement in Hindi–Urdu and its Phonological Implications. Doctoral dissertation University of Michigan.]

Silverstein, Michael. 1976. Hierarchy of features and ergativity. *Grammatical categories in Australian languages*, ed. by R.M.W. Dixon, 112–71. Canberra: Australian Institute of Aboriginal Studies.

———. 1979. Language structure and linguistic ideology. *The elements: parasession on linguistic units and levels*, ed. by Paul R. Clyne et al., 193–97. Chicago: Chicago Linguistics Society.

Van Olphen, Herman H. (1975). Aspect, tense and mood in the Hindi verb. *Indo-Iranian Journal* 16.284–301.

Verma, M.K. (ed.). 1976. *The notion of subject in South Asian languages*. Madison: Dept. of South Asian Studies, University of Wisconsin.

Verma, M.K. and **K.P. Mohanan** (eds). 1990. *Experiencer subjects in South Asian languages*. Stanford: Center for the Study of Language and Information.

Whorf, Benjamin Lee. 1956 [1945]. Grammatical categories. *Language, thought and reality: selected writings of Benjamin Lee Whorf*, ed. by John B. Caroll, 87–101. Cambridge, Mass.: MIT Press [*Language*, 21.1–11]

Zwicky, Arnold. 1991. Systematic versus accidental phonological identity. *Paradigms: the economy of inflection*, ed. by Frans Plank, 113–31. Berlin: Mouton de Gruyter.

Negative Contexts and Negative Polarity in Hindi

SHRAVAN VASISHTH

This is a study of the behavior of negative polarity items (NPIs) in Hindi. Dutch NPIs appear in three distinct negative contexts, and are accordingly classified as 'weak', 'medium', and 'strong'. A subset of the NPIs considered here behaves similarly to English and Dutch, but they only show a 'weak' vs. 'Medium' distinction. Other Hindi NPIs do not conform to the bi- or tripartite classification: the weaker the negative context, the greater the preference for the NPI appearing without any focus particle, and the stronger the negative context, the greater the preference for the NPI appearing with a focus particle.

This paper provides an empirically motivated account of constraints on the occurrence of negative polarity items (NPIs) in different kinds of negative contexts in Hindi, and ultimately seeks to develop a formalizable semantic account of NPI licensing that has cross-linguistic validity. Essentially, negative contexts in Hindi are shown to behave like those in other natural languages in that they have certain well-defined boolean algebraic properties, and these properties serve as a constraint on NPI licensing. The present research shows, however, that these boolean constraints, though present, are quite different in Hindi compared to English and Dutch.

■ 1. NPIs and Monotonicity

The role of monotone decreasing functors in NPI licensing is well-known since Ladusaw (1979). In this section, I begin by summarizing known facts about NPI licensing in English. These facts, along with related work on Dutch and German NPIs (see Zwarts [1986], Zwarts [1996], van der Wouden [1994], among others), seem to indicate that NPIs tend to present a hierarchical behavior cross-linguistically.

Next, I examine the logico-mathematical notion of monotonicity in natural language in order to set the stage for the discussion to follow.

I conclude this section by summarizing and extending van der Wouden's (1994) and Yoshimura's (1996) accounts of NPI licensing in English. Briefly, they have shown that monotone decreasing, anti-additive and antimorphic functors are distinct licensors of three kinds of NPIs, 'weak', 'medium' and 'strong' respectively, where 'weak' NPIs are by definition licensed in all downward entailing contexts (i.e. monotone decreasing, anti-additive, and antimorphic contexts); 'medium' NPIs are defined as being licensed only in anti-additive and antimorphic contexts, while 'strong' NPIs are those that are licensed only in antimorphic contexts.

■ 1.1. Some Facts About NPIs

It is well-known since Klima (1964) that certain words and phrases must appear within the scope of a negative element if they are to form a well-formed expression. Some simple examples from English, where the licensor in question is the expression **not**,[1] are given below. Comparing the pairs given in examples (1) to (3), it is clear that each of the NPIs shown must be licensed by (in other words, must appear in the presence of) the negative element **not**.

1. a. John has**n't** talked about *any* of these problems.
   b. *John has talked about *any* of these problems.
2. a. John was**n't** *a bit* happy about these problems.
   b. *John was *a bit* happy about these problems.
3. a. This new book on semantics is**n't** *half bad.*
   b. *This new book on semantics is *half bad.*

It turns out, however, that the presence of such a negative element is a sufficient but not a necessary condition, and that English NPIs display a hierarchical behavior with respect to their licensing environments.

As an illustration of this hierarchical behavior, consider the three NPIs *any*, *a bit* and *half bad* and the constraints on their appearance in the presence of the licensors **few students, no one**, and **not** [these examples are adapted from Yoshimura (1996)].

4. a. **Few students** are aware of *any* of these facts.
   b. **No one** is aware of *any* of these facts.
   c. John has**n't** read *any* of these books.
5. a. ***Few students** were *a bit* happy about these facts.
   b. **No one** was *a bit* happy about these facts.
   c. John was**n't** *a bit* happy about these facts.

6. a. ***Few amateur actors** were *half bad*.
   b. *Among the amateur actors, **no one** was *half bad*.
   c. This new book on semantics is**n't** *half bad*.

This licensing hierarchy may be conveniently summarised in tabular form:

Table 1

English	*any*	*a bit*	*half bad*
few students	✔	*	*
no one	✔	✔	*
not	✔	✔	✔

What is required here is an explanation of why *any* is licensed by all the three licensors **few students, no one**, and **not**, as in (4); while *a bit* is licensed only by **no one**, and **not** and not by **few students**, as in (5); and *half bad* is licensed only by **not** and not by **few students** or **no one**, as in (6). Van der Wouden (1994) and others, developing Ladusaw's (1979) ideas, have in fact provided an account of these English facts. Before describing van der Wouden's account of NPI licensing, first let us review the phenomenon of monotonicity in natural language.

■ 1.2 Monotonicity and Natural Language

Noun phrases (NPs) have long been regarded as generalized quantifiers (Zwarts 1996: 173–86), that is, as set-theoretic entities consisting of collections of sets. Moreover, certain quantifier NPs, such as *FEW* Ns and *AT MOST* n N(s), happen to have the set-theoretic property of being closed under subsets. That is, given a universe *U*, sets *X* and *Y*, and a (generalized) quantifier *Q*, if $X \in Q$ and $Y \subseteq X \subseteq U$, then $Y \in Q$. Such quantifiers are known as *downward entailing* or *monotone decreasing* quantifiers (Barwise and Cooper 1981).

Downward entailing quantifiers are distinct from *upward entailing* or *monotone increasing* quantifiers such as *every N*, and *at least n N(s)* which have the property of being closed under *super*sets. In set-theoretic notation, upward entailment amounts to the following statement: if $X \in Q$ and $X \subseteq Y \subseteq U$, then $Y \in Q$.

The word 'downward' in 'downward entailing' describes the fact that one can reason from sets to subsets. For example, consider an expression such as *no one ran* which contains the downward entailing quantifier **no one**. Given that this expression happens to be true, we can conclude that the expression *no one ran slowly* must also be true. Here, the set of slow runners is a proper subset of the set of runners. The converse, however, is not true. That is, given that *no one ran slowly* is true, we cannot conclude that *no one ran* must also be true. In other words, we can't reason from a set such as one characterizing the property of running slowly to one of its supersets, which in this case is the set characterizing the property of running.[2]

Zwarts (1986: 175) demonstrates that the above set-theoretic statement of monotonicity can be re-phrased in terms of boolean algebra. I adapt his results to present the following simplified schema.

7. SCHEMA 1
   An expression f is monotone decreasing[3] iff the following is valid:
   f (VP_1 *or* VP_2) $\leftrightarrow$ f (VP_1) *and* f (VP_2)

Note that the implicational statement in (7) mirrors one half of the first of De Morgan's laws, which I state here for convenience:

8. a. De Morgan's First Law:
      $\neg (p \vee q) \leftrightarrow (\neg p \wedge \neg q)$
   b. De Morgan's Second Law:
      $\neg (p \wedge q) \leftrightarrow (\neg p \vee \neg q)$

In English, several expressions qualify as monotone decreasing on the basis of the test given in (7); Zwarts (1996: 176) lists twenty-one such NPs but we consider only two, *few Ns* and at *most n N(s)*, by way of illustration.

Applying Schema 1 to the expression **few men**, we find that it does indeed satisfy the schema.

9. a. **Few men** drink or smoke $\rightarrow(\not\leftarrow)$ **few men** drink and **few men** smoke.
   b. **At most two men** drink or smoke $\rightarrow(\not\leftarrow)$ **at most two men** drink and **at most two men** smoke.

Next, van der Wouden (1994), relying on Zwarts (1986), provides a test for determining *anti-additive* expressions, which I present below in an adapted form.

10. SCHEMA 2
    An expression f is anti-additive iff the following is logically valid:
    f (VP_1 *or* VP_2) $\leftrightarrow$ f (VP_1) *and* f (VP_2)

Note here that the above schema for anti-additivity corresponds to the first of De Morgan's Laws in (8) in its entirety, as opposed to Schema 1, which only corresponds to one half of the biconditional statement of the first law.

Zwarts (1996: 184) lists eleven NPs that qualify as anti-additive on the basis of Schema 2 above, but we consider only two, *no N* and *none of the N*, for purposes of illustration.

11. a. **No men** drink or smoke $\leftrightarrow$ **no men** drink and **no men** smoke.
    b. **None of the men** drink or smoke $\leftrightarrow$ **none of the men** drink and **none of the men** smoke.

Finally, following van der Wouden (1994), *antimorphic* expressions may be defined as follows:

12. SCHEMA 3
    An expression f is antimorphic iff the following are logically valid
    $f(VP_1 \textit{ or } VP_2) \leftrightarrow f(VP_1) \textit{ and } f(VP_2)$
    $f(VP_1 \textit{ and } VP_2) \leftrightarrow f(VP_1) \textit{ or } f(VP_2)$

This schema corresponds exactly to both of De Morgan's laws. Now, it should be self-evident by comparing the schemas in (7), (10) and (12) that antimorphic expressions constitute a proper subset of anti-additive ones; and anti-additive expressions constitute a proper subset of monotone decreasing ones. This is so because antimorphicity is a condition satisfiable only by the two biconditional statements corresponding to De Morgan's laws, while anti-additivity is satisfied by a less restrictive constraint, that is, only the first of De Morgan's laws. Anti-additivity therefore encompasses a larger class of expressions, including all those expressions that satisfy antimorphicity. A similar relationship exists between monotone decreasing expressions and anti-additive ones. These relationships can be stated as follows.

13. Antimorphic ⊂ Anti-additive ⊂ Monotone decreasing

The significance of the above fact is that if an NPI is licensed in a monotone decreasing context, it must necessarily be licensed in an anti-additive one as well, but not vice versa. Similarly, if an NPI is licensed in an anti-additive context, it must necessarily be licensed in an antimorphic one as well, but not vice versa.

Put another way, all antimorphic contexts, which satisfy the most restrictive biconditionals in (12), are also anti-additive since they naturally satisfy the less restrictive biconditional in (10), but not vice versa. Similarly, all anti-additive contexts, which satisfy the more restrictive biconditional in (10), are also monotone decreasing ones since they naturally satisfy the less restrictive implication in (7), but not vice versa.

With these distinctions and relationships in mind, I now present a summary of Zwarts' ([1986] and [1996]) and van der Wouden's (1994) conclusions regarding the connection between monotonicity and negative polarity.

■ 1.3 'Strong', 'Medium' and 'Weak' NPI and Monotonicity in English

First, recall the case of English, as shown in examples (1) to (3). The NPI *any* is licensed by what we now recognize as a monotone decreasing context, *few Ns*. From this it follows that all other downward monotone expressions, including anti-additive and antimorphic ones, would be expected to license *any*. This is borne out by the facts in (1).

The NPI *a bit*, however, appears only in what we now know to be an anti-additive context, *none of the Ns*, and therefore in antimorphic contexts, as is evident from (2).

Furthermore, the NPI *half bad* appears only in an antimorphic context, as (3) shows.

Van der Wouden (1994) refers to NPIs like *any* as 'weak', to NPIs like *a bit* as 'medium' NPIs, and to NPIs like *half bad* as 'strong', on the basis of the following definitions.

14. *Definition 1*
    An NPI is 'weak' iff it is licensed in a monotone decreasing context.
15. *Definition 2*
    An NPI is 'medium' iff it is licensed in an anti-additive context.
16. *Definition 3*
    An NPI is 'strong' iff it is licensed in an antimorphic context.

According to van der Wouden, both English and Dutch have these three kinds of NPI, as summarized in Table 2 below.

Table 2

Type of NPI	*'weak' NPI*	*'medium'*	*'strong' NPI*
English	**any**	**a bit**	**half bad**
Dutch	**kunnen uitstaan**	**ook maar iets**	**mals**
monotone decreasing	✔	*	*
anti-additive	✔	✔	*
antimorphic	✔	✔	✔

Now, these results for English and Dutch would lead us to expect that other languages should also have van der Wouden's 'weak'-'medium'-'strong' distinction among their NPIs.

Upon examining Hindi, it turns out that although van der Wouden's distinction is not irrelevant, there are additional constraints imposed by the three kinds of licensors (monotone decreasing, anti-additive and antimorphic) on Hindi NPIs. We now turn to the details of Hindi NPIs.

■ 2. Hindi Negative Polarity Items

■ 2.1 Negative Polarity Licensors in Hindi

First consider **kam-hii Ns**, 'few-*encl* Ns', and **aadhe se kam Ns**, 'less than half Ns'. These turn out to be monotone decreasing but not anti-additive, as the bracketed invalid implications indicate.

17. a. **kam-hii** **bacce** naacte yaa gaate haĩ →(↚) **kam-hii**
    few-ENCL children dance or sing are few-*encl*

bacce naacte haĩ aur **kam-hii** **bacce** gaate haĩ
children dance are and few-**encl** children sing are
'Few children dance or sing →(↚) few children dance and few children sing'

b. **aadhe** **se** **kam** bhaaratiya jaapaanii bol yaa paḍh
half from less Indians Japanese speak or read
sakte haĩ →(↚) **aadhe** **se** **kam** bhaaratiya jaapaanii
can are half from less Indians Japanese
bol sakte haĩ aur **aadhe** **se** **kam** bhaaratiya jaapaanii
speak can are and half from less Indians Japanese
paḍh sakte haĩ
read can are
'Less than half Indians can speak or read Japanese →(↚) less than half Indians can speak Japanese and less than half Indians can read Japanese.'

By contrast, the expressions **agar**…, 'if…', **PN nahĩĩ**, 'not PN', where PN is a proper name, and **sirf NP**, 'only NP', exhibit anti-additivity and not anti-morphicity.

18. a. mujhe bahut dukh hogaa **agar** tum-ne sharaab yaa
me-to much sadness will-be if you-*erg* alcohol or
sigareṭ piinii shuruu kii ↔ mujhe bahut dukh hogaa
cigarette drink begin do me-to much sadness will-be
agar tum-ne sharaab piinii shuruu kii aur agar tum-ne
if you-*erg* alcohol drink begin do and if you-*erg*
sigareṭ piinii shuruu kii
cigarette drink begin do
'I'll be very unhappy if you start drinking or smoking ↔ I'll be very unhappy if you start drinking and if you start smoking.'

b. mujhe bahut dukh hogaa **agar** tum-ne sharaab aur
me-to much sadness will-be if you-*erg* alcohol and
sigareṭ piinii shuruu kii ↮ mujhe bahut dukh
cigarette drink begin do me-to much sadness
hogaa **agar** tum-ne sharaab piinii shuruu kii yaa **agar**
will-be if you-*erg* alcohol drink begin do or if
tum-ne sigareṭ piinii shuruu kii
you-*erg* cigarette drink begin do
'I'll be very unhappy if you start drinking and smoking ↮ I'll be very unhappy if you start drinking or if you start smoking.'

19. a. **samiir** **nahĩĩ** naactaa yaa gaataa ↔ **samiir** **nahĩĩ** naactaa hai
Samir not dance or sing Samir not dance is
aur **samiir** **nahĩĩ** gaataa hai
and Samir not sing is

(Lit.) 'Not Samir dances or sings ↔ not Samir dances and not Samir sings.'

b. **samiir nahĩĩ** naactaa aur gaataa ↔ **samiir nahĩĩ** naactaa
Samir not dance and sing Samir not dance
hai yaa **samiir nahĩĩ** gaataa hai
is or Samir not sing is
(Lit.) 'Not Samir dances and sings ↔ not Samir dances or not Samir sings.'

20. a. **sirf ravii** jaapaanii bol yaa paḍh saktaa hai ↔ **sirf**
only Ravi Japanese speak or read can are only
ravii jaapaanii bol saktaa hai aur **sirf ravii** jaapaanii
Ravi Japanese speak can are and only Ravi Japanese
paḍh saktaa hai
read can are
'Only Ravi can speak or read Japanese ↔ only Ravi can speak Japanese and only Ravi can read Japanese.'

b. **sirf ravii** jaapaanii bol aur paḍh saktaa hai ↮ **sirf**
only Ravi Japanese speak and read can are only
ravii jaapaanii bol saktaa hai yaa **sirf ravii** jaapaanii
Ravi Japanese speak can are or only Ravi Japanese
paḍh saktaa hai
read can are
'Only Ravi can speak and read Japanese ↮ only Ravi can speak Japanese or only Ravi can read Japanese.'

Finally, Hindi **nahĩĩ** and **naa**,[4] like their English counterpart **not**, are antimorphic:

21. a. rahul naactaa yaa gaataa **nahĩĩ** ↔ rahul naactaa **nahĩĩ** hai
Rahul dances or sings not Rahul dances not is
aur rahul gaataa **nahĩĩ** haĩ
and Rahul sings not is
'Rahul does not dance or sing ↔ Rahul does not dance and Rahul does not sing.'

b. rahul naactaa aur gaataa **nahĩĩ** ↔ rahul naactaa **nahĩĩ** hai
Rahul dances and sings not Rahul dances not is
yaa rahul gaataa **nahĩĩ** haĩ
or Rahul sings not is
'Rahul does not dance or sing ↔ Rahul does not dance and Rahul does not sing.'

Thus it is clear that in Hindi the three kinds of downward entailing expressions (i.e. monotone decreasing, anti-additive, and antimorphic) discussed in the case of English. Let us now look at the behavior of several Hindi NPIs in these licensing environments.

■ 2.2. 'Weak', 'Medium' and 'Strong' NPIs in Hindi

The grammaticality judgments presented here have been gathered by means of a questionnaire that 89 native speakers of Hindi responded to.[5] The intention here is to provide an empirically sound basis for determining the Hindi facts. However, it is clear that a sample of 89 is far too small[6] to allow any categorical assertions about the judgments presented here, and this fact of statistics is complicated by the slippery problem of defining 'native-speaker-hood' for Hindi, or of defining the language Hindi itself (see, for example, the discussion in Singh and Agnihotri 1997: 15–19). These constraints force us to limit ourselves to saying that the responses, presented below, of the 89 informants constitute a basis for a working hypothesis that remains to be confirmed through a much larger survey.

The sentences were evaluated by each informant on a four-point scale, where a score of 4 means that the sentence is perfectly grammatical, and 1 indicates clear ungrammaticality. The mean was computed of the score for each sentence, and this mean score is presented at the beginning of each sentence below, in square brackets. Due to the large number of sentences involved, only those were included in the questionnaire that were not clearly ungrammatical or grammatical in my opinion. Thus, among the sentences given below are some that have no mean score but a '*' or '✓', signaling ungrammaticality and ungrammaticality, respectively; this is because these sentences were not included in the questionnaire as their grammatical status was judged by me to be unproblematic. Finally, only the main results obtained through the questionnaire are presented here for reasons of space.

With these caveats in mind, we turn to the data.

2.2.1 *Hindi NPIs in negative contexts*

The discussion centers around the following three NPIs, which are illustrative of the behavior of NPIs in Hindi in general (see Vasishth [1997]):

- *sir pair (bhii/tak) samajh aanaa*, 'to make (even) head or tail of'.
- *tinkaa (bhii/tak) hilaanaa*, 'to lift (even) a finger'.
- *uf (bhii/tak) karnaa*, 'to complain (even) a bit'.

In each of the following sets of examples, I have considered each of the above three NPIs in the three distinct downward entailing contexts: monotone decreasing, anti-additive, and antimorphic. Moreover, each NPI is considered successively in its three possible *incarnations* (cf. Vasishth 1997): in its *focused incarnations*, which consist of the NPI's occurrence with the focus particle em *-bhii*, 'even', 'also' or with the focus particle em *-tak*, 'even', 'until'; and in its *bare incarnation*, i.e. its occurrence without either of these focus particles. Thus, each of these three NPIs gives us three sentence sets, with each set having one of the three kinds of licensors. For the reader's convenience I provide at the beginning of each set the name of the licensor being used: monotone decreasing, anti-additive, or antimorphic. Furthermore, each sentence set has three sentences each, corresponding to the three incarnations of the NPIs: NPI *-bhii*, NPI *-tak*, and the bare NPI.

So, to begin with, *sir-pair*, the first NPI to be considered, is first considered in its three incarnations in a monotone decreasing context, **kam-hii log**, 'few people'.

22. Monotone decreasing context
    a. * **kam-hii logõ-ko** us kitaab-kaa *sir-pair-bhii*
    few-*encl* people-*acc* that book-of head or foot-even
    samajh aayaa
    understand came
    (Lit.) 'Few people understood head or tail of that book.'
    b. * **kam-hii logõ-ko** us kitaab-kaa *sir-pair-tak*
    few-*encl* people-*acc* that book-of head or foot-even
    samajh aayaa
    understand came
    (Lit.) 'Few people understood head or tail of that book.'
    c. [3.2] **kam-hii logõ-ko** us kitaab-kaa *sir-pair*
    few-*encl* people-*acc* that book-of head or foot
    samajh aayaa
    understand came
    (Lit.) 'Few people understood head or tail of that book.'

Leaving the analysis of the results given above for later, next consider the same NPI in the anti-additive context **agar**, 'if'.

23. Anti-additive context
    a. * **agar** tumhe us kitaab-kaa *sir-pair-bhii* samajh
    if you-to that book-of head or foot-even understand
    aayaa ho to mujhe samjhaaoo
    came become-*subj* then me-to explain-*imp*
    'If you have understood anything at all about that book, please explain it to me.'
    b. * **agar** tumhe us kitaab-kaa *sir-pair-tak* samajh
    if you-to that book-of head or foot-even understand
    aayaa ho to mujhe samjhaaoo
    came become-*subj* then me-to explain-*imp*
    'If you have understood anything at all about that book, please explain it to me.'
    c. [3.4] **agar** tumhe us kitaab-kaa *sir-pair* samajh
    if you-to that book-of head or foot understand
    aayaa ho to mujhe samjhaaoo
    came become-*subj* then me-to explain-*imp*

'If you have understood anything at all about that book, please explain it to me.'

The last sentence set for this NPI consists of its three incarnations in the antimorphic context **nahĩĩ**, or **naa**, both meaning 'not'.

24. Antimorphic context

a. [3.3] mujhe us kitaab-kaa *sir-pair-bhii* **nahĩĩ** samajh
me to that book of head or foot even not understand
aayaa
came
'I couldn't make head or tail out of that book.'

b. [3.1] mujhe us kitaab-kaa *sir-pair-tak* **nahĩĩ** samajh
me-to that book-of head or foot-even not understand
aayaa
came
'I couldn't make head or tail out of that book.'

c. [2.7] mujhe us kitaab-kaa *sir-pair* **nahĩĩ** samajh
me-to that book-of head or foot not understand
aayaa
came
'I couldn't make head or tail out of that book.'

Similarly, the second NPI, *tinkaa hilaana*, 'lift a finger', is presented next.

25. Monotone decreasing context

a. [2.3] **kam-hii laḍke** ghar-me *tinkaa-bhii hilaatee* haĩ
few-*encl* boys home-at lift a finger-even are
'Few boys ever lift a finger (to help) in the house.'

b. [2.5] **kam-hii laḍke** ghar-me *tinkaa-tak hilaatee* haĩ
few-*encl* boys home-at lift a finger-even are
'Few boys ever lift a finger (to help) in the house.'

c. [2.8] **kam-hii laḍke** ghar-m' *tinkaa hilaatee* haĩ
few-*encl* boys home-at lift a finger are
'Few boys ever lift a finger (to help) in the house.'

26. Anti-additive context

a. [3.5] agar ramesh-ne karobar-mẽ madad karne-ke liye
if Ramesh-*erg* business-in help doing for
tinkaa-bhii hilaayaa hotaa to maĩ use jaidaad-kaa
lifted a finger-even had then I him property-of
hissedaar maanne-ko taiyaar hotaa, lekin us-ne
partner believe-*acc* ready would-be but he-*erg*
hamaarii madad kabhii-bhii nahĩĩ kii
our help never not did
'I would agree to have Ramesh as one of the beneficiaries of the business if he had ever lifted a finger to help; but he never helped us even once.'

b. [3.2] **agar** ramesh-ne karobar-mẽ madad karne-ke liye
if Ramesh-*erg* business-in help doing for
tinkaa-tak hilaayaa hotaa to maĩ use jaidaad-kaa hissedaar
lifted a finger-even had then I him property-of partner
maanne-ko taiyaar hotaa, lekin us-ne hamaarii madad
believe-*acc* ready would-be but he-*erg* our help
kabhii-bhii nahĩĩ kii
never not did
'I would agree to have Ramesh as one of the beneficiaries of the business if he had ever lifted a finger to help; but he never helped us even once.'

c. [2.4] agar ramesh-ne karobar-mẽ madad karne-ke liye
if Ramesh-*erg* business-in help doing for
tinkaa hilaayaa hotaa to maĩ use jaidaad-kaa hissedaar
lifted a finger had then I him property-of partner
maanne-ko taiyaar hotaa, lekin us-ne hamaarii madad
believe-*acc* ready would-be but he-*erg* our help
kabhii-bhii nahĩĩ kii
never not did
'I would agree to have Ramesh as one of the beneficiaries of the business if he had ever lifted a finger to help; but he never helped us even once.'

27. Antimorphic context

a. [3.2] ravii-kii bahin-kii shaadii-mẽ saaraa ghar
Ravi-of sister-of marriage-in whole house
kaam-mẽlagaa thaa lekin us-ne *tinkaa-bhii* **naa** em
work-in engrossed was but he-*erg* lift a finger-even not
hilaayaa
moved
'Everyone was busily preparing for Ravi's sister's wedding but he didn't lift a finger to help.'

b. [3.2] ravii-kii bahin-kii shaadii-mẽ saaraa ghar
Ravi-of sister-of marriage-in whole house
kaam-mẽlagaa thaa lekin us-ne *tinkaa-tak*
work-in engrossed was but he-*erg* lift a finger-even
naa em *hilaayaa*
not moved
'Everyone was busily preparing for Ravi's sister's wedding but he didn't lift a finger to help.'

c. [2.6] ravii-kii bahin-kii shaadii-mẽ saaraa ghar
Ravi-of sister-of marriage-in whole house
kaam-mẽlagaa thaa lekin us-ne *tinkaa* **naa** em
work-in engrossed was but he-*erg* lift a finger not
hilaayaa
moved

'Everyone was busily preparing for Ravi's sister's wedding but he didn't lift a finger to help.'

Finally, the last data set concerns the three incarnations of the NPI *uf karnaa*, 'to blink an eyelid' or 'to complain a bit'.

28. Monotone decreasing context

a. [2.2] **kam-hii maẽ** apnii santaan-ko jang-mẽ
few-*encl* mothers self's progeny-*acc* war-in
khone-par *uf-bhii kartĩĩ* haĩ
lose-on complain-even are
'Few mothers complain upon losing their progeny in war.'

b. [2.4] **kam-hii maẽ** apnii santaan-ko jang-mẽ
few-*encl* mothers self's progeny-*acc* war-in
khone-par *uf-tak kartĩĩ* haĩ
lose-on complain-even are
'Few mothers complain upon losing their progeny in war.'

c. [2.8] **kam-hii maẽ** apnii santaan-ko jang-mẽ
few-*encl* mothers self's progeny-*acc* war-in
khone-par *uf kartĩĩ* haĩ
lose-on complain are
'Few mothers complain upon losing their progeny in war.'

29. Anti-additive context

a. [3.4] **agar** sipaahii cot lagne par *uf-bhii kare* to vo
if soldier hurt get on complains-even then he
kamzor maanaa jaataa hai
weak believed go is
'If a soldier makes the smallest sound on getting hurt, he is regarded as a coward.'

b. [3.3] **agar** sipaahii cot lagne par *uf-tak kare* to vo
if soldier hurt get on complains-even then he
kamzor maanaa jaataa hai
weak believed go is
'If a soldier makes the smallest sound on getting hurt, he is regarded as a coward.'

c. [3.0] **agar** sipaahii cot lagne par *uf kare* to vo
if soldier hurt get on complains then he
kamzor maanaa jaataa hai
weak believed go is
'If a soldier makes the smallest sound on getting hurt, he is regarded as a coward.'

30. Antimorphic context

a. [3.1] jamiilaa-kaa laḍkaa jang-mẽ maaraa gayaa lekin
Jamila-of son war-in killed went but

us-ne *uf-bhii* **naa** kii
she-*erg* complain-even not did
'Jamila's son was killed in (the) war but she didn't bat an eyelid.'

b. [3.6] jamiilaa-kaa laḍkaa jang-mẽ maaraa gayaa lekin
Jamila-of son war-in killed went but
us-ne *uf-tak* **naa** kii
she-*erg* complain-even not did
'Jamila's son was killed in (the) war but she didn't bat an eyelid.'

c. [3.2] jamiilaa-kaa laḍkaa jang-mẽ maaraa gayaa lekin
Jamila-of son war-in killed went but
us-ne *uf* **naa** kii
she-*erg* complain not did
'Jamila's son was killed in (the) war but she didn't bat an eyelid.'

The above data present an interesting pattern regarding grammaticality judgments which I summarize below for ease of exposition and ease of reference.

Table 3: *sir-pair*

Context	*Monotone decreasing*	*Anti-additive*	*Antimorphic*
1. *sir-pair-bhii*	*	*	3.3
2. *sir-pair-tak*	*	*	3.1
3. *sir-pair*	3.2	3.4	2.7

Table 4: *tinkaa*

Context	*Monotone decreasing*	*Anti-additive*	*Antimorphic*
1. *tinkaa-bii*	2.3	3.5	3.2
2. *tinkaa-tak*	2.5	3.2	3.2
3. *tinkaa*	2.8	2.4	2.6

Table 5: *uf karnaa*

Context	*Monotone decreasing*	*Anti-additive*	*Antimorphic*
1. *uf-bhii*	2.2	3.4	3.1
2. *uf-tak*	2.4	3.3	3.6
3. *uf*	2.5	3.0	3.2

First of all, notice in Table 3 that the NPI *sir-pair* in its bare form is greatly preferred in the monotone decreasing and anti-additive contexts (row 3), but in its other incarnations, i.e. with one of the focus particles attached, this NPI is accepted only in the antimorphic context (rows 1 and 2). Comparing the columns, the monotone decreasing and anti-additive columns show that the bare incarnation is the only acceptable one, while the antimorphic column indicates that the focused incarnations are preferred to the bare one.

One way of interpreting these results is as follows. Consider first the fact that the three kinds of downward entailing contexts may be regarded as three different degrees of strength of negativity, with monotone decreasing contexts being 'weakly negative contexts', and antimorphic ones being the 'strongest negative contexts' (cf. Jespersen 1917). With negative contexts taken in this manner, one can then make the following assertions, based on the above comparison of the rows and columns in Table 3.

Fact 1: The stronger the negative context, the greater the preference for a focused incarnation of an NPI.

Fact 2: The weaker the negative context, the greater the preference for the bare incarnation of an NPI.

It turns out that these licensing principles for the NPI *sir-pair* are supported by the other two NPIs examined, with some further interesting variations.

Consider the second NPI, *tinkaa hilaanaa*, 'to lift a finger'. As shown in Table 4, this NPI in its bare incarnation is not too well-received in any of the three downward entailing contexts (see row 3), but is less unacceptable in the weaker negative context (i.e. the monotone decreasing context) than in the stronger ones. Second, the stronger the negative context, the greater the acceptability of the focused incarnations of this NPI (see rows 1 and 2 of Table 4). Moreover, comparing the columns, one finds that the bare incarnation is the most acceptable in the monotone decreasing (weaker negative) context, and that in the anti-additive and antimorphic (stronger negative) contexts the focused incarnations are preferred over the bare one.

These facts are in harmony with facts 1 and 2 given above.

However, *tinkaa hilaanaa* and *sir-pair* do not behave exactly similarly: note that *tinkaa hilaanaa* occurs less happily in its bare incarnation than *sir-pair* (compare rows 3 of Tables 3 and 4).

Finally, we turn to the third NPI *uf karnaa* in Table 5. This NPI behaves differently again from the above two NPIs in that the stronger the negative context, the em *greater* the acceptability of the bare incarnation (see row 3). This indicates that fact 2 is either not valid or is constrained by some other factor. It appears that the latter is the case and that fact 2 is not invalidated but needs revision. First of all, consider rows 1 and 2 of Table 5. Here, as fact 1 predicts, the stronger the negative context, the greater the acceptability of a focused incarnation. These facts in Table 5 together indicate that *uf karnaa* is an NPI that is what I shall call *inherently bare*: it *abhors* the presence of focus particles.[7] Furthermore, unlike the first two NPIs, *uf karnaa* conforms to the van der Wouden distinction as it is a 'medium' NPI (compare row 3 in Table 5 with rows 3 in Tables 3 and 4). This accounts for its behavior in row 3 in Table 5. However, if a focus particle em *does* occur with this inherently bare NPI, it is preferred in this focused incarnation in a stronger negative context, and rejected in a weak negative context.

If the above account for *uf karnaa* is along the right lines, then we need to amend fact 2 as follows.

Fact 2': For all non-inherently bare NPIs, the weaker the negative context, the greater the preference for the bare incarnation of an NPI.

2.2.2 *Some predictions of this account*

If Facts 1 and 2' are indeed true for Hindi, then we would expect that other NPIs would conform to them as well. This turns out to be the case.

The first NPI we look at is *ṭas-se mas honaa*, 'to budge an inch'.

This NPI behaves like (and therefore is) an inherently bare NPI, and moreover is a 'weak' NPI on van der Wouden's definition in (15), as should be evident from the following judgments. It is 'weak' because it is licensed in all the three downward entailing contexts:

31. a. [3.4] **kam-hii** **log** ramesh-ko girte dekhkar
few-*encl* people Ramesh-*acc* falling seeing
ṭas-se mas hue
budge an inch became
'Few people budged an inch (to help) on seeing Ramesh fall.'
b. [3.1] maĩ tumhe golii maar duungaa **agar** tum
I you-to bullet hit will if you
ṭas-se mas hue
budge an inch become
'I will kill you if you move an inch.'
c. ✓ ramesh-ne bacce-ko nadii-mẽ girte dekhaa lekin
Ramesh-*erg* child-*acc* river-in falling saw but
vo *ṭas-se mas* **naa** huaa
he budge an inch not became
'Ramesh saw the child fall into the river but he didn't lift a finger (to help).'

Recall that inherently bare NPIs abhor focused incarnations, but if the em *do* appear in their focused incarnations, then the stronger the negative context, the great the degree of acceptability of the NPI.

This is exactly how *ṭas-se mas* behaves, as the following examples show.

32. Monotone decreasing context
a. [2.6] **kam-hii** **log** ramesh-ko girte dekhkar
few-*encl* people Ramesh-acc falling seeing
ṭas-se mas-bhii hue
budge an inch-even became
'Few people budged an inch (to help) on seeing Ramesh fall.'
b. [2.7] **kam-hii** **log** ramesh-ko girte dekhkar
few-*encl* people Ramesh-acc falling seeing

ṭas-se mas-tak hue
budge an inch-even became
'Few people budged an inch (to help) on seeing Ramesh fall.'

c. [3.4] **kam-hii log** rameshko girte dekhkar
few-*encl* people Ramesh-acc falling seeing
ṭas-se mas hue
budge an inch became
'Few people budged an inch (to help) on seeing Ramesh fall.'

33. Anti-additive context

a. [3.2] maĩ tumhe golii maar duungaa **agar** tum
I you-to bullet hit will if you
ṭas-se mas *bhii* hue
budge an inch even become
'I will kill you if you move an inch.'

b. [2.8] maĩ tumhe golii maar duungaa **agar** tum
I you-to bullet hit will if you
ṭas-se mas *tak* hue
budge an inch even become
'I will kill you if you move an inch.'

c. [3.1] maĩ tumhe golii maar duungaa **agar** tum
I you-to bullet hit will if you
ṭas-se mas hue
budge an inch become
'I will kill you if you move an inch.'

34. Antimorphic context

a. ✓ ramesh-ne bacce-ko nadii-mẽ girte dekhaa lekin vo
Ramesh-*erg* child-*acc* river-in falling saw but he
ṭas-se mas-bhii **naa** huaa
budge an inch-even not became
'Ramesh saw the child fall into the river but he didn't lift a finger (to help).'

b. [3.3] ramesh-ne bacce-ko nadii-mẽ girte dekhaa lekin vo
Ramesh-*erg* child-*acc* river-in falling saw but he
ṭas-se mas-tak **naa** huaa
budge an inch-even not became
'Ramesh saw the child fall into the river but he didn't lift a finger (to help).'

c. ✓ ramesh-ne bacce-ko nadii-mẽ girte dekhaa lekin vo
Ramesh-*erg* child-*acc* river-in falling saw but he
ṭas-se mas **naa** huaa
budge an inch not became
'Ramesh saw the child fall into the river but he didn't lift a finger (to help).'

In (32), both the *-bhii* and *-tak* focused incarnations are degraded compared to the bare incarnation when they appear in a monotone decreasing context, but from (33) and (34) it is clear that the stronger the negative context, the greater the acceptability of the focused incarnations. I summarize these results for *ṭas-se mas* in Table 6 below.

Table 6: *ṭas-se mas*

Context	*Monotone decreasing*	*Anti–additive*	*Antimorphic*
1. *ṭas-se mas-bhii*	2.6	3.2	✓
2. *ṭas-se mas -tak*	2.7	2.8	3.3
3. *ṭas-se mas*	3.4	3.1	✓

Here, in the monotone decreasing column the bare incarnation is the most acceptable, and comparing the rows shows that the stronger the negative context, the greater the preference for the focused incarnations.

Other NPIs also behave similarly. Next, I present four other NPIs in monotone decreasing contexts to show that the prediction that weaker negative contexts prefer the bare incarnation of an NPI over the focused one is borne out.

This time I summarize the results first in a table so that the reader can confirm the results by comparing them with the examples given below.

Table 7: Four NPIs in a monotone decreasing context

NPI	*muh lagaanaa*	*muh-lagnaa*	*muh-kholnaa*	*juutii-ki no-bark*
1. *-bhii*	2.5	2.6	2.6	2.7
2. *-tak*	2.6	2.5	2.8	2.7
3. Bare	3.5	3.6	3.7	3.1

35. a. [2.5] us desh-mẽ **kam-hii log** sharaab-ko em
that country-in few-*encl* people alcohol-*acc*
muh-bhii lagaate haĩ
touch-even are
'In that country few people drink alcohol.'

b. [2.6] us desh-mẽ **kam-hii log** sharaab-ko em
that country-in few-*encl* people alcohol-*acc*
muh-tak lagaate haĩ
touch-even are
'In that country few people drink alcohol.'

c. [3.5] us desh-mẽ **kam-hii log** sharaab-ko em
that country-in few-*encl* people
muh lagaate haĩ
alcohol-*acc* touch are
'In that country few people drink alcohol.'

36. a. [2.6] **kam-hii log** us bevakuuf-ke *muh-bhii lagte* haĩ

few-*encl* people that fool-of even-interact with are

'Few people interact with that fool.'

b. [2.5] **kam-hii log** us bevakuuf-ke *muh-tak lagte* haĩ

few-*encl* people that fool-of even-interact with are

'Few people interact with that fool.'

c. [3.6] **kam-hii log** us bevakuuf-ke *muh lagte* haĩ

few-*encl* people that fool-of interact with are

'Few people interact with that fool.'

37. a. [2.6] us zamaane-mẽ **kam-hii log** apne pitaa-ke

that age-in few-*encl* people self's father-of

saamne *muh-bhii kholte* thee

in front of even-open their mouth were

'In those days few people ever opened their mouth in front of their father.'

b. [2.8] us zamaane-mẽ **kam-hii log** apne pitaa-ke

that age-in few-*encl* people self's father-of

saamne *muh-tak kholte* thee

in front of even-open their mouth were

'In those days few people ever opened their mouth in front of their father.'

c. [3.7] us zamaane-mẽ **kam-hii log** apne pitaa-ke

that age-in few-*encl* people self's father-of

saamne *muh kholte* thee

in front of open their mouth were

'In those days few people ever opened their mouth in front of their father.'

38. a. [2.7] kaam-ke maamle-mẽ praṇav-ke **kam-hii sahyogii**

work-of regarding-in Pravan-of few-*encl* colleagues

uski em *juutii-kii no-bark-ke* em *baraabar-bhii* haĩ

his shoe-of tip-of equal even are

'As regards work, few of Pranav's colleagues can equal him.'

b. [2.7] kaam-ke maamle-mẽ praṇav-ke **kam-hii sahyogii**

work-of regarding-in Pranav-of few-*encl* colleagues

uski em *juutii-kii no-bark-ke* em *bhii baraabar* haĩ

his shoe-of tip-of even equal are

'As regards work, few of Pranav's colleagues can equal him.'

c. [3.1] kaam-ke maamle-mẽ praṇav-ke **kam-hii sahyogii**

work-of regarding-in Pravan-of few-*encl* colleagues

uski em *juutii-kii no-bark-ke* em *baraabar* haĩ

his shoe-of tip-of equal are

'As regards work, few of Pranav's colleagues can equal him.'

■ 3. Conclusions

Van der Wouden and others have shown that Dutch and English exhibit a clear distinction among three kinds of NPI, and that the boolean properties of the various licensors are responsible for the distinction between 'weak', 'medium', and 'strong' NPIs.

In Hindi, it seems that NPI licensors also demonstrate boolean properties parallel to those in Dutch and English. However, they constrain the appearance of NPIs in a way that is significantly different.

The analysis presented in this paper hinges upon treating Hindi NPIs as generally appearing in two distinct *incarnations*, one being a *bare incarnation* of the NPI, and the other a *focused incarnation*, and I propose that there is a class of NPIs in Hindi, which I refer to as *inherently bare NPIs*, which *abhors* their focused incarnations.

The inherently bare class of NPIs em *does* conform to van der Wouden's 'weak', 'medium' and 'strong' distinction, except that there do not seem to be any 'strong' NPIs in Hindi. In other words, in the class of inherently bare NPIs, we find only 'medium' and 'weak' ones (see the last rows of Tables 5 and 7 respectively). Second, if any member of this class of inherently bare NPIs appears in a sentence in a focused incarnation, then the stronger the negative context, the greater the acceptability of this focused incarnation.

The other NPIs, that is, the non-inherently bare NPIs, do not conform to van der Wouden's distinction in any straightforward way: for example, from Tables 3 and 4 it could be argued that *sir-pair* is a 'strong' NPI in its focused incarnation, and that *tinkaa* is a 'medium' NPI in its focused incarnation.

However, this is problematic since in row 3 of Table 3 *sir-pair* in its bare incarnation is violating the boolean behavior predicted for NPIs by van der Wouden: the fact that it is licensed in monotone decreasing and anti-additive contexts implies that it must be licensed in an antimorphic one; this follows from the relationships between the three kinds of licensors, as shown in (13). But this does not happen, as is clear from row 3 in Table 3.

Furthermore, although it could be argued that *tinkaa* is a 'medium' NPI in its focused incarnation, it would be hard to account for row 3 in Table 4, where the same logical impossibility holds as discussed in the case of *sir-pair* above.

My alternative account for these facts is that, although van der Wouden's distinctions are not supported straightforwardly in this class of non-inherently bare NPIs, these NPIs do in fact exhibit principled boolean behavior in that the weaker the negative context, the greater the preference for the bare incarnation, and conversely, the stronger the negative context, the greater the preference for the focused incarnation.

■ NOTES

1. In subsequent examples I indicate the licensing environment in **bold** and the NPIs in *italic*.
2. The discussion is limited to noun phrases as generalized quantifiers, which take the verb phrase denotation as argument. However, it is also to consider a determiner as a two-place

functor which takes the noun and verb phrase as arguments. In such case, one can than speak of downward and upward entailment applying independently to both the left and right arguments of the determiner. For example, the determiner *every* can be regarded as taking to arguments, a left argument, such as *man*, with which it forms an NP, *every man* and a right argument, such as the verb phrase *runs*, to form the sentence *every man runs*. As the reader can verify from the relatively informal characterization of monotonicity given in the text, *every* happens to be downward entailing on its left argument, but upward entailing on its right argument. In this paper, when talking of quantifiers, in the case where I describe an expression as downward entailing, it should be clear that I am referring to the monotonicity property as applying to the right argument of the *determiner* within the (generalized) quantifier in question.

3. I depart from convention in regarding the terms 'downward entailing' and 'monotone decreasing' as distinct. In this paper, monotone decreasing expressions are defined as downward entailing expressions that are *not* anti-additive or antimorphic, these last two terms being defined further on in Schema 2 and Schema 3 respectively.
4. I do not present the sentences for **naa** here for reasons of space, but this can easily be done.
5. The survey was conducted in New Delhi over a period of two weeks in December 1996, and the respondents were a heterogeneous group of educated Hindi speakers.
6. Given the fact that there are an estimated 600 million speakers of Hindi (Singh and Agnihotri 1997: 17).
7. I have shown elsewhere (Vasishth 1997) that Hindi has other such inherently bare NPIs.

■ REFERENCES

Barwise, Jon and **Robin Cooper.** 1981. Generalized quantifiers and natural languages. *Linguistics and Philosophy* 4.159–219.

Jespersen, Otto. 1917. Negation in English and Other Languages. Historisk-fololigiske Meddeleser 1 (reprinted in *Selected Writings of Otto Jespersen*, London and Tokyo: George Allen and Unwin and Sejo Publishing Company Limited, 1962). 1–151.

Klima, Edward S. 1964. Negation in English. *The structure of language*, ed. by Jerry A. Fodor and Jerrold J. Katz, 246–323. Englewood Cliffs, New Jersey: Holt Rinehart.

Ladusaw, William A. 1979. Polarity sensitivity as inherent scope relations. Austin: University of Texas dissertation.

Singh, Rajendra and **Rama Kant Agnihotri.** 1997. *Hindi Morphology.* Delhi: Motilal Banarasidass.

Vasishth, Shravan. 1997. Monotonicity constraints on negative polarity in Hindi. Proceedings of the Eighteenth South Asian Languages Analysis Roundtable.

van der Wouden, Ton. 1994. Negative contexts. Groningen: University of Groningen dissertation.

Yoshimura, Akiko. 1996. Buuru tokusei to hitei no imironteki kaisousei. Osaka Gakuin University, ms.

Zwarts, Frans. 1986. Categoricale Grammatica en Algebraïsche Semantiek. *Studie naar Negatie en Polariteit in het Nederlands.* Groningen: University of Groningen dissertation.

———. 1996. A hierarchy of negative expressions. *Negation: a notion in focus*, ed. by Heinrich Wnasing, 169–94. Berlin: Walter de Gruyter.

C

■ Regional Reports, Reviews ■ and Abstracts

Regional Reports

■ AFRICA ■

RAJEND MESTHRIE

Since linguistic research pertaining to South Asian languages in Africa is not exactly a flourishing industry this initial report will provide a survey of research up to 1996, rather than for this year alone. The country in which the most research of concern to this journal occurs is South Africa, which until it was recently overtaken by Britain had the largest extraterritorial South Asian population for over a century. Accordingly it is convenient to divide this report into a section on South Africa and elsewhere in Africa.

■ 1. Africa, Excluding South Africa

No large scale projects pertaining to South Asian languages in this area currently exist. Hromnik's book *The Indo-Africans* contains a great deal of speculation about the influence of Indian culture and languages on Africa in the prehistorical period. He cites putative sporadic similarities linking the two sets of languages, but is unable to suggest even a semblance of a system of correspondences. Accordingly it is hard not to agree with reviewers like Hall and Borland (1982) who call into question the archaeological and linguistic basis of the work.

Two informative articles on the South Asian community in Kenya and its linguistic repertoire can be found in Neale (1974a and b). Arabic in Africa is, of course, the subject of a fair amount of research. It is not appropriate to give an overview of that research here, since there is not a direct South Asian connection involved (except to mention that Koranic Arabic continues to form an important part of the repertoire of South Asians of Islamic faith in Africa).

■ 2. South Africa

Prior to the 1990s most research into the South Asian languages of South Africa was confined to dissertations on education focusing on the acquisition of English, e.g. Kuppusamy (1946) and Bughwan (1970), a *précis* of the latter appearing as Bughwan (1979). Work that draws upon, and falls directly into the field of Linguistics (more specifically, Sociolinguistics), dates to 1985, when Mesthrie's 'A history of the Bhojpuri (or "Hindi") language in South Africa' appeared (University of Cape Town Ph.D. dissertation). This work was subsequently published in revised form as Mesthrie (1992a). It was followed by full-length studies of Urdu, Telugu, Gujarati and to a lesser extent, Tamil in South Africa. The works concerned are as follows:

Urdu: Aziz, A.K. 1988. An investigation into the factors governing the persistence of Urdu as a minority language in South Africa. University of South Africa M.A. thesis.
Telugu: Prabhakaran 1991. The Telugu language and its influence on the cultural lives of the Hindu 'Pravasandhras' in South Africa. University of Durban-Westville Ph.D. dissertation (revised and published by the author as *A Language Challenged.*)
Gujarati: Desai, U.K. 1992. The Gujarati language amongst Gujarati-speaking Hindus in Natal. University of Durban–Westville M.A. thesis.
Tamil: Murugan (in progress)

Two unpublished reports on Tamil (Mesthrie and Pillay 1992) and Telugu (Prabhakaran 1996) are lodged with the Centre for Science Development. Mesthrie and Prabhakaran have individually published a number of articles in the 1990s. Apart from his work on Bhojpuri, Mesthrie has covered topics including Gandhi and language politics in South Africa (1993), reversing language shift (1995a), and overviews of the situation pertaining to South Asian languages in South Africa (1995b). Prabhakaran has published a series of articles on topics pertaining to language contact, change and shift in Telugu in the *South Africa Journal of Linguistics* (1994). *The Journal of the Indological Society of Southern Africa* has devoted its latest volume (V of 1996) to topics pertaining to language. The contents page gives an indication of the dominant paradigm within which scholars are working:

The religio-cultural heritage of Hindu South Africans (R. Sitaram)
Generation as a factor in the obsolescence of the Gujarati language in South Africa (U.K. Desai)
Hindi in South Africa—a sociolinguistic perspective (U.D. Shukla)
The Sanskrit heritage in South Africa—domains of usage and efforts towards maintenance (S. Panday)
Shift and maintenance of the Tamil language in Natal (G. Murugan)
Retention of the Tamil language through the "Tevaram" among Natal Tamils (S. Subramaniyan)
Dravidian languages in contact—changes on South African Telugu (V. Prabhakaran)
Naitali—South African Bhojpuri (B. Rambilass).

With the transition to democracy and the changes in education and general public policy a great deal of attention has been paid to policy work pertaining to Indian languages in the country. The Institute of Indian languages based in Durban (under the current chairpersonship of Veena Lutchman of the Department of Indian languages at the University of Durban–Westville) has a repository of materials pertaining to the place of Indian languages in the post-apartheid curriculum, as well as memoranda and press releases issued by the Institute. Another resource is the LANGTAG (Language Task Action Group) report to the Minister of Arts, Culture, Science and Technology in 1996 on Heritage languages in South Africa, which contains information on *inter alia* Chinese, Indian languages and Malay.

South African Indian English has been studied extensively by Mesthrie in a series of articles and two books (1992b and c). Bughwan's dissertation (1970) is an important (if prescriptive) account of English usage amongst Indians; whilst Crossley (1988) is a dissertation attempting to devise a list of the main grammatical features of the sociolect for clinical purposes.

■ REFERENCES

(excluding items fully referenced above)

Bughwan, D. 1970. An investigation into the use of English by the Indians in South Africa, with special reference to Natal. Ph.D. thesis. University of South Africa.

———. 1979. Language practices. *South Africa's Indians: the Evolution of a Minority*, ed. by B. Pachai, 161–518. Washington: University Press of America.

Crossley S. 1988. The syntactic features of South African Indian English among students in Natal, with regard to use and attitudes towards usage. University of Durban–Westville. Master of Speech Pathology thesis.

Hromnik, C.A. 1981. *Indo-Africa: towards a new understanding of the history of sub-Saharan Africa.* Cape Town: Juta.

Hall M. and **Borland, C.H.** 1982. The Indian connection: an assessment of Hromnik's "Indo-Africa". *South African Archaeological Bulletin* 37.75–80.

Kuppusami, C. 1946. Indian education in Natal, 1860–1946. University of South Africa. M.Ed. dissertation.

LANGTAG 1996. Towards a national language plan for South Africa (Final report of the Language Plan Task Group—LANGTAG presented to the Minister of Arts, Culture, Science and Technology.).

Mesthrie, R. 1992a. *Language in indenture: a sociolinguistic history of Bhojpuri-Hindi in South Africa.* London: Routledge.

———. 1992b. *A lexicon of South African Indian English.* Leeds: Peepal Tree.

———. 1992c. *English in language shift: the history, structure and sociolinguistics of South African Indian English.* Cambridge: Cambridge University Press.

———. 1993. Gandhi and language politics. *Bua* 8(4).4–7.

———. 1995a. Reversing language shift: problems and possibilities. *Journal of the Indological Society of Southern Africa* 2 and 3.1–20.

———. 1995b. Language change, survival, decline: Indian languages in South Africa. *Language and Social History: studies in South African Sociolinguistics*, ed. by R. Mesthrie, 116–28. Cape Town: David Philip.

Mesthrie, R. and **Pillay, B.** 1992. South African Tamil: history, structure, change, obsolescence. Unpublished report submitted to the Centre for Science Development.

Neale, B. 1974a. Kenya's Asian languages. *Language in Kenya*, ed. by W.H. Whiteley, 69–86. Nairobi: Oxford University Press.

———. 1974b. Language use among the Asian communities. *Language in Kenya*, ed. by W.H. Whiteley, 263–317. Nairobi: Oxford University Press.

Prabhakaran V. 1994. Tamil lexical borrowings in South African Telugu. *South African Journal of Linguistics* 12(1).26–32.

———. 1996. A sociolinguistic analysis of South African Telugu: History, structure, change, obsolescence. Unpublished report submitted to the Centre for Science Development.

■ EUROPE ■

JOHN PETERSON

Most research currently being done in Europe falls into one of the following categories: 1. Himalayan Languages, 2. Hindi/Urdu, 3. Historical Linguistics, 4. Dravidian Languages. As far too much research is currently being conducted at European universities on South Asian languages to include everything in such a brief bibliography, a decision had to be made as to which articles and books were to be included. Thus, a thematic approach has been taken here. Most works which have appeared since 1990 belonging to topics 1 and 2 above are listed. Even here, however, not all information could be included—generally reviews have not been included. Next year's bibliography will then focus on Historical Linguistics and Dravidian Languages, as well as newer research in other categories.

■ Himalayan Language Research

Work on Himalayan languages is being conducted in many European countries, above all in the Netherlands, the United Kingdom, France and Germany. Especially worth mentioning is the "Himalaya–talenproject—Himalayan Languages Project" in Leiden. Information on this project is available under

http: //iias.leidenuniv.nl: 80/host/himalaya

A. Phonology

Driem, George van. 1990. The fall and rise of the phoneme /r/ in Eastern Kiranti. *BSOAS* LIII (1).83–86.

———. 1994. The phonologies of Dzongkha and the Bhutanese liturgical language. *Zentralasiatische Studien* 24.36–44.

B. Morphology

Driem, George van. 1990. An exploration of Proto-Kiranti verbal morphology. *AL* 22.27–48.

Driem, George van. 1991. Bahing and the Proto-Kiranti verb. *BSOAS* LIV (2).336–56.
———. 1991. Tangut verbal agreement and the patient category in Tibeto-Burman. *BSOAS* LIV (3).520–34.
———. 1992. Le proto-kiranti revisité, morphologie verbale du lohorung [in French: Proto-Kiranti revisited: The verbal morphology of Lohorung]. *AL* 21.33–76.
———. 1993a. The Proto-Tibeto-Burman verbal agreement system. *BSOAS* LVI (2).292–334.
———. 1993b. The Newar verb in Tibeto-Burman perspective. *AL* 26.23–43.
———. 1993c. Language change, conjugational morphology and the Sino-Tibetan Urheimat. *AL* 26.45–56.
———. 1994. The Yakkha verb: interpretation and analysis of the Omruwa material (a Kiranti language of eastern Nepal). *BSOAS* LVII (2).347–55.
———. 1995. Black Mountain conjugational morphology, Proto-Tibeto-Burman morphosyntax, and the linguistic position of Chinese. *New Horizons in Tibeto-Burman Morphosyntax*, ed. by Yoshio Nishi, James Alan Matisoff and Yasuhiko Nagano (Senri Ethnological Studies 41), 229–59. Osaka: National Museum of Ethnology.
Ebert, Karen H. 1991. Inverse and pseudoinverse prefixes in Kiranti languages: evidence from Belhare, Athphare and Dungmali. *Linguistics of the Tibeto-Burman Area* 14(1).73–92.
Hansson, Gerd. 1991. Polysynthetic paradigms in Tibeto-Burman: Bantawa verb affixation. *Lingua Posnaniensis* 32–33.91–103.
Tiffou, Étienne and **Yves-Charles Morin.** 1993. Le préfixe *d-* en bourouchaski du Yasin. *PICL* 1992 (1993) 15(2).385–88.

C. *Semantics*

Hansson, Gerd, Werner Winter, Alfons K. Weidert and **D.B. Ingwaba Subba.** 1996. *A synoptic glossary of Athpare, Belhare and Yakkha with further contributions.* München: Lincom.
Kölver, Ulrike and **Iswarananda Shresthacarya.** 1994. *A dictionary of contemporary Newari. Newari—English* (with the assistance of Daya Ratna Sakya, Nirmal Man Tuladhar). Bonn: VGH Wissenschaftsverlag. (*Nepalica*, Vol. 8).
Schmidt, Ruth Laila et al. (ed.). 1993. *A practical dictionary of Modern Nepali.* Kathmandu: Ratna Sagar.(L + 1006pp.).
Toffin, Gérard. 1990. Review of *Newar towns and buildings: an illustrated dictionary*, by Niels Gutschow, Bernhard Kölver, Ishwarand Shresthacarya. NewÁrÍ-English. Sankt August VGH—Wissenschaftverlag, 1987. (Nepalica, 3) *Indo-Iranian Journal* 33(2).139–42.

D. *Sociolinguistics*

Driem, George van. 1991. Taal en identiteit: Indo-Arisch expansionisme in oostelijk Nepal [in Dutch: Language and identity: Indo-Aryan expansionism in eastern Nepal]. Bijdragen tot de Taal-, *Landen Volkenkunde* 147(1).61–73.
Hutt, Michael. 1994. Nepal: language situation. *Encyclopedia of Language and Linguistics, Vol. 5*, ed. by R.E. Asher and J.M.Y. Simpson, 2777–8. Oxford: Clarendon Press.
Tiffou, Étienne. 1992. Towards an edition of Hunza Burušaski proverbs. In collaboration with H. Berger [et al.]. *ICANAS 1986* (1992) 32.491–492.

E. *General*

Berger, Hermann. 1990. Burushaski. *Encyclopaedia Iranica, Vol. IV/6: Burial II–Calenders II*, ed. by Ehsan Yarshater, 567–68. London: Routledge and Kegan Paul.
Bickel, Balthasar. 1993. Belhare subordination and the theory of topic. *Studies in clause linkage*, ed. by Karen H. Ebert. Papers from the first Köln-Zürich Workshop.
———. 1994. Spatial operations in deixis, cognition and culture. How to orient oneself in Belhare. Working paper 28. Nijmegen: Cognitive Anthropology Research group.

Chazot, Pascal and **Evelyne Chazot.** 1996. *Parlons Népali* [in French: Let's Speak Nepali]. Paris: Editions L'Harmattan. 280pp.

Driem, George van. 1990a. Review of La langue Hayu, by Boyd Michailovsky. *BSOAS* LIII (3).565–71.

———. 1990b. À propos de La Langue Hayu par Boyd Michailovsky Cahiers de Linguistique. *Asie Orientale* XIX (2).267–85.

———. 1991a. Report on the First Linguistic Survey of Bhutan (sKad-rigs Ma-'dra-ba'i dPye-zhib-thengs Dangs-pa'i sNyan-zhu). Thimphu: Royal Government of Bhutan (27-page internal publication of the Bhutanese government).

———. 1991b. Guide to official Dzongkha Romanization (gZhung-'brel rDzong-kha Ro-man ('Dzam-ling Nub-Phyogs-pa'i Yig-thog) 'Bri-lugs Lam-ston). Thimphu: Royal Government of Bhutan (x + 104 pp.).

———. 1992a. *The grammar of Dzongkha* (rDzong-kha'i brDa-sprod-pa'i gZhung). Thimphu: Royal Government of Bhutan (xviii + 388 pp.).

———. 1992b. In quest of Mahakiranti, contributions to Nepalese studies. *Journal of the Centre of Nepal and Asian Studies of Tribhuvan University* 19 (2).241–47.

———. 1993a. Sino-Tibetaanse talen [in Dutch: Sino-Tibetan languages]. deel 21, blz. 176–77, Tibetaanse taal [in Dutch: Tibetan language]. deel 22, blz. 464, Grote Winkler Prins Encyclopedie (9e druk). Amsterdam: Uitgeversmaatschappij Argus.

———. 1993b. *A grammar of Dumi.* Berlin: Mouton de Gruyter (xx + 452 pp.).

———. 1993c. Einige Bemerkungen zum Aspekt im Limbu [in German: Several observations on aspect in Limbu]. *Linguistische Berichte* 148 (Dezember 1993). 483–89.

———. 1994. Language policy in Bhutan. *Bhutan: aspects of Culture and Development*, ed. by Michael Aris and Michael Hutt, 87–105. Gartmore: Kiscadale Publications.

———. 1995. Een eerste grammaticale verkenning van het Bumthang, een taal van Midden-Bhutan -met een overzicht van de talen en volkeren van Bhutan [in Dutch: A first grammatical exploration of Bumthang, a language of central Bhutan—with a survey of the languages and peoples of Bhutan]. Leiden: Centrum voor Niet-Westerse Studiën.

Driem, George van and **Ksenia Borisovna von Kepping.** 1991. The Tibetan transcriptions of Tangut (Hsi-hsia) Ideograms. *Linguistics of the Tibeto-Burman Area* 14(1).117–28.

Driem, George van and **Suhnu Ram Sharma.** 1996. In search of Kentum Indo-European in the Himalayas. *Indogermanische Forschungen* 101.107–46.

Ebert, Karen H. 1990. On the evidence for the relationship Kiranti-Rung. *Linguistics of the Tibeto-Burman Area* 13(1).57–78.

———. 1993. Kiranti subordination in the South Asian areal context. *Studies in Clause Linkage*, ed. by Karen H. Ebert. Papers from the First Köln-Zürich Workshop. 83–110.

———. 1994. *The structure of Kiranti languages. Comparative grammar and texts.* (ASAS, Arbeiten des Seminars für Allgemeine Sprachwissenschaft, Nr. 13). Zürich: Seminar für Allgemeine Sprachwissenschaft.

Georg, Stefan. 1996. Marphatan Thakali. Untersuchungen zur Sprache des Dorfes Marpha im Oberen Kāli-Gaṇḍali-Tal/Nepal [in German: Marphatan Thakali. Studies of the Language of the Village Marpha in the Upper Kāli-Gaṇḍali Valley/Nepal] (*LINCOM Studies in Asian Linguistics 02*). München/ Newcastle: Lincom Europa.

Hansson, Gerd. 1991. *The Rai of Eastern Nepal. Ethnic and linguistic grouping. Findings of the Linguistic Survey of Nepal*, ed. and provided with an introduction by W. Winter. Kathmandu: Linguistic Survey of Nepal and Centre for Nepal and Asian Studies.

———. 1994. Topical report: lesser-known languages in Nepal. A brief state-of-the-art report. *European Bulletin of Himalayan Research* 7.8–17.

Hutt, Michael. 1991. Unbridgeable gaps? Some reflections on the translation of Nepali literature into English. *Nepalese Linguistics* 5–8.13–25.

———. 1990. The standardisation and development of Nepali. *Language Reform, Vol. IV*, ed. by Istvan Fodor and Claude Hagège, 459–69. Hamburg: Buske Verlag.

———. 1994a. Nepali. *Encyclopedia of Language and Linguistics, Vol. 5*, ed. by R.E. Asher and J.M.Y. Simpson, 2778–9. Oxford: Clarendon Press.

———. 1994b. Review Article: Nepali dictionaries—A new contribution. *European Bulletin of Himalayan Research* 7.1–5.

———. 1997. *Modern Literary Nepali. an introductory reader.* New Delhi: Oxford University Press.

Matthews, David. 1992. *A Course in Nepali.* Second Edition. London: SOAS (iv + 344pp.).

Mazaudon, Martine and **John B. Lowe.** 1992. Reconstruction assistée par ordinateur dans les langues tibéto-birmanes [in French: Computer assisted reconstruction in the Tibeto-Burman languages]. *BSL 1991* (1992) 86(1).v–vi.

Michailovsky, Boyd. 1993. Catégories verbales et intransitivité duale en limbu. *Actances* 7.241–58.

Winter, Werner. 1991. Introduction to Gerd Hansson, *The Rai of Eastern Nepal*, pp. i–ii.

———. 1992. Diversity in Rai languages: an inspection of verb stems in selected idioms. *Lingua Posnaniensis* 34.141–56.

———. 1992. The Linguistic Survey of Nepal. *Aspects of Nepalese traditions*, ed. by Bernhard Kölver, 171–75. Stuttgart: Franz Steiner.

———. 1993. Abstract mapping. *Historische Dialektologie und Sprachwandel. Sprachatlanten und Wörterbücher. Verhandlungen des Internationalen Dialektologenkongresses Bamberg* 29.7.–4.8.1990. 258–262. Stuttgart: Franz Steiner.

Winter, Werner and **Novel Kishore Rai.** 1990. Triplicated verbal adjuncts in Bantawa. "Linguistic fiesta" Festschrift for Professor Hisao Kakehi's sixtieth birthday. 135–50. Tokyo.

■ 2. Hindi/Urdu

Work seems to be in progress in Europe on virtually all aspects of Hindi/Urdu, with the possible exception of phonology, which is notably lacking here. Perhaps the most prominent tendency at the moment is on complex predicates ("compound verbs"). Also, a number of dictionaries and language-teaching materials have appeared in the past few years.

B. Morphology

Butt, Miriam. 1995. *The structure of complex predicates in Urdu.* Stanford, CA: CSLI Publications.

C. Semantics

Balbir, Nicole and **Jagbans K.** 1992. *Dictionnaire général hindi-français— framsisiśabdakoś* [in French: General Hindi–French dictionary]. Paris: L'Asiathèque (xxxviii + 1052pp.).

Butt, Miriam and **T.H. King.** 1991. Semantic case in Urdu. Papers from the 27th Regional Meeting of the Chicago Linguistic Society (CLS) 1, ed. by L. Dobrin, L. Nichols and R. Rodriguez. 31–46.

Nespital, Helmut. 1989. Verbal aspect and lexical semantics in Indo-Aryan languages: The typology of verbal expressions ("compound verbs") and their relation to simple verbs. *StII* 15.159–96. (appeared in 1990).

———. 1997. *Dictionary of Hindi verbs/Hindī Kriya-Koś* (containing all simple and compound verbs, their lexical equivalents in English, and illustrations of their usage). Ilāhābād: Lokbhāratī Prakāśan.

D. Sociolinguistics

Balbir, Nicole. 1990. The use of speech and speech style in some Hindi novels. *Language versus dialect*, ed. by Mariola Offredi. 191–96.

E. General

Butt, Miriam. 1993a. Hindi–Urdu infinitives as NPs. *South Asian Language Review: Special Issue on Studies in Hindi–Urdu, Vol. III*, ed. by Y. Kachru, (1).51–72.

———. 1993b. Object Specificity and Agreement in Hindi/Urdu. Papers from the 29th Regional Meeting of the Chicago Linguistic Society 1, ed. by K. Beals et al., 1.89–103.

———. 1994a. Complex Predicate Scrambling. *Theoretical Perspectives on Word Order Issues in South Asian Languages*, ed. by M. Butt, T.H. King and G. Ramchand. Stanford, CA: CSLI Publications.

———. 1994b. Machine Translation and Complex Predicates. Proceedings of the Konferenze "Verarbeitung natürlicher Sprache" 94, ed. by H. Trost. Vienna: KONVENS.

———. 1995. Clause union—then and now. *Proceedings of the Formal Grammar Conference*, ESSLI, Barcelona.

Damsteegt, Theo. 1990. Hindi and Sarnami as literary languages of the East Indian Surinamese. *Language versus dialect*, ed. by Mariola Offredi, 47–63.

Gatzlaff, Margot. 1990. Das Hindi als Staats- und Unionssprache in Indien [in German: Hindi as State and Union Language in India]. *PICL 1987* (1990) 14(2).1611–14.

Mavi, Baldev Singh. 1995. *Teach yourself Hindi. An audio visual course.* Walsall (UK): B.S. Mavi. (154pp.).

McGregor, R.S. 1993. *The Oxford Hindi-English Dictionary.* Oxford/Delhi: Oxford University Press. (xx + 1084pp.).

Montaut, Annie. 1991a. La réflexivisation en hindi/urdu: "empathie" et syntaxe [in French: Reflexivization in Hindi/Urdu: "Empathy" and syntax]. *LINX* 1990/1 22.55–79.

———. 1991b. La construction passive en hindi moderne [in French: The passive construction in modern Hindi]. *BSL 1990* (1991) 85(1).91–136.

———. 1991c. Constructions objectives, subjectives et déterminatives en hindi/urdu: où les paramètres sémantiques croisent les paramètres discursifs [in French: Objective, subjective and determinative constructions in Hindi/Urdu: Where semantic parametres and discursive parametres cross]. *LINX* 24.111–32.

———. 1991d. Aspects, voix et diathèses en hindi moderne [in French: Aspects, voices and diatheses in Modern Hindi]. Paris: Soc. pour l'information grammaticale/Louva Peeters (246pp.) (Bibliothèque de l'Information grammaticale 20).

———. 1991e. On the temporal reference of some peculiar uses of the perfective forms in Modern Hindi. *Indian Linguistics 1989* (1991) 50.95–110.

Négyesi, Mária. 1991. A tehénpásztortól a taxisig—egy hindi képzö története [in Hungarian: From cowboy to taxi-driver—the hist. of a derivational suffix in Hindi]. *AULAM* 1.122–26.

Nespital, Helmut. 1990. On the relation of Hindi to its regional dialects: the impact of dialects on the Standard Language in the speech of Hindi speakers (with regard to lexical, morphological and syntactic features). *Language versus dialect*, ed. by M. Offredi. 3–23.

———. 1994a. The development of literary Urdu in Delhi in the 17th and 18th centuries with regard to changes of its language structure. *Tender Ironies, A Tribute to Lothar Lutze*. Delhi: Manohar. 302–25.

———. 1994b. Fragesätze im Hindi und Urdu [in German: Interrogative Sentences in Hindi and Urdu]. *Festschrift Georg Buddruss = Studien zur Indologie und Iranistik*, 19.173–98.

———. 1994c. Zur Bezeichnung der Determiniertheit von Substantiv-Denotaten und zur Existenz von Artikeln im Neuindischen—dargelegt anhand des Hindi und Bengali und unter Vergleich mit dem Deutschen [in German: The marking of noun-denotates as determined and the existence of articles in new Indian languages—with reference to Hindi and Bengali and in comparison to German]. *Festschrift Klaus Bruhn = Studien zur Indologie und Iranistik*, 437–53.

Offredi, Mariola. 1990. The importance of literature and the relevance of its lay themes in the formation of supraregional languages: on the relationships between Bhojpuri and Rájasthání literatures and Hindi literature. *Language versus dialect: linguistics and literary essays on*

Hindi, Tamil and Sarnami, ed. by M. Offredi. Papers from Panel 10 of the 10th European conference on Modern South Asian Studies, Venice, 28 Sep.–1 Oct. 1988. 67–101. New Delhi: Manohar.

Plukker, D.F. 1995. Leerboek Hindi (met twee geluidscassettes) tweede, herziene druk (eerste druk 1993) [in Dutch: Hindi primer (with two tapes) Sec., rev. ed. (first ed. 1993)]. Amsterdam: India Instituut (204 pp.).

Snell, Rupert. 1992. *The Hindi Classical tradition. A Braj Bhāṣā reader*. New Delhi: Heritage Publishers (xvi + 260pp.).

■ 3. Miscellaneous

The following is a listing of mostly recent or forthcoming works (including a few dissertations) which do not fall under the above mentioned. The topics here range from Historial Linguistics to Dravidian and New Indo-Aryan Languages (excluding Hindi/Urdu).

B. Morphology

Martínez García, Fco. Javier. 1996. Abouth the -n- element in Old Indian declension. *Journal of the Indological Society of Southern Africa*. 37–41.

———. 1997. Review of Eva Tichy: die Nomina agentis auf -tar- im Vedischen. Heidelberg: Winter, 1995 *Language* 1997 (in press).

D. Sociolinguistics

Walle, Lieve Van de. 1993. *Pragmatics and Classical Sanskrit: a pilot study in linguistic politeness*. Amsterdam: Benjamins. (xii + 454pp.) Revised edition of 1991 Antwerp University dissertation.

Winter, Werner. 1993. Some conditions for the survival of small languages. Ernst Håkon Jahr, ed., *Language conflict and language planning*. 299–314. Berlin/New York: Mouton de Gruyter.

E. General

Brockington, John L. 1994. Sanskrit R.E. Asher (ed.): *The Encyclopedia of Language and Linguistics, Vol. 7*, 3649–51. Oxford: Pergamon Press.

Driem, George van. 1992. Moenda talen [in Dutch: Munda languages]. deel 16, blz. 216–17, Nicobarese talen [in Dutch: Nicobarese languages]. deel 17, blz. 128, Grote Winkler Prins Encyclopedie (9e druk). Amsterdam: Uitgeversmaatschappij Argus.

Dwyer, Rachel. 1995. *Gujarati. A complete course for beginners*. London: Hodder and Stoughton. (376pp. + cassette) (Teach Yourself Books).

Ebert, Karen H. 1996. Ko±ava. München/Newcastle: Lincom Europa. (Languages of the World/Materials, 104).

Garzilli, Enrica. 1996a. One birth from the encounter between Text and Translator and the Non-Other: the Translation of the Spandasaṃdoha of Kṣemarāja. *Translating, translations, translators from India to the West* (Opera Minora, Vol. 1), ed. by E. Garzilli, 11–23. Cambridge/Mass.: Harvard Oriental Series.

———. 1996b. Introduction. *Translating, translations, translators from India to the West*, ed. by E. Garzilli. Cambridge/Mass.: Harvard Oriental Series.

———. 1996c. Review of Giorgio Renato Franci (ed.): Studi Orientali e Linguistici. Istituto di Glottologia dell'Universitá di Bologna, Nuova Serie. V, 1996 *International Journal of Tantric Studies*, http: //www.shore.net/ india/ijts/, Vol. 2, No. 2 (November 29, 1996), "New Titles".

Hansson, Geıd and **Witold Stefansk.** 1993. Polypersonalität des Verbs im eurasischen Raum. Ein typologisch-pragmatischer Querschnitt. [in German: Polypersonality of the verb in the Eurasian area: A typological-pragmatic cross-section]. (8–12 Indo-Euopean (with Indo-Aryan), 49–50 Burushaski, 25–30 Munda, 65–91 Tibeto-Burman). Torun (Poland): Uniwersytet Mikolaja Kopernika.

Jayawardena-Moser, Premalatha. 1993. Grudwortschatz Singhalesisch-Deutsch: mit einer grammatischen Übersicht [in German: *Basic Vocabulary Singhalese-German: With a Grammatical Overview*]. Wiesbaden: Harrassowitz. (xiv + 211pp.).

Lehmann, Thomas. 1993. *A Grammar of Modern Tamil.* (2nd edition) Pondicherry: Pondicherry Institute of Linguistics and Culture.

———. 1994. Grammatik des Alttamil. Unter besonderer Berücksichtigung der Cankam-Texte des Dichters Kapila [in German: *A Grammar of Old Tamil*]. Stuttgart: Franz Steiner Verlag.

Martínez García, Fco. Javier. 1992. Review of Der Yasna HaptanhÁiti, by J. Narten. *Orientalistische Literaturzeitung* 87(2).179–82.

———. 1996a. El locativo singular histerodinámico [in Spanish: *About the hysterodynamic Locative singularis*]. Veleia 13.177–83.

———. 1996b. Das HTML-Format und seine (Un)benutzbarkeit für sprachwissenschaftliche Zwecke [in German: HTML and its (un)usability for linguistic aims]. *SIMA 2.*

Nespital, Helmut. 1996a. The use of non-perfective simple verbs and of perfective verbal expressions ("compound verbs") in new Indo-Aryan languages: grammatical, lexical and pragmatic criteria for their selection. (Dieter B. Kapp, ed.) Nānā Vidhaikatā. Festschrift für Hermann Berger. (Beiträge zur Kenntnis südasiatischer Sprachen und Literaturen, 3.) 145–63. Wiesbaden: Harrassowitz.

———. 1996b. Verbal aspect in Indo-Aryan and Dravidian languages. The relation of simple verbs to verbal expression ("compound verbs"). *Berliner Indologische Studien* 9.247–314.

Pant, Mahes Raj. 1991. Jātarūpa's commentary on the Amarakosa. For the first time critically edited together with an introduction, appendices and indices. Ph.D. dissertation at the University of Hamburg, Germany. Scheduled to appear in 1997 by Motilal Banarsidass, New Delhi.

———. 1993. On the meaning of Śabdakāra. Ābdakāra. Àdarśa 1.1–9. Kathmandu: Pundit Publications.

Parpola, Asko and **Sayid Ghulam Mustafa Shah.** 1991. *Corpus of Indus Seals and Inscriptions. Vol. 2: Collections in Pakistan.* Helsinki: Suomalainen Tiedeakatemia (xxxii + 448pp.).

Parpola, Asko. 1994. *Deciphering the Indus Script.* Cambridge: Cambridge University Press (xxii + 374pp.).

Peterson, John Michael. 1995. Grammatical Relations in Páli and the emergence of ergativity in Indo-Aryan. (with German summary). Unpublished dissertation, on microfiche at the Christian-Albrechts-Universität zu Kiel, Germany (iii + 278pp.).

■ JAPAN ■

TSUYOSHI NARA

Ever since an academic agreement was formally concluded between ILCAA (Institute for the Study of Languages and Cultures of Asia and Africa, Tokyo University of Foreign Studies, of Tokyo) and CIIL (Central Institute of Indian

Languages of Mysore) in 1987, these institutes have been carrying out a joint research project whose goal is to compile bilingual dictionaries of Japanese versus certain South-Asian languages, viz. Assamese, Bengali, Hindi, Gujarati, Kashmiri, Marathi, Oriya, Punjabi, Sanskrit, Sindhi, and Urdu (Indo-Aryan family); Kannada, Malayalam, Tamil, and Telugu (Dravidian family); Santali, Mundari, Khasi (Austro-Asiatic family); Manipuri, Mizo, Kheza Naga (Tibeto-Burman family). This work is based on comparative-cum-contrastive studies of these languages aided by the computer.

So far, 15 Japanese linguists and 25 Indian linguists have been involved in this collaborative project as joint researchers assisted by roughly as many research assistants and data input operators. Every year most of the Japanese researchers visited CIIL and spent a few weeks to five months there. In return yearly two Indian researchers visited ILCAA and spent a few weeks to 12 months in Japan.

In connection with this project, ILCAA issued some monographs and a series of annual reports including many papers by these researchers. During one year's stay in Japan, Dr. B.B. Rajapurohit of CIIL made all the fonts of scripts of Kannada, Telugu and Malayalam for the main frame computer in ILCAA. A contrastive word-list of Tamil, Kannada and Malayalam was published by Takanobu Takahashi, Taro Iemoto, Hiroshi Yamashita, Jun Takashima, Kazuhiko Machida and Makoto Minegishi (Annual Report on CIIL–ILCAA Joint Research Project Vol. 5, ILCAA, 1994–5: 81–145.

A Hindi–Japanese machine-readable dictionary developed by Kazuhiko Machida, Associate Professor at ILCAA is now available for public use at the home page of ILCAA (www.aa.tufs.ac.jp) on the Internet. From 1999 onwards the bilingual dictionaries are expected to be issued in instalments.

I was in-charge of the project from 1987 up to the end of March 1997. The charge was transferred to Professor Peri Bhaskararao at ILCAA on April 1st, 1997.

In 1987, ILCAA initiated another international joint research in collaboration with ISI (Indian Statistical Institute, Calcutta) to analyze the Bengali language used in the literary works of Rabindranath Tagore, the first Asian poet who was awarded the Nobel Prize for Literature in 1913. All his poems and short stories written in the language of prose style were studied linguistically from various angles aided by the computer. As a result of these analytic studies, ILCAA produced 7 volumes under the title *South Asian Data Series—Bengali* which include alphabetical lists of words as well as graphemes with their respective frequencies and with their pre- and post-contexts. These words are taken from *Prabhat-sangit*, *Sandhya-sangit*, *Gitanjali*, *Bhanusimha Thakurer Padabali*, *Sabhyatar Sankat*, *Katha o Kahini*, *Balaka*, *Manasi*, etc. They were published by ILCAA serially from 1987 to 1993 under the joint editorship of Tsuyoshi Nara, Bhakti Prasad Mallik and Yasuaki Sakamoto. Furthermore, ISI published a book called *Gitanjali—Linguistic Statistical Analysis* which shows the results of stylistic, syntactic, morphological, prosodemic and phonological analysis of the language used in *Gitanjali*.

Besides these two joint research projects, there is some individual research to report in the South-Asian field by various linguists in Japan during the last 5 years.

As for dictionary making, worth mentioning are the two dictionaries: (1) *A Japanese–Hindi dictionary* (893 pages) compiled and published in 1996 by Katsuro Koga (Osaka University of Foreign Studies), and (2) *A Hindi reverse dictionary* (996 pages) edited by Kazuhiko Machida and published by ILCAA in 1995.

It should also be mentioned here that in 1995 ILCAA reprinted, as *Syntactic Studies of Indo-Aryan Languages* (302 pages), three books of Sukumar Sen—*The Use of Cases in Vedic Prose*, *Syntactic Studies of Buddhistic Sanskrit* and *Historical Syntax of Middle Indo-Aryan*.

Turning to historical studies of South Asian languages, Muneo Tokunaga, at Kyoto University, has made a data base of the *Mahabharata* and some other Sanskrit works. Jun Takashima, ILCAA, has made a data base of almost all Sanskrit texts related to Shiva worship. S.K. Choudhury, Aichi Gakusen University, is studying the history of Sanskrit studies by Japanese scholars.

In the field of descriptive study, Tsuyoshi Nara, Kazuhiko Machida, Tomio Mizokami (Osaka University of Foreign Studies) are specializing in Indo-Aryan languages, and Norihiko Uchida (Sonoda Women's College), Taro Iemoto (Kyoto University), Nozomi Kodama (Kumamoto University), Takanobu Takahashi (Tokyo University), Hiroshi Yamashita (Tohoku University) are specializing in Dravidian languages. Toshiki Osada of International Centre of Japanese Studies and Makoto Minegishi, of ILCAA are specializing in Austro-Asiatic languages. Peri Bhaskararao (ILCAA) and Shiro Yabu (Osaka University of Foreign Studies) are specializing in Tibeto-Burman languages. Besides these specific fields, all these scholars are also working on other languages of the South Asian area.

A list of the names of linguists and their recent publications follows:

Chaudhury, Saroj Kumar. 1995. Sanskrit phonetics and Chinese. *Series of Humanities and Social Science*, Vol. 9, 9. 11–49. Aichi Gakusen University.

———. 1996a. Sanskrit in Japanese linguistic studies. *Series of Humanities and Social Science* Vol. 10, 1. 99–150. Aichi Gakusen University.

———. 1996b. Sanskrit—Its perception in Japan. *Series of Humanities and Social Science* Vol. 9, 10. 71–107. Aichi Gakusen University.

Kodama, Nozomi. 1994–5. Karhadi verb morphology. Annual Report on CIIL–ILCAA Joint Research Project Vol. 5, 15–32. ILCAA.

Iemoto, Taro. 1992. A Note on adjectives in Tamil and Kannada—with special reference to compounding process. *Journal of the Japanese Association for South Asian Studies* 4.79–87. JASAS (in Japanese).

———. 1993. Re-examination of adjectives in Tamil. Annual Report on CIIL–ILCAA Joint Research Project, Vol. 4, 16–29. ILCAA.

Iemoto, Taro. 1994. On Indian linguistic area from a viewpoint of Dravidian linguistics. *The Dravidian World.* Ed. by Noboru Karashima, The University of Tokyo Press (in Japanese).

———. 1995 A Note on Dr. Ohno's hypothesis—Japanese kinship with Tamil. Bulletin of International Research Center for Japanese Studies 13. 232–42. Kyoto: *IRCJS* (In Japanese).

Machida, Kazuhiko. 1993. List of Hindi Homographs. Annual Report on CIIL–ILCAA Joint Research Project, Vol. 4, 56–128. ILCAA.

Minegishi, Makoto. 1991. On Munda (Hassada) phonology—supplemented with the word-list Annual Report on CIIL–ILCAA Joint Research Project, Vol. 2, 61–108. ILCAA.

———. 1994a. On the phones and phonemes of Khasi. *Journal of Asian and African Studies*, ILCAA 45–47.161–74 (in Japanese).

———. 1994b. Basic vocabulary of Khasi language. *Bulletin of Cambodian Studies* 1.93–130. ILCAA (in Japanese).

Mizokami, Tomio. 1991. Word order in Kashmiri. Annual Report on CIIL–ILCAA Joint Research Project Vol. 2, 56–128. ILCAA.

———. 1992. On emotional expressions of Hindi–Urdu. Contrastive study of languages and language education. Osaka University of Foreign Studies, Osaka.

Nara, Tsuyoshi. 1991. An automatic segmentation parameter for Bengali affixes. *Lexicological Studies*, Vol. 3, 1–10. ILCAA.

———. 1994. A computer-aided phonetic instruction system for South Asian languages. Proceedings of International Conference on Spoken Language Processing, Vol. 3, 219–22. ICSLP, Yokohama. [with Peri Bhaskararao].

Osada, Toshiki. 1990. Notes on the Proto-Kherwarian vowel system. *Indo-Iranian Journal* 39.245–58.

———. 1991a. Serial verb in Mundari. Annual Report on CIIL–ILCAA Joint Research Project, Vol. 2, 21–28. ILCAA.

———. 1991b. The demonstrative system in Mundari. *Journal of Asian and African Studies* 42.59–70. ILCAA.

———. 1991c. Father Ponette's field note on Turi. *Journal of Asian and African Studies* 42.175–89 ILCAA.

———. 1992. A reference grammar of Mundari. 168. ILCAA.

———. 1993. Field notes on Birhor. Annual Report on CIIL–ILCAA Joint Research Project, Vol. 4, 30–40. ILCAA.

Bhaskararao, Peri. 1993a. Phonetic structure of Angami. In University of California Working Papers in Phonetics, Vol. 84, 127–42 [with Barbara Blakenship, Nichumeno Chase and Peter Ladefoged].

———. 1993b. Phonetics of Toda. In University of California Working Papers in Phonetics, Vol. 84, 89–126 [with Michael Shalev and Peter Ladefoged].

———. 1994a. The Rhotics of Toda. In University of California Working Papers in Phonetics, Vol. 87, 35–99 [with Sinisa Spajic and Peter Ladefoged].

———. 1994b. Tiddim Chin verbs and their alternants. *Journal of Asian and African Studies* 46–7.333–60. ILCAA.

———. 1994–5a. Phonology-Script mismatch and use of descriptive tags in Indian languages. Annual Report on CIIL–ILCAA Joint Research Project, Vol. 5, 8–14. ILCAA.

———. 1994–5b. An analysis of Telugu numerals for implementation in a text-to-phoneme system. Annual Report on CIIL–ILCAA Joint Research Project, Vol. 5, 33–41. ILCAA. [with Tsuyoshi Nara].

———. 1996. A computerized lexical database of Tiddim Chin and Lushai, Annual Report on CIIL–ILCAA Joint Research Project, Vol. 6, 27–143. ILCAA.

Takashima, Jun. 1996. KWIC Index to Sanskrit texts of Dharmakirti, p. 1, 211 ILCAA.

Yabu, Shiro. 1993. The Linguistic position of the Meitei language, Annual Report on CIIL–ILCAA Joint Research Project Vol. 4, 41–6. ILCAA.

■ NORTH AMERICA ■

TEJ K. BHATIA

Since *The Yearbook of South Asian Languages and Linguistics* makes its debut on the historic occasion of the observance of a half-century of Indian and Pakistani independence, it is appropriate to begin this report by offering some remarks of a historical nature which will set the stage for a discussion on research and teaching of South Asian languages, literatures and linguistics in this young and vibrant part of the world. These remarks will provide the needed perspectives on the nature and scope of research on South Asian languages and linguistics in North America in general and in the USA in particular.

This survey is based on published, gray, and unpublished materials from—but not exclusively—the 1990s. Whenever it is deemed necessary, reference is made to studies published prior to the 1990s to provide a context. In the process of doing so, the report will bring to light the salient findings of the current research and refer to theoretical, conceptual and descriptive issues surrounding South Asian linguistic research. In venturing to write a report on such a topic, one is at once made conscious of a number of difficulties. In the first place the scope of South Asian languages and linguistic is quite vast. Second, the North American continent, in addition to being highly diversified and prolific, is remarkably active and productive, and in many respects is credited with setting new trends and directions in the field. For these reasons, although an attempt is made to be as exhaustive as possible, it is naturally impossible to incorporate all the works and the trends of the 90s. The survey is presented in three major sections: (1) Historical and Diachronic linguistics; (2) Theoretical linguistics; and (3) Sociolinguistics and Applied linguistics. The classification of theoretical linguistics, sociolinguistics, and applied linguistics is by no means rigid.

A few preliminary remarks on the institutional organization of this research in North America may be useful. The South Centers (known as Asian Studies Departments in Canada) and Linguistics departments complement each other on language and linguistic research on South Asia. The Centers focus on what can be termed as Applied linguistic research, whereas the linguistics departments are naturally more inclined to theoretically grounded linguistic research. This complementary role is in part due to historical reasons.

Prior to World War II (1939–45), international studies in the United States were left primarily to missionaries, foreign-service agents, and some news organizations. This limited interest left serious gaps in the understanding of the world outside selected European countries. This situation began to change radically, however, during and after World War II with the perception that knowledge about other countries is not only critical for foreign studies but also intimately tied to economic and business interests. This shift radically changed the nature of research on South Asian linguistics. Although some scattered attempts had been made to promote South Asian Studies in the United States, such as the establishment of Professorship of Sanskrit at Yale (1844) and similar positions at Harvard and Columbia Universities and the Universities of Pennsylvania, Chicago, and California, the largest and most vigorous attempts had to wait until the passage of the National Defense Education Act in 1958. With this act, Foreign Language and Area Studies (FLAS) mushroomed in American universities. In the 1960s, a number of South Asian Studies Centers at various universities, including the University of California, Berkeley; the University of Washington, Seattle; the University of Texas at Austin; the University of Chicago; Columbia University; University of Wisconsin, Madison; and Cornell University, offered a wide variety of Programs including the teaching of South Asian languages. The Centers continue to play an important role in the applied linguistics of South Asia. The languages which continue to be popular in the 90s are the following: Hindi–Urdu, Sanskrit, Tamil, Bengali, Telugu, Marathi, Punjabi and Prakrit.

The Linguistics departments of the US universities, which are notable for their research on South Asian languages *per se* are: the Universities of California at Los Angles, Chicago, Cornell, Illinois at Urbana-Champaign, Iowa, Pennsylvania, Rutgers, Stanford, SUNY Stonybrook, Syracuse, Texas (Austin), Washington (Seattle), Wisconsin (Madison), and in Canada: Universities of British Columbia (Vancouver), Montreal and Toronto and Memorial University of Newfoundland.

Perhaps the single most important vehicle of research devoted to South Asian languages and linguistics is the yearly conference, affectionately called 'SALA' ('brother-in-law' in Hindi). The first conference was held in 1979 at the University of Illinois at Urbana-Champaign, as a forum for South Asian linguists, language teachers, and scholars of literature. So successful was the conference that the tradition of holding yearly SALA Roundtables continues to this day. The diversity of research topics and areas addressed by South Asian linguistics can best be exemplified by the proceedings published by SALA XV. The languages of five genetic groups: Indo-Aryan, Dravidian, Dardic, Tibeto-Burman and Munda are represented. Both Classical languages and modern languages are included. Of course, most of the articles are devoted to syntax but phonetics, phonology, and morphology are not neglected. Syntactic topics range from negation, coordination, relativization and subordination to clefting, anaphora and tense-aspect agreement system. Sociolinguistic topics such as diglossia and women's language are also included. Studies fall within the typological, descriptive and theoretical frameworks. The SALA Roundtable XIV which was held at Stanford University a year before resulted in two books: Gambhir (1995) and Butt, King and Ramchand (1994). Another important forum for South Asian linguistics is the Wisconsin yearly conference. In the 90s this conference yielded two important works devoted to the typology of subjects and complex predicates in South Asian languages (see Verma and Mohanan 1991 and Verma 1993).

■ 1. Historical and Diachronic Studies

A large body of research devoted to historical and diachronic linguistics of South Asia deals with both the linguistic and sociolinguistic aspects of Sanskrit, Tamil and Middle Indo Aryan languages. A large body of such studies is naturally devoted to Sanskrit in general and Paninian studies in particular (Deshpande and Bhate 1991; and several articles in Hock 1991). Topics covered by these studies range from the early history of Sanskrit (Aklujkar 1996a), interpretation of grammatical texts (Aklujkar 1991a, 1991b and 1993), to the treatment of syntactic topics such as word order (Aklujkar 1996b), nominal and pronominal objects (Bubenik 1991), pronominal systems (Bubenik 1992), passives and ergatives (Deshpande 1991a and 1991b; Bubenik 1995a and b), and tense-aspectal system (Bubenik and Hewson 1997).

Studies devoted to language contact and change address the issues of morphophonemic and morphosyntactic changes (Bubenik 1993a and 1993b), restructuring of cases (Bubenik 1993a) and Arabic and Persian influence on Indo-Aryan languages, particularly of the North-Western group (Bubenik 1990). Sociolinguistic issues of Sanskrit and Prakrits and their dialects are also detailed in the studies (Deshpande 1993 and Bubenik 1996). The state of Sankskrit studies in Canada is the subject of Aklujkar (1997).

■ 2. Theoretical Linguistics

■ 2.1 Syntax, Semantics and Universal Grammar

Word order in South Asian languages continues to draw attention from a variety of theoretical perspectives (e.g. Government and Binding and others). Word order represents a phenomena that is 'so close yet so far away'. On the one hand even a novice learner will be able to observe some crucial facts about the word order phenomenon while on the other hand it poses a serious challenge to linguists, universal grammarians, and theoreticians as well as to practitioners of language. The underlying reason for this is the problem of accounting for the range of variability found in South Asian languages and its syntactic, semantic and pragmatic determinants. The articles included in Butt, King and Ramchand (1994) set out to undertake the challenge of presenting some meaningful explanations of syntactic, semantic and pragmatic variability in the word order of South Asian languages and at the same time bring together theoretical and empirical perspectives on word order variability in selected South Asian languages. The term 'word order variability' by no means refers to the phenomenon of linguistic variability in term of sociolinguistic variation (spatial, class, gender and age distribution of linguistic feature), but in the sense used in universal grammar and language typology.

South Asian languages offer a dazzling array of flexibility in word order in spite of the fact they are not completely 'non configurational' languages. Data from South Asian languages has been the source of recent theoretical controversies. Mahajan (1994a) addresses the issue of word order with reference to the phenomenon of ergativity while papers in Verma and Mohanan (1991) consider word order and oblique subjects. Also noteworthy are Hook (1990), Bhatt (1993a and 1993b), and Hook and Koul (1996).

Other topics which received attention in the 90s are: Agreement and Case assignment (Gair 1992 and others), Null subjects (Davison 1993), Negation (Bhatia 1995); ACTIVE Passives (Mahajan 1995, Hook 1992), Imperfectivity–Genericity Correlation (M. Singh 1991), Interrogatives (Dayal 1996, Lahiri 1991), movement (Mahajan 1990), Scrambling (Mahajan 1994b), Pronominal and Reflexive clitics (Hock 1992a and b, Lidz 1995a and 1995b), Relative clauses and subordination (Hock 1993, Dayal 1996), Corelatives (Rajesh Bhatt 1996), Verbal predicates (M. Singh 1994, Bhatt 1994), Causative (M. Singh 1992), Aspetual system (Schiffman 1993a), and Compound verbs (Hook 1993 and M. Singh 1990).

Four notable works (Asher 1982, Sridhar 1990, Bhatia 1993, Wali and Koul 1996, on Tamil, Kannada, Punjabi, and Kashmiri, respectively) form a part of the *Croom Helm Descriptive Grammars Series* which aims at providing detailed descriptions of genetically and typologically diverse languages of the world in a uniform format in order to make direct comparison of the information pertaining to possible structures found in natural languages. In order to accomplish this goal, the volumes in the series follow the format outlined in the *Questionnaire*, developed by Comrie and Smith (1977), and originally published in *Lingua*, vol. 42. These grammars give a finely detailed and sophisticated account of the standard languages in question, drawing from the insights of traditional, structural, generative and universal-typological grammarians. Keeping the needs of both theoreticians and practitioners in mind, the typological grammars give a lucid, explicit, and in many cases original account of the syntax, morphology and phonology of the languages involved.

Masica (1991) represents another landmark of South Asian linguistics. This work presents an ambitious survey of the Indo-Aryan languages which is of great interest to both general and theoretical linguists. Von Munkwitz–Smith (1995), Masica (1994), D'souza, Furguson and Bhatt (in Dimock et al. 1992) present some new perspective on 'South Asia as a linguistic area' primarily from the syntactic point of view, while Ohala (1991) examines the areal phonological features of some Indo-Aryan languages.

Recent attempts to posit constraints on the grammar of bilingual language mixing within the Government and Binding framework (in particular, the Government constraint by Di Sciullo, Muysken and Singh (1986), and the

Functional Head Constraint Belazi, Rubin and Toribio (1994) have renewed interest in the grammar of code-mixing in South Asian languages. Drawing data from language mixing in South Asian languages, works by Bhatia and Ritchie (1996a and 1996b), Bhatt 1996, Singh 1995 are driven by deeper theoretical considerations and, thus, have serious implications for the study of Universal Grammar (UG) and language acquisition as well as linguistic performance.

The work by Mishra (1996) deals with the phonology of Avadhi, while Singh and Agnihotri (1997) deals with Hindi morphology. The works of Ohala and Ohala deal with a wide variety of phonetic and phonological topics such as nasals and nasalization (Ohala and Ohala 1991a and b, 1992, 1993a and b), segment duration (Ohala and Ohala 1992 and Ohala 1994) and syllables (Ohala 1994). The noteworthy works dealing with acoustic and auditory phonetics are as follows: Ohala (1996 and 1995) and Ohala and Ohala (1995).

■ 3. Sociolinguistics and Applied Linguistics

A new beginning in South Asian sociolinguistics is witnessed in the two pioneering works published in the collection of articles edited by Edward C. Dimock, Braj B. Kachru and Bh. Krishnamurti (1992), and in Singh, Dasgupta and Lele (1995). The synthesis of the research findings in these works is satisfying and instructive. The books are unfailingly stimulating and will provoke argument on almost every topic and issue pertaining to sociolinguistics and South Asian sociolinguistics.

The topic of the English Diaspora in general and of the spread of South Asian English in particular continue to generate a lot of enthusiasm and controversies in the field of socio- and applied linguistics. The recent provocative works of Kachru (in particular 1992, 1994, 1996a, 1996b, 1996c and his earlier works) have added new dimensions to the question of the spread, functions and models of native and nonnative Englishes. The question of English vs. World Englishes is a hotly debated topic today. The contact of English with many languages of South Asia has resulted in linguistic innovations in genres such as administrative writing, print media, literary creativity, and so on (Y. Kachru 1992, Sridhar 1992, Pandharipande 1992, and others). The dialogue on the diversification of English, nativization, acculturation, users and language acquisition is lively and gaining momentum with the growing body of literature on this topic. The publication of numerous articles, special symposia, discussion and debates, in journals such as *World Englishes*, *English World-Wide* and *World Literature Written in English* supports this claim. The topic has caught the fancy of journals not devoted to World Englishes *per se*. A case in point is the discussion devoted to 'new/non-native' Englishes in the *Journal of Pragmatics* (Afendras et al. 1995). The opening remarks of the editors of the journal are instructive in this regard. 'When we received the manuscript by Rajendra Singh, Jean D'souza, Karuvannar P. Mohanan and Nagur S. Prabhu called, "On 'new/non-native' Englishes", we immediately saw the opportunity of sending the paper as a target article to a number of colleagues for comments. We managed to assemble a group of distinguished scholars who we assumed to have something to say about the subject, and to collect their comments, which are presented here' (*Journal of Pragmatics* 1995, 24.295). In addition to the issues surrounding some of the central concepts of linguisitic theory (e.g. native speakers, grammaticality judgments) and methodology, the questions of ideologies, and assumptions that have gone into the 'native and non-native' distinction in linguistic research and World Englishes are also addressed by this stimulating volume. Ten distinguished scholars who have participated in the discussion are: Evangelos A. Afendras, Sheron Millar, Eoghan Mac Aogáin, Ayo Bamgbose, Yamuna Kachru, Anjum Saleemi, Bent Preisler, Peter Trudgill, Florian Coulmas and Probal Dasgupta. The discussion ends with the last word on the topic by R. Singh, entitled "Coda". The 'Coda' revisits the issues raised by the discussion in a perceptive and timely fashion. As the editors of the journal rightly point out, "This is, of course, not the final note of this polyphonic debate, which we hope will trigger many encores." (*Journal of Pragmatics* 1995, 24.295). Needless to say that the debate on the World Englishes will continue to be more vibrant and colourful in future research.

The topic of variation and particularly of diaglossic variation in South Asian languages in the subject of notable studies such as by Bright (1990) and Schiffman (1993b).

■ 3.1 Discourse Analysis

South Asian discourse has been the topic of many theoretical and empirical investigations. It has received the attention of syntacticians interested in topics such as zero anaphora, null subjects, and word order, and of discourse analysts who set out to investigate strategies, styles and domains involved in South Asian discourse. See Y. Kachru (1996, 1992) for cross cultural discourse; Pandharipande (in Dimock et al. 1992) for religious discourse; Bhatia (1992) for advertising discourse. Attempts are also being made to use technology for teaching and research of South Asian discourse.[1]

■ 3.2 Language Acquisition Studies

The first language and second language acquisition studies devoted to South Asian languages are still very sparse. Some recent noteworthy studies are as follows: Lust, Bhatia, Gair, Sharma and Khare (in Gambhir 1995) deals with children's acquisition of Hindi Anaphora in 'jab' (when) clauses within the "Principles and Parameters" approach to Universal Grammar. Bhatia (in

Gambhir 1995) explores the acquisition of Hindi voicing and aspiration by adult English-speaking learners of Hindi as a second language.

■ 3.3 South Asian Language Pedagogy

A report of the National Foreign Language Center at the John Hopkins University (1996) characterizes the state of foreign language teaching as a 'system in crisis'. The report singles out primarily seven areas of concern: (1) dramatic shifts in language choice, (2) diversity of learners, (3) intra-institutional needs, (4) resources and staffing, (5) governance, (6) campus attitudes, and (7) technology. (For details, see NFLC 1996: 2–3). Although not all the seven areas of concerns have received adequate attention in the context of teaching of South Asian languages. Two new issues however, which figure prominently in the South Asian field are the following: the diversity of learners (e.g. Heritage language education) and technology in addition to the traditional concerns such as course materials, language testing and assessment, and language acquisition. See Gambhir (1995) for more details; Aklujkar (1992) and Bhatia (1996) for recent language courses.

■ 3.4 Technology

The South Asian Language Teachers Association held a 'very special meeting' of the Association in conjunction with the Annual Meeting of the Association of Asian Studies in April 1996 in Honolulu, Hawaii. The topic selected for a panel of discussion and a roundtable discussion was: Teaching of South Asian Languages in the 21st Century. While the field confronts some exciting challenges on the use of technology in the teaching of South Asian languages,[2] some new developments are worthy of attention. Here is the list of some South Asian language programs which make use of computer and multimedia technology.

3.4.1 Softwares and Internet

The Hyper Hindi computer-based course is called "Story Teller: An Interactive Literary-Linguistic Approach to the teaching of the Hindi language." The conceptual framework of the program incorporates the building blocks of the language. The students have access to graphemic, transliterational, syllabic, word and sentence structure of the text in question. The program has the following four major components: The Devanagari Script, Text Analysis, Vocabulary Stacks and Sounds.

The Hindi Writer Program is a pilot program which teaches the Devanagari writing system on microcomputers using Hypercard 2.0. Both software programs were developed at the Syracuse University. A Hindi teaching program is available on the World Wide Web from the University of Pennsylvania.

A Tamil learning software system containing computer-assisted language learning facilities have been developed and is being used as part of the Tamil courses offered at the University of Pennsylvania. This software, developed using the authorware Hypercard, consists of one hundred and four lessons. The lessons in this software are designed in such a way that both a speech content and grammatical information are illustrated in detail in each lesson to enhance self-guided learning. Since this software is made available through a local network server at the university, students are able to use it in any Macintosh computer connected to the network on campus.

Here is a list of the internet resources that I discovered which may be of interest to South Asian linguists:

Tamil on WWW:[3]
http: //ccat.sas.upenn.edu/~plc/tamilweb/tamil.html
Association of Indian Languages:
http: //hertz.njit.edu/~ais/stuff/lang.html
Course Catalog (as of Aug 1995)—Hindi (full curriculum at the Univ. of Illinois):
http: //www.uiuc.edu/admin_manual/Courses/C_D/latest/courses.HINDI.html
Hindi (tourist language basics):
http: //canada.canacad.ac.jp/elementary/mo1/hindi.html
Index of/COAST/dict/dictionaries/Hindi/:
http: //ftp.sterling.com/COAST/dict/dictionaries/Hindi/
Yamada Web Guide to Hindi–Urdu:
http: //babel.uoregon.edu/yamada/guides/hindiurdu.html

■ 4. Conclusion

From the above survey it becomes readily clear that the mosaic of South Asian language and linguistic research in North America is colorful and diverse. Although an attempt has been made to be as exhaustive as possible. Given the amount and the nature of research being done on this vast continent, I am sure there will be many omissions. I hope these gap will be filled in future issues by focusing on important debates and issues. Nevertheless, readers are encouraged to send their material and comments to the author in order to make future reports as comprehensible as possible. Please send your comments and list of publications through the feedback page of my webpage on the following address: http://web.syr.edu/~tkbhatia/

■ NOTES

1. The use of technology for research and teaching of South Asian discourse was the subject of a recent workshop held at University of Pennsylvania, Philadelphia. It was organized by the South Asia Regional Studies in conjunction with the Penn Language Center. The workshop was co-organized by Professors Harold Schiffman and Ralph Ginsberg. The principal objective of the workshop was to identify ways in which computer-based multimedia tools and data could enhance teaching and research in the South Asian context and to design an authoring

framework which would enable South Asianists to develop their own applications. The collaborative use of data and applications across the South Asian teaching community was another salient feature of the workshop which was built on a powerful hypermedia system (IDE) running on a Macintosh platform which has proven effective and usable in several educational contexts. A case in point is the French film analysis course at the University of Pennsylvania which manages and analyzes complex, multimedia microethnographic data. During the workshop Satyajit Ray's movie, The Chess Players was used to analyze various aspects of South Asian Discourse (e.g. genderlects, code-mixing and switching, etc.) and film analysis. The project is an on-going one and *The Yearbook* will continue to report further developments on this project of immense importance to sociolinguists, computational linguists and film analysts.

2. In addition to fiscal problems, there are a number of issues involving the use of technology in a South Asian language curricular context. The growing demands to integrate technology into teaching strategies can be very unsettling even for the teachers well-versed with trends in computer-assisted and multimedia instructions. Much needs to be known about distance learning techniques which should be of particular interest to the teachers of South Asian languages since the demand for learning South Asian languages is geographically so diversified that even the larger universities and South Asian Centers cannot cope with such demands.
3. Although still in developmental stages, this is an excellent site which may be accessed at the above URL address. The site is managed by Vasu Renganathan. The Penn Language Center and the Department of South Asia Regional Studies at the University of Pennsylvania undertook this project to build a polyvalent web site for teaching and learning the Tamil language. This project funded by the Consortium for language teaching and learning was initiated with the aim of using all possible resources that web technology can offer for teaching and learning a second language. The course materials available in this web site range from learning how to write the Tamil alphabets to getting familiar with many idiomatic and cultural expressions of the language. This multimedia web site offers various kinds of resources to improve listening comprehension and reading comprehension in Tamil using many audio and video files. The other significant feature of this site is the online approach to dictionary reference, taking proficiency tests, doing writing exercises and corpus look-up.

■ REFERENCES

Afendras, Evangelos et al. 1995. Discussion on 'new/non-native' Englishes: a gamelan. *Journal of Pragmatics* 24.295–321.

Aklujkar, Ashok. 1991a. Vakyapadiya. *Encyclopaedia of Indian philosophies: grammarians volume*, ed. by Karl Potter, 121–74. Princeton, NJ: Princeton University Press.

———. 1991b. Interpreting Vakyapadiya 2.486 historically (part 3). *Paninian studies: Professor S.D. Joshi felicitation volume*, ed. by Madhav Deshpande and Saroja Bhate. 1–47. Ann Arbour: CSAS.

———. 1992. *Sanskrit: an easy introduction to an enchanting language.* 3 vols. Richmond: Svadhyaya Publications.

———. 1993. An introduction to the study of Bhartrhari. *Asiatische Studien/Etudes Asiatiques* XLVII (1).7–36.

———. 1996a. The early history of Sanskrit as supreme language. *Ideology and status of Sanskrit: Contributions to the history of the Sanskrit language*, ed. by Jan E.M. Houben. 69–85. Leiden: E.J. Brill.

———. 1996b. Some theoretical observations on word order in Sanskrit. *Studien zur Indologie und Iranistik, Festschrift Paul Thieme.* 1–25.

———. 1997. Sanskrit studies in Canada. Sanskrit studies outside India. [Published] on the Occasion of [the] 10th World Sanskrit Conference, ed. by K.K. Mishra, 12–30. New Delhi: Rashtriya Sanskrit Sansthan.

Asher, R.E. 1982. *Tamil.* Lingua Descriptive Series 7. Amsterdam: North Holland.

Bagchi, Tista. 1993. Control, reflexives, and automodularity in Bangla imperfective participial complements. Papers from the Regional Meeting of the Chicago Linguistic Society 28.17–32.

Belazi, H.M., E.J. Rubin and **A.J. Toribio.** 1994. Code-switching and X-bar theory: The functional head constraint. *Linguistic Inquiry* 25(22).221–37.

Bhatia, Tej K. 1992. Discourse Functions and pragmatics of mixing: advertising across cultures. *World Englishes* 11(2–3).195–215.

———. 1993. *Punjabi: A cognitive-descriptive grammar.* London: Routledge.

———. 1995. *Negation in South Asian languages.* Delhi: Institute of Indian Languages.

———. 1996. *Colloquial Hindi: the complete language course.* London: Routledge.

Bhatia, Tej K. and **William C. Ritchie.** 1996a. Bilingual language mixing, universal grammar, and second language acquisition. *Handbook of second language acquisition*, ed. by William C. Ritchie and Tej K. Bhatia [Chapter 19], 627–82. San Diego: Academic Press.

———. 1996b. Light verbs in code-switched utterances: derivational economy in I-Language or incongruence in production? Proceedings of the Annual Boston University Conference on Language Development 20(1).52–62.

Bhatt, Rajesh. 1996. The matching parameter and correlatives. *Proceedings of Console 4*, ed. by Joao Costa, Rob Goedemans and Ruben van der Wijver, 15–30. Amsterdam: Holland Academic Graphics.

Bhatt, Rakesh. 1992. Language identity, conflict, convergence in South Asia. *Studies in Linguistic Sciences* 22(1).17–37.

———. 1993a. Word order and case in Kashmiri. Urbana: University of Illinois Ph.D. dissertation.

———. 1993b. Psyched out—Analyzing quirky construction. *Papers from the Regional Meeting of the Chicago Linguistic Society* 28.77–89.

———. 1994. On experiencers and subjects in perfective predicates. *Studies in Linguistic Sciences* 24 (1–2).73–4.

———. 1996. On the grammar of code-switching. *World Englishes* 15(3).369–75.

Bright, William. 1990. *Language variation in South Asia.* Oxford: Oxford University Press.

Bubenik, Vit. 1990. Structural influence of Arabic and Persian on the North-Western Indo-Aryan languages. Proceedings of the 14th Annual Meeting of the Atlantic Provinces Linguistic Association. St. John's. 11–20.

———. 1991. Nominal and pronominal objects in Prakrit. *Sanskrit syntax: Traditional and modern approaches*, ed. by Hans H. Hock, 19–30.

———. 1992. On the use of pronominal clitics in Late Middle Indo-Aryan. Wiener zeitschrift fur die kunde sudasiens und archiv fur indische philosophie, Band XXXVI, 1992. Supplement, ed. by G. Oberhammer, 7–18.

———. 1993a. Morphological and syntactic change in Late Middle Indo-Aryan. *Journal of Indo-European Studies* 21.259–81.

———. 1993b. Contact-induced morphosyntactic change in the North-West Indo-Aryan languages. *Annals of the Bhandarkar Oriental Research Institute*, LXXII–LXXIII, 701–3.

———. 1993. Restructuring of the nominal case and the evolution of phrasal case in Late Middle Indo-Aryan. *South Asia Horizons* [Ottawa: Carleton University] 1.229–48.

———. 1995a. Passives and ergatives in Middle Indo-Aryan. *Historical linguistics: Current issues in linguistic theory* 124.49–57.

———. 1995b. On typological changes and structural borrowing in the history of European Romani. Romani in contact. The history, structure and sociology of a language. *Current issues in linguistic theory*, ed. by Y. Matras, 1–24. Amsterdam: Benjamins.

———. 1996. *The structure and development of Middle Indo-Aryan dialects.* Delhi: Motilal Banarsidass.

Bubenik, Vit and **John Hewson.** 1997. Tense and aspect in Indo-European languages: Theory, typology and diachrony. *Current Issues in Linguistic Theory* 145. Amsterdam: Benjamins.

Bubenik, Vit and **Chitra Paranjape.** 1996. Development of the pronominal systems from Apabhramsa to Early New Indo-Aryan. *Indo-Iranian Journal* 39.111–32.

Butt, Mariam and **Tracy Holloway King.** 1992. Semantic case in Urdu. Papers from Regional Meeting of the Chicago Linguistic Society 27.31–45.

Butt, Mariam, Tracy Holloway King and **Gillian Ramchand** (eds). 1994. Theoretical perspectives on word order in South Asian languages (CSLI Lecture Notes 50). Center for the Study of Language and Information, Stanford: Stanford University Press.

Comrie, Bernard and **Norval Smith.** 1977. Lingua Descriptive Studies: Questionnaire. *Lingua* 42.1–72.

Davison, Alice. 1993. Controlled Experiencer Subjects: Implications for Phrase Structure. *South Asian language Review* III (2).46–58.

Davison, Alice and **Frederick M. Smith** (eds). 1994. *Papers from the fifteenth South Asian language analysis roundtable conference 1993.* Iowa: University of Iowa.

Dayal, V. 1996. *Locality in Wh-quantification: questions and relative clauses in Hindi.* Dordrecht: Kluwer.

Deshpande, Madhav. 1991a. Ditransitive passives in Panini. *Indo-Iranian Journal* 34(1).19–35.

———. 1991b. Prototypes in Paninian syntax. *Journal of the American Oriental Society* 111(3).465–480.

———. 1993. Sanskrit and Prakrit: sociolinguistic issues. Delhi: Motilal Banarasidass.

Deshpande, Madhav and **Saroja Bhate** (eds). 1991. *Paninian studies: Professor S.D. Joshi Felicitation volume.* Ann Arbor: CSSAS, University of Michigan.

Dimock, Edward C., Braj B. Kachru and **Bh. Krishnamurti** (eds). 1992. *Dimensions of sociolinguistics in South Asia.* New Delhi/Oxford: Oxford and IBH Publishing Co.

Di Sciullo, Anne–Marie, Peter Muysken and **Rajendra Singh.** 1986. Government and code-mixing. *Journal of Linguistics* 22.1–24.

Gair, James W. 1992. AGR, INFL, Case and Sinhala Diglossia or: Can linguistic theory find a home in variety. *Dimensions of sociolinguistics in South Asia*, ed. by Edward C. Dimock, Braj B. Kachru and Bh. Krishnamurti. New Delhi/Oxford: Oxford and IBH Publishing Co.

Hock, Hans H. (ed.). 1991. *Studies in Sanskrit syntax.* Delhi: Motilal Banarsidass.

———. 1992a. What's a nice word like you doing in a place like this? Syntax vs. Phonological form. *Studies in Linguistic Sciences* 22(1).39–87.

———. 1992b. Swallow tales: Chance and the "world etymology" MALLQ'A 'swallow, throat'. Papers from the Regional Meeting of the Chicago Linguistic Society 28. 215–34.

———. 1993. Some peculiarities of Vedic-prose relative clauses. *Winer Zeitschrift für die Kunde Südasiens.* Supplementband, 9–29.

Hook, Peter E. 1990. A note on the expressions of involuntary experience in the Shina of Skardu. *Bulletin of the School of Oriental and African Studies* 53.77–82.

———. 1991. On identifying the conceptual restructuring of Passive as Ergative in Indo-Aryan. *Paninian Studies: Professor S.D. Joshi Felicitation Volume*, ed. by Madhav Deshpande and Saroja Bhate, 177–99.

———. 1993. Seven variables influencing the use of compound verbs in Hindi–Urdu texts. *South Asian Language Review* III(2).59–70.

———. 1995. Covert Absolutivity in Vedic. *Stha:pakashra:ddha*, ed. by N.V. Gurov and Y.V. Vaislkov, 82–93. St. Petersburg: Russian Academy of Sciences, Institute of Oriental Studies.

Hook, Peter and **Onkar N. Koul.** 1996. Kashmiri as a V-2 language. *Word order in Indian languages*, ed. by V.S. Lakshmi and A. Mukerjee, 95–105. Hyderabad: Osmania University.

Kachru, Braj B. 1994. The speaking tree: a medium of plural canons. Georgetown University Round Table on Languages and Linguistics. 6–22.

———. 1996a. *The other tongue: English across cultures.* (South Asian edition). New Delhi: Oxford University Press.

———. 1996b. Transcultural creativity in World Englishes and literary canons. *Principle and practice in Applied Linguistics*, ed. by G. Cook and B. Seidlhofer, 272–87. Oxford: Oxford University Press.

———. 1996c. South Asian English: toward an identity in diaspora. *South Asian English: Structure, use and users*, ed. by Robert J. Baumgardner, 9–28. Urbana: University of Illinois.

Kachru, Braj B. and **C.L. Nelson.** 1996. *World Englishes. Sociolinguistic and Language Teaching*, ed. by Sandra L. Mckay and Nancy H. Hornberger, 71–102. Cambridge: Cambridge University Press.

Kachru, Braj B. and **Larry Smith** (eds). 1994. *World Englishes in Contact and Convergence.* Special issue of World Englishes.

Kachru, Yamuna. 1992. Speech Acts in World Englishes. *World Englishes* 10(3).299–306.

———. 1996. Language and cultural meanings: expository writing in South Asian English. *South Asian English: Structure, Use and Users*, ed. by Robert J. Baumgardner, 127–40. Urbana: University of Illinois.

Lahiri, Utpal. 1991. Embedded interrogatives and predicates that embed them. Cambridge, MA: MIT Ph.D. dissertation.

Lidz, Jeffrey. 1995a. On the non-existence of Reflexive Clitics. *Papers from the Regional Meeting of the Chicago Linguistic Society* 31(2).181–97.

———. 1995b. Morphological reflexive marking: evidence from Kannada. *Linguistic Inquiry* 26(4).705–10.

Mahajan, Anoop. 1990. The A/A-bar distinction and movement theory. Cambridge, MA: MIT Ph.D. dissertation.

———. 1994a. The ergative parameter: Have–Be alternation, word order, and split ergativity. Proceedings of NELS 15.286–301.

———. 1994b. Toward a unified theory of Scrambling. *Studies on Scrambling: Movement and non-movement approaches to free word-order phenomena*, ed. by Norbert Cover and Hank van Riemsdijk, 301–30. Berlin: Mouton de Gruyter.

———. 1995. ACTIVE Passives. Proceedings of the Thirteenth West Coast Conference on Formal Linguistics. Stanford: Center for the Study of Language and Information. 286–301.

Masica, Colin P. 1991. *The Indo-Aryan Languages.* Cambridge: Cambridge University Press.

———. 1994. Some new perspectives on South Asia as a linguistic area. *Papers from the fifteenth South Asian language analysis roundtable conference 1993*, ed. by Alice Davison and Frederick M. Smith, 187–200. Iowa: University of Iowa.

Mishra, Mithilesh. 1996. Aspects of Maithili Phonology. Urbana, Illinois: University of Illinois Ph.D. dissertation.

Ohala, John, and Manjari Ohala. 1993a. Nasals and nasalization in Hindi. Proceedings of the 3rd International Conference on Language and Linguistics: Pan-Asiatic Linguistics, Chulalongkorn University, Bangkok, Vol. 3. 1030–41.

———. 1993b. The phonetics of nasal phonology: theorems and data. *Nasals, nasalization, and the velum*, ed. by M.K. Huffman and R.A. Krokow, 225–49. San Diego, CA: Academic Press.

———. 1995. Speech perception and lexical representation: the role of vowel nasalization in Hindi and English. *Phonology and phonetic evidence: papers in Laboratory Phonology IV*, ed. by B. Connell and A. Arvaniti, 41–60. Cambridge: Cambridge University Press.

Ohala, Manjari. 1991. Phonological areal features of some Indo–Aryan languages. *Language Sciences* 13.107–24.

———. 1994. Experiments on the syllable in Hindi. *Proceedings, International conference on spoken language processing, Acoustical Society of Japan* 24(1).487–90.

———. 1995. Acoustic study of VC transitions for Hindi stops. *Proceedings of the XIIIth International Congress of Phonetic Sciences, Stockholm.* Vol. 4. 22–5.

———. 1996. Connected speech in Hindi. *Sound patterns connected speech: Description, models and explanation*, ed. by A.P. Simpson and M. Pätzold, 75–82. Kiel: Inst. für Phonetik und digitale Sparchverabeitung.

Ohala, Manjari and **John Ohala.** 1991a. Epenthetic nasals in the historical phonology of Hindi. Proceedings of the XII International Congress of Phonetic Sciences, Aix-en-Provence. Vol. 3. 126–29.

———. 1991b. Nasal epenthesis in Hindi. *Phonetica* 48.207–20.

———. 1992. Phonetic universals and Hindi segment duration. Proceedings, International conference on spoken language processing, Edmonton, University of Alberta. 831–34.

Pandharipande, Rajeshwari. 1992. Defining politeness in Indian English. *World Englishes* 2–3.241–50.

Schiffman, Harold F. 1993a. Intervocalic-v-deletion in Tamil: evidence for aspect as a morphological category. *Journal of the American Oriental Society* 113(4).513–28.

———. 1993b. The balance of power in multiglossic languages: implications for language shift. *International Journal of the Sociology of Language* 103.115–48.

Singh, Mona. 1990. The Aspectual Content of Compound Verbs. *Proceedings of the Eastern States Conference on Linguistics, Columbus, Ohio.* 260–72.

———. 1991. The Perfective Paradox: how to eat your cake and have it too. *Proceedings of the Berkeley Linguistic Society, Berkeley.* 469–80.

———. 1992. An Event Based Analysis of Causative. *Papers from the Regional Meeting of the Chicago Linguistic Society* 28.515–29.

Singh, Rajendra. 1995. *Linguistic theory, language contact, and Modern Hindustani.* New York: Peter Lang.

Singh, Rajendra and **Rama Kant Agnihotri.** 1997. *Modern Hindi morphology.* Delhi: Motilal Banarasidass.

Singh, Rajendra, Probal Dasgupta and **Jayant K. Lele.** 1995. *Explorations in Indian Sociolinguistics.* New Delhi: Sage.

Singh, Rajendra, Jean D'Souza, K.P. Mohanan and **Nagur S. Prabhu.** On 'new/non-native' Englishes: A quartet. *Journal of Pragmatics* 24.283–94.

Sridhar, S.N. 1990. *Kannada.* London: Routledge.

———. 1992. The ecology of bilingual competence: language interaction in indigenized varieties of English. *World Englishes* 11(2–3).141–50.

Verma, M.K. and **K.P. Mohanan.** 1991. *Word Order in South Asian languages.* Stanford: CLSI.

von Munkwitz–Smith, Jeffrey Clark. 1995. Substratum Influence on Indo-Aryan Grammar. Minneapolis: University of Minnesota. Ph.D. dissertation.

Wali, Kashi and **Onkar N. Koul.** 1996. *Kashmiri: a cognitive-descriptive grammar.* London: Routledge.

■ PAKISTAN: INDO-EUROPEAN ■

TARIQ RAHMAN

Pakistan does not have a university department or institute of higher education and research in linguistics. It is taught as a part of English studies, especially of English language courses at the University of Karachi at the M.A. level and some courses are offered at other universities in those aspects of linguistics—such as phonetics, varieties of English, etc.—which are relevant for teachers of English. Departments of other languages—Urdu, Punjabi, Pashto, Sindhi, Balochi, Brahvi, Arabic, Persian—also focus on literature though sometimes a linguistics thesis gets written, as will be described later.

The language academies—National Language Authority for Urdu; Sindhi Language Authority; Pashto Academy; Balochi Academy; Brahvi Academy; Punjabi Adabi Board—focus on that aspect of language planning (LP) which is defined as corpus planning (Cooper 1989: 154). They write dictionaries, standardize spelling and orthography and create technical terms (neologisms) to express new concepts. But their language planning efforts are guided by political imperatives, as we shall see later, and they are generally run by experts in literature whose knowledge of modern linguistics is very inadequate.

This being the scenario, there is little wonder that serious research in linguistics is not being produced by Pakistanis at least not by those who live in Pakistan.

■ 1. The Continuation of Philology and Sociolinguistics in Pakistan

The philological–comparativist tradition still dominates Pakistani linguistics. The revolution in linguistics following Ferdinand de Saussure and then Noam Chomsky remains almost unnoticed in Pakistani writings of this tradition. Most of these writings, even about the other languages of Pakistan, are in Urdu and their major focus remains words (as understood in common parlance) rather than other more precise units of analysis such as morphemes or phonemes. If the sound system is referred to there is often a confusion between phonemes, allophones and the symbols which represent them. Thus Sabzwari (1966: 50–78), Badakshani (1973), and Mehr Adbul Haq (1967), to name only three, do not differentiate between the letters of the alphabet and the sounds of the language. They sometimes appear to think that the letters actually represent the sounds of the language.

One major theme of the people writing in this tradition is discovering the origin, the family, and the roots of a language. In the case of Urdu, this is an obsession. Almost everyone of note has devoted considerable time on the origin and development of Urdu. Opinions on this subject are many and diverse: that Urdu was born out of Brij Bhasha (Azad 180.1); Hariani (Husain 1966: 183); the indigenous language (Prakrit) of Maharashtra (Bukhari 1975: 156–7; 1991: 349); Khari Boli (Sabzwari 1966: 38) and so on. Probably the best known work of Pakistani origin on this subject is Hafiz Mahmood Shirani's thesis that Urdu was born in the Punjab and traveled to northern India (Shirani 1928). Another interesting thesis, and one which seriously challenges Grierson's assumption that all the Indo-Aryan languages are the daughters of Sanskrit (Greirson Vol. 1. 121–7), is that Urdu is the descendant of the languages of the Dravidian and Munda tribes of this region and is, in essence, a pre-Sanskritic language (Faridkoti 1972, 1992). In fact Grierson himself acknowledged that the Indo-Aryan languages borrowed words from the Dravidian ones and that 'the borrowings have been much more considerable than has been admitted by many scholars of late years' but he also added 'that they were nothing like so universal as was once contended' (Grierson Vol. 1.130). Emeneau and others have given lists of such borrowings as well as Dravidian influences on the phonology of the languages in question (Burrow

1973: 378–88; Emeneau 1954 and 1956). But influence is one thing, origin quite another. If Faridkoti's work is substantiated—and it might well be true (Rahman 1996c)—it will be a significant piece of new research.

That the question of the roots of Urdu still absorbs the minds of Pakistanis writing in the philological–comparativist tradition is evident from the large number of studies still being undertaken in it (for a list see Akhtar 1995: 86–9). It is also in this tradition that other well-known studies—Mehr Abdul Haq's thesis (1967) on Multani (now called Siraiki), Yusuf Bukhari's comparative study of Urdu and Kashmiri (1986)—and Razzak Sabir's thesis on the relationship between Balochi and Brahvi (1994) have been written. Basically all these writers compare words of one language with another without taking into account contemporary theories, especially those dealing with phonology. However, Sabir has made efforts to refer to morphology, grammar and phonology though his sources are dated and inadequate.

Mehr Abdul Haq's major concern is ideological—to prove that Siraiki and Punjabi are different languages. It is this difference which enables Siraiki to function as an identity symbol of the people of the southern Punjab. Other Sikairi linguists, such as Ahsan Wagha (1990), have also tried to advance similar arguments. Razzak Sabir, who compares Balochi and Brahvi as competently as possible in the absence of the latest sources in linguistics, appears to go out of his way to argue that Brahvi is not a Dravidian language (Sabit 1994: 76–80) as Bray (1907) and Emeneau (1980) claimed. The problem is that Sabir does not know the Dravidian languages of India and his assertions are based on similarities between Balochi and Brahvi which could be explained on other grounds.

Similar to this is Ali Nawaz Jatoi's claim that Sindhi is a Semitic language (Jatoi 1983). Indeed, there are some people in Pakistan who argue that all languages came out of Arabic but their arguments are almost always based on comparisons of a few words. In fact, since language is an important symbol of ethnic nationalism in Pakistan (Rahman 1996g), such theses appear to be based upon arguments which the writers are emotionally committed to on non-linguistic grounds. For the same reason, most of the interest in the old indigenous languages of the country has come from the activists of the language movements. They have been active in corpus planning both in the official language academies and in their individual capacities.

In the official institutions for language planning the standardization of the script, modernization of the vocabulary by the creation of new technical terms (neologism) and research on languages and literature is undertaken. But orthography and neologism are both related with identity and thus with enthnic politics (Rahman 1995a). Thus, those who emphasize the Pakistani–Islamic identity insist upon the use of Arabic based scripts and the creation of new terms based upon Perso-Arabic roots whereas ethnic nationalists sometimes reject this script and coin words from the roots of their own languages. A number of private individuals too are promoting their languages because they feel that they are part of their identity and should not be allowed to become extinct. Not all such works are linguistic; there are many which are literary and cultural but in which language serves as a focal point. One such work, for instance, is Ghulam Haider Buriro's thesis, which compares Sindhi with the other languages of Pakistan to prove how developed and widely used it is in Sindh (Buriro 1980). Another is Abdur Rahman Brahvi's study (1982) of Bravhi, which is more historical and literary than linguistic. Most such works are written by very committed and identity-conscious people from the less powerful language groups, who write about their languages to make them better known and make their own people take pride in them. The names of the works on the following languages come to mind: Siraiki (Mughal 1987; Rasoolpuri 1976), Shina (Ali 1991), Wakhi (Ali, H n.d), Wanechi (Askar 1972), Balti (Yusuf 1990), Hindko (Nayyar 1976), Balochi (Hashimi 1962), Burushaski (Nasir n.d), etc. Most of these works are either primers or deal with orthography and the historical aspects of language at a very elementary level. Private efforts on behalf of the larger languages—Punjabi, Pashto, Sindhi and Urdu—are too numerous to be described (for details see Rahman 1996g and 1995a).

Unfortunately, these language planners too are mostly unaware of the contemporary developments in the theories of language planning. The only exception is Atash Durrani, whose book on neologism called *Urdu Istilahat Sazi* (1993) shows awareness of some of the developments in this field. Works by Raj Wali Khattak on Pashto orthography (Khattak 1991), by Syed Hashimi on Balochi technical terms (Hashimi 1962); by Khair Muhammad Baloch (1993) on the parts of a vehicle in Sindhi and by Qais Faridi in Sikairi (Faridi n.d) do not refer to the theoretical basis of similar work elsewhere in the world. However, G.A. Allana's book on Sindhi orthógraphy (1993) is an exception since the author is quite aware of the concepts of modern linguistics and has created terms which can be used to describe Sindhi in the light of modern concepts. But Allana's work falls in the modern linguistic tradition to which we turn now.

■ 2. The Contemporary Scene

It has been mentioned earlier that linguistics is not taught as an autonomous discipline in Pakistan. Among those who tried to establish it as a university subject is Anwar Dil, presently living in the United States. Dil could not establish either a department or an institute of linguistics but he did manage to establish the Linguistic Research Group in Pakistan in 1961, which published a number of monographs containing scholarly articles and papers read out at linguistic conferences in Pakistan (see Dil 1963). Some of the articles in the series are of a high standard but there are shoddy, ideologically inspired pieces too which mar most Pakistani publications. Such writings are published because there is no anonymous reviewing nor, indeed, the means to do good research. Moreover, most publications are supported by the state which influences the ideological contents of the publications. The Pakistani linguistic series—the organ of Dil's Linguistic Research Group—published work on most of the languages of Pakistan but it never became a permanent part of the academic establishment. Thus, when Dil went abroad, the series became defunct. However, Dil contributed to the field of sociolinguistics by editing a large, and highly significant, collection of the works of distinguished scholars. He is active in editing, compiling and generally trying to get linguistics recognized as an autonomous discipline in Pakistan. His wife Afia Dil, although counted amongst Bangladeshi linguists, has contributed earlier to Pakistani linguistics too. Her book on the Muslim variety of Bengali is highly relevant for Pakistanis, who used to think that Bengali was only a 'Hindu' language (Dil 1993).

In the seventies and eighties the British Council and the educational agencies of the United States started emphasizing the teaching of English as a second or other language—TESOL/TESL/ELT were among the acronyms to describe the enterprise.[1] However, when the University Grants Commission and the Allama Iqbal Open University started offering diploma courses in TESOL in 1985, a number of young lecturers with vested interest and knowledge of English language teaching formed a pressure group which brought about changes in the English departments.[2]

Apart from the efforts of the British Council, ELT also got a boost from the activities of the Society of Pakistani English Language Teachers (SPELT) which was established in 1984 by Zakia Sarwar (Interview 25 Sept 1994). SPELT holds lectures, workshops and conferences on a regular basis—the 12th conference was held in Karachi and Islamabad in October 1996—which increase awareness about the teaching of English. Although SPELT and other ELT programs do not focus on linguistics as such, they do contribute indirectly to the teaching of the rudiments of phonetics, varieties of language or stylistics. However, their concern is the teaching of English and not theoretical analysis. Books produced by SPELT (such as Sarwar 1991) or by those involved in ELT are concerned with English, and that too with its teaching. A survey of English language teaching, for instance, has recently been produced by Farida Malik (Malik 1996).

However, it is because of this increased concern with English as a language that some scholars have written about its role in Pakistan (Abbas 1993; Rahman 1996d). Even more significant is the questioning of the traditional prescriptivist notion that only British Standard English (BSE) and RP should be considered 'correct' and only it should be the pedagogical norm. This questioning is a consequence of the notion of the non-native varieties of English which are partly endonormative rather than being wholly exonormative as the RP and BSE ideal was. The work of Kachru (1965; 1983), the Indian linguist, laid the foundation of the idea that the English used in India—and, of course, other similar English-using countries—has its own norms and is different in certain systematic, rule-bound ways from native varieties of English. This notion was first introduced in Pakistan by Robert J. Baumgardner (1987), who later explored the grammatical and lexical features of Pakistani English (PE) in more detail (1993). The first detailed description of PE—including its phonetic and phonological features and sub-varieties which Baumgardner had not touched upon—was published by the present author (Rahman 1990). The notion of 'Pakistani Urdu', advanced by the present author in a newspaper article (1995g), has still not been described in detail. In Pakistan, however, there is not much advance upon this earlier work while elsewhere in the world there is much debate about the concept, and features, of non-native varieties of a language. To this debate only one Pakistani linguist, Anjum Saleemi, has contributed. His comment is that 'native and non-native varieties of English are valid linguistic entities only to the extent that "a language L" and "a particular variety of L" are legitimate concepts' (Saleemi 1995a: 311).

But Saleemi lives abroad and works in the mainstream tradition of Chomskyan theoretical linguistics, which is hardly understood in Pakistan. This is why his study of language learnability (1992), which should have been discussed by linguists as well as English language teachers, has gone unnoticed. In the only review of the book in Pakistan, the present writer confessed his own ignorance of some of the theories used by Saleemi because research journals and books are not available on such a highly technical subject (Rahman 1996f). Similarly, the work of Ruqaiya Hasan, who collaborated with Halliday on the well-known book *Cohesion in English* (Halliday and Hasan 1976) is unknown in Pakistan. Indeed, discourse analysis and systemic grammar—the linguistic tradition associated with Halliday in which Ruqaiya Hasan worked (Hasan 1964)—is even less known in Pakistan than the Chomskyan one. Indeed, it is in the Chomskyan tradition that some studies on Urdu by Baber S. Khan (Khan 1987; 1989) and, once again Saleemi (1994; 1995b), have been written. There is also a dissertation on Punjabi morphology in this tradition (Raja 1992). However, a study of 'word form' in Urdu (Moizuddin 1989) and the phonology of the verbal phrase in Hindko are not in this tradition (Awan 1974). The present author has helped in introducing some basic Chomskyan theories to students in Pakistan (Rahman 1992). However, most of the works in modern linguistics were completed in Western universities and it is significant that the authors did not produce any further studies on similar lines in Pakistan.

A linguist, who, though trained in the U.S.A., did produce some work in Pakistan is Elena L. Bashir. The work is along modern lines though it is contrastive. Bashir has contrasted Urdu with Pashto (1991a), Balochi (1991b) and Brahvi (1991c). According to her this 'contrastive analysis will provide a set of statements about similarities and differences between' Urdu and these other languages of Pakistan (1991a: 1). Although the aim of the analysis is pedagogical—to help teachers design instructional material and teach Urdu to children who speak Pashto, Balochi and Brahvi at home—the comparison of the languages gives useful data to those interested in these languages as such.

As mentioned earlier, there is very little work on linguistics in Pakistani languages. There is not even a study of Urdu on modern lines in Pakistan though there is one written in India in Urdu (Javed 1981). This is known only to a few experts because the technical vocabulary used in it is not taught in Pakistan. In India there are also studies of Sindhi (Khubchandani 1961; Rohra 1971), Punjabi (Bhatia 1993) and other languages in English. But, since the focus of this report is on Pakistan, these works cannot be explored here. In Pakistan there are only a few recent works written in Pakistani languages which show some awareness of contemporary terminology and concepts. Most of these works are wrtitten in Urdu and Sindhi. There is, for instance, G.A. Allana's (1967) book on the phonetics of Sindhi and his study of the dialects and spread of the language (Allana 1979). Also worth mentioning are Nabi Baksh Baloch's historical studies of Sindhi (Baloch 1962) and Hidayat Ullah Akhund's thesis on the same subject (Akhund 1994). In Urdu there are studies by Suhail Bukhari (1991) and Abdul Salam's Urdu book on general linguistics (Salam 1993). Although of a rudimentary level, Abdul Salam provides technical terms in Urdu which can help linguists describe modern linguistic concepts. After Mohiuddin Qadri Zor's similar introductory work entitled *Hindustani Lisaniyat* (1932), this is the most adequate attempt to provide an introductory book giving equivalents of the terminology of linguistics in Urdu.

A brief study of Pashto where the terminology of linguistics is introduced in that language is by Khial Bukhari (1964–65). Bukhari touches upon dialectology and phonetics which are generally ignored by Pakistani linguists. His grammar of Pashto, also written in Pashto, is also worth mentioning though it does not touch upon recent grammatical theories (Bukhari 1983). There are such works in Afghanistan, of course, but they also fall outside our purview.

Indeed, for Pakistani linguists it is difficult not to ignore theoretical complexities, because the sources and the level of training available, is not conducive to the study of the more technical aspects of contemporary phonetics, phonology, morphology, syntax and semantics. What then is left for a Pakistani linguist is language planning and lexicology of which examples have been given earlier (Rahman 1995a) or some aspects of sociolinguistics. There are, for instance, studies of politeness in Shina (Shah 1995) and Urdu (Rahman 1995d) and so on. The former work describes verbal politeness patterns in Shina while the latter argues that the norms of verbal politeness in English-speaking cultures—such as the use of the first name without honorifics irrespective of the age differentials of the interlocutors—are influencing English-using Pakistanis. Another kind of work is that of surveying the attitude of people towards different languages. This has been done in great detail by the authors of the *Sociolinguistics Survey of Pakistan* (1992). Even more relevant from the point of view of education is the survey of student's attitudes towards Urdu, English and Punjabi by Sabiha Mansoor in Lahore (Mansoor 1993). The point made in this survey is that students respond pragmatically to the apparent social prestige of a language and evaluate it positively if it increases chances of upward social mobility.

This brings one to the relationship between language and politics; the way language policy can make one language more pragmatically useful, and therefore of higher status, than another language. An example of this is the increase in the social status of English with the corresponding decrease in that of Persian because of British language policies (Rahman 1996b). Another aspect of this relationship is the way language becomes a symbol of ethnicity and may be used to mobilize people against the ruling elite. This has been investigated by the present author in a book-length study (Rahman 1996g) out of which articles on the Hindi–Urdu controversy (1994b) and the Siraiki (1995b), Sindhi (1995c), Pashto (1995e), Bengali (1995f), Balochi/Brahvi (1996a) and Hindko (1996e) language movements are available.

Other Pakistanis interested in linguistics focus on history. The investigation of the history of Urdu and other languages have been mentioned. Among the more scholarly works in other fields are the Proto-historical works of A.H. Dani on the Kharoshthi script (1979), the languages of 'Sind and Sauvira' (1981: 35–42) and archaeological research shedding light on the undeciphered script of the Indus Valley civilization (Dani 1971: 1–77). F.A. Durrani, for instance, suggests that the symbols on Kot Dijian artefacts may be the beginning of writing in the Indus Valley (Durrani 1981). But on this subject too Western scholars, with their immense resources, have written more detailed studies (Parpola 1994, Southworth 1984, Fairservis 1992) while Rashid Akhtar Nadwi, the only Pakistani writer who has written a book on this subject in Urdu (Nadwi 1995), shows neither any awareness of the state of contemporary research in the subject nor of modern techniques in this field of research. The present author's article on the languages of the Proto-Historic Indus Valley is also historical in nature. Although it brings evidence from history in one place it presents no linguistic evidence to support the conjecture that the languages of the Indus Valley were Dardic or any other (Rahman 1996c).

In short, then, linguists working in Pakistan actually work on the periphery of the field of linguistics. Since they do not find material on linguistic theory they wander off into history, political science and sociology or stop producing research altogether. The present author too has undergone this shift from the study of language *per se* to fields which are touched by language or those in which language provides a focal point or serves as an analytical device. Thus, in a sense there is no authentic theoretical (or micro) linguist working in Pakistan. The present author has the reputation of being a linguist but that only reflects the state of ignorance of the country. Those who really are linguists—such as Anjum Saleemi or Ruqaiya Hasan—do not live and work in Pakistan. Such is the state of affairs now but it is only by acknowledging it that we may be able to move forward.

■ 3. Conclusion

Pakistan is perhaps the most backward country of South Asia in the field of linguistics. This is not because there is a dearth of talent but because the subject is not taught anywhere in the country. The few courses which departments of English do offer in it are meant to help in teaching English and not to equip the student to undertake research in linguistics proper. In any case they do not touch upon Pakistani languages. Worst of all, very few books and even fewer journals of linguistics are available in the country so that it is only when one goes abroad that one learns what is happening in the field.

Those who are interested in languages either write in the nineteenth century philological tradition ignoring all recent advances in linguistics or produce prescriptive manuals of 'good usage'. Activists of language movements also write in an amateur and tendencious quality either to air their views or to promote their languages. There are no academic journals of linguistics in the country nor professional groups holding conferences and responding to research. Those who write in this field are virtually isolated. That is why, as in the case of the present writer, linguists turn away from linguistics proper to interdisciplinary areas in which the resources of the established social sciences—such as politics, history or sociology—are available. To sum up, Pakistan has not even started crawling in the field of linguistics.

■ NOTES

1. Up to this time the departments of English focused almost exclusively on English (which generally meant only British) literature up to T.S. Eliot.
2. The present writer, when appointed to the Chair of English at the University of Azad Jammu and Kashmir (Muzaffarabad) in 1987, started the first M.A. in English Language Teaching and Linguistics. This M.A. was unique in that it had courses on general linguistics, socio- and psycho-linguistics as well as English language teaching. However, upon the present writer's relocation at the Quaid-i-Azam University in Islamabad the contents of this M.A. became more traditional as the linguistics courses were replaced with literature ones. At Quaid-i-Azam University, however, a course in anthropological linguistics and on language planning and language problems in Pakistan have been added by the present writer.

■ REFERENCES

Abbas, Shemeem. 1993. The power of English in Pakistan. *World Englishes* 12(2): 147–56.

Akhtar, Saleem. 1995. *Urdu zaban ki mukhtasar tareen tareekh.* [Urdu: The briefest history of the Urdu language]. Islamabad: National Language Authority.

Akhund, Hidayat Ullah. 1994. Sindhi boli jo tarikhi pas manzar. [Sindhi: The historical background to the Sindhi language]. Unpublished Ph.D. thesis, University of Sind, Hyderabad, Pakistan.

Ali, Haqiqat. n.d. *Wakhi language book* [primer]. Hunza: Wakhi Culture Association.

Ali, Usman. 1991. *Shinalogy* [Urdu]. Gilgit: Usmani kutab khana.

Allana, Ghulam Ali. 1967. *Sindhi sautiyat* [Sindhi: Sindhi phonetics]. Hyderabad, Pakistan: Adabiat Publications.

———. 1979. *Sindhi boli ji lisani jagrafi* [Sindhi: The linguistic geography of the Sindhi language]. Hyderabad: Institute of Sindhology.

———. 1993. *Sindhi suratkhati* [Sindhi: Sindhi orthography]. Hyderabad, Pakistan: Sindhi Language Authority.

Askar, Umar Gul. 1972. *Wanechi* [Pashto]. Quetta: Pashto Academy Balochistan.

Awan, Ealhi Baksh. 1994. *The phonology of the verbal phrase in Hindko*. Peshawar: Idara Farogh-i-Hindko.

Azad, Mohammaed Husain. 1880. *Aab-e-hayat* [Urdu: The elixir of Life]. Repr. Lahore: Sang-e-Meel, 1985.

Badakhshani, Maqbool Beg. 1973. *Qawaid-e-Punjabi*. Lahore: Punjabi Tahqeeqati Markaz.

Baloch, Kahair Muhammad. 1993. *Motor vehicles and its parts*. Hyderabad, Pakistan: Sindhi Language Authority.

Baloch, Nabi Baksh. 1962. *Sindhi boli e adab ji makhtasar tarikh* [Sindhi: A brief history of Sindhi language and literature]. Hyderabad, Pakistan: Zeb Adabi Markaz.

Bashir, Elena S. 1991a. A contrastive analysis of Pashto and Urdu. Typescript report. Prepared for the Directorates of Primary Education, NWFP and Balochistan, Pakistan.

———. 1991b. A contrastive analysis of Balochi and Urdu. Typescript report Prepared for the Directorates of Primary Education, NWFP and Balochistan, Pakistan.

———. 1991c. A contrastive analysis of Brahvi and Urdu. Typescript report. Prepared for the Directorates of Primary Education, NWFP and Balochistan, Pakistan.

Baumgardner, Robert J. 1987. Utilizing Pakistani newspaper English to teach grammar. *World Englishes* 6(3).241–52.

——— (ed.). 1993. *The English language in Pakistan*. Karachi: Oxford University Press.

Bhatia, Tej K. 1993. *Punjabi: a cognitive descriptive grammar*. London: Routledge.

Bordi, John G. 1981. An inquiry into the glotto-chronology of Sindhi phonology. *Sind through the centuries*, ed. by Hamida Khuro. 29–80. Karachi: Oxford University Press.

Brahvi, Abdur Rahman. 1982. *Brahvi zaban o adab ki makhtasar tareekh*. Lahore: Markazi Urdu Board.

Bray, Denis. 1907. *The Brahvi language*. Repr. Quetta: Brahvi Academy, 1977.

Bukhari, Khyal. 1964–65. Da Pashto jabe buniadi mas'ale [Pashto: the basic problems of the Pashto language]. Pukhto [Pashto Academy Peshawar] 3–4, Vols 7–8. 119–234.

———. 1983. *Da Pakhto sarf-o-nahaw* [Pashto: Pashto Grammar]. Peshawar: University Book Agency.

Bukhari, Suhail. 1975. *Urdu ki kahani*. Lahore: Maktaba-e-Alia.

———. 1991. *Lisani muqalat*. Part 3. [Urdu: Linguistic dissertations]. Islamabad: National Language Authority.

Bukhari, M. Yusuf. 1986. *Kashmiri aur Urdu zaban ka taqabli muta'ala* [Urdu: The comparative study of Urdu and Kashmiri]. Lahore: Markazi Urdu Board.

Buriro, Ghulam Haider. 1980. Pakistan ji subai e ilaqai zabanan me Sindhi zaban ji ilmi, adabi e lisani haisiat [Sindhi: The linguistic, literary and scholarly position of Sindhi among the other provincial and regional languages of Pakistan]. Unpublished Ph.D. Thesis, University of Sind, Hyderabad, Pakistan.

Burrow, T. 1973. *The Sanskrit language*. London: Faber & Faber.

Cooper, Robert L. 1989. *Language planning and social change*. Cambridge: Cambridge University Press.

Dani, A.H. 1971. Excavations in the Gomal valley. *Ancient Pakistan* 5.1–79.

———. 1979. *Kharoshthi primer*. Lahore: Lahore Museum.

———. 1981a. Sindhu-sauvira: a glimpse into the early history of Sind. Khuro, Hamida (ed.) 1981: 35–42.

——— (ed.). 1981b. *Indus valley: new perspectives*. Islamabad: Quaid-i-Azam University.

Daoodi, Khalil Ur Rahman (ed.). 1962. *Qawaid-e-zaban-e-Urdu* [Urdu: The rules of the Urdu language]. Lahore: Majlis-e-Taraqqi-e-Adab.

Dil, Afia. 1993. *Two traditions of the Bengali language.* Islamabad: National Institute of Historical and Cultural Research.

Dil, Anwar S. 1963. *Pakistani linguistics.* Lahore: Pakistani Linguistics Series.

Durrani, Atash. 1993. *Urdu istilahat sazi* [Urdu: Neologism in Urdu]. Islamabad: Anjuman Sharqia Islamia.

Durrani, F.A. 1981. Indus valley, evidence West of Indus. *Indus valley: new perspectives*, ed. by A.H. Dani, 133–37. Islamabad: Quaid-i-Azam University.

Emeneau, M.B. 1954. Linguistic prehistory of India. *Proceedings of the American society* 98.282–92.

———. 1956. India as a linguistic area. *Language* 32.3–16.

———. 1980. The position of Brahvi in Dravidian languages. *Pakistani linguistics*, ed. by Anwar S. Dil. Lahore: Pakistani Linguistic Series.

———. 1980. *Languages and linguistic area.* Los Angeles and Berkeley: University of California Press.

Fairservis, Walter A. 1992. *The Harappan civilization and its writings: a model for the decipherment of the Indus script.* Leiden: E.J. Brill.

Faridi, Qais. n.d. *Chand Sikairi istalahat o mutradifat* [Urdu/Siraiki: Some Siraiki terms and equivalents]. Khanpur: Dahreecha Adabi Academy.

Faridkoti, Ainul Haq. 1972. *Urdu zaban ki qadeem tareekh* [Urdu: The ancient history of the Urdu language]. Lahore: Orient Research Centre.

———. 1992. *Pre-Aryan origins of the Pakistani languages: a monograph.* Lahore: Orient Research Centre.

Grierson, George. 1901–21. *The linguistic survey of India.* Vols. I–X. Calcutta: Govt of India. Repr.: The linguistic survey of Pakistan. 5 Vols. Lahore: Sang-e-Meel, n.d.

Halliday, M.A.K. and **Hasan, Ruqaiya.** 1976. *Cohesion in English.* London and New York: Longman.

Haq, Mehr Abdul. 1967. *Multani zuban aur us ka Urdu se ta'aluq* [Urdu: The Multani language and its relationship with Urdu]. Bahawalpur: Urdu Academy.

Hasan, Ruqaiya. 1964. A linguistic study of contrasting features in the style of two contemporary English prose writes. University of Edinburgh Ph.D. thesis.

Hashimi, Sayyid. 1962. *Balochi siyahage rastnibisag.* [Balochi: Balochi orthography]. Karachi.

Husain, Masood. 1966. *Tarikh zaban Urdu.* Lahore: Urdu Markaz.

Jatoi, Ali Nawaz. 1983. *Ilm ul lisan aur Sindhi zaban* [Urdu: Linguistics and the Sindhi language]. Hyderabad, Pakistan: Institute of Sindhology.

Javed, Asmat. 1981. *Nae Urdu gawaid* [Urdu: The new grammar of Urdu]. New Delhi: Taraqqi-e-Urdu Bureau.

Kachru, Braj B. 1965. The Indiannes in Indian English. *Word* 21.391–410.

———. 1983. *The Indianization of English: the English language in India.* Delhi: Oxford University Press.

Khan, Baber S. 1987. The ergative case in Hindi–Urdu. *Studies in the Linguistic Sciences* 17(1).91–101.

———. 1989. A note of disagreement on verb agreement in Hindi–Urdu. *Linguistics* 27.71–87.

Khattak, Raj Wali. 1991. *Navi imla* [Pashto: New orthography]. Peshawar: Pashto Academy.

Khubchandani, L. 1961. The phonology and morphophonemics of Sindhi. Unpublished M.A. thesis, University of Pennsylvania.

Khuhro, Hamida (ed.). 1981. *Sind through the centuries.* Karachi: Oxford University Press.

Mansoor, Sabiha. 1993. *Punjabi, Urdu, English in Pakistan: a sociolinguistic study.* Lahore: Vanguard.

Moizuddin, Mohammad. 1989. *Word forms in Urdu.* Islamabad: National Language Authority.

Mughal, Shaukat. 1987. *Qadeem Urdu ki lughat aur Siraiki zaban* [Urdu: The dictionary of Old Urdu and the Siraiki language]. Multan: Siraiki Isha'ati Idara.

Nadvi, Rahid Akhtar. 1995. *Pakistan ka qadeem rasmul khat* [Urdu: The ancient script of Pakistan]. Islamabad: National Institute of History and Culture.

Nasir, Nasiruddin. n.d. *Buruso birkis* [Burushaski/English primer]. Hunza: Bursaski Kisarc Ekodami.

Nayyar, Moukhtar Ali. 1976. *Hindko gawaid* [Hindko: Hindko grammar]. Peshawar: Maktaba Hindko Zaban.

Parpola, Asko. 1994. *Deciphering the Indus script.* Cambridge: Cambridge University Press.

Rahman, Tariq. 1990. *Pakistani English.* Islamabad: National Institue of Pakistan Studies, Quaid-i-Azam University.

———. 1992. MA TEFL: *Modern grammatical theory: Guide.* Islamabad: Allama Iqbal Open University.

———. 1994a. Sociolinguistic survey of Northern Pakistan. *Language* 70(4).840–3.

———. 1994b. Urdu-Hindi controversy. *Pakistan journal of history and culture.* 15(2).19–45.

———. 1995a. *Language planning and politics in Pakistan.* Islamabad: Sustainable Development Policy Institute.

———. 1995b. The Siraiki movement in Pakistan. *Language problems and language planning* 19(1).1–25.

———. 1995c. Language and politics in a Pakistan province: the Sindhi language movement. *Asian survey* 35(11).1005–16.

———. 1995d. Imperialism and the pragmatics of Urdu in Pakistan. *Journal of Central Asia* 18(1).16–44.

———. 1995e. The Pashto language movement and identity formation in Pakistan. *Journal of comtemporary Asia* 4(26).151–70.

———. 1995f. The Bengali language movement. *Pakistan Journal of history and culture* 16(2).1–32.

———. 1995g. Urdu of another kind. *News* [English Daily] 29 Apr., 1995. Opinion page.

———. 1996a. The Balochi/Brahvi language movements in Pakistan. *Journal of South Asian and Middle Eastern Studies.* 19(3).71–88.

———. 1996b. British language policies and imperialism in India. *Language problems and language planning* 20(2).91–115.

———. 1996c. Languages of the proto-historic Indus valley. *Mankind quarterly* 36(3–4). 221–46.

———. 1996d. The English-Urdu controversy in Pakistan. *Modern Asian studies* 31(1). 177–207.

———. 1996e. The Hindko language movement in Pakistan. *Kashmir journal of language research* 1(1).30–40.

———. 1996f. Insights into language-learning: review of Universal grammar and language learnability, by Anjum Saleemi. *News* [English daily] 28 Aug., Opinion page.

———. 1996g. *Language and politics in Pakistan.* Karachi: Oxford University Press.

Raja, Nasim Akhtar. 1992. Punjabi compounds: a structural and semantic study. Unpublished M. Litt. dissertation, University of Strathclyde.

Rasoolpuri, Aslam. 1976. *Siraiki rasmulkhat ki makhtasar tareekh* [Urdu: A short history of Siraiki orthography]. Multan: Bazme Saqafat.

Rohra, S.K. 1971. Sindhi, kacchi and emigrant Sindhi. *Indian Linguistics* 32(2).130–1.

Sabir, Abdul Razzak. 1994. Balochi aur Brahvi zabanon ke ravabit [Urdu: The relations between the Balochi and Brahvi languages]. Unpublished Ph.D. thesis, University of Balochistan, Quetta.

Sabzwari, Shaukat. 1966. *Urdu lisaniyat* [Urdu: Urdu linguistics]. Karachi: Maktaba Takhleeq Adab.

Salam, Abdul. 1993. *Umumi lisaniyat* [Urdu: General linguistics]. Karachi: Royal Book Co.

Saleemi, Anjum P. 1992. *Universal grammar and language learnability.* Cambridge: Cambridge University Press.
———. 1994. Case and agreement in Hindi–Urdu. *Papers from the fifteenth Asian language analysis roundtable conference*, ed. by A. Davison and F.N. Smith. Iowa City: University of Iowa.
———. 1995a. Discussion: On new/non-native English: a gamelan. *Journal of pragmatics* 24.295–321.
———. 1995b. On the acquisition of split ergativity: some evidence from Urdu. *The proceedings of the twenty-sixth annual child language research forum*, ed. by E. Clark. Stanford California: CSLI, Stanford University Press.
Sarwar, Zakia (ed.). 1991. *English study skills.* Karachi: SPELT.
———. Interview. 25 Sept. 1994, Karachi.
Shah, Ijlal Hussain. 1994. The Pragmatics of formality and politeness in Burushaski and Shina. Unpublished M.Phil. thesis, Quaid-i-Azam University, Islamabad.
Shirani, Hafiz Mahmood. 1928. *Punjab mein Urdu* [Urdu: Urdu in Punjab]. Lahore: Kitab Numa.
Southworth, F.C. 1984. Some aspects of Dravidian prehistory based on vocabulary re-construction. Paper presented at the American anthropological meeting, Denver, November.
Wagha, Ahsan. 1990. *The Siraiki language, its growth and development.* Islamabad: Ddewar Publications.
Yusuf, Mohammad. 1990. *Balti zaban* [Urdu: The Balti language].
Zor, S.M. Qadri. 1932. *Hindustani lisaniyat* [Urdu: Indian linguistics]. Repr. Lahore: Panjnad Academy.

■ PAKISTAN: NON-INDO-EUROPEAN ■

ÉTIENNE TIFFOU

■ 1. Introduction

All the languages spoken in Pakistan are Indo-European, except three: Balti, a Tibeto-Burman language, spoken at the foot of the Karakoram, just south of K2; Brahui, a Dravidian language, spoken in some parts of Balochistan and of Sind, and, finally, Burushaski, an isolated language, spoken in the valley of Hunza located in the Karakoram and also used in the valley of Yasin located in a transitional area where these mountains meet the Hindukush (about the two languages spoken in the north of Pakistan and the surrounding languages, see Backstrom and Radloft [1992] on the languages and Irmtraud–Stellrecht [1995] for a bibliography).

■ 2. Balti

We have to go beyond the last ten years to find monographs dedicated to Balti.[1] The most important grammars of this language are: the grammar written by A.F.C. Read published in 1934, and the grammar of R. Bielmeier published in *Das Märchen vom Prinzen Čobzaŋ* (1985a). The latter is a reprint of the part one of the author's habilitation thesis: *Deskriptive und historisch-vergleichende Untersuchung zur Stellung des tibetischen Balti-Dialekts*. On the other hand, this book offers, up to the date of its publication, an excellent bibliography of the works produced on the Balti. More recently, Muhammad Yusef Hussainabadi has written, in Urdu, a small grammar of Balti (1990). Very shortly after, one year later, came out another book whose author, Ghulam Hassan Lobsang, produced in Balti a grammar which has just been published in English (1995). As for the book giving short sketches of the languages of the concerned area, and in particular on Balti (*Languages of Northern Areas*, 1992), the data are too often inaccurate. Finally, since Balti offers very precious information for historical linguistics, it is very often taken in consideration in more general studies (cf. R. Bielmeier 1985b, 1986a, 1986b, 1988a, 1988b, 1988c, 1993, 1994).

For the vocabulary, a glossary will be found in R. Bielmeier (1985a). On the other hand, R.K. Sprigg is about to publish a dictionary which integrates the dictionary Read had undertaken approximatively sixty years earlier. Read had practically finished his book, but he lost half of his work when he left Kashmir around 1947. Only the first part (from A to M) remained. R.K. Sprigg has just completed what was missing and re-appraised what was left. At the same time, R. Bielmeier and his team are preparing an edition of a Balti–Urdu–English dictionary, compiled by the actual raja of Shigar, Muhammad Ali Saba, and rewritten and translated in English by Fakhruz Zaman. Actually the authors are proceeding to the phonological notations. Finally, in his dictionary, H. Berger (see the Burushaski section), has identified the words borrowed in Hunza from Balti.

As for to the texts, R. Bielmeier (1985a) offered the edition and the translation of a Balti story. A good and interesting overview of the oral literature will be found in K. Sagaster's article (1995). R. Bielmeier and his team are also preparing an edition of 850 Balti proverbs gathered by Gh. Hassan Hasni. There is a computerized version of these proverbs transcribed, explained and translated in Urdu. They have just been transcribed in Roman script and a translation is under way.

■ 3. Brahui

Brahui which, as Emeneau wrote (1980: 315–16), "is in some ways the most interesting of the languages of the Dravidian family,…has been known to the Westerners since 1816." One will find in Emeneau (1980: 316–18) a good presentation of the first studies on this language. One of the major works is the book of Sir Denys Bray (1909 and 1934), the other one is the Dravidian etymological dictionary of T. Burrow and M.B. Emeneau (1961) in which are included

Brahui items of Dravidian origin. Because of its special features, Brahui is quoted very often in the numerous studies dedicated to other Dravidian languages. Emeneau (1961) deals with this kind of a comparative grammar. From another point of view, E. Bashir's valuable work (1991) proposes a contrastive approach to this language (with Urdu). The English version of Andronov's study offers a good grammar of Brahui itself, but it relies, as this scholar recognizes it (1980: 317), on Bray's work.

Among the recent articles on Brahui, the two by Elfenbein (1987 and 1989) offer good perspectives of this language. Emeneau's analysis of pronouns and reflexives (1991) is convincing. R. Parkin's study intersects linguistics at a lexicographical level, but, as far as kinship terminology is concerned, this article pertains to anthropology and it is valuable to compare this terminology with those used in surrounding or related languages.

Finally it is worth noting that Brahui is the only Pakistani non-Indo-European language which is taught and specially studied at the university level. There is a department of Brahui in the University of Balochistan (located in Quetta). The professor, Abdul Razzaq, can be contacted for further information.

■ 4. Burushaski

Being an isolate, Burushaski has always aroused the interest of linguists, and, compared with other languages, particularly since the end of the precedent century, a lot of studies have been dedicated to this language (D.L.R. Lorimer's works of 1935–38 and 1963 remain even now very important). Burushaski splits into two main dialects (Hunza-Nagar and Yasin). The first one subdivides into two sub-dialects (Hunza and Nagar). Paradoxically, Hunza, which has been celebrated by a lot of journalists and travellers, has not led to any recent monographs, except the publication of a book on proverbs by the present author and some of his colleagues (E. Tiffou and all, 1993). That is not the case for Yasin Burushaski on which H. Berger has written in 1974—a fundamental work. Since then the present author (E. Tiffou 1989, with the collaboration of J. Pesot) has published a book with tales, grammar and a glossary, and a small dictionary (1989, with the collaboration of Y–C. Morin) which brings some additional information to H. Berger's work. In actual fact, this linguist is about to publish the book of a lifetime on Hunza and Nagar Burushaski. This one will consist of three volumes: I grammar; II texts with notes and remarks; III dictionary. I am sure this book, eagerly awaited by specialists, will increase the knowledge of Burushaski. The same linguist has also published a booklet on the fate of this language (1992). For the record, we will mention the book already quoted about the languages of the area (*Languages of Northern Areas*, 1992), but the data in it are rudimentary and the notations have to be reconsidered. On the other hand, in one of the three booklets he has edited, N. Uḍḍin Hunzai (1991a) offers an interesting point of view of a speaker on his native language, and the other two (1991b and c) give a very rich corpus of proverbs and riddles. Finally, besides linguistic considerations, A.H. Dani (1989) has written a substantial book on the history of the area and the present author (Tiffou 1995) a book on life in Yasin, which includes a chapter on the language.

The articles about Burushaski are various and numerous and interestingly in very different fields: 1) linguistics: H. Berger (1994), D´jačov (1988), R. Patry and E. Tiffou (forthcoming, ms.), E. Tiffou and R. Patry (1993, 1995a, 1995b, 1995c, forthcoming), B. Tikkanen (1991a, 1996, ms.), S.R. Willson (1996); 2) texts: B. Tikkanen (1991b); 3) origins et survival of the language: J. Bengtson (ms.1; ms.2), M. Morvan (1992), E. Tiffou (1995, 1996), B. Tikkanen (1988); 3); history and civilisation: A. Frémont (1993), H. Kreutzmann (1989, 1991). As is clear from the linguistic references, Burushaski has been studied from phonological as well as from a morphological, syntactic and semantic angle. An exploration, according to linguistics principles, is also under way. In this exploration, grammatical coherence (play of anaphorics, function of connectors) is chiefly considered (at the Université de Montréal).

■ NOTE

1. I want to thank my colleague R. Bielmeier who sent all the information on Balti I needed for the present survey.

■ REFERENCES

I. General

Backstrom, P.C. and **C.F. Radloff** (eds). 1992. *Languages of Northern Areas.* National Institute of Pakistan Studies. Qaid-i-Azam University, Summer Institute of Linguistics.

Irmtraud-Stellrecht, I. 1995. *Bibliography. Northern Pakistan.* Reinbek bei Hambourg. Verlaf für Orientalische Fachpublicationen.

II. Balti

Bielmeier, R. 1985a. Das Märchen vom Prinzen Čobzaŋ. Eine tibetische Erzählung aus Baltistan. Text, Übersetzung, Grammatik und west-tibetisch vergleichendes Glossar. Sankt Augustin. VGH Wissenschaftsverlag.

———. 1985b. A survey of the development of western and southwestern Tibetan dialects. Proceedings of the 1982 Seminar of the International Association for Tibetan Studies. *Soundings in Tibetan Civilization*, ed. by B.N. Aziz and M. Kapstein, 3–19. New Delhi: Manohar.

———. 1986a. Zur Stellung des Dialektes vom Mustang in Nepal. Formen kulturellen Wandels und andere Beiträge zur Erforschung des Himalaya. Nepalica II. Colloquium des Schwerpunktes Nepal. 1984, ed. by B. Kölver, 433–50. Sankt Augustin (VGH Wissenschaftsverlag).

———. 1986b. Die tibetische Sprache und ihre Dialekte. *Tibet-Forum* 5/1.15–18.

———. 1988a. Tone in Tibetan. Proceedings of the 4th seminar of IATS. Tibetan Studies. München. 43–54.

———. 1988b. A Preliminary Survey of the Dialect Mustang. *Journal of the Nepal Research Center* 8.31–7.

———. 1988c. The Reconstruction of the Stop Series and the Verbal System in Tibetan. Festschrift for T. Nishida. *Languages and History of East Asia.* Kyoto. 15–27.

Bielmeier, R. 1993. Sprachvielfalt im Himalaya. *Tibetische Dialektforschung in Bern,* ed. by A. Etter. 78.31–33. Bern: Universität Bern.

———. 1994. Zu den Bono-Na Liedern der Darden von Da-Hanu. *Festschrift Georg Budruss,* ed. by R. Söhnen-Thieme and O. von Hinüber. 11–32.

———. Muhammad Ali Saba and Fakhruz Zaman: Forthcoming. *Balti-Urdu-English dictionary.*

Hassan (Lobsang), Gh. 1995. *Short sketch of Balti grammar. A tibetan dialect spoken in Northern Pakistan.* Bern: Universität Bern, Institut für Sprachwissenschaft.

Hussainabadi, M.Y. 1990. *Balti zaban.* Skardu.

Sagaster, K. 1995. Mündliche epische Tradition in Westtibet (Baltistan). Norrhein-Westfälische Akademie der Wissenschaften, 95 ed. by W. Heissig. 121–31. Formen und Fonktion mündlicher Tradition, Westdeutscher Verlag.

Sprigg, R.K. Forthcoming. *Balti-English dictionary.*

III. Brahui

Andronov, M.S. 1980. *The Brahui language.* Moskva. Nauka.

Bashir, E. 1991. *A contrastive analysis of Brahui and Urdu.* Washington DC: Academy for Educational Development.

Bray, Denys (Sir). 1909. *The Brahui language: part I, Introduction and grammar.* Calcutta.

———. 1934. *The Brahui language: part II, The Brahui problem; part III: Etymological vocabulary.* Delhi.

Burrow, T. and **Emeneau, M.B.** 1961. *A Dravidian etymological Dictionary.* Oxford: Clarendon Press.

Elfenbein, J. 1987. A periplus of the 'Brahui problem'. *Studia Iranica* 16(2).215–33.

Elfenbein, J. 1989. Brahui 2: language. *Encyclopædia Iranica 4,* ed. by E. Yarshater, 438–43. London, Routledge and Kegan Paul.

Emeneau, M.B. 1961. Brahui and Dravidian comparative grammar. UCPL 27.

———. 1980. *Language and linguistic area.* Essays by Murray B. Emeneau, selected and introduced by Anwar S. Dil. Stanford: Stanford University Press (the third part of this book is dedicated to Brahui, S. 315–49).

———. 1991. Brahui personal pronouns: 1st singular and reflexive. *Studies in Dravidian and general linguistics: a festschrift for Bh. Krishnamurti,* ed. by B. Lakshmi Bai and B. Ramakrishna Reddy. 1–12. Hyderabad: Centre of Advanced Study in Linguistics.

Parkin, R. 1989. Some comments on Brahui kinship terminology. *IIJ* 32(1). 37–43.

IV. Burushaski

Bengtson, J. *Ms1.* A comparison of Burushic and (North) Caucasian.

———. *Ms2.* Burushaski 'Nose', 'Nostril'.

Berger, H. 1992. *Das Burushaski: schicksale einer zentralasiatischen Retsprache.* Heidelberg. Winter.

———. 1994. 'Kombinatorischer Lautwandel im Burushaski.' *Festschrift Georg Budruss,* ed. by R. Söhnen-Thieme and O. von Hinüber. 1–9.

———. Forthcoming. *Die burushaski Sprache von Hunza und Nagar.* Teil I: Grammatik. Teil II Texte mit Übersetzungen und Anmerkungen. Teil III: Hunza-Wörterbuch.

Dani, A.H. 1991. *History of Northern Areas of Pakistan.* Islamabad: National Institute of Historical and Cultural Research.

D'jačov, M.T. 1988. Burušaski-cyganski jazykovyekontakti: (po povodu sta'i Ch. Bergera). *Grammatičeskaja i semantičeskaja struktura slova v jazykach norodov Sibiri: skornich trudov,* ed. by B.V. Boldyrev and L.V. Petropavlovskaja. Novosibirsk.

Frémont, A. 1993. Remarques sur les activités commerciales des pays Burushos de 1761 à nos jours. Fiction et réalité. Circulation des monnaies, des marchandises et des biens. Res Orientales 5. Groupe pour l'Étude de la Civilisation du Moyen–Orient. Bures-sur-Yvette. 179–87.

Kreutzmann, H. 1989. Hunza: ländliche Entwicklung im Karakoram. Abhandlungen—Anthropogeographie. Institut für geographische Wissenschaften 44. Berlin: Dietrich Reimer Verlag.

Kreutzmann, H. 1991. The Karakoram Highway—The impact of road construction on mountain societies. *Modern Asian Studies* 25. 711–36.

Lorimer, D.L.R. 1935–38. *The Burushaski Language.* 3 vols. Oslo: Instituttet forsammenlignende kulturforskning.

———. 1962. Werchikwar English Vocabulary (with a few Werchikwar Texts). Oslo: Instituttet forsammenlignende kulturforskning.

Morin, Y.-Ch. and Tiffou, E. 1988. Passives in Burushaski. *Passive and Voice*, ed. by M. Shibatani, 493–524. Typological Studies in Language 16. Amsterdam/ Philadelphia: John Benjamins.

——— 1989. *Dictionnaire complémentaire du bourouchaski du Yasin.* Paris: Peteers/ SELAF.

Morvan, M. 1992. Remarques au sujet des comparaisons macro-caucasiques de John P. Bengtson. *Bulletin de la Société Linguistique de Paris* 87(1).357–65.

Patry, R. and **E. Tiffou.** Forthcoming. An analysis of grammatical anaphora within corpus of tales in Yasin Burushaski. To appear in *Himalayan Languages*, ed. by G. van Driem. Berlin: Walter de Gruyter.

——— and **Tiffou, E.** Forthcoming. Etude sur les connecteurs de liaison en bourouchaski du Yasin.

Tiffou, É. and **Pesot, J.** 1989. *Contes du Yasin. Introduction au bourouchaski du Yasin avec grammaire et dictionnaire analytique.* Paris: Peeters/SELAF.

Tiffou, É., Morin, Y.–Ch., Berger, H., †Lorimer, D.L.R. and **Uḍḍin Hunzai, N.** 1993. Hunza Proverbs. Calgary. University of Calgary Press.

——— and **Patry, R.** 1993. L'expression de la cohésion lexicale en bourouchaski: de la continuité du discours. Working Papers of the University of Toronto. 14 p.

———. 1995a. La relative en bourouchaski du Yasin. *Bulletin de la Société Linguistique de Paris* 110(1).335–90.

———. 1995b. La notion de pluralité verbale: Le cas du bourouchaski. *Journal Asiatique* 282(1).407–44.

———. 1995c. L'expression de l'antériorité et de la postériorité en bourouchaski du Yasin. *Cahiers de l'Institut de Linguistique de Louvain* 21(3–4).139–71.

———. 1995. About Trask: Basque and Dene–Caucasian: A critique from the Basque side. *Mother tongue* 1.159–62.

———. 1996. Le bourouchaski, langue en danger? Actes du XIXème congrés International de la Fédération des Langues et Littératures Modernes. Brasilía. Universidade de Brasília. T. 2.572–84.

———. Forthcoming. Verbal plurality and the notion of mulitple-event in Yasin Burushaski. To appear in Proceedings of the 3rd International Hindukush Conference, ed. by E. Bashir. Chitral.

Tikkanen, B. 1988. On Burushaski and other ancient Substrata in North-Western South Asia. *Studia Orientalia* (ed. by the Finnish Oriental Society) 64.303–25.

———. 1991a. Review of 'Contes du Yasin' (Étienne Tiffou and Jurgen Pesot) and of 'Dictionnaire complémentaire du bourouchaski du Yasin' (Yves-Charles Morin and Étienne Tiffou). *Studia Orientalia* 67.215–31.

———. 1991b. A Burushaski folktale, transcribed and translated: the Frog as a Bride, or, the Three Princes and the Fairy Princess Salaasír. *Studia Orientalia* 67.65–125.

———. 1995. Burushaski converbs in their South and Central Asian areal context. Converbs (adverbial participles, gerunds) in cross-linguistic perspective, ed. by M. Haspelmath and E. König. 487–528. *Empirical Approaches to Language Typologie* 13. Berlin and New York. Mouton de Gruyter.

———. Ms. The verb *hurúṭ* 'sit, stay, dwell,' as an aspectual auxiliary in Hunza Burushaski: a South Asian areal feature in the Karakoram?

Uḍḍin Hunzai, N. 1991a. Burušo birkiṣ. Hunzo, Giilt, Karaači: Burušaski Risarč Ekaḍemi.

———. 1991b. Saweene bariŋ. Hunzo, Giilt, Karaači. Burušaski Risarč Ekaḍemi.

Uḍḍin Hunzai, N. 1991c. Burušaski burjooniŋ. Hunzo, Giilt, Karaači. Burušaski Risarč Ekaḍemi.
Willson, S.R. 1996. Verb agreement and case marking in Burushaski. Working Papers of the Summer Institute of Linguistics. 40.1–71. University of North Dakota.

■ SOUTHEAST ASIA ■

ANJUM P. SALEEMI

The South Asian Diaspora in Southeast Asia is mainly represented by South Indian minorities, some of which, notably the Tamil communities in Malaysia and Singapore, are quite large in size. There are also (typically much smaller) minorities of the North and East Indian origin. As many of these immigrant minorities continued to speak their languages in at least some contexts of use, several South Asian languages, e.g. Tamil, Malayalam, Bengali, Gujerati, Hindi, Punjabi, etc. became part of the current linguistic scene of South Asia, thus adding a new dimension to the immense linguistic richness and diversity inherent in the region. Given the relatively small numbers of the immigrant or expatriate speakers of these languages, there is simply no critical demographic mass to generate a lot of research on them. Some such research, however, does get done, depending on individual interests of researchers working at academic institutions in the region. In what follows, the publications described are those which have originated in the somewhat sporadic research activity devoted to the investigation of South Asian languages conducted wholly or partly in South Asia (in fact, mostly in Singapore and Malaysia). Moreover, since this is the first report to be compiled for the present journal, instead of confining my commentary merely to the past year, I'll take the liberty of extending its scope further back to include work published or presented during 1994. That will provide a relatively more enriched and wider perspective, meant to serve as a broad enough backdrop for future commentary and discussion.

Much of the work to be discussed is syntactic in orientation, though semantic, acquisitional, phonetic, and sociolinguistic studies will also be reported.

In the domain of syntax, there is a set of closely related publications by K.P. Mohanan and Tara Mohanan, perhaps the most notable of which is T. Mohanan (1994a). This is a revised version of the author's doctoral dissertation, completed at Stanford University in 1990. Based on extensive Hindi data, it is a study of argument structure, construed as a distinct level of syntax, and of its place among the other levels of syntax. The latter are specified as semantic structure, grammatical function structure and grammatical category structure, and it is argued that these, together with argument structure, constitute a multi-dimensional, parallel and non-transformational system of syntactic organisation. The spirit of the argumentation, if not the actual technical detail, is fairly close to Joan Bresnan's Lexical Functional Grammar. The range of Hindi data examined is considerable, encompassing case marking, agreement, noun incorporation, complex predicates, anaphora and control.

The approach presented in T. Mohanan (1994a) resurfaces in both T. Mohanan (1994b) and Mohanan and Mohanan (1994), and indeed continues in these authors' subsequent work. The arguments of T. Mohanan (1994b) rest on the view that Hindi exhibits a constraint, akin to the Obligatory Contour Principle in phonology, whereby adjacent nouns are prevented from having identical case endings. In Mohanan and Mohanan (1994), some facts pertaining to the freedom of word order in Hindi and Malayalam are analyzed and it is claimed that the analysis provides further support to the multi-dimensional approach to the architecture of syntactic representations developed in T. Mohanan (1994a). Reaching down to the level of morphology, the foregoing concerns are reflected, once again, in T. Mohanan (1995), which, having argued that certain verb-object sequences in Hindi are in fact instances of noun incorporation, goes on to conceptualize lexicality and wordhood in a fashion that is consistent with her general approach to linguistic architecture, an approach further extended to an investigation of complex predicates in Hindi in T. Mohanan (to appear). Finally, using data from Kannada (along with Malay and English data), Mohanan and Mohanan (to appear) treats lexical reflexives and reciprocals within a theory of the projection of arguments.

A number of recent papers by David Gil utilize data from South Asian languages to capture various historical, typological and theoretical insights. Gil (1994) discusses conjunctive operators: in particular, Malayalam *-um* and Punjabi *-vi*. Drawing upon the work of Murray Emeneau, he proposes a framework to account for the diverse range of interpretations that conjunctive operators like *-um* and *-vi* can have. The historical predecessors of such operators in South Asian languages, namely the Classical Sanskrit *api* and the Proto-Dravidian *-um*, are discussed in Gil (to appear, a). In Gil (to appear, b) the focus is shifted to some reduplicative expressions in Punjabi, Hindi and Bangla. Gil analyzes the process involved in the construction of these expressions as consisting of mutation and reduplication, both of which are claimed to be iconic in nature. The former, transforming one word into another similar-sounding one, is argued to denote associativity, whereas the latter, involving the repetition of a word, is considered to be a marker of plurality.

Some research has concentrated on certain aspects of Hindi–Urdu syntax and the acquisition of the syntax. In Saleemi (1994a), a child's acquisition of Urdu is described and an attempt is made to explain the systematic incompleteness of children's early language in terms of economy of derivations. It is suggested that children's derivations may converge prematurely and that their syntax tends to be more LF-oriented than the adult syntax of the ambient language.

Saleemi (1994b) considers the systems of case and agreement in Hindi–Urdu from the principles-and-parameters perspective, and suggests that the interaction between case and agreement in this language is far more complex than is commonly acknowledged. For instance, the nominative–ergative split is shown to exist systematically only in respect of imperfective vs. inflectional perfective aspect. When the aspect is encoded in one of the few perfective auxiliaries, the ergative pattern is no longer determined by perfectivity alone; in fact, it is possible only when the particular perfective auxiliary in use possesses certain semantic properties. The syntactic arguments of Saleemi (1994b) find at least partial support in the acquisition data discussed in Saleemi (1995), where the acquisition of case and agreement in an Urdu-speaking child is analyzed. Further, the Hindi–Urdu and Punjabi systems of case and agreement form part of the empirical motivation for questioning the notion of a unified language/grammar in Saleemi (1996), which outlines a radical rethink of the standard learnability assumptions in the generative paradigm.

The phonetics of some South Asian languages has also been the focus of investigation in Southeast Asia. Thus, Nihalani (1994) presents an acoustic study of the stop consonants in Malayalam. Nihalani has been working on the phonetics of Sindhi for many years. His papers on apical and laminal stops (Nihalani 1995a) and implosives (Nihalani, to appear) are a consequence of that long-standing interest, also reflected in his sketch of Sindhi composed for the *Journal of the International Phonetic Association* (Nihalani 1995b). Note that Nihalani (to appear) takes into account the relevant Malayalam data as well.

Further, there is a study of code choice among multilingual Malaysian–Bengali women. Although it is the author's Texas A & M University doctoral dissertation, part of the research for Mukherjee (1995) was conducted in Malaysia. This work relies considerably on results obtained from extensive fieldwork, and can be described as an ethnography of communication. Also notable, though pertaining to Southwest Pacific rather than Southeast Asia, are a number of studies conducted by France Mugler and his co-researchers (e.g., Mugler 1997, Mugler and Lal 1995) that investigate the place of South Indian languages in Fiji. Most of the Indian population of Fiji speaks Fiji Hindi, and these researchers claim that the vocal varieties of Tamil, Telugu and Malayalam are undergoing structural attrition, particularly in the mophosyntax. Further, they are facing a continuing and precipitous loss of speakers and are thus threatened with extinction.

As can be judged from the foregoing outline, South Asian linguistics in Southeast Asia is hardly a large-scale enterprise. Many aspects of linguistics and several facets of the empirical phenomena remain understudied or even unexplored, including the potentially prolific and insightful domain of comparison between South Asian and Southeast Asian languages. It is, however, hoped that the relevant linguistic research in the region will expand with the passage of time, and will eventually succeed in establishing the necessary symbiotic links with the study of the original local languages. I might as well mention that there is a possibility that some relevant research conducted in Malaysia, Indonesia, the Philippines, and the rest has escaped my notice due to poor channels of communication or sheer ignorance on my part. If so, let's hope such deficiencies will get corrected in due course, and consequently the coverage will be much better in the next report.

■ REFERENCES

Gil, David. 1994. Conjunctive operators in South Asian languages. *Papers from the fifteenth South Asian language analysis roundtable conference 1993*, ed. by Alice Davison and Frederick M. Smith, 277–95. Iowa City: South Asian Studies Program, University of Iowa.

———. (to appear, a). Sanskrit *api*, Proto-Dravidian *-um*, and their descendants. Professor D.S. Dwivedi felicitation volume, ed. by R.E. Asher and R. Harris.

———. (to appear, b). An iconic associative plural construction: mutation cum reduplication in South Asian languages. *Papers from the eighteenth South Asian language analysis roundtable conference*, New Delhi, 1997.

Mohanan, K.P. and **Tara Mohanan.** 1994. Issues in word order: enriched phrase structure or multidimensionality? *Theoretical perspectives on word order in South Asian languages*, ed. by Miriam Butt, Tracy Holloway King and Gillian Ramchand: 153–84. Stanford: CSLI Publications.

———. To appear. Strong and weak projection: lexical reflexives and reciprocals. *Projection of arguments: Lexical and syntactic constraints*, ed. by Miriam Butt and Wilhelm Geuder. Stanford: CSLI Publications.

Mohanan, Tara. 1994a. Argument structure in Hindi (Dissertations in Linguistics). Stanford: CSLI Publications.

———. 1994b. Case OCP: A constraint on word order in Hindi. *Theoretical perspectives on word order in South Asian languages*, ed. by M. Butt, T.H. King and G. Ramchand, 185–216. Stanford: CSLI: Publications.

———. 1995. Wordhood and lexicality: noun incorporation in Hindi. *Natural Language and Linguistic Theory* 13.75–134.

———. To appear. Multidimensionality of representation: NV complex predicates in Hindi. *Complex predicates*, ed. by Alex Alsina, Joan Bresnan and Peter Sells. Stanford: CSLI Publications.

Mugler, France. 1997. South Indian languages in Fiji: languages contact and attrition. *Proceedings of the second international conference on oceanic linguistics*, ed. by Jan Tent and France Mugler. Canberra: Australian National University (forthcoming).

Mugler, France and **Sam Mohan Lal.** 1995. Fiji Tamil: the structure of a language under threat. *International Journal of Dravidian Linguistics* 24(2).118–33.

Mukherjee, Dipika. 1995. Ethnic identity and language use by women in the immigrant Malaysian–Bengali community. Texas A & M University doctoral dissertation.

Nihalani, Paroo. 1994. Acoustic properties of stop consonants in Malayalam. *Journal of Acoustical Society of India* 22.328–36.

———. 1995a. Distinguishing apical and laminal stops: a relevant study of articulatory and acoustic properties. *The proceedings of XVth International Congress on Phonetics, Vol. 3.* 117–20. Trondheim.

———. 1995b. Sindhi. *Journal of the International Phonetic Association* 25.27–30.

———. To appear. Implosives revisited. Submitted to: *Journal of the International Phonetic Association.*

Saleemi, Anjum P. 1994a. Derivational constraints in early Urdu syntax. Paper presented at the 18th Boston University Conference on Language Development, Boston.

———. 1994b. "If that's the Case I don't agree": Case, agreement and phrase structure in Hindi–Urdu. *Papers from the fifteenth South Asian language analysis roundtable conference*

1993, ed. by Alice Davison and Frederick M. Smith, 277–95. Iowa City: South Asian Studies Program, University of Iowa.

Saleemi, Anjum P. 1995. On the acquisition of split ergativity: some evidence from Urdu. The proceedings of the twenty-sixth annual Child Language Research Forum, ed. by Eve V. Clark, 82–93. Stanford: CSLI.

———. 1996. Syntax learnability: the problem that won't go away. Paper presented at the Linguistics Association of Great Britain Autumn Meeting, Cardiff.

Reviews

Josef Bayer, *Directionality and Logical Form: On the Scope of Focussing Particles and Wh-in-situ*. Dordrecht: Kluwer, 1996, Pp. xv, 328. Price not available.

Reviewed by Tanmoy Bhattacharya, University College, London.

The subtitle of the book under review—*On the Scope of Focussing Particles and Wh-in-situ*—probably covers a larger range of the topics discussed within than the title *Directionality and LF*, both of which work as lifelines connecting Chapters 1–6 and Chapter 7. The title is also an attempt to reinstate our faith in matters severely dislodged recently by Kayne (Kayne, R. 1994. *The Antisymmetry of Syntax*. Cambridge, Mass.: MIT Press). But that is only half the truth. As far as LF is concerned, the main thesis that Bayer pushes is that there must be a level of representation of LF. This is not an earthshaking proposal by itself; but combined with promises to show that

- abstract and visible movements are subject to the same constraints, and
- syntax of LF is more transparently derivational than overt syntax.

It is a rather awesome task that Bayer sets himself. In this context, it does not so much matter that the latter of the two promises never really gets fulfilled; the reader gets more than s/he can bargain for in a book of modest length (pp. 328).

The importance of this study, for many readers of this *Yearbook*, may however lie in its attempt to resurrect the directionality parameter from—what we may call—the post-Kaynean ruins of the syntax of head-final languages. Notwithstanding Chomsky's attempt to reduce word order to the PF—therefore playing no part in the computation from the numeration to LF—and his integration within the bare theory of a modified Linear Correspondence Axiom (i.e. essentially rejecting the conceptual arguments for LCA), the range of evidence that Bayer garners in Chapters 3–7 constitutes, what may surely be considered, a successful attempt in maintaining directionality as a 'supervising force' in government.

Crucially, this also brings across an 'uncomfortable' or, in my view, 'alternative' stance that the work is forced to take. A book published in 1996, that broadly accepts the minimalist framework and insists on government as a crucial notion deciding directionality, must clearly *imply* (since Bayer never clearly *states* this point) an alternative view of syntax. I will be inclined to read it as a matter of conscious choice rather than a mere chronological accident. Be that as it may, the third major thrust of the discussion in this connection

- directionality is not only important in syntax but in LF too

can be taken to be a direct stand against minimalism which decisively pushes LCA to the PF (see above and p. 340 of Chomsky, N. 1995. *The Minimalist Program*. Cambridge, Mass.: MIT Press).

Ironically, it is from Kayne's earlier work (Kayne, R. 1983. Connectedness. *Linguistic Inquiry 14*. 223–49) on g-projections (which define an 'extraction domain'), that Bayer initiates his directionality argument. This and its extension in Koster's (Koster, J. 1987. *Domains and dynasties: The radical autonomy of syntax*. Dordrecht: Foris) Condition on Global Harmony (CGH), which informally states that extraction is only possible if all the governors "point" in a uniform direction, is the first step that Bayer takes in building his case. Chomsky (Chomsky, N. 1986. *Barriers*. Cambridge, Mass.: MIT Press), on the other hand, as Bayer himself points out, does not take directionality as a defining notion for extraction domain. Rather, he uses other syntactic notions, e.g. adjunction, to escape barrierhood. These other notions, according to Bayer, do not 'constrain derivations sufficiently' (43). Specifically, they do not work for mixed word order systems such as Dutch or German.

Although superior and empirically richer, Bayer's theory of directionality remains essentially Kosterian. For example, the simple explanation that CGH offers for the possibility of P-stranding in (1a) would not be greatly improved in the present study.

1a. DP_i [$_{PP}$ e_i P] V] b*. DP_i [$_{VP}$ [$_{PP}$ P e_i] V]

However, one respect in which it crucially differs from Koster's account is in terms of movements at LF. For Koster, CGH doesn't apply at LF which, for him, does not exist as a syntactic level of representation. Scope, for example, is not constrained by directionality in Koster's theory. Bayer's goal, as we have seen, is to show that syntactic movements are replicated (under similar constraints) in the LF. To prove this, he looks at

- focusing particles like *only* and *even* (Chapters 1–6)
- Wh-in-situ (Chapter 7)

He shows that the theory of scope assignment for focusing particles relies on syntactic principles and it makes correct (LF) predictions as to their quantificational versus scalar interpretation. This forms most of Chapters 1–3 in the book.

Based on Rothstein's (Rothstein, S. 1991. Head, projections, and category determination. *Views on phrase structure*, ed. by K. Leffel and D. Bouchard. Dordrecht: Kluwer) classification, focusing particles are considered as *minor functional heads* (p. 14). The only PS requirement is that they attach to a maximal category which is able to bear stress. This type of head does not project categorial features. Early in the book, Bayer presents the Jacobs (Jacobs, J. 1983. Fokus und skalen: Zur syntax und semantik der gradpartikeln im deutschen. Tübingen: Niemeyer) and Rooth (Rooth, M. 1985. Association with focus. University of Massachusetts, Amherst Ph. D. dissertation) approaches to these focusing particles and adopts the latter approach of 'non-movement' focus association as the basis of his analysis.

In Chapter 2, Bayer builds upon the scope of these focusing particles by distinguishing their quantificational and scalar uses. A quantified XP, [PRT XP] must move to a position from which it can have access to its domain of quantification. The important result that Bayer derives is that a constraint similar to CGH holds for these quantificational expressions (or [PRT XP]s). The difference between quantificational and scalar interpretations is to be ascribed to the access that the PRT can have over a particular domain of quantification. He appeals to semantic feature checking (in addition to morphological) to satisfy last resort.

In Chapter 3, alongside the main argument that PPs (and DPs and APs in later chapters) are barriers to syntactic and LF movement, a sub-motif that enters at this stage of the development of the theory, is that effects like P-stranding are not observed in case of other quantifiers, negatives or Wh-operators. This is to be expected, given that focusing particle constructions are a different kettle of fish. This seems to sufficiently clinch the main thesis of the book that LF is a separate level of representation. However, this does not go to show the equivalence between overt and abstract syntax—that is quite another matter.

Non-canonical government is introduced in the definition of barriers (p. 93) to allow stranding dependent upon directionality—the original CGH story. Looking at mainly non-P stranding languages (Romance) and the H-initial languages like Scandinavian, Bayer shows that if a language allows P-stranding in syntax, it allows it in LF too. Again, it is shown that LF barrierhood of PP is seen only in case of quantificationally focusing particles and not in the case of quantification rooted in the agreement system.

Chapter 4 looks at extraction from DP and shows that the Left Branch Constraint—no extraction from the left branch—holds at LF. This satisfies a part of the theme of the book. The definition of barrier (with a directionality clause) is shown to be insufficient for extraction from DPs in German as in (2b):

2a. $[_{DP} [_{D'}$ der $[_{NP} [_{N'}$ Blick $[_{PP}$ auf's Meer]]]]]
the view at-the sea
'The view of the sea'

2b. $[_{DP}$ $[_{PP}$ auf's Meer$]_i$ $[_{D'}$ der$[_{-\text{ā}}$ $[_{N'}$ Blick e_i $]]]]$ ([1a,b] p. 123)

Bayer follows other DP researchers and assumes that Spec DP provides the escape-hatch. But with (2c) both CGH and the modified barrier definition run into problems:

2c. $[_{PP}$ Auf's Meer$]_i$	haben	leider	nicht	alle $[_{DP}$ e_i $[_{D'}$	den $[_{NP}[_{N'}$
	have	unfortunately	not	all	the

Blick $e_i]]]]]$	geniessen	konnen
view	enjoy	can

'Unfortunately, not everyone could enjoy the view of the sea'

([1c] p. 123)

The leftward directionality pattern in German breaks down in the N–D system. According to Bayer, fluidity of movement inside this system is related to a sharing of the agreement index between N and D. The barrier definition is suitably modified to include agreement as in $[_{ZP} \ldots Z^{agr} \ldots [_{XP} \ldots X^{agr} \ldots YP]]$ which obliterates the distinction between Z and X. This revision, however, makes a number of wrong predictions for LBC violations—a DP in Spec DP is not included in DP and therefore should be able to extract:

3a*. Whose did you see girlfriend?
3b*. Wessen hast du Frenndin gesehen? ([8a,b] p. 127)

Since in these cases Spec DP is filled (*whose*, *wessen*), extraction from DP would lead to strong subjacency violations. The expectation that extraction from such genitive DPs should be difficult in LF is borne out. Similar to the PP cases, the focusing particles do not take part in feature percolation and pied-piping—and since percolation is through the agreement system, the minor functional heads not being part of the agreement system, percolation does not take place. So QR must apply directly to the phrase quantified by a particle. Scope facts are thus predicted by the theory of syntactic movements. A copy theory of movement gives the right results for the quantifications ([52–54] on p. 144).

Unlike in PPs, in DPs the Spec DP can be accessed by QR which hides the barrierhood status of the DP. QR, crucially for Bayer, is a movement to a specific Spec position. This makes the parallelism between overt and covert movement striking. This is also in tune with one school of research in Neg-criterion/wh-criterion where QR is through spec-head.

Adjectival phrases (topic of discussion of Chapter 5) select a DP complement to the left but a PP complement can occur on either sides of A. For Bayer, the post-adjectival position of the PP is a case of extraposition. The fact that extraposition from the DP selected by A is possible again points towards CGH. Most of the chapter develops the theme initiated in the previous chapter—i.e. to show that QR is not adjunction.

In the case of PPs, extraposition is not obtained if the PP is quantified by a focusing particle. Bayer then goes on to argue against the traditional rightward movement analysis of extraposition and an analysis based on Kayne's (1994) claim that SVO as the universal word order. To argue against the latter, he cites the possibility of allowing optional movement as the necessary evil. However, he had earlier (p. 133) mentioned a similar possibility in connection with preference matrix between an ambiguous state and an unambiguous but QRed state. Bayer adopts an analysis similar to Hoekstra (Hoekstra, T. 1987. Extrapositie en SOV. *Tabu* 17. 133–42). This third option is to do with the availability of the post-adjectival PP in an A (rather than A')-position. However, he rejects the option of its being base generated to the right of A as that would violate UTAH. He settles for an "argument shift" approach to extraposition which looks at an output like [$_{AP}$[$_{AP}$ e_i A] PP_i] with partial blindness where the PP bears a *head* relation to A and "A simply selects PP to the right" (on p. 166). This would be considered strange within Chomskyan linguistics.

This brings us back to my reading of the book which is that it offers us an alternative way of looking at systems within the broader boundaries of a mainstream Chomskyan framework. This tension is becoming increasingly visible in current syntactic research. This voice, coupled with the long-standing tradition of German linguistics in providing solid alternatives brings about a successful, and bold, recipe that is at the same time commendable and useful. Such studies gently nudge students of generative syntax to wake up from the overdose of "mainstream" linguistics. This also applies to complex cases of PP extraction ([20–21] on p. 167) which uses the notions of complex heads (like {A+I}) and head percolation that essentially carry over from Bayer's earlier works.

I am, however, not entirely sure how far such alternatives can be stretched. For example, in section 5.4, while discussing the motivation for extraposition, Bayer talks about "softer" constraints. Extraposition for him seems to be 'linked in a transparent way' (p. 169) to the human processing system. If we agree that rightward movement exists then it would be meaningless to propose a different *type* of constraint. Whether extraposition 'optimises the sentence for the processing system' (p. 170) is far from decided in the current state of generative grammar and can at best be a speculation.

Bayer also proposes a 'semantic' head, Prt, which is 'created' in the course of the LF derivation and projects PrtP which dominates the AP undergoing extraction. SpecPrtP, which is licensed by the empty head Prt, accommodates the moved [PRT XP]. A landing site for QR strengthens his argument, initiated in the last chapter, that QR rather than being an adjunction, targets a specific position like SpecPrtP. In providing a landing site for QR, Bayer broadly anticipates similar moves made by the advocates of the Landing Site Theory at UCLA (Stowell, Beghelli, Szabolsci et al.). Although, the spirit of this analysis carries over to a large extent to the analysis of scope marking in Bangla discussed in Chapter 7, the process of semantic identification, like semantic feature checking, is not independently motivated. In fact, in order to cover the full range of data, Bayer is forced to formulate a sub-rule of spec-head agreement ([33] on p. 174). However, his main contention that quantified PPs which end up on the *wrong* side of the adjectival head behave as islands in terms of scope facts, remains.

The rest of the book (Chapters 6 and 7) covers almost half its size. They look at bigger structures. Chapter 6 looks at VPs and extraposition of clausal complements and Chapter 7 discusses the scope of *wh* in Bangla. Chapter 6 does three things: it carries on the move suggested in Chapter 5 to build an adjacency requirement between C and V based on "complementiser visibility", it claims that CPs with [PRT XP] are different—a sub-plot that we encountered in Chapters 3–5—and it shows certain CPs to be islands for LF movement but not overt movement. The parallelism between overt/covert syntax seems to break down but the resulting differences are exactly the ones motivated by the directionality parameter.

In German, the (finite) clausal complement of the verb appears to the right (*Nachfeld*), in violation of the directionality parameter. For reasons of Uniformity of Theta Assignment Hypothesis, a post-verbal base-generation approach is unsuitable. Computation of operator-variable relation leads to complications due to A' traces present in a standard extraposition analysis. One complication for C-visibility is "short" centre-embedded CPs which occur pre-verbally ([10] on p. 192). Bayer circumvents the problem posed by these 'marked' options by reanalyzing them as NPs. This point probably deserves far greater attention than it gets considering that a vast literature exists on reanalyzed non-finites.

Bayer argues for a rightward argument-shift of CPs on the basis of the fact that this movement is 'almost' obligatory and that extraction is permitted from extraposed complements. This would argue against such positions being considered as A'. What drives argument-shift, however, remains unclear since the only thing it achieves is C-visibility which is only a descriptively sound observation. After CP extraposition, the computable structure of $[_{VP} [$ V CP]] that reorients the CP is in a sister relation with the V but in the non-canonical direction, VP and therefore, must be a barrier for CP. This is shown to be operating most clearly at LF (inability to reconstruct, for example). The theory correctly accounts for cross-linguistic evidence that, for example, in English, quantified CPs canonically selected to the right will undergo movement to a scope position.

Giving evidence from verb raising, Bayer claims that right branching structures are exceptional in head-final languages which follows from Bayer's theory that head-final setting of the directionality parameter implies that right branching VPs are directionality barriers.

Another major theoretical claim of this chapter is that there is no long *wh* movement from right hand complements in German. As an alternative to the movement analysis, Bayer considers the operation of Generalized Transformations (GT)—free insertion of one phrase marker into another; after all, *wh* scope is logically independent of movement. Bayer's mechanism involves a free insertion of a *wh*-phrase at the root Spec CP. The inserted *wh*-phrase is included in a *wh*-chain extended from lower clause(s). This implies that chain formation is more basic than movement. Thus, Bayer advocates a mixed system involving both derivational and representational systems, which purists may find difficult to accept. However, there is no *a priori* reason not to opt for a mixed system.

In the concluding chapter Bayer looks at complementation and *wh* scope in Bangla to test the theories developed in Chapters 1–6. Since Bangla does not allow *wh*-movement but exhibits complement clauses on both sides of the verb, it serves as a good testing ground for the theory. Thus the theory would predict that extraposed clausal complements would only permit narrow scope readings (since they are on the non-canonical or "wrong" side the V), while canonically selected complements allow for wide scope construal as well. Bangla, and other Indo-Aryan languages, bear this out.

Bayer's initial apologetic statement, that the chapter remains sketchy because of 'looking through the optics of instruments which have been developed in the study of languages very different from eastern Indo Aryan languages', undermines the basis of UG. However, in the same breath, the claim that the explanations offered for one IA language (Bangla in his case) need not apply cross-linguistically to other languages (like Hindi, Marathi and Oriya) of the same language family, reinstates UG as operative. Again, Bayer shows convincingly that classical extraposition analyses do not explain a number of facts about binding into and focusing of extraposed CPs. The analysis from earlier chapters carries over as the verb "reselects" the rightward extraposed CP as a sister which explains the binding and focusing facts.

In Bayer's analysis both *je* and *bole* are complementizer heads, the former being clause-initial and the latter, clause-final. C-visibility, developed in the previous chapter, predicts that *je*-clauses can appear only to the right of the matrix verb. According to the theory developed so far, the Bangla VP, therefore, must be a directionality barrier for movements from a rightward A-position.

This sets the stage for Bayer to investigate scope of wh-in-situ in Bangla. He argues that unlike in Japanese, Chinese or Korean, Bangla K-words (for example *ki* as a clitic element) have an inherent +*wh* feature that needs checking at LF. He argues strenuously, adducing data from Assamese, that *wh*-movement in Bangla cannot be a QR-type adjunction and that LF movement targets essentially the same position as overt operator movement (as in the case of the relative operator *je* moving to Spec CP)—the standard wh-in-situ stance. Bayer provides empirical arguments against treating rightward complements in IA languages as adjuncts and in keeping with his general theory, accounts for the data by ascribing argument status to the extraposed CP. This explains why in (9), *ke* can never get wide scope:

6. ora Suneche [ke aSbe] "they heard-PTS3 who come-FUT3"

(i) they have heard who will come (ii) # who have they heard will come?

By being "included" in the VP, the extraposed CP turns the VP into a directionality barrier for the complement. If it were an adjunct, VP could not have been a barrier and the scope facts would remain unexplained. However, in the last section, Bayer discusses an apparent case of *wh*-movement where the barrier status is circumvented by the process of feature-absorption and GT. By providing a clause-internal projection (CLP or Clitic-P) above the VP ([88] p. 295), this is shown as *not* a case of trans-clausal movement.

If we take the metaphor of a mixed system seriously, Bayer's book certainly manages to create a place for itself among the modern day tensions of generative linguistics. If the currently prevalent theory were to posit that not all movement is feature-driven, then a Bayer-type rightward argument-shift extraposition would become more 'acceptable'. This, however, would only serve to put Bayer's account back in the 'permissible' realm of the 'mainstream' program, a move which—going by the reading of the book offered in this review—deviates from the spirit of the work.

■ ■

Ashok R. Kelkar, *Language in a semiotic perspective: the architecture of a Marathi sentence*. Pune: Shubhada Saraswat Prakashan, 1997. Pp. xxiii, 656. Rs 575.

Reviewed by Probal Dasgupta, University of Hyderabad, India.

This book is, needless to say, a monument, and hard to summarize. Equally obviously, I will have to try and summarize it in my own way to have a basis for the discussion that its author (hereinafter ARK) wishes to launch. I therefore stick my neck out, as follows, in a mixture of the book's terms and those more often used.

A: Users of language exchange spoken/written signs. B: The S(entence) is a strategically important type of sign. C: Languages are systems whereby sign-vehicles can effectively carry sign-messages back and forth between interlocutors. D: Sign systems invite analysis in terms of a semiotic design where structured vehicles and structured messages have their structures matched—but not conflated—at Nodal (in the case of language this means morpho-syntactic) interfaces. E: In principle, language as a human categorizing practice is both a Medium of understanding reality and a Means of communicating with others to indicate and to control aspects of reality. F: In fact, S is Nodally structured both Mediumwise, as a field of semantic arguments of predicates, and Meanswise, as an array of more salient or less salient items in a message. These structurations are equally Nodal: each of them operates both at the Speech-Form levels of the S-vehicle and at the Notional-Form levels of the S-message. G: The present book, by arguing that S is so structured in the

Marathi language, underwrites claims E and F, shows how they are connected to other thinking, and invites future work on whether smaller signs like Phrases and Words and bigger signs like S-Sequences also turn out to combine an outward or Means-oriented structuration with an inward or Medium-oriented structuration.

But ARK does not primarily intend this book as an account of Marathi, although it spends most of its energies there. He wants us to notice that 'Human categories are fundamentally rough and ready, crude and ordinary, full of interstices and fuzzy margins' and in general 'messy. But there is no denying that human categories are abstractive' (p. 409). Faced with this fact that 'All grammars leak' (p. 434, a quote from Sapir who first said it this way, as we are reminded on p. 556—these endnotes, unsignaled by obtrusive note numbers in the main text, provide resources but leave you free)—and that more generally human organizations are rough and yet real—what does one do? ARK's answer is that if 'Sentence formation is then, like architecture, created by men…' (p. 433), then it makes sense to look at it in terms of design: 'Design is meaningful or motivated form, and architecture is essentially a design art… [which] reflects man's coming to terms with the environment he lives in' (p. 434). Thus the architecture metaphor for the organizing principle of this study proposes a general methodology for the human sciences. People cope, abstractly but messily; their self-understanding in and as the human sciences must face this coping in its situated specificity.

To read such a text we must situate it. ARK has always taken the linguistics-pedagogy link seriously. One thing he offers in this book is a model presentation, by a presenter who has learnt it thoroughly, of his knowledge of his own language. But what will guarantee that a learnedness which is also a taughtness does not produce a dry, pedantic, and therefore unreal replica of speech, in the manner of the direct-method-wielding grandfather Schweitzer whose inauthenticity dominated Sartre's childhood? ARK's response seems to be to reteach yourself your language as a flowing constancy or a *pravaaha-nitya* in the sense of Bhartrihari, and to depend for success in this effort on poetry as a guarantee against the mere grammarian's rigid constants or *kuutastha-nitya* constructs taking over. For the community, in remembering its poetry, remembers that, to quote the passage from p. 433 fully, 'Sentence formation is then, like architecture, created by men *and also created by a man*.' What social memory preserves as poetry is the fact that individuals, as authentic creators, keep sociality afloat. The question that has consistently made ARK's project tick is: How does one build a thought accountable both to the fact of poetry and to the dryness-risking craft of grammar?

My reading of ARK's response to this question is that he has been exploring the lineaments of a Delicate Code. Let me unpack this as follows. Any grammar plus dictionary apparatus must treat a language as apparatizable in lexicogrammatical terms. If you assume a system merits and fits such apparatus, I will say you take it to be a Code. A given Apparatus may be relatively Gross or Delicate, according as it fits the Code loosely or tightly. Consider a gross apparatus gA(C) that describes a code C by listing a host of Nouns and the Adj *tall*, writing a rule combining this with any N, and leaving it up to interlocutors to figure out which combinations are going to work. Compare it with another apparatus dA(C) which does the job delicately. It says to each Noun, good morning, have you slept well, are you feeling physical, would you like a physical Adj? Not that dA(C) prevents interlocutors from speaking or hearing of tall theories. But it would encourage all involved to listen to the unusualness of such a combination and its paradigmatic contiguity to tall stories, the latter an extension of physicality. In contrast, gA(C) would push all that out of language and be unconcerned where any or all of it lands. ARK exemplifies the art of resisting gA(C), tries to build some pieces of dA(C) as works of this art, and suggests rather than argues that this at least is where the grammarian, no slave of the dry sands, is accountable to the beaches of the sea of social creativity where poets' boats sometimes land.

This preference leads to a nationalism that wants speakers of each C to build dA(C)s for it as part of their communitarian self-teaching which in turn forms part of their social coping, and to resist missionaries trying to write a gA(C) for them. The human sciences should be a coalition of societies that watch themselves codally as they cope with life as part of their natural living.

In the Nehruvian India where ARK came of age, a serious nationalism had to cope with all the Three Languages of the Formula. And his biography has been marked by a triple inheritance: the Paninian tradition, through Damle on Marathi; classical Western grammatical artistry, through Jespersen on English; and the structuralist implementation, through ARK's teachers from the American fifties, of formal modernity as total and publicly accountable explicitness, which the preference for dA(C) situates, with interesting consequences, in the European structuralist adventure.

Given the industrial imperatives of efficiency that the Nehruvian projects had made their own, it was structurally given that any account of language willing to inherit and therefore, continuingly, to challenge the American structuralist endeavour would attempt to build the general type of system that glossematics had adumbrated "prepractically" (to echo the new chestnut "pretheoretically"). The path forked in two directions when the generative approach extended the grammar into the lexicon and the stratificational alternative extended the lexical into the grammatical. Now, the word had always been the prototype for sign theory; it was easier for stratificational approaches to keep construing every message as a sign composed of signs; and ARK needed to cleave to this construal. So his path was chosen for him.

And he has now finished fashioning his apparatus which lovingly begins with lexicography and continues into grammar, instead of finding its first joy in formal generalizations and regretfully relegating exceptions to some residuary lexicon.

Why has ARK needed to keep construing messages as signs composed of signs? Because his impulse has forced him, unlike stratificational grammar or glossematics, not to take it for granted that S was a sign, but to question S in the semiotic mode in which one interrogates signs. Where does this impulse come from? In his study of literature, ARK found quite early that his desire for a publicly explicit account of private processes leads to an appropriation of Langer and through her of Whitehead on the crystallization of feelings as forms. ARK's program implies that semiotics will eventually have to come to terms with that crystallization at the level of specificity that the Whitehead–Langer tradition brought within the reach of literary studies. Rooted as he was in the grammatical tradition and in the linguistic enterprise of reaching beyond that metawriting to a less formal and more humanly feelable metaspeech, ARK was able to form a proportion like, private Feeling is to public Thought as Speech is to Writing.

This connection committed ARK's vision to semiotics as a field that becomes crucial to human self-understanding once the natural sciences and their industrial corollaries have identified and begun to deploy ways to stop letting natural contingencies and calamities overtake most human plans. For semiotics deals with feelings and their formalizations, and is presupposed in any serious interrogation of our plans themselves. It is perhaps the logic of this reading of currently vital exigencies that leaves ARK impatient with plan-obsessed Left "alternatives" to mainstream modes of industriality. It may be useful for many of us to read ARK's impatience as a response to the dismaying but obvious fact that, contrary to what the apparently high intellect levels of many recruits to the cause might have led one to expect, the Left has glibly remained oriented to an "economics" that leaves wishes and plans unexamined as categories, refusing to open its agendas to a semiotics or a linguistics capable of forging tools for the serious peace that the Left would like to think it is working for.

So delicately apparatused, how has the code fared in ARK's project? My reading is that his enterprise of forcing the highbrow concept to be accountable to the middlebrow percept without conceding the territory to the purely lowbrow sensation has shown that the communicative public and the thoughtful private become accountable to each other at the point of the S(entence). He has worked on the S to the point where it becomes apparent to the serious viewer of his show that S is at the same time the biggest possible sign for a continuist Code to be built around, as ARK shows directly, and the smallest possible stretch of an eventist Discourse that might resist codification from its inaugural gesture onwards, as an anti-ownership thinker today wishing to inherit ARK's work will have to demonstrate to his or her own satisfaction.

For an environmentally sensitive free and liberating discourse today will want to travel light, serving as its own null metadiscourse, and thus choosing to belong without claiming possession. On such a journey, the traveller will want to inherit ARK's self-consciousness about what the Technical is and how to tame the animal, so that one can feed it and continue one's trip without being pursued by it.

Why and how do I think ARK's narrative of the perfect self-possession of a speech community helps someone who might wish to, in the *tyaagii* mode, enter such a dispossession, obligatory at least as a presence on the screen of thinkers shaped by the devastations wrought by industriality? It seems to me that the ARK narrative stylizes a prototypically ethnic community's self-possession as perfect by introducing just the right—non-ethnic—kinds of counterfactuals to aid those of us who would resist the positivist abridgement that binds Reason to factual appearances. What is specific about Kelkar's tacit counterfactuals is the poise with which he invokes the sense of community with a public that has in fact not, the evidence shows, been listening. In other words his counterfactuals do not embody a scheme that claims to outwit positivism by a higher science ('A scheme is not a vision, / And you never have been tempted / By a demon or a god', sings Leonard Cohen, addressing 'You who build these altars now / To sacrifice our children'). Their poise bespeaks a community—not a particular ethnic mafia successfully hogging the limelight in a province, but an anywhere-located Community—whose individual representative is strong enough to face long seasons of nonresponse from potential peer groups, and precisely by means of this quiet patience to continue to build a basis for Listening, another name for strong communities.

To understand the courage encoded in this book's rhetorical gentleness, one needs to appreciate the fact that yet again, after the successful publication of an account of Hindi-Urdu phonology in the sixties, ARK has given linguistics a reasonably finished product of lasting interest. I mean by this more than a professionally important set of hypotheses and examples. In his phonology, ARK had suggested that we domesticate the dual existence of Hindi and Urdu by describing the shared linguistic core as "Hirdu"—a daring hybridity ahead of his climes. In his architecture, as the present work will inevitably come to be called, ARK juxtaposes *aayaa nahiiN, gayaa* with *aayaa, nahiiN gayaa* for Hindi-knowing readers, providing the glosses 'he-came not, he-went' and 'he-came, not he-went' for others. The glosses make the point just as well as the Hindi forms, with the genial simplicity of an author who can choose such examples and glosses.

How best can the community of linguists make optimal use of such resources as an author like this? Surely by reversing the throwaway style of American industriality in the academic domain. How, specifically? By debating thoroughly what is proposed, and thus by avowing a multiple inheritance going back to earlier layers of the field, not appealing just to a public memory that one populistically encourages to remain short. Now that the generative enterprise has found it necessary to reinstal GT from the fifties and to juxtapose phonological and syntactic with morphological versions of Blocking, the field's own inner drives will propel it away from the throwaway culture, one hopes.

Brief reviews of large books are not where thorough debating can be done. But it may be possible to throw up a suggestion or two that could start a debate. Here's one from this reviewer. ARK departs from glossematics in his decision to place a third Modal form between the expression and content systems, where glossematics did it by having the form principle directly link expression-form and content-form and thereby indirectly associate expression-substance with content-substance. But ARK treats Means and Medium as simply two roles language plays, with consequences for the structuration of S, as we have seen. My suggestion is to go glossematic about this, redesignate these roles as the Means-Flow and the Medium-Flow of language, and say that Flowing is that whereby language interfaces its Means and Medium identities. What is Flowing? Its formal side is the recursion stuff that the Chomsky revolution has a mathematics for. Its substantive side, I would conjecture, is the fact that some stretches are, within each Flow and across the boundary dividing Means-Flow from Medium-Flow, heard as repeating or recycling other stretches. Call it message recycling—an intrinsically inexact but vital art, like all human actions that ARK helps us to view and value. If forms of linguistic inquiry now beginning can zero in on message recycling and identify the ways in which the Flows flow, it begins to be possible to dream that we discursors will some day get the key to the way Discourse carries its own Metadiscourse, lightly, on its normal Flow mechanisms themselves, making Codes optional devices for a stage of social community-building that has found them necessary to keep itself confident. It is important to be able to visualize such options, even if they are currently of purely utopian significance, to see how the pedestrian jobs that we must continue to persevere in are related to the tougher, and more delicate, jobs which give them their ambience—and which we don't have to put off, for the discourse of dispossession can play poetry to the prosaic codes of possession which we as lexicographers and grammarians will remain addicted to.

■ ■

Amar Nath Malik, *The Phonology and Morphology of Panjabi*. New Delhi: Munshiram Manoharlal Publishers, 1995. Pp. xiii, 376. Rs 500.

Reviewed by Tej K. Bhatia, Syracuse University, New York

When I glanced at the title of the book under review, my first reaction was I wished I had this book during the years when I was frantically working on my own book on Panjabi. During that period I experienced a serious scarcity of material on Panjabi morphology. I spent an entire summer sifting through the pages of the dictionaries of Panjabi to construct an adequate sketch of Panjabi morphology. These anecdotal remarks make it readily clear that the book under review offers a rich harvest of data to researchers of linguistics as well as to scholars of Panjabi.

As is self-evident from the title, the scope of the book is restricted to phonology and morphology. However, the interface with syntax is also provided, whenever it is deemed necessary. The book offers a synchronic analysis of Panjabi phonology and morphology. In his introductory remarks, Malik claims, 'There have been a few traditional grammars of Panjabi, but there is a complete lack of studies of any variety of it on modern linguistic principles. A few diachronic or historical-comparative of the language have been made, but almost no complete and systematic descriptive treatment of the language as it obtains today is available.' (Introduction: viii). This statement is a rather gross misrepresentation of the state of the modern linguistic studies on Panjabi. A number of studies published in India and abroad support my claim. The excellent works of Bahl (Bahl, Kali Charan. 1957. Tones in Punjabi. *Indian Linguistics* 17, 139–47; ———. 1969. Punjabi. *Current Trends in Linguistics*, Vol. V, ed. by T.A. Sebeok, 153–99. The Hague: Mouton and Co.), Chandra (Chandra, Duni. *Punjaabii bhaashaa daa vyaakrana* [A grammar of the Punjabi language]. Chandigarh: Schuster), Sethi (Sethi, J. 1971. *Intonation of statements and questions in Punjabi* (monograph 6). Hyderabad: Central Institute of English), Sandhu (Sandhu, Balbir Singh. 1974. *The articulatory and acoustic structure of the Punjabi vowels*. Parakh II. Chandigarh: Punjab University), Kalra (Kalra, Ashok Kumar. 1982. Some topics in Punjabi phonology. Delhi: Delhi University Ph.D. dissertation), Dulai (Dulai, Narinder K. 1989. *A pedagogical grammar of Punjabi*. Patiala: Indian Institute of Language Studies), Bhatia (Bhatia, Tej K. 1975. The evolution of tones in Punjabi. Studies in Linguistic Sciences 5(2), 12–24; ———. 1993. *Punjabi: A cognitive–descriptive grammar*. London: Routledge), and others have been totally overlooked by this book. These works may not deal exclusively with phonology and morphology of Panjabi, but they offer a wealth of material on the synchronic treatment of these aspects of the Panjabi language with varying depth and details. Therefore, a lack of knowledge of these works, regrettably, leaves a serious gap in the book in terms of its understanding of the issues involving Panjabi phonology and morphology and their treatment in the modern linguistic literature.

On the basis of his review of earlier works on Panjabi phonology, Malik concludes 'As far as I know a complete and concise statement of phonology and morphology of Panjabi (Majhi dialect) has been attempted for the first time on modern linguistic principles' (Introduction: ix). This statement is not only misleading and self-serving but is also uncharitable to the works of his predecessors who demonstrated a better understanding of modern linguistics more than a decade ago than exhibited by Malik's work some two decades later. Consider, for example, the phonological treatment of Panjabi by Kalra (1982) conducted within the generative framework. It is rather puzzling to note Malik makes no mention of Kalra whose Ph.D. dissertation was submitted at the same university where Malik submitted his work.

Although Malik claims his book is a pioneering work based on modern linguistic principles, this reviewer must note that it is actually written within the structural linguistics framework and does not go beyond the Pike's Tagmemics approach, let alone the generative approach exemplified in Kalra (1982).

As is evident by the following remarks, the main approach to data elicitation seems to be primarily introspective in nature: 'Apart from being my own informant, I have closely observed the speech of other Majhi speakers, not excluding the broadcasters of the language who speak the colloquial dialect in its purest form' (Introduction: viii). The latter part of the statement, indicating prescriptive rather than descriptive considerations, have also gone into the selection of the data. This indicates that the methodology followed in the book is not free from shortcomings.

The book is divided into sixteen chapters. The first ten chapters are devoted to phonology and the remaining six to morphology. The phonological treatment includes segmental phonology which is covered in five chapters: Phonemics (Chapter 1), Vowels (Chapter 2), Diphthongs (Chapter 3), Consonants (Chapter 4), Distribution of Consonants (Chapter 5). In the remaining five chapters the suprasegmental phonology is dealt with: Suprasegmental Phonemes: Nasalization, Length, and Aspiration (Chapter 6), Suprasegmental Phonemes: Stress (Chapter 7), Suprasegmental Phonemes: Tones (Chapter 8), Juncture (Chapter 9), and Morphophemics (Chapter 10). One wonders why aspiration is treated as suprasegmental.

The treatment of morphology is carried out in the following six chapters: General morphemic (Chapter 11), Form-classes: Noun (Chapter 12), Non-Paradigmatic Form-classes: stems, adverbs and particles (Chapter 13), Form-classes: Verb (Chapter 14), Verbal composition (Chapter 15) and Intonation or Phrase Pitch (Chapter 16).

The analysis presented in this work is often confusing and is full of contradictions. Although the author claims that the analysis presented is *synchronic* in nature and makes use of the insights of 'the American and European linguisticians of today' (ix). Let us consider the treatment of voiced aspirates in Panjabi offered in the book. However, before we do that, here are some facts about voiced aspirates and tones in Panjabi. At the synchronic level, Panjabi does not have voiced aspirates. There is a close correlation between *h* and voiced aspirates of Hindi and Panjabi tones. Thus, in place of Hindi voiced aspirates, Panjabi shows unvoiced unaspirated segments in initial position followed by low tone; and in non-initial position, it shows voiced unaspirated stops either preceded by high tone or followed by low tone. (For further details see Bhatia 1975). The book under review presents Panjabi voiced aspirates in the Table of Majhi consonants (p. 5); voiced aspirates as phonemes are claimed to occur in the word–initial position (pp. 38–39); and yet another place it is claimed that voiced aspirates are not 'simple but compound phonemes, which are comprised of plosives accompanied by low-rising or high falling tone' (p. 26). On page 6, the readers are informed that the high-falling tone is represented by the /'/ over and above a vowel or the exponent /ʰ/ over and after a vowel. From the synchronic view not only is the treatment of Panjabi tones (or voiced aspirates) confusing but also makes the whole transcription scheme involving voiced aspirates and tone idiosyncratic, which is in turn totally unmotivated. If the claim is being made that some dialects of Panjabi do not have tones and instead show the 'exponent /ʰ/', one can understand the motivation behind the two ways of transcribing tones. Otherwise, it makes the whole analysis baffling and the transcription scheme perplexing.

The treatment of syntax and morphology is equally full of errors. Complex Predicates such as *kamm karna* 'to work' are treated as 'Nominal Compounds' which are "intransitive" (p. 322) whereas *kamm hona* "to succeed in any business" are 'intransitive, and are the passive forms of the corresponding compounds with */karna/*' (pp. 322–3).

In short, the book is rich in data, and if used with care, the data will be of enormous use to the future researchers of Panjabi. However, my main regret is that the failure of the author to capitalize on the findings of his predecessors and insights of modern linguistics makes the book take a step backward rather forward in the state of research on Panjabi.

■ ■

Tariq Rahman, *Language and politics in Pakistan*. Karachi, Oxford, New York and Delhi: Oxford University Press, 1996. Pp. xviii, 320. Price not available.

Reviewed by William Bright, University of Colorado, USA.

The partition of Pakistan from India in 1946 was motivated by the desire for a unified Islamic state, and from the beginning the Urdu language was regarded as a major symbol of national unity. But the Pakistani nation has been troubled from the beginning by disunity in language, and the role of Urdu has been problematic: although it is widely known and used as a second language, it has never been used as a first language by more than a minority of Pakistanis—mainly the Mohajir ('immigrant') families who moved from India to Pakistan subsequent to partition. In the meantime, the majority of native Urdu-speakers in the Indian subcontinent are still citizens of India.

The majority of Pakistanis speak a variety of first languages (other than Urdu), and they associate varying degrees of emotional allegiance with these local tongues. As the nation was originally constituted, the native language with the largest number of speakers was Bengali, as spoken in East Pakistan—but also, of course, in the neighboring West Bengal state of India. The association of the Bengali language with ethno-nationalistic aspirations was, as the world now knows, responsible for the split of Pakistan and the formation of independent Bangladesh in 1971. In present-day Pakistan, approximately half the population are speakers of Punjabi, a language also spoken by large populations (Hindu, Sikh, and Muslim) in India. Other languages of Pakistan with speakers numbering in the millions include Pashto, Sindhi, Balochi, and Brahui (also called Brahvi, a Dravidian language). Superimposed on this diversity is English, which remains an important language within the nation as well as internationally. But each of these languages is the center of social and political controversy, which has on various occasions turned into open violence.

Rahman's book is a clear and often eloquent account of this situation, written from the viewpoint of history and political science, rather than linguistics. Chapter 1, 'Introduction', gives an overall linguistic portrait of Pakistan; Chapter 2, 'Theoretical preliminaries', characterizes such notions as language planning and standardization. Chapter 3, 'British language policies and imperialism,' and Chapter 4, 'The vernacular-English controversy', describe the historical role of English before the subcontinent became independent. Chapter 5, 'The Urdu–Hindi controversy', discusses the position before partition of these two languages—so nearly identical from the standpoint of colloquial speech, so different from the standpoints of formal speech, of written language, and of religious associations. Since then, of course, the confrontation of Urdu and Hindi has continued in India, while in Pakistan the position of Urdu has shifted: it is the unquestioned national language, yet has entered into new conflicts with local vernaculars.

Chapter 6, 'The Bengali language movement', details the earliest and most violent of these conflicts, in which the *ashraf*, the elite Urdu-speaking community of East Pakistan, attempted to exalt Urdu in the face of local Bengali ethno-nationalism. The father of Pakistan, Mohammad Ali Jinnah, refused in 1948 to recognize Urdu and Bengali as equal languages of the nation, because of 'his fear of the disintegration of the country' (p. 88); but in the sequel, it was just this inflexibility that brought about disintegration, in which East Pakistan became independent Bangladesh.

Chapter 7, 'The Sindhi language movement', describes the movement for recognition of the vernacular language of Sindh province. The dominant fact here is the conflict between Urdu-speaking Mohajirs and the local Sindhi-speaking population in the Karachi area, which has been especially serious since 1971. The problem is not simply one of language allegiance, but also involves fundamental economic needs: What language will be used, for instance, in examinations taken by university students? As Rahman describes events,

> Mohajir students brought out processions… from 9 January 1971 onwards. Sindhi students in their turn brought out processions… Events took an ugly turn on 17 January 1971 when buses were burnt … [In July 1972] the bloodiest language riots witnessed in Pakistan followed. The Mohajirs

attacked Sindhis in Karachi and the Department of Sindhi at the University of Karachi was burnt… (p. 125)

When Rahman was completing his book (in January 1995, according to his Preface), he wrote: 'Given this intransigence on both sides, Sindh is in danger of violence, riots, and perhaps a civil war' (p. 132). His prophetic powers were proven correct all too soon, as reported later in 1995 by the international press. Thus a headline in the New York *Times*, on 19 July 1995, announced: 'Ethnic battles in Karachi claim 30 more lives,' and the article stated: 'There have been more than 200 deaths in the city this month related to the violence.'

Chapter 8, 'The Pashto language movement', points out that the position of Pashto in Pakistan—its speakers are called Pakhtuns—is complicated by the fact that the language has official status in neighboring Afghanistan. One result has been outbreaks of Pashto separatism, and there have been calls for an independent 'Pakhtunistan', supported by the Afghan government. In recent decades, however, the capital of Pakistan was moved to the new city of Islamabad, in the Pashto area; a long civil war broke out in Afghanistan, which still continues; and finally, 'as the Pakhtuns have become more prosperous and better integrated in the economic and power structure of Pakistan, the Pashto movement has decreased' (p. 154). Chapter 9, 'The language movements of Baluchistan', also describes a situation in which militant separatism was once a problem, with 600 lives lost in battles during the 1970s. But the problem has abated, and Urdu is increasingly accepted in Balochistan.

Chapter 10, 'The Siraiki movement', introduces a term which will be unfamiliar to some readers; it refers to the speech of the southern Punjab—around Multan, Muzaffargarh, and Bahawalpur—which has sometimes been called Lahnda. It had some 12.6 million speakers in 1993 (1). Although 'Siraiki and Punjabi are mutually intelligible' (p. 175), Siraiki shares some features with neighboring Sindhi, such as implosive voiced consonants. A writing system has been developed, but only two Siraiki periodicals were published in Pakistan during 1992 (see Rahman's Appendix A); and ethno-regionalist feeling is relatively weak.

Chapter 11, 'The Punjabi movement', presents a somewhat paradoxical situation: the Punjab is 'the most populous and prosperous province of the country, notorious in the army and the bureaucracy'; however, 'most Punjabis of the upper and the middle classes do favour Urdu, and submerge their Punjabi identity in the Pakistani one' (p. 191). To some extent, there seems to be a continuation of the view held by British officers during the Raj, 'that Punjabi was a rural patois of which Urdu was the refined form' (p. 193). Punjabi regionalism remains weak—only two periodicals are published in the language, the same as for Siraiki!—and this is perhaps understandable, Rahman suggests, 'because Punjabis already have power which ethnicity would only threaten' (p. 209). Chapter 12, 'Minor language movements', discusses languages including Gujrati, Burushaski, and Kashmiri.

Chapter 13, 'The Urdu–English controversy', returns to the controversial position of English, which remains an important language of ruling circles in Pakistan. Rahman describes how the government of Benazir Bhutto in the 1990s, 'being unable, or unwilling, to oust English from the domains of power, ... mooted the idea that English should be taught in all schools and not merely in elitist ones ... These steps, said the government, would "bring children of poor [sic] at par with privileged class"' (p. 243; the 'sic' is Rahman's). But this is pure hypocrisy, as Rahman says, and he minces no words:

> The government will not provide teachers who can speak and teach English competently for all the schools in the country. [To do so,] the government would have to spend much more money. This the government is neither prepared to do, nor is it indeed capable of doing, because the military, the higher bureaucracy, and the other members of the elite would be impoverished if such an enormous investment was made for the education of the common people (pp. 243–4).

Rahman makes the significant point that 'the official language of communication in the officer-training military academies remains English and cadets are still forbidden to use any other language' (p. 247).

In his 'Conclusion', Rahman considers alternatives for public policy. First he discredits the conspiracy theories which see all problems of Pakistani disunity as originating in India. The problem, he says, is homegrown, linguistically based ethno-regionalism—'a matter which the ruling elite will have to confront' (p. 253). He continues:

> One possibility is to continue the existing language policies which keep power in the hands of the English-using elite at the Centre. This will continue to threaten the culture of the peripheries, keep them weak, and leave them feeling that they are being exploited. Such a policy may appeal to those who believe in a unitary system of rule or in the efficacy of the integrative potential of Islam and Urdu. But, in the face of perceived injustice, as we have seen, Islam and Urdu have not prevented the rise of militant ethnicity in Bangladesh, in Balochistan, or in Karachi. The other possibility would be to divide the present provinces of Pakistan so as to form smaller units.

In the upper Indus Valley, Rahman feels, such a reorganization could be beneficial: 'Punjab will no longer be seen as dominant, and ethnic bitterness will be reduced' (p. 254). However, in the present province of Sindh, 'the consequences of creating an Urdu-speaking province may be even worse than the present state ...' (ibid.) In the end, 'The greatest impediment[s] in the way of political decentralization are the conspiracy theories and the self-interest of the ruling elite ... A truly multi-ethnic, multilingual polity, like Switzerland, can live in equilibrium on the basis of perceived justice and equity' (p. 256).

Pakistan is, to be sure, far from unusual among the world's nations as regards linguistic diversity and language conflicts, and India has had such problems in abundance. Even so, Pakistan may be unique in the problems which are raised by the problematic position of Urdu. In the nation as a whole, it is a symbol of national identity, yet a minority mother-tongue, and primarily used as a second rather than a first language. In Karachi, the nation's largest city and economic capital, Urdu is the mother-tongue of the majority, yet its speakers are viewed as 'outsiders'. Rahman's comparison with Switzerland is, perhaps, unrealistic. But at the beginning of his book, he gives us two epigraphs—the first, for pessimists, from Shakespeare's Caliban: 'You taught me language; and my profit on't is I know how to curse.' The second epigraph, for (qualified) optimists, is from the *Dhammapada*, the teachings of the Buddha: 'Hatreds never cease by hatred in this world; by love alone do they cease.'

Abstracts

INDIRA AYYAR, Language Crossover in the Syntax of Spoken Indian English. Ph.D. 1993, State University of New York, Stony Brook.

Supervisor: S.N. Sridhar

This thesis aims to expand the empirical base of research on Indian English (IE henceforth). It examines conversations of educated speakers of IE whose mother tongue is Tamil, and native speakers of American English (AE henceforth). A number of recurrent syntactic patterns found to be systematic in the IE data are isolated for detailed analysis.

Through a comparison with AE data, it is shown that these patterns are "ungrammatical", infrequent, stylistically marked, or absent from the point of view of the native English system. In accounting for their use by IE speakers, it is argued that they result from language crossover or the bilingual's tendency to freely extrapolate from mother tongue syntax when using a second language to communicate with fellow bilinguals.

Language crossover is discussed in relation to specific non-native patterns, and in a number of cases shown to reflect functions and discourse strategies associated with the mother tongue—in this case Tamil. It is also argued that non-native patterns are used by IE speakers in addition to, and not necessarily as substitutes for, native English patterns. As such, they are optional patterns in the bilingual rule system of the IE user.

The theoretical model adopted in this study acknowledges the sociolinguistic reality of IE, sees its users as forming a speech community sharing communicative norms, and views mother tongue transfer as a major influence in the indigenization process of IE. In adopting this model and presenting its findings, this study argues that there is a need to describe the patterns of use resulting from the contact between English and Indian languages, and that such descriptions lead to a better understanding of the processes of change affecting IE and, by extension, other indigenized varieties of English.

■ ■

TANMOY BHATTACHARYA, A Computational Study of Transitivity.
Ph.D. 1996, University of Hyderabad, India.

Supervisor: P. Dasgupta

The central issue that the dissertation addresses is: In what form is language available to the language user? One of the claims is that: clauses *stage* events (or actions) like a camera staging a film/frame. The utterance/understanding of a sentence is a spectacle. A major part of the thesis, therefore, is concerned with the *presentational* aspect of a clause.

Another aspect is the connection that a language user makes with the staged spectacle. We capture this through the notions of accommodation and field which constitutes a modified DRT. This is the formal tool that is used to capture this connection. The main tension of the thesis is of using a particular formal method to capture concepts that lie beyond the boundaries of the formalism. The answer to the question: How does the user get a grip on the presented clause? has been the major thread of discovery in this dissertation—the notion of **salience**. We claim that salience is a general cognitive apparatus through which the user *computes* the clause and thus gets a grip on it. We capture salience of clause through various asymmetries that are part and parcel of a clause—like topic/focus, AGRs/AGRo, etc. Our claims are the following in this regard:

(i) asymmetries can be subsumed under a general notion of a new versus given opposition
(ii) asymmetries are reflected at each level of abstraction

Transitivity is the clearest of the asymmetries which represents the cognitive/perceptive notion of salience. Psycholinguistic evidence show that for a child, the basic conceptual structure is that 'persons perform actions and things are affected by actions'. We read this as transitivity. We construct a syntactic account of transitivity where certain syntactic configurations and operations reflect extra-sentential notions like staging, scening, and event. Regarding (ii) above, a slow reading of the dissertation displays a general narrowing down of the scope from discourse structure to clausal structure to phrasal structure (Chapters 1–4). Crucially, the claim is that at each level, the complexities involved is but a refraction of the complexities at a higher level. For the purpose of this dissertation these complexities are asymmetries. In the introduction (Chapter 1), we elaborate the interconnections that obtain between various asymmetries and the given/new distinction. We further discuss the syntactic impact that such interconnections may have on concepts like Staging, Scening and Event which together define the consequences of a clause in the totality of a discourse.

We extend DRT to a **camera angle view** of discourse (Chapter 2). Discourse, in this model, is to be seen in terms of photographs. Language understanding takes place through the camera lens. We propose that **field** is the theoretical construct to capture a camera angle view. A camera which is sensitive to changes in the scene and records or arranges the snaps in an album. There is a universal set of *fields* which are part of human language processing/understanding. Implementation of the theory demands a field to file mapping in terms of a salience gradient called the *zoom potential.* Zoom potential is calculated in terms of the transitivity of the clause. Transitivity is further reduced to predication and agreement. Connections between the head and the tail of asymmetries are established through agreement. The notion of field, we claim, will lead to a more efficient correspondence between the Kamp (1981) and the Heim (1982) versions of DRT.

In Chapter 3 we discuss the notion of agreement as much as it bears upon our agenda. Agreement for our purpose serves the goal of identifying the participants for evaluating syntactic transitivity and therefore, ultimately, salience—the major thrust of this study. Agreement provides finer details in a particular subroutine of an algorithm that we presented in the previous chapter.

The bulk of the chapter is devoted to the thesis that the object relation is more important; we try to see this in the light of a more general term like *landmark.* In this chapter, unergative clauses are first shown (section 3.2) to consistently contain a deep object position. The following sections discuss ergatives, transitives unaccusatives to argue that all of them have an object at some level of derivation. This discussion also includes revisions of the Split-VP Hypothesis and the Obligatory Case Parameter.

In section 3.5 we present our analysis of the phenomenon of long-distance agreement in Hindi, based on Watanabe's (1993) Three-Layered Case Theory and claim that the analysis has an advantage over existing analyses in terms of the data that it covers as also the computational edge that it packages. In our terms an (actually) L-related position can be detected if we are able to track the different features like Fs (section 3.5 and 3.6) located/created during the derivation. This makes the task of producing a list of the typology of positions (in terms of the A/A' distinction, for example) easier. This is claimed to be the computational advantage of the present theoretical account.

In Chapter 4 the phenomenon of (Noun) Classification in Bangla (and Hindi, to some extent) is discussed in conjunction with our drive towards discovering newer asymmetries down the clause highway. The inner stories of strength resolution of B(adge) and D(eclension) are revealed in order to flesh out the relevant phrase picture as much as it contributes to the clause picture. Definiteness, in this connection, seems to correlate strongly with the new/given distinction (section 4.1). Thus, the classifier as a cognitive category and its definiteness import is presented in section 4.3.

In section 4.10 we discuss Principle-Based Parsing (PBP) in connection with the Bangla classifier system and show that a PBP approach along with a strong KB will give us the right results as far as the DPs in Bangla/Hindi are concerned. We propose (section 4.10.2.1) that **Frames** are phrase level computational variants of the thematic concept of **scening** which we claimed (section

1.4.3) determines the modality aspects of a clause and thus the parsing technique that we suggest enables a computation of scenes. Lastly (4.10.3), we propose a KB called WISE which solves certain residual problems of Bangla nominal syntax.

■ ■

AYESHA KIDWAI, Binding and Free Word Order Phenomena in Hindi and Urdu. Ph.D. 1995, Jawaharlal Nehru University, New Delhi.

Supervisor: Anvita Abbi

This dissertation explores the syntactic and semantic/pragmatic properties of Hindi and Urdu scrambling within the framework of Chomsky (1992). It argues for a uniform analysis of Hindi and Urdu scrambling as adjunction to XP, and formalizes the link between clause-internal leftward (CIL) scrambling and preverbal WH-focusing in Hindi and Urdu. It therefore departs from standard assumptions of scrambling as optional and/or semantically vacuous.

Chapter 1 outlines the theoretical framework within which the phenomenon of CIL scrambling is investigated, and explores the problems that it poses for the minimalist program.

Chapter 2 investigates the syntactic properties of CIL from the perspective of the theory of movement and finds that the movement involved in scrambling cannot be characterized as either movement for Case/agreement, WH-movement, Topicalization or (S-Structure) QR. Following Muller and Sternefeld (1993), the discussion here suggests that, cross-linguistically, scrambling can only be characterized as adjunction to XP. The chapter concludes with a discussion of the status of XP-adjunction in the minimalist program, and proposes that the theoretically optimal characterization of adjunction would be one which provided the operation with a morphological motivation—i.e. one in which XP-adjunction would, like substitution, be feature-driven movement.

Chapter 3 is designed to explain the facts in scrambled configurations, taken by Mahajan (1990) to be evidence for an A-movement analysis of the operation. Chapter 2 shows that the binding-theoretic evidence Mahajan presents is not only inconclusive with regards to an A-movement analysis, but also that if the binding facts in Hindi and Urdu default order are studied carefully, even Mahajan's data actually points in the direction of an adjunction analysis of CIL scrambling. Chapter 3 develops a Binding Theory that can explain the binding judgments obtained in scrambled configurations and still maintain CIL scrambling to be adjunction to XP. In this context, the structure of double object constructions in UG, the LF-raising approach to pronouns and reflexives, the theories of binding and coreference of Reinhart (1991) and Reinhart and Grodzinsky (1993), and the theory of reconstruction are examined and developed. The Binding Theory that emerges from these explorations is shown to have coverage beyond scrambling data, as it can provide an explanation for binding in double object constructions in a number of languages, as well as a principled distinction between Weak and Strong Crossover.

With this last argument against an adjunction analysis of CIL scrambling dispensed with, Chapter 4 turns to a consideration of the related issues of morphological motivations for XP-adjunction in general, and CIL scrambling in particular. The chapter claims that scrambling is employed for focusing elements in the preverbal focus position. The thesis describes this position as a Focus Phrase projection immediately dominating VP, which is activated by the scrambled XP. The mechanisms of head-activation are hypothesized to involve a version of dynamic agreement (Rizzi 1991), by which the scrambled XP transmits an N-feature to the head of the Focus Phrase. By this account, scrambling is no longer characterizable as optional (since it must take place whenever the [+FOCUS] feature is involved), or semantically vacuous (since scrambling has an expressed LF-effect—focusing).

Chapter 5 considers the specificity effects noted in scrambled configurations. It suggests that with a few modifications to Diesing's (1992) Mapping Hypothesis, these facts can be explained by an adjunction analysis of scrambling. The chapter contradicts assumptions of a causal link between object agreement and specificity and makes some informal speculations regarding the sites of (in)definiteness in Hindi and Urdu.

Chapter 6 concludes the dissertation with a brief consideration of the issues of rightward and long-distance scrambling. It is claimed that rightward scrambling is actually base-generated, and that long-distance scrambling across tensed clause boundaries is ungrammatical.

Besides the issues surrounding scrambling, the dissertation offers some new theoretical and empirical proposals. In Chapter 2, an analysis of the Hindi and Urdu *-to* particle as a topic particle is offered; in Chapter 3 the impossibility of raising X-reflexives across tensed boundaries is explained in terms of Watanabe's (1993) layered Case theory. In the same chapter, a universal proposal for the structure of ditransitives in UG is developed, that maintains a strict version of UTAH and involves Case checking in a VP internal AGR-oP. Dative shift is argued to require IO Case checking in a broadly L-related position to this AGR-o. This is used to explain the binding and extraction facts in double object constructions in a number of languages, including Albanian, English and Italian.

■ ■

ARA SHAH, Complement Clauses in Hindi and Gujarati.
Ph.D. 1995, University of Hyderabad, India.

Supervisor: P. Dasgupta

The syntactic approach chosen for this dissertation seeks to describe complement clauses, their structure, their idiosyncrasies, and attempts to understand their behavior in terms of wider linguistic principles. This dissertation is within the generative paradigm. I have chosen the current version of this paradigm which seemed most appropriate for this work in that it has a certain inbuilt freedom which is necessary when working on relatively uncharted grounds.

However, this dissertation maintains two attitudes. The first ensures that the dissertation provides a useful account for translators in the form of an exhaustive compilation of complements selecting verbs in Hindi and Gujarati and a thorough description of the types of complement constructions; it is this attitude, infused with the applicability spirit which prompts me to base the chapters on construction types, rather than have a syntactically more insightful arrangement (grouping participials, say with small clauses and not with other non-finite verb constructions would be an example of such an arrangement). On the other hand, the other attitude channelizes the focus of this dissertation in a direction which attempts to raise certain theoretical issues regarding the Hindi/Gujarati language pair. The two attitudes serve to create a completeness. The applicability of an enterprise ultimately depends on the degree of descriptive adequacy achieved by the conceptual framework that one is working within and the validity of the theoretical assumptions of that framework.

Chapter 1 is the Introduction. It spells out the approach and the attitudes underlying this dissertation as well as the motivation behind them. Chapter 2 deals with finite complement clauses in Hindi and Gujarati. The major issues taken up in this chapter are (i) the nature of *ki* and (ii) the non-canonical position of the finite complement clause. This is a phenomenon common to several Indo-Aryan languages, as well as to certain Germanic languages, as is evident from the discussion. We report a number of accounts regarding this phenomenon. A controversy exists over the occurrence of the finite complement clause to the right of the verbal head. Essentially, the complement clause could either be base generated in that position or adjoined to the matrix verb by means of extraposition. I argue that the complement clauses in Hindi/Gujarati are extraposed to the right in order to be licensed by the matrix verbal complex. Issues of adjacency, directionality of government and theta marking will be discussed in the course of this chapter.

Chapter 3 deals with non-finite complement clauses. It is a fairly exhaustive account, the three main sections dealing with gerunds, infinitivals and participials. We will situate our discussion of gerunds within the minimalist framework, which we will modify in order to account for the Hindi/Gujarati *kaa naa* constructions. We then discuss infinitivals, that is, complement clauses with a postpositional complementizer. Using Kayne (1984) as a point of departure, we account for the null subject in infinitivals and postulate a phonetically null P/C in Hindi and Gujarati. This chapter also throws light on certain difficult to classify constructions, thereby contributing to the debate on "nominal clauses".

Small clause complements are discussed in Chapter 4. The interesting fact about small clauses in Hindi/Gujarati is that the subject of the construction is assigned Accusative Case. In this chapter we will review two major contributions to this issue, Mahajan (1990) and Sinha (1991). We will attempt to reformulate the hypotheses offered in these two works in order to account for the alternative range of interpretations that are available due to factors of animacy, specificity and definiteness.

Chapter 5 is a lexicographic exercise. Essentially, the aim is to provide a working bilingual dictionary for a closely related language pair. In this chapter we will present the agreement patterns available for verbs in Hindi/Gujarati. The main purpose of this chapter is to collate information for designing a specific purpose dictionary, a sample of which will be presented. An index of complement selecting verbs in Hindi and Gujarati is provided at the end of the chapter.

D

■ Dialogue ■

South Asian Languages and Linguistic Typology

BERNARD COMRIE

■ 1. Introduction

While many researchers will feel—with justification—that South Asian languages are worthy objects of study purely in their own right, the success of the field of South Asian linguistics will obviously be greatly enhanced if it can reach out to other disciplines, including both other disciplines that are concerned with South Asia (such as history) and, of particular interest in the present context, the broader field of general linguistics. In this brief paper, I want to address in particular relations between South Asian linguistics and language typology, both pointing to some of the fruitful past collaborations between South Asian linguistics and language typology, and to some ongoing and future possibilities for such cooperation.

■ 2. Areal Typology

Given that the concept of "South Asian" languages comprises languages from at least four different language families—the Indo-Aryan branch of Indo-European, Dravidian, the Munda branch of Austro-Asiatic, and parts of the Tibeto-Burman branch of Sino-Tibetan—plus the language isolates Burushaski and Nihali, it is clear that for this concept to have linguistic, as opposed to purely cultural validity, it must reflect a sharing of areal features among the languages of the diverse genetic groupings. And indeed South Asia has come to be accepted as one of the paradigm cases of a linguistic area, alongside the traditional Balkan sprachbund (with, let it be noted, far fewer languages and far less genetic diversity), Southeast Asia, and Meso-America. The classic statement remains Masica (1976), now supplemented by a large number of substantial studies of particular topics across the variety of South Asian languages, of which I will cite only a small selection: Verma (1976) on subjects; Bhat (1991) more generally on grammatical relations; and Wali, Subbarao, Lust, and Gair (forthcoming) on anaphora and pronouns, the last named being particularly interesting in that it has involved the long-term research cooperation of scholars in South Asia and North America. It is clear that the areal linguistics of South Asian languages is a vital research domain, and that scholars will continue to investigate the striking similarities that have spread across the genetic boundaries that characterize this area.

But documenting these similarities, however important, is in a sense only the first step of a more ambitious project, which is providing the detailed historical background to these similarities. Where—in which language or language family—did the striking features of South Asian languages originate? When did they originate? How did they spread to other languages and language families? and when? Until these questions are investigated in detail, a large part of the question concerning South Asia as a linguistic area will remain unanswered. In one sense, South Asian language specialists are in an enviable position for historical research, since Sanskrit, or more specifically Vedic, is one of the world's oldest attested languages, and there is a near-continuous record (first orally transmitted, then written) from then to present-day Indo-Aryan. A Dravidian language like Tamil has a documented history that would be the envy of many a European language. But as so often with the historical record, we find ourselves in the position that it would be nice to go just one step further back. (And no doubt we would then want to be able to go yet another step further back—and so on to the dawn of human language.)

I will illustrate this with the example of retroflex consonants in South Asian languages, in particular in Indo-Aryan and Dravidian languages. The synchronic data are clear. Retroflex consonants are rather rare cross-linguistically—Maddieson (1984: 32) finds retroflex stops in only 11.4% of the languages in his sample but are salient features of the phonological systems of nearly all Indo-Aryan and Dravidian languages (Masica 1991: 131, for Indo-Aryan). Outside Indo-Aryan, retroflex consonants are rare even in other Indo-European languages. Some of those that do occur in non-Indo-Aryan Indo-European languages, such as those that arise from sequences of dental consonant in most varieties of Norwegian and Swedish, are clearly too far remote in space and time to be areally relevant to South Asia, though as I will note below there are also some more disturbing parallels closer to the geographical area of interest. The retroflexes in Indo-Aryan are clearly an innovation relative to earlier Indo-European, appearing partly in loans from Dravidian and partly as the result of sound changes internal to pre-Indo-Aryan. The details of the adoption of retroflexes into Indo-Aryan are not available for historical inspection, since from the earliest texts, the Vedas, they are already in place. The traditional historical account is that retroflex consonants are indigenous to Dravidian languages and that they arose in Indo-Aryan under Dravidian influence. The first part of this explanation finds no counter-evidence, to my knowledge, and the second part still strikes me as the most plausible historical account. But there is the disturbing fact that the highest incidence of retroflection, at least as measured in terms of the number of distinct retroflex phonemes, is found not in a location where one might have expected to find early contact between Indo-Aryan and Dravidian, but rather in the far northwest of South Asia, spreading indeed to adjacent Iranian languages (although phonemic retroflection is not a characteristic of Iranian languages in general) (Masica 1991: 132). If the languages in question had been spoken in Scandinavia, we would have dismissed similarities between the two retroflex areas as coincidental. It is of course conceivable that the pocket of intense retroflection in the northwest of South Asia could be an independent phenomenon (or conceivably also the result of an independent innovation interacting with the general South Asian retroflection phenomenon), but given the areal contiguity this solution is suggestive rather than compelling. We are left therefore with a nagging doubt, one that the gaps in the historical record for the languages of the far northwest of South Asia may leave unresolvable.

In studying the historical mechanisms by which language areas arise, the general study of ongoing language contact is of course an important ingredient, because here we can see in operation the kinds of mechanisms that are relevant. We can therefore gain insight into the general phenomenon of the formation of language areas by the study of more local phenomena that are amenable to contemporary observation, or that reflect a shorter time-depth and are therefore more likely to be amenable to available techniques of historical reconstruction. One feature that strikes me as potentially rewarding in this respect is the kind of focus construction that is found in the south of South Asia, not only in the Dravidian languages (where it could reflect different developments of an inherited construction), but also in Sinhala, where it most plausibly reflects contact with Dravidian, in particular Tamil. In Comrie (1995) I tried to work out some of the details of the focus construction of one variety of Malayalam, as in (1), inevitably relying on the earlier work by K.P. Mohanan (1982):

1. raaman kuTTiy-ey aaNï kaN-T-a-tï
   Raman child-ACC be-PRS see-PST-ADJ-NT
   'is the child that Raman saw.'

Existing descriptions of Tamil, Kannada, Telugu, and Sinhala make it clear that very similar phenomena exist across these languages. A detailed comparison of the possibilities in the various languages, including reconstruction of their historical development in Sinhala in particular, would seem a rewarding research project—and one that might perhaps find a place in *The Yearbook of South Asian Languages and Linguistics*?

■ 3. Anaphora

At the beginning of 1996 I had the opportunity to participate in a joint US–Indian workshop on anaphors and pronouns at the University of Delhi. The workshop was part of a larger project whose main end product will be the volume Wali et al. (forthcoming), which presents, from the perspective of a unified typological framework, information on the behavior of anaphors and pronouns across a range of South Asian languages. I believe that this volume will be a major contribution from South Asian languages to linguistic typology and I therefore wish to discuss some of the reasons why data from South Asian languages should prove particularly important for our general understanding of anaphora and related phenomena.

A language like English has, in order to express coreference, a two-way opposition between reflexive and non-reflexive pronouns, e.g. *himself* versus *he*, the former being used in more local domains (e.g. within a clause, especially among the arguments of the predicate), the latter in more global domains (for instance across a clause boundary), as in the contrast between (2) and (3):

2. $John_i$ hit $himself_i$.
3. $John_i$ said that he_i would leave.

Many South Asian languages, including in particular both Indo-Aryan and Dravidian languages, belong to a type of language that makes a three-way distinction here. Thus, Hindi has a distinction among what I will call the ordinary reflexive, *apnee*, the emphatic reflexive, *apnee aap*, and non-reflexive pronouns like *us*. These distribute, as expressions of coreference, from most local to most global domains in the following order: most local is the emphatic reflexive, next comes the ordinary reflexive, finally the non-reflexive pronoun. In Hindi, for instance, the emphatic reflexive is used for arguments of the same predicate (often alternating with the ordinary reflexive), the ordinary reflexive optionally with a subject antecedent across a clause boundary (in so-called logophoric use), the non-reflexive pronoun elsewhere across a clause boundary, as in (4)–(6):

4. Siilaa nee apnee (aap) koo SiiSee meeM deekhaa.
   Shila ERG self ACC mirror in saw
   'Shila saw herself in the mirror.'
5. Siilaa nee vijay koo apnii praSamsaa kar-nee see manaa kiyaa.
   Shila ERG Vijay to self's praise do-INF from prohibit did
   '$Shila_i$ prohibited $Vijay_j$ from praising her_i (also: $himself_j$).'
6. Siilaa nee vijay koo uskii praSamsaa kar-nee see manaa kiyaa.
   Shila ERG Vijay to his/her praise do-INF from prohibit did
   '$Shila_i$ prohibited $Vijay_j$ from praising her_i.'

(These data were provided by Alice Davison.)

Similar three-way patterns, though often with differences in detail as to the precise dividing line between adjacent, are reasonably well known from outside South Asia. For instance, some East Asian languages have a similar pattern, as in Mandarin emphatic reflexive *ta ziji*, ordinary reflexive *ziji*, non-reflexive *ta*, or Japanese emphatic reflexive *zibun zisin*, ordinary reflexive *zibun*, non-reflexive *kare* (or null). Likewise, Danish distinguishes emphatic reflexive *sig selv*, ordinary reflexive *sig*, and non-reflexive *ham* 'him'. Indeed, languages with such a three-way opposition have played an important role in the recent generative literature, the distinction between the domains of emphatic and ordinary reflexives being accounted for in purely formal syntactic and morphological terms. I have myself preferred an alternative account, and South Asian languages provide data that might be relevant to this alternative.

My approach has been more in terms of semantics and pragmatics, in particular noting—as has often been done in the earlier literature—that there is an expectation that the arguments of a single predicate will be noncoreferential, thus leading to preference for a more marked form when they are in fact coreferential. This covers, for instance, the use of the more marked reflexive in English to express coreference among the arguments of a single predicate. But one can in fact generalize this, so that there is not a purely binary contrast between local and global domains, but rather an ordering from most local to least local (most global) domains. In this sense, the domain including the arguments of a predicate would be more local that the relation between the adjuncts and the arguments in a clause, although this would in turn be more local that the relation between noun phrases in different clauses. This ordering of domains can then be mapped onto the ordering from emphatic reflexive to ordinary reflexive to non-reflexive pronoun, which in turn reflects an ordering from most marked to least marked morphological form. This is fully consistent with the variation that is found cross-linguistically. For instance, for languages with a two-way opposition—reflexive versus non-reflexive, the cut-off point may occur at different points, so that Russian, for instance, allows reflexives in certain infinitival complements to be coreferential with the subject of the main clause while English does not, as in Russian (7) versus its English translation (8):

7. Kolja velel Vere dat' sebe (reflexive) knigu.
8. Kolya told Vera to give him the book.

Similar variation occurs in languages with a three-way opposition. For instance, Hindi allows the ordinary reflexive, alongside the emphatic reflexive, for a direct object coreferential with the subject of the same clause, while Danish requires the emphatic reflexive here.

But more importantly, the extra marking that characterizes the emphatic reflexive does not have be indicated in the reflexive pronoun itself, and Tamil provides crucial evidence here. In Tamil, in addition to the form of the reflexive pronoun itself, reflexivization can also be indicated by the auxiliary verb 'hold'. The addition of this extra reflexive morpheme has the same effect as an emphatic reflexive: it restricts coreference to the most local domain. In (9), therefore, the antecedent of the object of the subordinate clause can only be the subject of that clause, not the subject of the main clause; without the auxiliary 'hold', the latter interpretation is permitted.

9. kumaar raajaa tann-aip parrip peec-ik koN-T-aan enru
   Kumar Raja self-ACC about talk-CVB hold-PST-3SM that
   ninai-tt-aan.
   think-PST-3SM
   'Kumar$_i$ thought that Raja$_j$ was talking about himself$_j$'

In other words, evidence from South Asian languages shows that what is relevant here is the distinction between an emphatic (morphologically heavier) expression of reflexivity and a morphologically less heavy expression; in all the instances I am aware of, the morphologically heavier one simply involves one or more extra morphemes. The extra morpheme can form part of a reflexive pronoun, as in (4), or can be in a completely different part of the clause, as shown by the use of the auxiliary in (9). Here we have an instance where South Asian data patterns contribute both to evaluating proposals in formal syntax and to illuminating the general typology of coreference relations cross-linguistically.

■ 3. Ergativity and Grammatical Relations

One of the issues that first aroused my interest in South Asian languages was the phenomenon of ergativity, and the broader related issue of grammatical relations. Published results of this interest include Comrie (1979), and also the exchange Saksena (1981), Comrie (1984), Saksena (1985), and Comrie (1985). The last mentioned exchange came to an end but not, I think, a conclusion, since the issues that separated the participants were never resolved to our mutual satisfaction. Indeed, the current situation is rather paradoxical. On the one hand, South Asian languages are often held up as model illustrations of particular points concerning grammatical relations in a cross-linguistic perspective, for instance experiencer subjects (Verma and Mohanan 1990), while on the other hand we find works like Bhat (1991), and on a more specific point Saksena (1981; 1985) arguing that grammatical relations do not play a role in the syntax of South Asian languages, that those phenomena elsewhere handled in terms of grammatical relations are better handled in other terms, appealing for instance to morphology, word order, pragmatics and the vest.

While I am not committed *a priori* to the view that every possible human language has to make reference to grammatical relations in its syntax, I am committed to the view that alternative approaches must be subjected to just as rigorous criteria of falsification as must accounts couched in terms of grammatical relations. For instance, I am not aware of any data internal to Hindi, at least the varieties of Hindi under consideration, that would distinguish between the positions taken by Comrie and Saksena in the above mentioned exchange, which boils down basically to the following: Is verb agreement in Hindi governed primarily by grammatical relations (Comrie), or rather by case marking supplemented by word order (Saksena). But whatever the situation in Hindi, it is clear that there are other South Asian languages to which Saksena's analysis for Hindi would not be directly applicable, for instance Marathi, where personal pronouns do not show a case distinction between ergative and citation forms. Saksena's analysis of Hindi, whereby the first of two citation-form noun phrases triggers agreement in the perfective aspect, would work fine in (12) and (13) below—two-place verbs that nonetheless take a citation-form subject, even for nouns, in the perfective—but not for (11), which has exactly the same case marking as (13) but behaves syntactically, in particular for purposes of verb agreement, like (10) with an ergative subject (which cannot trigger verb agreement, relinquishing this to the neuter plural direct object in the citation form):

10. ram ne kame keli.
    Ram ERG jobs did-3PNT
    'Ram did the jobs.'
11. mi kame keli.
    I jobs did-3PNT
    'I did the jobs.'
12. ram khup goSTi boll-a.
    Ram many things said-3SM
    'Ram said many things.'
13. mi khup goSTi boll-o.
    I many things said-1S
    'I said many things.'

So South Asian languages may differ in the contribution that such factors as grammatical relations, word order, and nominal morphology make to the definition of syntactic structure. Moreover, I suspect that there is much more information from South Asian languages that could be brought to bear on this range of problems.

One factor that almost certainly has to be taken into account is the variation that exists not only across, but also within South Asian languages. Often, moreover, it is not clear exactly what kind of variation is at issue: variation among different well-defined dialects (whether geographical or social)? variation among individuals? or even within a single individual manifested on different occasions? I will mention two examples that have come to my attention, both of which relate to the general issue of grammatical relations. I will mention both of them briefly, although I will also note that they have important implications for the place of South Asian languages within a general typology of languages according to the role played by grammatical relations.

The first concerns conditions on the antecedent of the possessive reflexive pronoun *apnaa* in Hindi. In the most recent appeal that I am aware of to grammatical relations in the treatment of Hindi reflexives, T. Mohanan (1994: 125) argues that in the variety of Hindi that she is describing, the relevant condition is that the antecedent must be a subject, although she notes that there are also other varieties of Hindi for which this constraint does not hold. Clearly, if there are well-defined distinct varieties, then great care needs to be taken in presenting Hindi data relating to this question, since data taken from the dialect that does not have the subject-as-antecedent condition would not be usable as evidence that "Hindi", as an abstract entity, lacks the subject-as-antecedent condition, since there would be other varieties of the language that do have this condition. And unfortunately much of the literature is couched in terms that leave the reader unclear which variety of Hindi is under consideration, or indeed if all the data are from the same consistent variety of Hindi. After all, in a speech community of hundreds of millions of people, some variation is hardly surprising. But what would be nice would be to see more care being taken in defining the varieties that are being described, and in ascertaining the kinds of variation that exist. It is not, for instance, immediately obvious that we are dealing with distinct well-defined varieties; at least, it would be nice to see this established if it is true—then we could progress more confidently in the description of individual varieties.

My second point in this section concerns subject–object asymmetries, specifically in Malayalam. One of the important claims in K.P. Mohanan (1982, especially 524–26) is that Malayalam lacks subject–object asymmetries, whence his justification for representing Malayalam clause structure as "flat", with the S-node immediately dominating all of subject, object, and predicate, and without an intervening node dominating object and predicate to the exclusion of subject. This would thus constitute an important typological difference between Malayalam and English, since the latter has well-defined subject–object asymmetries. Now, in work that I carried out together with a graduate student in linguistics who is a native speaker of Malayalam, Suchitra Sadanandan, it transpired that in her variety of Malayalam, there are subject–object asymmetries. Since K.P. Mohanan and Suchitra Sadanandan come from different regions of Kerala, this could be a well-defined geographical dialect distinction, but only further detailed work with a variety of speakers of Malayalam would give us reason to accept or reject this account of the variation.

The scenario that these data suggest is intriguing, namely that there might be considerable variation not so much among as within South Asian languages concerning the extent to which native speakers make appeal to grammatical relations and differences in grammatical relations as opposed to other features, such as word order and case marking. A detailed study of this variation, perhaps initially for a single phenomenon in a single language, would throw valuable light on the precise place that South Asian languages hold in a typology of grammatical relations.

■ 5. Conclusions

Inevitably, in the space at my disposal. I have only been able to say a few things about a few of the problems and areas that seem to me to be of interest in South Asian languages from a typological perspective. But I hope that I have succeeded in showing that South Asian languages have an important contribution to make to linguistic typology, and conversely that typological considerations are important to our understanding of South Asian languages. I look forward to following the success of *The Yearbook of South Asian Languages and Linguistics* as, among other things, a forum for the fruitful interaction of South Asian linguistics and language typology.

■ ABBREVIATIONS

ACC–accusative, ADJ–adjective, CVB–converb, ERG–ergative, INF–infinitive, NT–neuter, PNT–plural neuter, PRS–present, PST–past, S–singular, SM–singular masculine.

■ REFERENCES

Bhat, D.N.S. 1991. *Grammatical relations: the evidence against their necessity and universality.* London: Routledge.

Comrie, Bernard. 1979. Some remarks on ergativity in South Asian languages. *South Asian Languages Analysis* 1.211–19.

———. 1984. Reflections on verb agreement in Hindi and related languages. *Linguistics* 22.857–64.

———. 1985. Reply to Saksena: further reflections on verb agreement in Hindi. *Linguistics* 23.143–5.

———. 1995. Focus in Malayalam. *Journal of Asian and African Studies* 48-49.577–603.

Maddieson, Ian. 1984. *Patterns of sounds.* Cambridge: Cambridge University Press.

Masica, Colin P. 1976. *Defining a linguistic area: South Asia.* Chicago: University of Chicago Press.

———. 1991. *The Indo-Aryan languages.* Cambridge: Cambridge University Press.

Mohanan, K.P. 1982. Grammatical relations and clause structure in Malayalam. *The mental representation of grammatical relations*, ed. by Joan Bresnan, 504–845. Cambridge, MA: MIT Press.

Mohanan, Tara. 1994. *Argument structure in Hindi.* Stanford: CSLI.

Saksena, A. 1981. Verb agreement in Hindi. *Linguistics* 19.467–74.

———. 1985. Verb agreement in Hindi : part II. *Linguistics* 23.137–42.

Verma, M.K. (ed.). 1976. *The notion of subject in South Asian languages.* South Asian Studies, University of Wisconsin-Madison Publication Series 2.

Verma, M.K. and **K.P. Mohanan** (eds). 1990. *Experiencer subjects in South Asian languages.* Stanford: CSLI.

Wali, Kashi, K.V. Subbarao, Barbara Lust and **James Gair** (eds). Forthcoming. *Lexical anaphors and pronouns in selected South Asian languages: a principled typology.* Berlin: Mouton de Gruyter.

Knowing the Word *Trikkhe*: Against Purism in the Study of Language

PROBAL DASGUPTA

Dear A.M.,

This open letter seeks to convince you that the generative linguistics program needs to identify and discard certain current assumptions which overvalue what I shall call Purism in linguistics. I will recommend strengthening other assumptions, also current. These take us away from a geometry of pointed locations towards a geography of nonsimple habitations.

The letter is organized as follows. Section 1 sets the stage. Section 2 touches base with a consensus that linguists should help resist language use purism. Section 3 links this injunction to the antipuristic drift in linguistic thought which we can identify and should consciously continue. We obviously gave up on a religious purism and on a historicist purism when we embarked on a linguistic science. Section 4 makes the less obvious proposal that when we started the generative program we also abandoned a structural–formalist purism focused on an inner form that would be defiled by contact with substance. Section 5 notes the recent decline of the purism of a logically interpretable deep structure with single referential interfaces. Section 6 suggests that the minimalist program invites such a construal, and that all contemporary models are with it on this. Section 7 places the struggle against purism in syntax in a larger mental and social context with respect to some morpho-lexical facts from the Bangla multiplication table featuring *tin* 'three' and *trikkhe* 'times three', arguing that threeness is a body-purity which they may share but which we never find maskless. Section 8 examines syntagmatic Displacement and paradigmatic Delegation as fundamental properties of language, suggesting specific mechanisms for extending to the paradigmatic domain the form of the knowledge we have of syntagmatic chains. Section 9 studies the sentence's formal impurity in terms of the substantive impurity that constitutes the act of speaking, which brings the new to bear on the old. Section 10, finally, proposes a Grammar and Composition model, returns to your debate with N.C., and argues that resisting the purism latent in these positions as they now stand will make the debate more pursuable.

■ 1. Purpose

Let me begin to set the stage. My context is the debate between you and N.C. Permit me to avoid side issues. My notation will impersonally treat you, A.M., as just the proposal that the meaning of sentence S is the set of all the real choices that constitute S—all the unforced steps in S's linguistic derivation. In contrast, N.C. for present purposes will mean the proposal that the entire derivation of S is not what bears meaning. However one may redistribute the goodies for some technical task, N.C. says, an S is a pairing of some representation pi at PF with some representation lambda at LF. Pardon this Roman spellout of Greek letters. If LF does not fully determine S's meaning, maybe some aspects are fixed at PF, but no other determinants are available.

I find this debate interesting mainly in relation to the possibility that we may need to push Head Movement—or whatever we call the factor responsible for Verb-Second clauses—into the PF component. If Head Movement, Scrambling, and other "syntactic" phenomena affecting phonological sentence rhythm and contextual meaning (however distributed between semantics and pragmatics) move out of the c/overt syntax into the "sentence morphology", questions about choice will become murkier.

Intuitively, one thinks of the overt and covert syntax as making all the choices, including the lexical ones, and the PF component seems to just spell all that out, unable to affect what any of it means. Standard work reflects these intuitions even in the formalism.

But one is now apparently going to let certain PF processes affect the ups and downs of meaning-prominence in some sense. This makes it possible to ask, with A.M., if there is any reason left why derivations should not do some (or even all) lexical choosing ("insertion") in the PF.

N.C. replies that there is a reason, namely, that an optimally simple lexicon should make it easy to read an LF at the interface with the C(onceptual)-I(ntentional) system. Therefore all lexical choices—however coded—should be available at LF and not have to be hunted for all over the LF-PF couple S, let alone all over S's entire derivation.

This response would have sounded prima facie unanswerable if one was not going to shift some of the meaning-affecting choices to the PF component. But it seems that independent reasons compel such a shift anyway. This loosens LF's once-complete grip on "interpretation"—some of it possibly sitting at the

"C-I interface", and some of it at PF which one must accordingly redefine not as an "A(rticulatory)-P(erceptual)" interface in some physical sense, but in some richer way which gives more rights to Perception and to corresponding productive acts. This means that A.M. vs. N.C. becomes in principle a real debate, not a case where most of us can reasonably back only one side.

How does that set the stage for a paper about purism? I am going to argue that we need to move away from puristic ways of asking and answering linguistic questions. Having argued my case, I return to the A.M. vs. N.C. issue, not to resolve it to either side's satisfaction, but to suggest that the issue looks even more interestingly pursuable, once we have removed the purism from the way both sides look in this introductory presentation. I propose to end, then, with a nonpurist rewrite of A.M. and N.C., and argue that such a debate gives us a 'better' issue than what we have just been looking at. Does such rewriting contribute to this or any other discussion? The readers will judge.

■ 2. Linguists and Purism

My first point concerns the general social imperative to resist purism which also obliges the linguist to help. Scientists may claim that they have no scientific opinion on whether a society should leave mixed norms or behaviors as they are or modify them towards some purity. But social decisions of this sort are often associated with a belief that a pure language, say, is a real object in a way that a mixed or hybrid one is not. Common sense then says to the linguist, Hey you, come and tell us how these pure objects should be described, surely your science is about purity.

It then becomes a public duty for linguists to explain that the field rejects this agenda, that neither generative grammar nor sociolinguistics can retain the structuralist first approximation to languages as ideally single and homogeneous codes, that we are sure that pure codes are not more real than anything else. Our failure to tell the public this does not exactly help the situation, which is rather grim in some cultures and contexts.

Some linguists who refuse to talk to the public may however be willing to look at issues of purism and resistance to it within the work of linguistics itself. One hopes that even internal rethinking will help prepare for and fortify our approach to the public. This is one basis for this paper.

It is difficult to imagine that the general imperative can or should be argued for. So we proceed to the specifics.

■ 3. The Antipuristic Legacy

The very gesture of starting a science of language that sees each contemporary language as coming from older ones via lawful sound changes rejects a religious narrative of the origins of language in some act of God, and a consequent privilege for some pure Hebrew or Sanskrit or whatever. In other words the foundation of our discipline made the rejection of religious purism in the case of language an emphatic presupposition of our work itself. We must inherit and strengthen this antipuristic legacy.

Some of us place the birth of scientific linguistics not at the Indo-European hypothesis but at Saussure. This need not alter the main point. Structuralism made us face a language before asking where it comes from. It thus gave equal rights in principle to dynastically descended royal languages and the lowliest creole of mixed origins. These gestures amounted to abandoning an incipient historicist purism that might otherwise have unintendedly allied the field with Aryan or other racisms. Here, too, we begin by constitutively renouncing a potentially puristic option. Our science then owes it to itself, not only to some public, to deepen the understanding of the antipuristic current that carries this field along. If there were no antipurists, there would be no linguists.

So far, we have merely been dressing up the textbook claim that linguistics pits its descriptions against unreasonable social authority's prescriptive grammars. That we can learn from a re-examination of the obvious will only become clear when we are on to something less obvious.

■ 4. Abandoning the Purism of Form

I would like to propose that one of the core impulses of the generative grammar program has been to reject a certain structural–formalist purism of an inner Form that would be defiled by contact with Substance if linguistics were to let Substance in. Far from being obvious, this proposal may even be wrong.

My point is not that generative work lets substance into the study of form or erases the boundary between knowledge and action. On the contrary, competence vs. performance if anything sharpens such a boundary, and may at first sight seem to reinforce the purism which I am claiming generative work rejects.

Rather, my point is that generative grammar recasts Linguistic Form quite fundamentally; generative representations in and as pure Form already participate in the work of Substance. I will unpack this as a first point about underlying and superficial representations and a second point concerning the flow of time.

Generative grammar distinguishes abstract/deep from concrete/surface representations both in syntax and in phonology. Does this simply continue structuralist thinking about levels? Or does it mark a decisive break of the sort I am suggesting?

I shall take the position that it does continue the work of structuralism, but with the radical innovation of permitting two or more levels of representation to use the same alphabet (the same set of elements taken to constitute a given level). Thus, the same features rearrange to turn a phonological into a phonetic representation. The same nodes reconfigure to change a deep into a surface syntactic tree.

Earthshakingly obvious? Perhaps. But what makes this innovation tick? What are distinct levels doing with the same alphabet?

They are marking the breakdown of structuralism's unitary point-sign. Saussure's well-known arbitrary sign is a socially packaged single interpoint where a stretch of sound /arbr/ contingently contacts a stretch of meaning 'tree'. At that point, every alphabet of linguistics comes into play, exactly once.

Generativism's use of the same alphabet over two levels (say, the phonological feature system over underlying phonology and superficial phonetics or the syntactic category system over deep syntax and surface syntax) provides an extended interface, not a unique interpoint. This extended interface in its internal dynamics actively reflects the duality of substances. Deep syntax sets up a relation with surface syntax which reworks the duality of semantic substance and phonetic substance, for instance. It is by deploying the same alphabet over a stretch of the derivation that the play within the form of language takes part in, and in that sense brings into play, the distinct realities of the substances. This is what I mean by the claim made earlier that "generative representations in and as pure Form already participate in the work of Substance".

That was point One, about the "sign-interface" stretching the Saussurean interpoint over several derivational steps. We turn to point Two. Generativism abandons the notion of the Sign insofar as its essential commitment is to the Sentence. Even though the competence abstraction represents knowledge and suspends the real time of action, the knowledge of a sentence brings time sequentiality into play quite crucially, a point that has become especially clear in recent work. Here again a property of Substance, the flow of time, enters the system of linguistic Form under generativism. The sign-point stretches not only over derivational steps, but over moments of the abstract time in language Form that anticipates and shapes the concrete temporal flow in the Substance of language use.

Generativism is thus committed by its inaugural gestures to a twofold rejection of the pointed purity of the Saussurean sign, the prototypical building block embodying language as a pure form uncontaminated by the vicissitudes of the concrete phonetic and semantic substance of speaking and understanding. The generative sign-equivalent, the Sentence as generated by a grammar, mimics crucial properties of the language-external actions of speech and comprehension. In the space of the sentence, word meets word, a meeting that brings time and other externalities into play. In the ordering of the computation, the structure readjusts itself so as to reflect the sound-meaning duality of substance, one of the biggest externalities of language.

Of course this formulation cannot stand still through the development of the generative account of language. A current version might focus on the Chain as the core fact corresponding to what the portrait given just now does with derivational steps. With this type of mutatis mutandis understood, we can look at the obvious and learn something less obvious. Namely, we generatives have been abandoning a structuralist version of purism.

A Structure of a Language was supposed to look like a Pure set of Norms, imposed by arbitrative Society, Sign by Sign. This was supposed to be spontaneous and unconscious and therefore not prescriptive. But linguistics in its structuralist period visualized this structure in the image of prescription by authority. Generativism has been undermining that visualization in ways we need to identify and consciously strengthen. Hence the necessity of explicit antipuristic work.

■ 5. The Importance of Impure Reference

Explicit antipurism is a voyage, not a particular destination. Generative grammar itself in its classical form crystallized a type of purism it has been shedding in phase two.

Classical generativism assumed processes such as pronominalization, reflexivization, relativization. These projected purified deep structures, where all the *hims* and *whoms* and *himselves* turned right back into the John they cross-referred to, from the messy surface structures with all sorts of bleached or empty 'shadows' that lacked referential power because surface structure was not in that business.

This purism of a conceptually interpretable deep structure with ideally single referential interfaces between language and reality became untenable when those 'shadows' turned out to have logically interesting properties and could not be left out of the reckoning. Current programs are busy examining the cross-referential properties of various shadow elements in the languages of the world. Now that it is clear that reference to 'real' entities often goes through the play of 'shadows', one's general picture of how language refers to reality must view Reference as Impure. Hence the title of this section.

The field of linguistics may have been focusing excessively on one way in which reference is impure—its mediation through chain-held empty categories, through overt anaphors and pronominals, and other referentially dependent elements. Future work will no doubt examine also the pervasive formal fact of linguistic gender, once the obvious and non-negligible social issues of patriarchal coding of asymmetry are addressed—by society, not just by linguists—and recedes from view, permitting other facts to emerge.

Under such conditions, future work will be able to address the striking formal fact that language everywhere classifies nouns into genders or classes, marking this codification in agreement systems or pronouns or other grammatical devices. There is nothing this pervasive for verbs. Gender/Class, call it GG for Generalized Gender, is obviously a deep fact about how N talks to its D support system. Reference conceivably works through GG. The system seems to first consider a GG-carried subworld and then pick out some denizen thereof. In that case even an R-expression at the head of a syntactic chain does not face the referential trial alone, but is spoken for by various as yet unexplored support mechanisms, perhaps some of them GG-linked.

Existing work on empty categories and overtly dependent-referential elements already shows—even without the future work I have been handwaving at—that the 'referential dependence' between a John and a himself is, in an important sense, mutual, not one-way. The idea that only a himself depends on a John, enshrined in the terminology of referential dependence, is a relic from the period which believed that N heads an NP in which D plays a satellite role. We now assume that D sets the syntagmatic stage on which N can occupy a syntactic position. I think it is useful to construe the GG question—which we know we will have to address, though we don't yet know how the answers will look—as something like, "Precisely how do pronouns, affixes, and other GG markers set the paradigmatic stage on which N can do any referring?"

In other words, not only syntagmatically, but also in the paradigmatics of the system of reference, the dependence between name-like Nouns and their 'dependent' grammatical support systems is a matter of two-way traffic. None of the relevant items works alone. We have been learning how to examine the syntagmatic company an item keeps. We are on the verge of serious work on what its paradigmatic neighbors are like and how it cooperates with them.

Work along such lines will obviously continue to distend the naively pure picture of a referential interpoint between language and reality over an interregion in which referential identification gets worked out. We already have familiar proposals like N moving to D (proper names, Swedish definiteness, etc.) and anaphoric D moving to I (subject-oriented monomorphemic overt anaphors). These concern the derivational stretching of the erstwhile referential interpoint into chains and other syntagmatic stretches. But we also need to use GG and other probes to explore the paradigmatic neighborhood of items that refer variously. Then the interpoints will fan out in a different direction. That might provide a base from which we as linguists can meet halfway some proposals outside the field about how referential expressions compel a detour through paradigmatic neighbors in the language system and thus postpone the content-cashing of their expression-checks. One version of such thinking underlay classical deconstructionism, a remark that need not be construed as an endorsement of any particular implementation of the idea of deferred reference.

We have accumulated enough material from the current scene in linguistics—bearing in mind both what has been on the anvil and what we have tended to shelve but hope to return to—to try a characterization of the adversary that this paper targets, Purism in linguistic study:

1. Characterization of Purism in Linguistic Study: Purism in linguistics is the tendency to hope to detect, and to base your analysis of the entire language on, some decisive effect visible in the primary data reflecting particular absolute principles such as "Names refer" or "Core morphology

survives language change" which directly, unhedged by other principles, shape some characteristic core facts of language Antipuristic workers, on such a view, always try to preserve the results obtained under puristic assumptions but jiggle around the importance of the criteria so that yesterday's factual core loses its primacy. Thus first approximations give way to second and third versions, and old purisms shrink into narrower, subtler purisms, which successive generations have to notice and overcome.

So much for a broad perspective that abstracts away from idealizations people have been actually operating with. What concretely available program does or can make room for serious antipuristic work in generative linguistics?

■ 6. Minimalist Syntax

I wouldn't blame you, A.M., for assuming that minimalism was the last thing I would vote for in this mood. It might seem to you, after all this, that I should find the minimalist program unacceptably austere, pure, segregative in its approach to highly specific and cut-the-crap interfaces between pieces of language and of non-language. But in fact I find the minimalist program an excellent base for antipurism to operate from.

Minimalism forces us to face lexical entries and their irregular edges directly, without evasions. And we find a mess. Minimalist inquiry asks how best to deal with this mess without looking beyond the tools the lexicon itself makes available. This approach forecloses the fake mopping-up options which bother me and which I've been calling puristic.

At the heart of the actual mechanisms of minimalist syntax lies the operation of comparing potential derivations that converge on the same output couple <pi, lambda>. This optimality comparison operation must admit the most economical such derivation and block the others, thus identifying the Admissible proper subset of the set of derivations which are Convergent (which have non-crashing outputs at PF and LF).

If minimalism had not resolutely abandoned the referential purism of classical generative work, one would inevitably start asking: Why confine optimality comparison to a reference set of derivations all of which converge on exactly the same sentence with PF pi and LF lambda? Why not ask the question for a bigger reference set of ways of saying the same thing? For instance, why not carry out optimality comparisons between *John$_i$ expected that he$_i$ would win* and *John expected to win* and conclude that the latter is less marked, leaving the present identifications of the Admissible from among the Convergent as a special effect of this broader operation?

It is only because minimalist work inherits a firm commitment to lexico-syntactic reality that it leaves such looser jobs to pragmatics, and restricts its own agenda to working out how to manage the traffic of one bunch of words used for saying one thing. Adherence to the specific reality of a task is one's best guarantee against purism. Inappropriate clean-up jobs arise from a false sense of knowing how to reduce one task to another.

I am only saving time by focusing on minimalism and handwaving at the other approaches to syntax. It should be clear to readers interested in alternatives that all viable syntaxes since the decline of generative semantics have shared this commitment to lexico-syntactic reality and this division of jobs between grammar and pragmatics. The old purism of a homogeneous single linguistics using a single set of tools for both jobs is dead in everybody's work. Minimalism simply serves to make the story stand out sharply.

■ 7. The Mental Context of Word Use

One important methodological property of a minimalist syntactic account of a sentence S is that it is accountable to the words that have been chosen in the numeration of S. Syntax thus begins the study of words in the context they create for each other. A minimalist program in syntax will then have to work as a cutting edge for some larger program which does for the comprehensive study of words and their labor what the minimalist program tries to do for the syntactic sector of that inquiry.

The welcome reduction of potential space for purism in syntax, then, which comes from this faithfulness to lexical choices (in the non-negotiable numeration that initiates the work of syntax), needs to be set in the larger study of all mutual relations between words. We must do this without sacrificing the specificity of syntactic inquiry.

I shall take the position that this task involves setting the resistance to purism in syntax in a specifically mental context of social action. I know, A.M., that you will suspect me of sociologism at this point. Please give me some space to clarify. Surely you agree with me that linguistics is about knowledge. Can I try on you a particular way, please, of developing the surely askable question "What is it to know a word?"? I would like to push the question towards a clear intersection with current grammatical thinking.

To this end, consider a particular context, the Bangla (a.k.a. Bengali) *namta* or multiplication table, the word *trikkhe* embedded therein, and the question of what it is to know this word. Here is the three times subtable:

2. a. tin ekke tin — $3 \times 1 = 3$
   b. tin dugune chOY — $3 \times 2 = 6$
   c. tin trikkhe nOY — $3 \times 3 = 9$
   d. tin care baro — $3 \times 4 = 12$
   e. tin paMce ponero — $3 \times 5 = 15$
   f. tin chOk aTharo — $3 \times 6 = 18$
   g. tin Satte ekuS — $3 \times 7 = 21$

h. tin aSTe cobbiS $3 \times 8 = 24$
i. tin nOng SataS $3 \times 9 = 27$
j. tin dOSe tiriS $3 \times 10 = 30$

Compare these '× n' forms with the bare 'n' forms given in (3):

3. a. Ek
 b. duy
 c. tin
 d. car
 e. paMc
 f. chOY
 g. Sat
 h. aT
 i. nOY
 j. dOS

Obviously, every normal Numeral n differs from its corresponding Times-Numeral × n. These differences do not reduce to any simple conversion formula. Why, then, do we focus on the word *trikkhe* 'times-three' and not on the whole *namta*? Why should *trikkhe* be special?

If you inspect the *namta*, you will find that every other Times-Numeral form occurs at least twice in the table. Only *trikkhe* occurs exactly once, in the line $3 \times 3 = 9$ alone. Therefore, what is special about *trikkhe* is that, arguably, to know the word *trikkhe* is to know that line of the *namta*. Thus, the word *trikkhe* poses in an extreme form the question of knowing a word.

On reflection, so do all the Times-Numerals. They are all embedded in the educational practice of the *namta*. It is true, of course, that a speaker can know the words and not know the *namta*, in the sense of being able to believe or to say, as a bad mathematician, that *tin trikkhe dOS* '$3 \times 3 = 10$'. But even an incorrigible speaker who makes such persistent errors and yet knows the words does know a *namta*, albeit a normatively invalid one. You cannot know the Times Numerals and yet truthfully claim you don't know the multiplication table from Adam.

Likewise, as a fuller data base would have illustrated, knowledge of the Date Ordinals *pOYla* 'first', *doSra* 'second', *teSra* 'third', etc. is embedded in the operative knowledge of locating dates in a month. Knowledge of the Playing Card Serials *Tekka* 'ace', *duri* 'two', *tiri* 'three' etc. is hard to separate sharply from rudimentary knowledge, however unused or unusable, of a pack of cards.

To a considerable extent, knowing such words is not sharply distinguishable from a specialized knowledge of the contexts (or, if you prefer, the practices, or the language games) they pertain to. To that extent, the shapes *trikkhe* '× 3', *teSra* 'the third [of a month]', *tiri* 'three [of a card suite]', and the general context item tin 'three' are used by the mind to cross inter-context boundaries at particular correspondence points. Words help as embodied links between these practices that we have operative knowledge of.

Knowing an embodied inter-practice link, then, is a good first approximation to the notion of knowing a word.

What about the morphology of a word? Suppose for a moment that one might wish to describe *teSra*, along the lines of the common notation *3ra*, as '*tin* plus date ordinal morphology'. Given this point of departure, how do we extend our account of words as embodied cross-practice links?

The morphology, so conceived, modifies words in ways that help them to serve as such links. You add, say, date ordinal material to 'three' to get 'third'. And you subtract that material from 'third' to obtain 'three'. In the case of date ordinals, the material settles down to an affix *-oi* from five to eighteen, and then another affix *-e* from nineteen to thirty-two (months in Bengal don't stop at thirty-one). Times numerals and playing card serials stay suppletive throughout; they never settle down. But even suppletion is an extreme case of material co-modifying expression and content if a series of such modifications gives each member at least the paradigmatic company of the rest.

These additive and subtractive modifications are the morphology (the co-modifications of expression and of content) and enable each word-shape involved to be construed as a reshaping of the corresponding word-shape, of its opposite number in the morphological correspondence. This option of construing one word as a re-embodiment of another word extends and underwrites our account of words as inter-practice link-bodies.

Consider now the problems of squaring these moves with the imagery of a broadly Saussurean system of signifying expressions and signified contents. The closest we can now come to signification is within one of the practices, by noting, say, that *teSra* means 'the third' (however we might then choose to unpack 'means "the third"') at a point on the date ordinal line. But this is hardly a simple and separable location. The term *teSra* in the date ordinal system can only do this in solidarity with its fellow threenesses in the playing card system, in the cardinal system, and so forth. We might at best place some limits on how much cross-reference is called for and how often. But clear and distinct point-particulars are obviously not an option.

Note that this places morphology at the very heart of our sincerest reconstruction of signification and thus of Saussurean arbitrariness. The word *tin* or the word *teSra* can so signify, each within its system, only in a metasystem hooked up by the morphological connectors that 'cross-signify'—the plus-ordinal addition that takes significant *tin* into significant *teSra* or the minus-ordinal subtraction taking *teSra* into *tin*.

In other words, A.M., and this bears on any theory of lexical choice, there is no innocent Saussurean signifier that can just sit and signify. For a word to signify, within its system, it must wear a hat that both qualifies it to access that system and morphologically trades with other hats mapping it into congeners in other systems.

In general, then, you expect a word to have both a body proper, the invariant core that underpins its correspondences with congeners, and a hat that marks which side of a correspondence a particular word is on (say, the cardinal *tin* side or the date ordinal *teSra* side). This basis for expecting word complexity dissociates generative morphology, as unpacked here, from the structuralisms that we tend to assume, often harmlessly, as points of departure.

Surely you, A.M., can see that such an account allows us to finish a business the generative journey started when we abandoned the right of an early nominalization theory to derive unproductive nominals from transparent sentences. Today, nominals are supported by specific functionals, and every contentive lexical item in general floats in a functional support pool.

The older kind of theory permitted an S to pretend to be true body and a nominalization to say it was an S-body plus a nominalizing mask. Today we need to say that each body always appears masked (i.e. active) in an act. You get no pure bodies. Such an account allows no lapsarian derivation of purity-destroying mask from pure body.

Not that such a system makes it impossible to speak of inter-mask relations. One masked body may correspond to another masked body. Such correspondences help make sense of the system as a whole and belong to the knowledge that the speaker has. We need the body-mask duality to be able to formalize such notions. Body remains as an inter-practice domain for stating such correspondence, not a purity. The word is then the body in the relevant sense, but the body is always masked, it's just that you can ask it to think across masks and thus across contexts/practices. You can ask *tin* 'three' and *trikkhe* 'times-three' to look at each other in their shared body-threeness across the gap between their masks of cardinality and times-numerality, for example, without appealing to any pure threeness embodied in some neutral maskless form. In particular, *tin* 'three' is not a pure form.

The nature of language makes impurity necessary.

■ 8. Necessity the Mother of Inflection

The Saussurean approximation's pure point-signs made inflection contingent and slightly mysterious. We have been looking at the need to extend the typical expression-content interface over an inter-region. Instead of point-signs that can in principle ignore each other, we have a situation where word accommodates fellow word by stretching. Such mutual accommodation in a syntagmatic construction is inflection, which thus becomes necessary on language design grounds.

When words accommodate to paradigmatic fieldmates we get the more general body-mask effect, with affixation as a special case of masking. Masking in general and inflection in particular are thus rooted in the nature of language.

Minimalism's commitment to such a view—and my project here is to convince you that there is such a commitment in practice which merely needs to become also theoretical—has grown with independently motivated moves like the decision to treat subject Agr as a non-(LF-)interpretable feature rather than as a PRO, as in the early eighties, sitting in Infl and inviting control by the subject. Today's non-sovereign Agr is a true mask in my sense.

Such a view does not work if it remains word-bound. Not only affixes mark inflection and accommodation. An accusative case affix in Sanskrit and a object marker particle in Japanese are equally non-interpretable at Logical Form. Masking is a general function. Extensive study of expletive subjects like *it* and *there* has accompanied the development of hard core minimalism. Expletives are masks of clausal nuclei. Current conceptions of Move Alpha as Attract F plus Generalized Pied-Piping may be read as: in movement, only mask calls, and only mask responds; bodies seem to tag along for PF purposes. "Interpretability" in general says that Body is what comes out in the wash at LF.

LF under minimalism is turning into an area where heavily masked Latin morphology can talk to lightly masked Mandarin morphology through Universal Grammar's syntax and make sense of each other as possible expression-content systems. LF concerns itself with the preservation of body, with content remaining intact across diversity of contexts/practices/games. This antipurist manifesto develops the proposal that this invariant body never directly appears as a pure form.

For any expression, from word size upwards, is always a sprawl, never a point. Minimalist work already recognizes this in chain theory as a syntagmatic fact. But an expression also lies athwart its paradigm, spread over a circle of friends—its heavier and lighter synonyms that provide or accept support. This paradigmatic type of extendedness has proved relatively difficult to investigate. We attempt here to address these issues on the basis of what is believed to be understood syntagmatically.

We know language design includes a syntagmatic displacement property. Minimalist work suggests this has to do with non-interpretable formal features triggering movement and extending items into chains. We just saw that it might be reasonable to construe the necessity of formal features in terms of mutual accommodation between word and fellow word in syntagms. It then follows that "derivation", in the sense of the always realized potential relatedness between word and fellow word in fields or families, is as fundamental paradigmatically as "inflection" is syntagmatically. To put it differently, language has a design feature prohibiting solitary, paradigmatically disconnected words. The question is how to derive predictions that give such thinking empirical teeth.

Let us take a closer formal look at chains and FFs (formal features), in terms of phi-features (Number, Gender, and Person as a bridgehead for deictic and anaphoric features) and TATAM-features (Tense, Aspect, Transitivity, Aktionsart, and Mood as a bridgehead for much that is murky):

4. The Fauna and Phenomena Diagram
   Nominal chains must bear:
   Verbal chains must bear: (i) phi (nominal) features
   (i) TATAM (verbal) features for identity
   (ii) para-TATAM (Case) features (ii) para-phi (Agr) features for connection

The non-interpretable FFs reduce to type (4-ii), the para-phi and para-TATAM connection features. Some paradigmatic formal mechanisms can now be postulated

5. Paradigmatic Support for item Alpha's Identity: Alpha's phi (if nominal) or TATAM (if verbal) features liaise with the support group of noun/verb subtypes sponsoring alpha's identity
6. Paradigmatic Support for item Alpha's Connections: Alpha's para-TATAM (if nominal) or para-phi (if verbal) features liaise with the support networks sponsoring alpha's syntagmatic connections and connectees

We have now found a place to keep paradigmatic material. The verb kick knows it is connected to feet, for example. That knowledge can now sit at the edge of the verb's non-interpretable para-phi feature matrix. The noun sister knows that its identity receives support from sisterhood (at the edge of the noun's interpretable phi feature matrix) and that it is connected to nurture and other key verbs (at the edge of the noun's non-interpretable para-TATAM feature matrix).

The ground is now prepared for our basic proposal in this domain—somewhat new, and quite possibly wrong:

7. The Delegation of Meaning Hypothesis. Every expression-content interface involves an item acting at a distance from the sources of its right to mean what it does

This point is best unpacked by referring to a concrete example, like the metaphoric use of kick in (8) as distinct from its literal use in (9):

8. Minimalists should kick Attract F and see what survives
9. The policeman kicked the prisoner

We all agree that these uses are different. But (7) claims that even the verb in (9) acts at a distance from where its meaning comes from. It is possible that serious work, when it settles down to an account, will replicate the core of our intuition that (8) brings the verb of (9) to bear on this abstract scene. But what (7) proposes, either against or at least without much help from our intuitions, is that even the verb in (9) brings an entire support group—feet and hitting, to be crude about it—to bear on the concrete scene. We can summarize proposal (7) by saying that the verb in (8) is a metaphoric Ladder (a paradigmatic counterpart to the syntagmatic Chain) one rung bigger than the one in (9).

Membership counts depend on arbitrary decisions. I would give the shortest Ladder, in literal (9), one overt(ly active lexical) member, kick, and one set of supportive members, call it one hinterland. That gives the shortest nontrivial Ladder, in metaphoric (8), two overt members, extended kicking and 'real' kicking, which we see before we reach the same hinterland, yielding a total of three members if (9) has two.

It may be useful to recall that early Chain Theory had one-member chains as a trivial special case, and that we soon found that one never needed such short chains in real S-structures once the findings were in. Ladder Theory may likewise find that the initially needed minimal ladders are an optical illusion associated with the early period of a proposal.

Summarizing so far, language has a Displacement property on the syntagmatic axis and a Delegation property on the paradigmatic one. Both properties spread the content-expression interface over an extended region in systematic ways. The better understood theory of syntagmatic chains may provide some hints for an account of paradigmatic ladders. But systematic plagiarism, as in most domains, is unlikely to help.

What is going to help is the obvious formal fact that affixes traditionally called derivational seem to systematize the paradigmatic semantic extension of items to new contexts. Date Ordinals in Bangla look as though they reapply Cardinals. This means that the territory of derivational morphology will provide a firm base for the paradigmatic formal research for which the issue now is no longer how to start it, but rather, how to not impede it from taking off. Such old purisms as the lingering belief that Cardinals are somehow more real than Date Ordinals will impede. One must remove such impediments. Hence this elaborately defended proposal that every 'signifying' operates under delegation, at some distance from the delegating forces which enable the 'signifier' to signify.

■ 9. The Sentence as Impurity

The discussion in section 8 deliberately ignores the growing recognition of the impurity of what used to seem endocentric noun phrases and verb phrases. Everybody now realizes that the functional head D of a "noun phrase" and the functional heads, whose number and scope are under negotiation, of a "verb phrase" must do what we had been attributing to the nouns and verbs; and at the same time that the jobs of many of these functional heads can only be done when the N or V wearing its various affixal or abstract features moves into those slots, lexicalizing them. This is one obvious kind of impurity that we know and love.

But I was leaving it out, A.M., not just because I could take the recognition of its reality for granted. I also wanted to invite some thinking about the specific impurity of being a sentence at all. Left to itself, current thinking makes a sentence a glorified verb phrase, with much complexity but still verbal. And one can see the compelling reasons for this belief's monopoly over current thinking. But we must pay attention to the growing evidence that the sentence is at the same time nominal.

We already know—from the necessity of moving or inserting some nominal phrase into the subject of IP (the Extended Projection Principle) and the near-necessity of moving some phrase into the specifier of CP (principles governing the licensing of C)—that sentences require what is again beginning to be called Thematization, reviving the old bipartite division of the Message into Theme and Rheme. This is very different from the behavior of other maximal projections.

I would like to add the obvious but fundamental fact that, when a clause gets embedded, the formal devices permit conversion into either a noun-like Complement Clause or an adjective-like Relative Clause, often using some item within or cognate to a WH family morphologically definable for the language, but never conversion into a specifically verb-like structure with a characteristic verbal complementizer of the WHERB type combining recognizably WH and verbal properties. Thus, we never have 'verbal relative' (11) or 'verbal complement' (12) with such morphology in any language:

10. The butter melted *The snow melted [WHERBED the butter t]
    'The snow did the same thing (melt) as the butter did'
11. *The cook did [WHERB the butter melt]
    'The cook made the butter melt'

One might argue that (11) is independently ruled out by whatever principles prevent verbs from referring and therefore coreferring. Since tense is referential, it is unclear to me what these principles are. But assume that they exist. I will allow that they exclude (11). What, then, prevents UG from finding a way around the problem in (12), where reference is not at stake? Why this apparent disinclination to have a WH-verbal Comp in any shape or form, and thus to verbalize the clause?

The answer, surely, is that clauses have a verbal inside and a nominal outside. Any embedding must use packaging that respects the outside and is accordingly nominal. This reinforces the realization that the clause is an emphatically impure structure.

I would like to propose, not a formal mechanism, but an interpretation of this impurity of sentences in terms of the essential, constitutive impurity of speaking. The idea runs like this. Speakers and hearers know that the number of sentences is infinite which makes it very likely that any particular sentence will be new to the experience of the addresser or the addressee. Each time a sentence is used, then, there is a sense that the message is presumed to be novel. One would then expect the addresser to provide and the addressee to respond to some sort of staging of whatever is new relative to some helpful anchoring in background material familiar to both parties.

On such a view, one expects a topic-comment articulation for every message, and typical topics are going to be nominal. This reasoning derives from first principles the nominal outside of a sentence and, if verbs typically derive the expression of new content against a familiar background, the verbal inside as well. The behavior of embedding devices now follows.

Looking at the matter backwards, from the point of view of the finitely many relatively familiar topics one can talk about and not from the mathematics of infinity, the use of sentences appears to unpack the sorts of messaging these topics sponsor. If unpacking topics is another valid view of the task of messages, we begin to see clauses, in addition to the chains and ladders they unleash, as a way for expressions as compactions to get unpacked.

Expressions, then, are compactions—they depend on the apparent pointedness of one item used in one position but invoking many other positions—and make sense under the reverse operation of rediffusion, which I am informally calling unpacking because we don't exactly have a mature theory of these matters.

■ 10. Grammar and Composition

I have spoken of three kinds of unpacking. Chains unpack by considering a series of copies which are exactly equivalent. Ladders juxtapose inexact equivalents, hence the looseness of metaphor and other delegations. Sentences qua messages unpack topics by bringing distinct ideas into connection. Observe the diminishing equivalence. Notice also the growing sociality. Chain Theory is a game where syntacticians can learn very little from lay advice or informal reflection on one's intuitions about what the chains are. Ladder Theory is perhaps semi-formal. Message Theory requires even greater dialogue with informal hunches.

Thus, unpacking refers crucially to the social exchange of equivalents, at least as imaged in the life of one's cognitive system. This being so, I must propose that we take seriously the option of a Grammar and Composition model.

Such a model says that the moment word meets word to form structure two things start happening. The grammar of the sentence begins, and invites syntax; the composition of the message and the discourse also begin, inviting pragmatics. These proceed on parallel but possibly connected tracks. Paradigmatic work seems to be an as yet diffuse meeting ground, possibly supposed to remain diffuse for reasons of principle.

There never was any *a priori* reason to assume that speech act-relevant units must be of sentence size. A Grammar and Composition model has been available, then, as a formal option. My suggestion is that we now have good *a posteriori* reasons for really trying it. My way of working out this suggestion, A.M., is to return to the debate between N.C. and you.

Let me begin with the other side. N.C.'s notion of a language diversity minimizing LF—with the non-interpretable formal features dropping out by getting eliminated in the overt component by the movement-inducing process "Attract Feature", so that LF consists only of interpretable features and can satisfy the Full Interpretation imperative—crucially requires that the real-time-free perfect part of the derivation be on the track that runs right through the c/overt syntax. This leaves all on-line imperfections for the morphology that leads to the PF. I will take the position that LF, the site where cross-language identifications in translation preserve interpretable bodies but ignore varying masks, explores the inter-practice of Perfect Translation as an ideal-type of potential mutual accountability between languages. Why "potential"? Because languages in real life often differ on matters that spoil translations in practice but leave this level of potential accountability unaffected. Such an LF encodes the important pretheoretical intuition that perfectly symmetric cross-language hospitality is possible. It thus deserves a niche in any programme for a complete linguistic theory.

Do I see you, A.M., as unable to accommodate such ideas? Let me not prejudge that point. I note that you also, wishing to act accountably, will try to capture the cross-language accountability intuition. The way your visualization of the computation seems to me to work, idiosyncratic decisions in the derivation, especially lexical ones, are taken on what I shall call the M/Orphic track. This track begins with the Orphic (overt) derivation and takes the left-hand, Morphic route to PF, while the right-hand route to LF performs covert jobs that affect scope like QR and abstract *wh*-movement. (Some lexical-choice-dependent string-vacuous jobs like moving toothless features from object to small v may need to—or at least can—get done on the Morphic route to PF, under your assumptions; in that case non-pied-piping follows from being toothless, not from occurring en route to LF.) You leave for the Covert road to LF only scope issues of logic proper. Your LF holds operator/functor-specified proposition formats, not real sentences. Lexicals and real–temporal choices converge on the information package at PF, in your system which says that the total meaning of a sentence S summates all the unforced choices in S's derivation.

N.C.'s story seems to me to bring out the utopian nature of the pretheoretical intuition that S(LA) in language A can be potentially perfectly equivalent to some S(LB) in B. For N.C.'s LF prescinds from the PF-affected imperfections of both and yet has enough lexical content left that one can, in an interesting subrange of cases, speak of optimal translation as manifesting accountability.

In contrast, your story seems to do better in meshing the pragmatics, which many of us think must play a role in translation and its reckonings, with what you will need to see as the site of translation. For you must, like all of us, put the pragmatics on the left, where time is real, and there it meets your lexical choices. So you can claim that, although your equivalences will always be hedged in by the pragmatics, you are dealing in real currency, so you image the accountability better.

I had promised not to try to settle your debate for you, but only to etch the lines sharply. Let me bring the debate into the heart of a single language. Translational equivalence arises as an issue also across contexts associated with the differences we are calling derivational. Accountability is about practices. What does knowing the Bangla word *trikkhe* mean? We have seen that the word is completely trapped in one particular line of the three times table. Does that leave us with any possible word-content for *trikkhe* alone? Can the word be said to signify precisely that subcontext where it appears, no more, no less? These are the questions that are going to arise, with some unresolved 'analytic philosophy' issues that usually get attached to them. They need not interest us. We wish to characterize knowledges.

One knows some practices, contexts, games. One mentally links them to each other. Words are best seen as aids that add tangibility and constancy to some of these links and thus help us to remember, know, use them. The word's morphology, a co-modification pointing both ways across an inter-context gap, helps this helping.

Such reasoning makes it reasonable to want to describe *trikkhe* as 'three plus times-numeral derivational morphology' or *tin* as 'three plus null or default morphology' as a way to say this. Even null is a morphology; even the apparent lack of mask is a mask; we are resisting purism's desire for a maskless body.

To see how such descriptions can actually help, imagine a new *ziro* line added to the Bangla multiplication table. You get *Ek ziroe ziro, duy ziroe ziro* for '$1 \times 0 = 0$, $2 \times 0 = 0$'. The pattern you extend to obtain this is presumably the morphological pattern that links *caar, paaMc* 'four, five' to *caare, paaMce* 'times four, times five'.

This extendability of the series to zero indicates that there is indeed a continuable series, a sustainability, and therefore a knowledge. The assumption, I hope reasonable, is that a knowledge is a pattern that enables the creative continuation of a systematic action-series. This assumption lets us know practices, and inter-practice links, and words that embody such links, and systematic co-modifications of these words that help carry our knowledge of them. If in our mental knowledge words ride piggyback on the morphologies that correlate them, then they are mentally represented without simple locations. Every location is viewed as a link between practices, between action-systems.

Such nonsimple locatedness in the word's home, the lexicon, should be unsurprising if sentenced words always appear in chains. Apparent one-pointed objects always unpack into series and contexts. Such unpacking provides multiple interfaces over which the 'same' thing unravels links between these contexts, helping them to illuminate each other.

Now we are ready to say some inconclusive last words, on the basis of what we have gone over, about the debate pitting an A.M. against an N.C.

A.M.'s picture of the meaning of S as the set of the unforced choices in the derivation of S looks puristic in the sharp boundary it draws between choice and compulsion. As phenomena like rhyme show, surely a syntagmatic pattern can signify even if some elements or stretches of it were not specifically chosen for those locations as they appear in the final product relative to other elements or subpatterns.

Likewise, N.C.'s pairing of a spelled-out PF and a lexically specified but non-spelled-out representation LF looks puristic for essentially the same reason. Like A.M., N.C. also assumes that S's PF representation pi meets its LF representation lambda only through lexical entries pairing word-size pieces of pi and of lambda. A serious Grammar and Composition model may well find principled ways for bigger chunks of pi and of lambda to meet on some other basis. There is something excessively pointed and Saussurean about the 'lexicon' of our first approximations.

Our stage-setting section 1 had nodded towards recent mainstream options that affect the debate, such as the idea of doing head movement (of the Verb-Second kind) and/or scrambling on the PF route. Now that this paper is over, we also see that there is a whole paradigmatic world that must enter any meaningful reckoning. Conceivably the lexicon is not uniform, but differentiates into two or more layers, with some entries riding piggyback on others which assemble 'glosses' for them. This could even be systematic, as in configurations studied under Diglossia Theory. Such considerations point towards a greater role, in theories of Meaning and Choice (two independent matters), for the emerging equations between grammar proper and the pragmatic buffer that presents messages in whatever settings they may be Conceived-Intended for. Provided that this 'may be' shields the potentials of competence from the online actualities of performance, we are still in a theory of knowledge, and thus in a linguistics and not an immediacy-enslaved communicology. No *a priori* thoughts will keep such issues out, and one is accountable to them.

Under these circumstances, A.M., your debate with N.C. is all set to shed its puristic first draft and turn into a full-blown engagement between two compelling sets of intuitions which initially look equally convincing to the community. I hope all who participate in a serious version of the debate will work against all purisms old and new to make such debates accountable to the many issues now coming into Visibility, to invoke a notion related to Interpretability.

E

■ Announcements ■

Announcements

■ The Chatterjee–Ramanujan Prize

The editorial board is pleased to announce that starting next year it will, in cooperation with Sage Publications, award the above yearly prize to the most outstanding student contribution to the *Open Submissions* section of *The Yearbook*.

■ Housekeeping: *The Yearbook (1999)*

As the inaugural issue goes to press, we are making preparations for the second issue. It will, we are happy to report, contain, amongst other things, invited contributions by Ashok Kelkar ("What Has Bhartṛhari Got to Say on Language?") and Mario Palaschke and Wolfgang Dressler ("Middle Indic Aspirate Formation: Syllable Structure vs. Natural Processes"), Regional Reports from India, Sri Lanka, and several other parts of the world, and reviews of L. Khubchandani, *Revisualizing Boundaries*, A. Parakrama, *De-Hegemonizing Language Standards*, and Rajendra Singh, *Grammar, Language, and Society*.

Potential contributors to the third and subsequent issues should get in touch with the Chief Editor as soon as possible. They are requested to please make sure that both their manuscripts and diskettes conform with our style-sheet. Authors of articles should make sure that an abstract is included. The Editors reserve the right to make non-substantive, minor editorial changes and to decline to process manuscripts and diskettes requiring unnecessary editorial work. While e-mail inquiries are welcome, manuscripts must be sent by ordinary post.

About the Chief Editor

Rajendra Singh is Professor of Linguistics, Philology and Translation at the Université de Montréal, Canada. He was a Fulbright Scholar in the USA before moving to Canada. Professor Singh has held visiting appointments at the Massachusetts Institute of Technology, and the universities of Amsterdam, British Columbia, Delhi, Passau, Singapore and Vienna. His research interests include phonology, morphology, sociolinguistics, language-contact and modern Hindi, areas in which he has written extensively.

Professor Singh's recent books are: *Explorations in Indian Sociolinguistics* (co-edited); *Towards a Critical Sociolinguistics* (edited); *Trubetzkoy's Orphan* (edited); *Pace Pāṇini: Towards a Word-based Theory of Morphology* (with Alan Ford and G. Martohardjono); *Grammar, Language, and Society: Contemporary Indian Contributions* (edited); *Modern Hindi Morphology* (with R.K. Agnihotri); *The Native Speaker: Multilingual Perspectives* (edited); *Linguistic Theory, Language Contact, and Modern Hindustani: The Three Sides of a Linguistic Story;* and *Lectures Against Sociolinguistics.*

Notes on Contributors

Prasanna Rekha Abel holds a Master's degree in linguistics (Deccan College, Pune, 1987), and did research at the University of Hyderabad, completing her M. Phil. in 1990 (on translation studies and semantic theory) and defending her Ph.D. (on diglossia and semantic theory) in 1997.

Asif Agha received his Ph.D. in linguistics from the University of Chicago in 1990. His main areas of research include grammatical theory, discourse analysis, and sociolinguistics. He has worked on Sino-Tibetan and Indo-Aryan languages, especially Lhasa Tibetan and Urdu–Hindi. He is currently Assistant Professor of Applied Linguistics and Anthropology, and Director of the Program in South and Southeast Asian Languages at UCLA.

Indira Ayyar teaches linguistics, applied linguistics, and TESOL related courses at the University of Western Ontario. She is also the coordinator of the university's training program for international Teaching Assistants. She has taught in India and the United States, and her research interests include Indian English, Tamil linguistics, and teacher training.

Tej K. Bhatia is professor of Linguistics at Syracuse University. Author of the Routledge *Grammar of Punjabi* and of *History of the Hindi Grammatical Tradition*, he has published extensively in the domains of descriptive, applied, and sociolinguistics.

Tanmoy Bhattacharya has done graduate work in linguistics at the University of Delhi, at Yale, at the University of Hyderabad, and at University College, London, where he is now finishing doctoral work on the Bangla determiner phrase. He has published several articles on syntax, pragmatics , and computational linguistics.

William Bright is Professor of Linguistics at the University of Colorado. For a number of years, he was the editor of *Language*. He also edited the 1996 classic *Sociolinguistics*. He now edits *Language in Society*. Professor Bright has always been interested in South Asia and has published several important papers on South Asian linguistics.

Bernard Comrie is Professor of Linguistics at the University of Southern California, Los Angeles. His publications include *Aspect* (Cambridge: 1976), *Language Universals and Linguistic Typology* (Oxford: 1981), *Tense* (Cambridge: 1985) and several important articles on syntax and typology.

Probal Dasgupta, Ph.D. (New York) is Professor and Chair of Applied Linguistics and Translation, University of Hyderabad. He has written extensively on Syntax and Sociolinguistics. His recent books include *Explorations in Indian Sociolinguistics* (1995, co-edited with R. Singh and J.K. Lele) and *The Otherness of English* (1993).

K.A. Jayaseelan holds a Ph.D. in English from Visvabharati University, Santiniketan (1970) and one in Linguistics from Simon Fraser University, Burnaby (1981). He teaches syntax and ELT at the Central Institute of English and Foreign Languages, Hyderabad. Professor Jayaseelan has published several collections of Malayalam poetry and many papers in formal syntax, with special reference to Malayalam.

Ayesha Kidwai did her Ph.D. (on scrambling in Hindi–Urdu) in 1995 at Jawaharlal Nehru University, New Delhi, where she teaches linguistics at the Centre for Linguistics and English. She is currently engaged also in the formal study of Indian varieties of English.

Paul Kiparsky is Professor of Linguistics at Stanford University. Well-known for his work in phonology, morphology, and historical linguistics, Prof. Kiparsky is the author of several influential papers in these domains as well as of *Panini as a Variationist* (1979), *Some Theoretical Problems in Panini's Grammar*, and of several important papers on Sanskrit.

Bh. Krishnamurti, Ph.D. (Pennsylvania), recently retired as the Vice-Chancellor of the University of Hyderabad. Well-known for his *Telugu Verbal Bases* (1961), *A Grammar of Modern Telugu* (1985) and for his work on Dravidian diachrony, he is the acknowledged Dean of Dravidian linguistics in India.

Rajend Mesthrie is Associate Professor of Linguistics at the University of Cape Town. His research interests are in Sociolinguistics generally, pidgin and creole languages, English in multilingual societies, especially in India and South Africa and the Indian diaspora, especially Bhojpuri.

Tsuyoshi Nara is Professor of Indian Languages at Seisen University, Tokyo. He studied Linguistics at the University of Tokyo and later at the University of Calcutta, from where he earned a doctorate in Indo-Aryan linguistics under the supervision of Professor Sukumar Sen. For a number of years, he was at the Institute for the Study of Languages and Cultures of Asia and Africa at Tokyo University of Foreign Studies, where he actively promoted research on Indian languages and also participated in the Institute's socio-historical study of Chengalaptu district in Tamil Nadu. His publications include computerized concordances of Tagore's *Gitanjali* and Premchand's *Godan* and a collection of Sen's papers on historical Indo-Aryan. He is currently finalizing a computerized dictionary of Hindi and preparing a text book of folk tales in translation from South Asian languages to be used in schools in Japan.

John Peterson completed his doctoral degree in General Linguistics at Kiel University while working as a "wissenschaftlicher Mitarbeiter" in Indology. He is presently employed as an assistant professor at the Department of General Linguistics, University of Zurich, Switzerland, where he is also actively engaged in a project on the topic of "South Asia as Linguistics Area". He runs *Vyākaran*, the indispensable list for all Indianists.

Tariq Rahman is Associate Professor of linguistics at the National Institute of Pakistan Studies, Quaid-i-Azam University, Islamabad, Pakistan. He has held the first chair of linguistics and professorship at the University of Azad Kashmir, Muzaffarabad. He has a Ph.D in English from the University of Sheffield and M. Litt. in linguistics from the University of Strathclyde (U.K.). He has published about 50 research papers and book reviews on literature, linguistics and the relationship between language and politics. His books include: *Pakistani English* (1989), *A History of Pakistani Literature in English* (1990) and *Language and Politics in Pakistan* (1996).

Anjum P. Saleemi, currently a visiting scientist at M.I.T., was for many years Senior Lecturer in the Department of English Language and Literature, National University of Singapore. He has been engaged in work on linguistic theory, the acquisition and learnability of syntax, and the grammar of Hindi–Urdu, Punjabi and other South Asian languages. His publications include the book *Universal Grammar and Language Learnability* (Cambridge University Press, 1992), and several papers contributed to journals, books and conference proceedings. Another major area of his interest is the philosophy of language and mind.

Ara Shah did her Master's in linguistics at the University of Bombay (1986), her M.Phil. at Deccan College, Pune (1988), and her Ph.D. at the University of Hyderabad (1996). She is doing postdoctoral research in London.

Étienne Tiffou is Professor Emeritus of Linguistics at the Université de Montréal and a fellow of the Royal Society of Canada. He has worked extensively on the non-Indoeuropean languages of Pakistan, particularly on Burushaski. His recent books include *Hunsa Proverbs* (1993) and *Dictionnaire complementaire du Bourouchaski du Yasin* (1989) (with Yves-Charles Morin).

Shravan Vasishth is currently a research assistant in Linguistics at the Ohio State University, Columbus. An Associate of the U.K. Institute of Translating and Interpreting, he has published articles on 'honorifics' and computational linguistics. His current research interests are: the syntax-semantics interface and computational linguistics.

Atlas of the Languages and Ethnic Communities of South Asia

ROLAND J–L BRETON

This geographical atlas constitutes the first systematic presentation of the spatial and quantitative characteristics of the distribution of languages in the seven countries of South Asia. Utilizing a semiographic analysis and combining and comparing language data from various national censuses covering a forty year period, this atlas enables readers to actually see the geographical location, extension and linguistic affinities of any of the numerous languages spoken in South Asia.

> Extremely well written...indispensable for any library...would serve as a reference for linguists, ethnologists and anthropologists.
>
> *Business Standard*

Contents: *Preface/Introduction*/PART I: General Presentation of the Languages and Ethnic Communities of South Asia: India as an Exemplary Laboratory for the Coexistence of Languages and Ethnic Communities/Language Compared to Other Ethnic Traits: Congruences and Discrepancies/From Language Dynamics to Linguism/PART II: The Sixty Plates with their Commentaries: Introduction: The Regional Semiographic Analysis/Indian Languages Throughout the Subcontinent and the World/The Northwest/The Hindi Belt/The Himalayas and the Northeast/The Peripheral Indo-Aryan and the Central Adivasi Belts/The Dravidian South and Sri Lanka/The Non-Regional Languages/The Linguistic States, the Media and the Metropolitan Situations/Ethno-Linguistic Issues Throughout the Subcontinent and Around/The Linguistic Situation up to the 1991 Census/*Annexures/Select Bibliography/Language Classification and Plate Index/Subject and Author Index*

440 mm x 280 mm/1997/236pp/hb